Relational Psychoanalysis: Volume III

New Voices

RELATIONAL PERSPECTIVES BOOK SERIES

Volume 34

Relational Psychoanalysis

Volume III

New Voices

Edited by
Melanie Suchet
Adrienne Harris
Lewis Aron

THE ANALYTIC PRESS

2007   Mahwah, New Jersey   London

The Analytic Press
10 Industrial Avenue
Mahwah, New Jersey 07430
www.erlbaum.com

Cover design by Kathryn Houghtaling Lacey

Library of Congress Cataloging-in-Publication Data

Relational psychoanalysis, Volume III : New voices / edited by Melanie Suchet, Adrienne Harris, Lewis Aron.

p.   cm.

ISBN 978-0-88163-456-3 — 0-88163-456-5 (pbk.)

Books published by Lawrence Erlbaum Associates are printed on acid-free paper, and their bindings are chosen for strength and durability.

Printed in the United States of America
10 9 8 7 6 5 4 3 2 1

For
Paul Stepansky

Contributors

Steven Botticelli, PhD, is a candidate in the NYU Postdoctoral Program in Psychotherapy and Psychoanalysis. He is the editor of *The Psychoanalytic Activist,* the newsletter for Section 9, the Section for Social Responsibility of Division 39, and a supervisor for the Clinical Psychology Program at City College, CUNY.

Anne Anlin Cheng is Associate Professor of English and American Literature at the University of California, Berkeley. She is the author of *The Melancholy of Race: Psychoanalysis, Assimilation, and Hidden Grief* (Oxford University Press).

Jeffre Cheuvront is a faculty member at the National Institute for the Psychotherapies; graduate of, and continuing education instructor at, the Institute for the Psychoanalytic Study of Subjectivity; clinical supervisor at the Ferkauf Graduate School of Psychology and St. Vincent's Hospital and Medical Center; and maintains a private practice in New York, NY.

Gilbert W. Cole, PhD, LCSW, is on the faculty of the Institute for Contemporary Psychotherapy, the National Institute for the Psychotherapies, and is on the faculty and is a supervisor at the Psychoanalytic Psychotherapy Study Center. Articles he has written have appeared in *Contemporary Psychoanalysis* and *Gender and Psychoanalysis,* and the *Psychoanalytic Quarterly.* He is on the editorial boards of *Studies in Gender and Psychoanalysis* and the *Journal of Gay and Lesbian Psychotherapy.* He is the author of *Infecting the Treatment: Being an HIV Positive Psychotherapist* (The Analytic Press, 2002). He is in private practice in New York City.

Margaret Crastnopol, PhD, is co-founder, past associate director, and a faculty member of the Northwest Center for Psychoanalysis (NCP) in Seattle, Washington. She is a supervisor of psychotherapy and a faculty member of the William Alanson White Institute of Psychiatry, Psychoanalysis and Psychology in New York City, a contributing editor of *Psychoanalytic Dialogues,* and an associate editor of *Contemporary Psychoanalysis.* Dr. Crastnopol is on the board of directors of the International Association for Relational Psychoanalysis and Psychotherapy.

Muriel Dimen, PhD, is Adjunct Clinical Professor of Psychology, New York University Postdoctoral Program in Psychotherapy and Psychoanalysis. Her most recent book, *Sexuality, Intimacy, Power* (The Analytic Press, 2003), won the Goethe Award for Psychoanalytic Scholarship as the best book published in 2003, given by the Section on Psychoanalytic and Psychodynamic Psychology of the Canadian Psychological Association.

David L. Eng, PhD, is Associate Professor of English at Rutgers University, New Brunswick. He is author *of Racial Castration: Managing Masculinity in Asian America* and coeditor of *Loss: The Politics of Mourning* and *Q&A: Queer in Asian America*.

Elaine Freedgood is an associate professor at New York University.

Katie Gentile, PhD, is Assistant Professor of Counseling and Women's Center Director at John Jay College of Criminal Justice in New York City. She is the author of the book *Creating Bodies: Eating Disorders as Self-Destructive Survival* (The Analytic Press, 2007), and is a Contributing Editor for the interdisciplinary journal *Studies in Gender and Sexuality*.

Sue Grand, PhD, is faculty and supervisor at the NYU Postdoctoral Program in Psychoanalysis and Psychotherapy, supervisor at the Manhattan Institute for Psychoanalysis, and faculty for the Psychoanalytic Institute for Northern California.

Robert Grossmark, PhD, is on the teaching faculty, National Institute of the Psychotherapies, and adjunct teaching faculty, doctoral program in clinical psychology, City University of New York. He is a clinical supervisor, doctoral program in clinical psychology, City University of New York; doctoral program in clinical psychology, Ferkauf Graduate School of Yeshiva University and National Institute of the Psychotherapies. He is in private practice in New York City.

Shinhee Han, PhD, is in private practice in New York City. Previously, she was a staff psychotherapist with the counseling services of Northwestern University, the University of Chicago, and Columbia University.

Stephen Hartman graduated from the NYU Postdoctoral Program in Psychotherapy and Psychoanalysis. He is a contributing editor for *Studies in Gender and Sexuality* and an assistant editor for *Psychoanalytic Dialogues*. Stephen supervises doctoral candidates in the clinical psychology program of City College, CUNY, and works in private practice in Manhattan.

Marsha Aileen Hewitt is Professor of Religion and Social Ethics at Trinity College in the University of Toronto. Her areas of research, teaching, and publishing include psychoanalysis, religion, and critical theory. Dr. Hewitt is also a psychoanalyst in private practice, and faculty member of the Toronto Institute for Contemporary Psychoanalysis in Toronto, Canada.

Debra Roth is a faculty member at the Institute for Contemporary Psychoanalysis and a contributing editor to *Studies in Gender and Sexuality*. She is in private practice in Manhattan.

Sandra Silverman, LCSW, is a faculty member and supervisor at the Psychoanalytic Psychotherapy Study Center and the Institute for Contemporary Psychotherapy. She is in private practice in New York City.

Ruth Stein, PhD is Associate Clinical Professor, New York University Postdoctoral Program for Psychotherapy and Psychoanalysis and on the Advisory Board of the International Association for Relational Psychoanalysis and Psychotherapy. She is Training Analyst, Israel Psychoanalytic Society; Faculty, Institute for Psychoanalytic Training and Research; Member, the American Psychoanalytic Association; Faculty, National Institute for the Psychotherapies; and Faculty, the Institute for the Psychoanalytic Study of Subjectivity. She is International Editor of *Studies in Gender and Sexuality*; Associate Editor, *Psychoanalytic Dialogues*; and on the Editorial Board of *The International Journal of Psychoanalysis*. She has published extensively on affect, sexuality, perversion, the philosophy of psychoanalysis, religious terrorism, and other topics. She currently lives and practices in New York City.

Gillian Straker, PhD, is Clinical Professor of Psychology, University of Sydney. She teaches Psychotherapy (Psychoanalytic Integrations) at the Metanoia Institute, London, and is an organizational consultant to Encompass Australia.

Melanie Suchet, PhD, is a faculty member at the Institute for Contemporary Psychotherapy. She is a contributing editor of *Studies in Gender and Sexuality* and an assistant editor of *Psychoanalytic Dialogues*. She is in private practice in New York City.

Contents

Introduction:
Pushing the Envelope

Melanie Suchet
Adrienne Harris
Lewis Aron

▼   ▼   ▼   ▼   ▼

This volume has a different agenda from the preceding two volumes of the Relational Tradition series. The first, edited by Stephen Mitchell and Lewis Aron before Mitchell's death in 2000, was a collection of essential early papers in relational theory. The second volume, undertaken by Lewis Aron and Adrienne Harris, picked up on the initial project, finding and presenting central papers in the evolution of relational thinking and relational practice.

This volume looks to a different group of writers and sets a gaze more towards the horizon than the current central landscape. We three co-editors represent two different generations of relational psychoanalysts. The older generation looks for heirs and new life, even if we do so with fear and mixed pleasures. The new generation longs to have a voice. Yet we come together to do this volume on new writing, new styles, new voices, and new ideas with a common wish to see what happens when you push the envelope.

We speak now from these distinct perspectives.

Lewis Aron

I have a very happy memory of spending time with Stephen Mitchell one day in the early 1990s. I recall that we were walking along West End Avenue after having Chef's Salad at the Allstate Cafu as we so often did together. It must have been soon after launching *Psychoanalytic Dialogues* and, as I recall, Steve and I were giddy, celebrating the success of the journal, the relational track at NYU, and other ventures that we were setting up. We enjoyed sharing our manic defenses and, on this particular day, we must have been planning next steps. I remember our laughing as Steve began to imagine what it would actually be like if relational theory ever became the dominant paradigm in psychoanalysis. Steve said that would never do; he couldn't stand being part of the establishment. We'd have to start another revolution. We laughed hard together—he, I think, because he so enjoyed his antiauthoritarian stance. I laughed because his excitement was contagious and I was so thrilled that he would include me in his imaginary future.

The story is not altogether comical. Steve was concerned that relational psychoanalysis not repeat the mistakes of previous psychoanalytic schools. He did not want relational theory to congeal into a fixed or stagnant paradigm. He didn't want us to become overly bound by rules of inclusion and exclusion. There would be no secret rings in this circle.

From the moment that Steve assembled our first meeting to plan the board of Psychoanalytic Dialogues, I knew how lucky I was to be a part of this group. I will never forget the magic of sitting with Steve, Mannie Ghent, Phil Bromberg, and Adrienne Harris planning how to begin this new venture. I knew at the time that this was going to be an unforgettable moment in my lifetime, and so it has been, of course, made infinitely more precious by the so unexpected loss of Steve and then of Mannie. One aspect of the memory is my appreciation, even at the time, that these senior analysts were making a choice to include younger analysts with them on this venture right from the start. We had already launched the relational track at the New York University Postdoctoral Program and this had been a consistent feature of the new orientation, namely, in every phase the most senior and established leaders included and invited young analysts and those who had been on the margins and the periphery of the program into the center of the new relational track.

And so now, it has been 18 years since we began the relational track. Now we have a relational journal, a relational book series, a relational training program, an international Association for Relational Psychoanalysis and Psychotherapy, and this is our third in a series of collections of key papers in relational psychoanalysis.

Dominant or not, we are certainly a strong presence on the international psychoanalytic scene. And indeed, we have become the establishment. What would Steve have done now? This volume is true to the spirit of the origin or the relational track. The early leaders of the track—Mannie, Steve, Phil, Bernie Friedland, and Jim Fosshage—followed the spirit of Bernie Kalinkowitz (who had begun and led the NYU program for many years) and emphasized democratic principles, inclusiveness, openness, dialog, and respect for numerous perspectives and multiple subject positions.

In this book we continue to insure a place at the center of relational psycho-analysis for those voices that might otherwise be pushed into the margins.

Adrienne Harris

I think that the last half decade, with its great promise, its huge stores of work in building relational psychoanalysis infrastructure and institutions, and yet above all, its devastating deaths and losses, has made me feel my mortality. And, of course, this is personal as well as institutional/profes-sional. I see the evolution and transformations in my own family, as well as my friend's, and see my cohort, building and assessing lives, families, work, and politics. And to set this in our larger context, the political world, seems overwhelmingly dangerous. There is perhaps no other setting but the polit-ical in which I so feel my age.

When I think about the two decades of relational psychoanalysis as idea, vision, practice, theory, and infrastructure, I feel many things, both sad and happy. But I do feel blessed to have had the great mentorship of Mitchell, Ghent, and Bromberg. Through the luck of timing and interest, the training with Mannie Ghent in an object relations perspective in the NYU postdoctoral program made many of us ripe for relational ideas. I, and others in my generation, have had many opportunities to make a ca-reer in which I feel happy and fulfilled. The lucky accident of being in the right place at the right time is, for me, coordinated with the powerful for-mative experiences in the late 1960s and 1970s of activism, antiwar work, and blessed feminism. My generation was both formed and tested in situa-tions of political gravity. We got to ride on the long waves and swells from liberation movements that began in the 1950s with the civil rights move-ments, moving through antiwar, feminism, and gay liberation and on-ward. This formation makes for romantic nostalgia, of course, but also it makes for a freedom from a certain kind of authoritarian training within psychoanalysis, and a strong formation in being critical and self-critical, in questioning the hegemonic discourses. Psychoanalytic concepts can be offered up to us as though ideas were as natural as the weather. I think it is consistent with the best hopes of the relational tradition of Steve Mitch-ell's own antiauthoritarian spirit that many chapters in this volume owe some of their lineage to this social history of resistance. I feel proud of the relational turn and proud to be an analyst within it. We need many things so that pride is not complacency and enforced compliancy. We need many deepening discourses, both critical and creative.

So, it is for all these reasons that I am looking for, and listening to, the next generation, the new voices. And I have learned that new voices often come in new registers, new tones. This volume is a beginning presence of the newer and emerging perspectives, both new in topic and new in modality.

But it is not without tension that I am doing this looking; Lew Aron's introduction has the marvelous insistence on history, on Mitchell's ideas, and on the founding fathers and mothers. My voice has a somewhat depressive tone, nostalgic, elegiac, wistfully turned to the future. Melanie's voice is of the arriving future, ready and tired of waiting. But, in a sense, it was important to see and hear all three individual voices, to see that we could not be fully in agreement. How could we be? Our interests as well as our history are different. So I think each of us has worked on this book with the compatible and competing wishes: Should we continue this history. Change it? Renew it? Alter it? Maintain it?

Melanie Suchet

Unlike psychoanalysis in a different era, relational psychoanalysis offered me the possibility of integrating the social and political with the intrapsychic. Growing up in South Africa, where the political informs every aspect of the psychological, I could not imagine divorcing the two. I was thus inspired by my early analytic mentors, Adrienne Harris, Jessica Benjamin, and Muriel Dimen, specifically, by how they incorporated theories of sexuality and gender within the political milieu of feminism, cultural studies, and, later, queer theory. I am propelled by this vision of relational psychoanalysis as transgressive, remaining at the edges and struggling with how to ensure our relevancy in the political and social currents of the time.

Twenty-five years later, having moved into a new century, we stand at a different threshold as the question arises: "Where do we go from here?" I wonder if it is inevitable that the innovation and creativity of a start-up venture and the flurry of ideas and excitement it generates, develops into a more rigid form as the organization grows and becomes more established. I ask myself, how do we maintain a liberated state of mind? And can we construct a space that allows for ongoing transformations, for shapes that cannot be anticipated, to emerge? Given the many criticisms and attacks that have been lobbied at relational concepts, it is difficult to resist the urge to hunker down. Yet we know, only too well, that it must be from a nondefensive position that we move forward. Can we embrace critical discourses that reveal our weaknesses and blind spots and use them to further our revolutionary initiative?

Unfortunately, we do carry the burden of our psychoanalytic history, transmitted through many generations, of internecine and fractured schools at the sighting of critical feedback. Yet, the hope is that relational psychoanalysis can be different. With its broad umbrella, it has resisted any pull towards a uniform dogma, toward being closed off or pinned down to any simple theoretical school of thought or view of the self. Further, we have always accommodated differences. At no time is this more important than now, when there are so many viewpoints as to what constitutes relational psychoanalysis and who may claim to be a relational psychoanalyst.

Certainly, Adrienne Harris, Lewis Aron, and I are united in our pride at challenging the hierarchy and authoritarianism of the classical analyst.[1] No longer is the analyst the hegemonic interpreter of reality, but a co-participant in a complex, intertwined dialogue of conscious and unconscious processes. Yet, power remains one of the least theorized and analyzed aspects of our work. And in its insidious way, power reappears despite our best attempts to undermine it. This is true in both the consulting room and in psychoanalytic organizations. We may need to resign ourselves to the fate of always having to uncover the ways in which power will inevitably reinstate itself. By ushering in new voices, we are attempting to redistribute power and counter the danger of an accumulation of power in the hands of too few.

It is with deep gratitude and respect that I embark on this project with two of the architects and visionaries of relational theory.

Organization of the Book

One may well wonder how a book about newness and vitality, a book that advertises the wish to push the envelope, is published as part of a traditional series, which appears as an apparent contradiction. However, if traditions have change and freshness to new ideas as part of the guiding philosophy, then there is room for the shape of the landscape to be continuously altered. In fact, change becomes embedded in the foundational concepts. To return to the words of Mitchell and Aron (1999) in the first volume of the traditional series, "the vitality of any psychoanalytic tradition derives, most centrally, from its power to generate new ideas" (p. xix). It is both the power to generate new ideas and the willingness to receive them that ensures our vitality.

We have always enriched our theories by embracing concepts from disciplines beyond psychoanalysis. Postmodernism has had an especially powerful impact on relational sensibilities. It has exposed how each of our subject positions are structured around differences in power. It has also opened up the fixity of structure, challenging us to find fluidity, movement,

---

[1]The word *classical* in this context refers to a conservative trend in psychoanalysis crossing different schools of thought, not simply classical Freudians.

and multiplicity. We have been able to deconstruct oppositions and tolerate tensions, holding in mind the inevitable contradictions that pull us in different directions.

Furthermore, for many decades the psychoanalytic establishment tended to accept the notion that mental health was a matter of accepting differences—between the generations and between the sexes. Psychosis was thought to be based on the blurring of these distinctions and the acceptance of reality was conflated with the acceptance of generational and sexual difference. Relational psychoanalysis, and this book in particular, is transgressive in specifically challenging these neat and clear distinctions.

In line with our dynamic and subversive history, spawned as it was in the midst of the revolutionary uprising of the 1960s, this book welcomes the contributions of dissident and disenfranchised voices. We are committed to continuing to integrate politics and psychology, furthering a vision of psychoanalysis that holds in mind race, class, power, and social consciousness. Six of the 19 chapters deal with these three topics directly, which is a rare occurrence in any edited compilation of psychoanalytic papers.

Furthermore, in encouraging independent and creative thinking, we wanted to select writers who were prepared to play with pushing the margins of established writing. It is a challenge to find different ways to capture the complexities of the treatment and to draw the reader into the page in a similar manner to how the analyst feels drawn in by the patient. Through experimenting with different styles and forms of the writing, the analyst can be freer to explore herself in text. This raises issues of how to use language and literary forms of writing to help us get closer to actual experience. Both writing and psychoanalysis require us to enter our unconscious, go deep inside ourselves, and capture what feels quite elusive and beyond words; it asks us how far we are prepared to go and what risks we are willing to take to allow something authentic and deep to be portrayed on the page.

We have divided the book into three parts. In Part I, "New Forms of Writing, Seasoned Voices," we have senior relational analysts exploring themes that cover religion, race, sexuality, gender, transgender, and intimacy. Using clinical material, poetry, lyrics, and personal history the authors experiment with different ways of enhancing psychoanalytic texts. Taking two readings of the story of the Garden of Eden, Lewis Aron's chapter (chap. 1) brings a psychoanalytic lens to understanding the Jewish interpretive tradition. Using poetry and lyrics, Margaret Crastnopol (chap. 2) explores the coopting into an emotional embrace that appears to offer nourishment but is, in fact, toxic. Muriel Dimen (chap. 3) gives a subjective reading of the film *Ma Vie en Rose* to explore the source of her anger. Venturing into the space of disembodied, deadened things, Sue Grand (chap. 4) explores the unsexed, ungendered nonhuman selves that exist in the aftermath of sexual violation. Adrienne Harris (chap. 5) uses her personal relationship to a family artifact to explore her fetishistic attachment to whiteness. Ruth Stein (chap. 6) takes us on her personal journey of discovering relational theories and, in so doing, articulates and contrasts the different theories.

Part II, "New Ideas, New Voices," introduces some newer generation relational writers. The common theme is the integration of subjectivity with social and political discourses. Two cultural theorists, David Eng (chap. 9) and Anne Cheng (chap. 8), are included for their contribution to the psychoanalytic understanding of race and melancholia. With Shinhee Han, David Eng (chap. 9) explores transnational adoption, the ways in which psychoanalytic concepts are racialized, including the racialization of good and bad objects. Anne Cheng (chap. 8) is focused on the melancholic constitution of the racial subject and how to build an ethics of relationality. Two chapters on class explore the issue from different perspectives. Steve Botticelli (chap. 7) explores class as a shadowy presence that can be known and not known simultaneously. Stephen Hartman (chap. 12) presents the class unconscious as a different kind of thirdness built on an early history of material relations. Directly addressing the political arena, Marsha Hewitt (chap. 13) reclaims psychoanalysis' subversiveness as a performative enactment of democratic principles. Looking at eating disorders from a feminist perspective, the paradox of resisting the social order to survive or self-destructing to resist is elaborated by Katie Gentile (chap. 10). In a different vein, a relational perspective on group therapy is introduced by Robert Grossmark (chap. 11), exploring the use of unformulated experience.

In Part III, "Experiments in a New Key," we have new writers experimenting with literary styles: Two fictional pieces are included. Jeffre Phillip Cheuvront (chap. 14) traces the themes of repetition and time in an evocative, mysterious piece filled with loss and longing. Melanie Suchet (chap. 19) explores the transformations entailed in transgender work by fictionalizing both analyst and analysand. The other four chapters explore a variety of ways the analyst can be used, both in the room and on the page. In holding and being identified as the Other, Gilbert Cole (chap. 15) explores what it means to be an HIV-positive analyst. Sandy Silverman (chap. 17) follows the trajectory of treatment when analysand and analyst share a parallel history of family mental illness. Gillian Straker (chap. 18) takes us into the co-constructed terrain of perversion, and the mechanisms that force us into entanglement. And finally, Elaine Freedgood and Debra Roth (chap. 16) interrogate the homo of sexuality, exposing how sameness is constituted along genitally based conceptions.

Reference

Mitchell, S., & Aron, L. (1999), *Relational psychoanalysis: The emergence of a tradition.* Hillsdale, NJ: The Analytic Press.

Acknowledgments

I want to express gratitude to my co-editors for their encouragement, wisdom, and this remarkable opportunity to work together.

For creative inspiration and dedicated support, I thank, with warmth, my writing group and especially Carole Maso, our muse. For the many years of intellectual enrichment I thank my study group, for whom my gratitude is enormous.

Most importantly, I thank my family, deeply, for the understanding and support that has always sustained me, to my children for the ways in which they delight me, and to Abby, whose love has never waivered.

—*MS*

I want to thank my co-editors, whose wonderful mix of spirit and responsibility made this task an adventure and a pleasure. As always, I thank my family for so much support, I thank Bob Sklar for all his steady, graceful love, and I thank Jake Tentler for 16 months of fun.

Paul Stapansky shepherded this book through some big changes at The Analytic Press, continuing his great support for relational psychoanalysis. Anyone who undertakes psychoanalytic publishing is much in his debt.

—*AH*

I too wish to thank my co-editors for their enthusiasm, dedication, creativity, and collegiality. I also want to acknowledge the continued support of New York University and the professional community of the Postdoctoral Program in Psychotherapy and Psychoanalysis.

I thank my wife, Janie, and my children, Benjamin, Raphi, and Kirya, for their constant love, support, and encouragement.

—*LA*

Part I

New Forms of Writing, Seasoned Voices

Relational psychoanalysis has given a great deal of attention to the relation between the old and the new, how they interpenetrate and dialectically define each other. The old object is re-found in the new object, and aspects of new experience are often constituted as new renditions of old experience. We begin this collection with "New Forms of Writing, Seasoned Voices." Here we feature six articles by well established psychoanalytic author/analysts writing in novel or unusual idioms. As much as we wish to highlight new voices, it seemed even more important to bring together older and newer voices, to mix generations, styles, and registers, to bring out new aspects of the old and to recognize old elements within the new.

Lewis Aron's "The Tree of Knowledge: Good and Evil" (chap. 1) draws on traditional and modern Jewish theological interpretations of the biblical story as well as on psychoanalytic elucidation of the myth, and explores a central controversy reflecting differences in world views concerning the good life, autonomy and relatedness, assertion and submission, will and surrender, obedience and rebellion, independence and interdependence, and subjectivity and intersubjectivity. Aron draws links to a variety of contemporary psychoanalytic theories, developments, and controversies including the relation of intersubjectivity to law and boundaries. Whereas psychoanalysis has historically been at some odds with religious and spiritual traditions, here Aron considers that the promotion of human self-creativity, rebirth, or transformation as a religious obligation may be a model for an understanding of psycho-analysis as a spiritual act.

Margaret Crastnopol's chapter "Uneasy Intimacy, A Siren's Call" (chap. 2) creatively explores the dark underbelly of intimacy. She carefully considers the phenomenology of a particular form of closeness that is, in some ways, more toxic than nourishing. She evokes a vexed and bittersweet form of closeness that most of us have experienced at one time or another, sometimes as therapists, where two people become involved too intensely or too quickly. It is not the conscious manipulation of seduction or boundary violation, although it may in fact be a prelude to such a violation. Crastnopol provides a detailed and engaging case illustration and relates her description to relational ideas about the inevitability of enactment and the analyst's co-participation.

In "Ma Vie En Rose: A Meditation" (chap. 3), Muriel Dimen uses her own affective reactions to Alain Berliner's film to draw out some lessons about psychosexuality and cultural sexuality. Bravely, Dimen utilizes her own subjectivity to elaborate on both one- and two-person aspects of gender and sexuality and on the film's challenge to conventional heterosexual mores. She insightfully observes the links between embarrassment, shame, narcissism, and sexuality, commenting along the way on class differences and on the difficulties that we have in recognizing the very otherness of the other.

Sue Grand's "Unsexed and Ungendered Bodies: The Violated Self" (chap. 4) presents a detailed case narrative that grippingly compels the reader's attention. Drawing deeply on the early work of Harold Searles, Grand proposes that trauma splits the psyche into a human and a nonhuman dimension. In the theater of the analysis, the patient needs to be able to reach the analyst's nonhuman, disembodied, inanimate self. Patient and therapist are forced to reenact two dimensions of experience in working through trauma and, in so doing, the analyst has to be prepared to become de-personalized, de-gendered, disembodied, and de-humanized to the point of almost literally hallucinating the image of the nonhuman in the countertransference, while also maintaining an empathic human relatedness. Grand's writing is haunting in its depiction of evil and courageous in its exploration of the consequences evoked in the analyst.

Adrienne Harris (chap. 5) masterfully examines a wide sweep of academic and psychoanalytic literature on racism and draws on her own personal experience growing up in a privileged "snowy white" Canada in order to deconstruct the categories of race and to argue that whiteness is the unmarked category of a social construction that privileges and perpetuates white power. As in other chapters in this volume, we see what may be described as a typical relational approach in which the author/analyst makes use of his or her own subjectivity, analysis of his or her own affective response, introspection, and self-analysis to open up a previously unexplored dimension of experience. Harris confronts elements of her own disavowed "whiteness" in order to shed light on a racist construction of the mind. Opening up for re-examination a classic essay by Joan Riviere entitled "Womanliness as a Masquerade," Harris is able to bring to light elements of race that have been heretofore missed by generations of psychoanalytic and feminist scholarship.

Part I ends with "Waystations on a Psychoanalytic Journey" (chap. 6), in which Ruth Stein quickly engages the reader in her own personal narrative of developing and evolving as a psychoanalyst. Stein explores the contemporary psychoanalyst's polygamous allegiances to theory and to multiple analytic communities. With openness she draws on postmodern notions of multiplicity to consider the analyst's hybrid identity. Because of her detailed personal experiences with different parts of the international psychoanalytic world and the plurality of psychoanalytic cultures and perspectives, Stein is in a unique position to provide a richly comparative psychoanalytic study. Stein's meditation of the plurality of analytic positions allows for a thoughtful examination of the specific contributions of relational psychoanalysis from her own singular perspective.

The reader can see throughout this collection of chapters a distinctive relational approach whereby analysts and authors utilize aspects of their own subjectivity, and especially their own affective responsiveness and personal values, in order to shed fresh light on heretofore neglected dimensions of experience or clinical stalemate.

1

The Tree of Knowledge: Good and Evil
Conflicting Interpretations*

Lewis Aron

This article examines a debate concerning the exegesis of the story of the garden of Eden and the tree of knowledge, as told in Genesis. Two contradictory interpretations of the garden narrative are examined, the first as the story is elucidated by the psychoanalyst and social theorist Erich Fromm and the alternative interpretation by the Talmudic scholar and philosopher Rabbi Joseph Soloveitchik. This article compares and contrasts their exegeses and the respective implications of each view. The controversy, which has profound implications, reflects differences in world views concerning the good life, autonomy and relatedness, assertion and submission, will and surrender, obedience and rebellion, independence and interdependence, subjectivity and intersubjectivity. Links are drawn to a variety of contemporary psychoanalytic theories, developments, and controversies.

AROLD BLOOM (1987) WROTE, "FREUD'S MOST PROFOUND JEWISHNESS, voluntary and involuntary, was his consuming passion for interpretation" (p. 52). It is by now well accepted to think of psychoanalysis, like Judaism and biblical exegesis, as a hermeneutical or interpretive tradition. The Jewish interpretive tradition is radically open. The compilers of the midrashic collections—and there have been numerous anthologies over many centuries—were quite comfortable presenting a range of interpretive options without suggesting any single definitive, monolithic, or authoritative reading

---

Lewis Aron, Ph.D., ABPP is director, New York University, Postdoctoral Program in Psychotherapy and Psychoanalysis.

A much abbreviated version of this article was presented on the panel, "Seduction in the Garden of Eden," as a discussion of Avivah Zornberg's presentation, "Seduced into Eden: The beginning of desire," at the William Alanson White Institute conference "Longings: Psychoanalytic Musings on Desire," October 24, 2004, New York.

*From *Psychoanalytic Dialogues*, 15(5): 681–707, 2005. Reprinted with permission.

of the biblical text. The Talmudic literature is filled with disagreements and differences of opinion. The mark of a Talmudic scholar is the ability to read and analyze the text and to explain both sides of any rabbinic disagreement by offering imaginative and compelling reasons for both sides of an argument (Hartman, 1999). "Indeed, matters go so far that in the course of a talmudic discussion, an argument that threatens to resolve a controversy is considered a difficulty [*kushia*], while one that restores the controversy is called a solution [*teruz*]!" (Boyarin, 1993, p. 27).

This article will examine a debate concerning the interpretation of the story of the garden of Eden as told in Genesis. In this article, I present two contradictory interpretations of the garden narrative as the story is interpreted by the psychoanalyst and social theorist Erich Fromm and by the Talmudic scholar and philosopher Rabbi Joseph Soloveitchik. I will compare and contrast their exegeses and the respective implications of each view.[1] The controversy, which has profound implications, reflects differences in worldviews concerning the good life, autonomy and relatedness, assertion and submission, will and surrender, obedience and rebellion, independence and interdependence, subjectivity and intersubjectivity. I draw links to a variety of contemporary psychoanalytic developments and controversies. "No aspect of Genesis 1–3 escapes scrutiny and rabbinic comment; no gap in the story lines goes unfilled. Modern readers of these compilations are likely to be overwhelmed by the plethora of

---

[1] After writing early drafts of this article, I read David Hartman's (1997) *A Living Covenant* and found that Hartman begins his chapter on Soloveitchik by comparing his views to those of Fromm and the Israeli philosopher Yeshayahu Leibowitz. Hartman argues that Fromm represents one side of a polarity (autonomy), Leibowitz represents the other extreme position (submission), and that Soloveitchik's position is dialectical (holding in tension autonomy and submission). Nevertheless, by the end of his chapter on this topic, Hartman concludes that Soloveitchik gives more weight to submission.

In contrast to Hartman, I argue here that although Soloveitchik attempts a dialectical approach, in my view his effort fails because the tension of his argument collapses to the side of submission. Therefore, there is much to be learned by holding both Fromm's and Soloveitchik's views in mind, as complementary. In addition, Hartman does not compare and contrast the thinker's views in regard to the Genesis narrative. Hartman's chapter on Soloveitchik's thought, as well as his full-length book (2001) on the topic, are exceptionally clear and systematic studies of the Rav's thought, and my own thinking is greatly indebted to Hartman's truly dialectical approach.

opinions offered and the dissonance between authoritative rabbinic 'voices'" (Kvam, Schearing, and Ziegler, 1999, p. 69).

For psychoanalysts, the rabbinic approach to interpretation should be familiar indeed. David Bakan (1958) persuasively argued that Freud applied to the study of individual behavior the traditional Jewish methodological principle of interpretation, in which every word—even every letter—of the Torah, even the decorative adornments of the letters, even the spaces between letters, was assumed to be meaningful and subject to multiple understandings. For psychoanalysts, the human being, created in the image of God, is like a holy text, subject to ongoing and interminable analysis and interpretation.

Our Eden story is told as part of the narrative of the creation of the world and specifically of humanity. "It has been taught: R. Meir used to say: the dust of the first man was gathered from all parts of the earth" (from the Talmud, quoted Fromm, 1966, p. 84). Creation universalizes the sanctity of all life, extending it beyond the narrow confines of any particular tradition, even beyond the particular revelations to Abraham and then at Sinai recorded later in the Hebrew Bible (see Hartman, 1999, p. 161). The Mishnah, in *Sanhedrin*, explains:

> Therefore humankind was created singly, to teach you that whoever destroys a single soul, Scripture accounts it as if he/she destroyed a full world; and whoever saves one soul, Scripture accounts it as if he/she saves a full world. And for the sake of peace among people, that one should not say to his fellow, "My father is greater than yours"; and that heretics should not say, "There are many powers in Heaven." Again, to declare the greatness of the Holy One, blessed be He, for a human being stamps out many coins with one die, and they are all alike, but the King, the King of Kings, the Holy One, blessed be He, stamped each human being with the seal of Adam, and not one of them is like another. Therefore each and every person is obliged to say, "For my sake was the world created" [quoted in Hartman, 1998, p. 161].

Rabbi Joseph Soloveitchik explained that the Torah tells the tale of creation not to reveal cosmology and metaphysical mysteries but rather to teach practical *halachah*, legal obligations. Soloveitchik's bold interpretation, drawing on the mystical work of Kabbalah, is that human beings, who are commanded to walk in God's ways, are obliged to engage in creation. "The Creator, as it were, impaired reality in order that mortal man could repair its flaws and perfect it" (Soloveitchik, 1983, p. 101)[2] But Soloveitchik gives a new and specifically existential refinement to this conviction. "The most fundamental principle of all is that man must create himself" (p. 109). For Soloveitchik, this is not simply abstract moralizing, rather he demonstrates that there are practical and specific *Halachic* (legal) implications, using as one example, the laws governing repentance which he interprets as reflecting the person's act of creating himself or herself anew. The promotion of human self-creativity, rebirth, or transformation as a religious obligation may be a model for an understanding of psychoanalysis as a spiritual act.

Another author, a psychoanalyst writing at about the same time as Soloveitchik, made quite a similar point. Erich Fromm (1966, p. 70) noted that the human being was created in God's likeness, meaning that human limits were not set. He quotes a Hasidic teaching to the effect that after creating the human, God did not say that it was good. The inference here is that the human's creation was incomplete and that human beings must develop themselves toward perfection. We will see that the theme of creativity and interpretation are central to both biblical exegesis and psychoanalysis.

Among the greatest challenges to a contemporary reading of Eve and Adam is the impossibility of a naive reading. It is too late to go back, you can't go home again to the nakedness of an interpretation-free textual reading. The road is blocked by the *cherubim*, awesome winged beasts, as well as by a whirling sword. We are prejudiced by centuries, no—by literally millennia, of previous readings and interpretations. Not only can we not interpret innocently, but we cannot even agree on translations of key terms without imposing millennia of layered traditions and interpretive understandings.

It may be helpful to spell out some general, if not absolute, differences between the Jewish and Christian traditions of reading

---

[2] Much of the discussion in this essay examines articles that were written by Soloveitchik and by Fromm before the feminist critique of the late 1960s and 1970s. The reader may well be struck by their use of *man* where today we would be more likely to speak of *humanity*, as well as by their masculine pronouns in speaking of God.

Eden. In his recent, beautiful, and integrative study, Dennis Shulman (2003) examines the story of Eden and provides a rich overview of rabbinic and psychoanalytic commentaries. He comments that it is the interpretation of the Eden text more than any other in the book of *Genesis* that differentiates Christian from Jewish understanding. In the entire Hebrew Bible there is no reference to Eden's being a place where the first couple sinned, nor is there any reference to the Fall of mankind or to sin's being introduced into a previously unmarred world. There is also no mention of how the first couple's sin was transmitted to future generations, no reference to sexual desire as being the cause of disobedience and exile. Much of this is of course to be found in the Apocrypha and in later Hellenistic and Christian literature, but the sin, the Fall, inherited sinfulness, and sexuality as evil never became dominant in Jewish tradition as in Christian belief. Having stated this broad distinction, it remains true that the midrashic literature is replete with echoes of Adam's having sinned and brought death into the world. Still, there is much less emphasis on sexuality as inherently sinful and certainly no acceptance of the Augustinian notion that the original sin was transmitted to future generations.

Daniel Boyarin (1993) explored the differences between rabbinic and Greek assumptions. In the classic age of rabbinic Judaism, in contrast not only to Christianity but even to Hellenstic Judaism, the rabbis defined a human being as a body animated by a soul, rather than as a soul housed in a body. The rabbis believed in the generation of offspring as a religious principle and in sexual intercourse as a God-given commandment and thus did not split off body from soul as did the Hellenists. The rabbis strongly opposed mind/body dualism and view the human being as sexual and embodied. Since the rabbis did not disavow their corporeality, they did not construct it as feminine and thus had no need to devalue it. In rabbinic Judaism, in contrast to Hellenistic Judaism and Patristic Christianity, the Fall was not elevated to the unique status of a paradigmatic event initiating universal sin and sexuality. In opposing dualism, rabbinic Judaism could not equate man with mind and woman with body and so could not equate man with culture and woman with nature in a simple privileged set of dichotomies. Boyarin recognizes that there was evidence of woman-hating in rabbinic culture and that sex itself was not always viewed affirmatively, and he is a strong critic of rabbinic sexism and homophobia; nevertheless, the opposition to dualism had consequences well beyond the rabbinic attitude toward sex and the body. Christianity adopted Paul's reading of "Israel in the spirit," that is, universalism, whereas rabbinic Judaism, unable to accept the underlying dualism that would separate spirit from body, continued to be bound by "Judaism in the flesh." Similarly, just as body cannot be separated from spirit and the body of Israel could not be separated from Israel in the spirit, in their method of interpretation the rabbis could not assume that there was a binary opposition between text and meaning. We will see that in modern Jewish understanding these interpretive trends become complexly interwoven and the distinctions become less stable.

Erich Fromm[3] was born to a long line of distinguished rabbinic families and received an intensive orthodox education. Indeed, the name *Fromm* means "observant" or "pious." He was strongly influenced by the radical humanism of Herman Cohen's neo-Kantian philosophy. It is well known that in his 20s he became involved with (and married) Frieda Reichmann in Frankfurt; they participated in a movement that their friend Gershom Scholem called "torahpeutic." Torahpeutic philosophy was an attempt to link Jewish and psychoanalytic traditions, and it may well have been the forerunner of Fromm's later attempt to link psychoanalysis and Marxism (see Hornstein, 2000).

Fromm (1966) proposes a radical humanistic reading of the bible, and he repeatedly refers to the Eden story throughout his major writings.[4] "The Old Testament is a *revolutionary* book; its theme is the liberation of man from the incestuous ties to blood and soil, from the submission to idols, from slavery, from powerful masters, to freedom for the individual, for the nation, and for all of mankind" (p. 7). Listen to his sharp and pithy remarks on Eden:

---

[3] I feel a special connection and allegiance to Fromm, who was among the founding faculty of the New York University Postdoctoral Program in Psychotherapy and Psychoanalysis, of which I have been the director since 1998.

[4] In his (1941) *Escape from Freedom*, Fromm spells out quite clearly and fully the gist of his interpretation of Eden (see p. 34), which he repeated in each of his later works. In the main body of this article I draw mostly from his 1950 and 1966 works. See also Fromm, 1947, p. 210; 1951, p. 246; 1955, p. 52; 1956, p. 68; and 1960, pp. 128–129. I am specifying these pages to help the interested reader pursue further research, as Fromm's books generally do not have indexes or bibliographies. Fromm does not specify who influenced him in this interpretation of Eden, although it seems likely that he drew inspiration from Martin Buber. Perhaps because he was writing for a wider public, Fromm included relatively few scholarly footnotes or citations of others' work.

The Christian interpretation of the story of man's act of disobedience as his "fall" has obscured the clear meaning of the story. The biblical text does not even mention the word "sin"; man challenges the supreme power of God, and he is able to challenge it because he is potentially God. Man's first act is *rebellion*, and God punishes him because he has rebelled and because God wants to preserve his supremacy. God has to protect his supremacy by an act of force, by expelling Adam and Eve from the Garden of Eden and by thus preventing them from taking the second step toward becoming God—eating from the tree of life. Man has to yield to God's superior force, but he does not express regret or repentance. Having been expelled from the Garden of Eden, he begins his independent life; his first act of disobedience is the beginning of human history, because it is the beginning of human freedom [1966, p. 23].

For Fromm (1966), the human being is

beset by the existential dichotomy of being within nature and yet transcending it by the fact of having self-awareness and choice; he can solve his dichotomy only by going forward. . . He has to experience the split between himself as subject and the world as object as the condition for overcoming this very split. Man creates himself in the historical process which began with his first act of freedom—the freedom to disobey—to say "no." This "corruption" lies in the very nature of human existence" [p. 88]. [Fromm continues with his interpretation, emphasizing freedom and independence:] In the process of history man gives birth to himself. He becomes what he potentially is, and he attains what the serpent—the symbol of wisdom and rebellion—promised, and what the patriarchal, jealous God of Adam did not wish: that man would become like God himself [p. 123].

Fromm's book, written only a few decades ago, is already a product of its time and context. In my view, his emphasis on freedom and independence goes too far and is one-sided. His radical humanism considers the human goal to be "complete independence" (1966, p. 13), going so far as to argue that the covenant prepares the way for the complete freedom of humanity, "even freedom from God" (1966, p. 25). In my view, this is an expression of Fromm's own nontheistic interpretation of Judaism and of his own fiercely independent and rebellious spirit. (We learn from any interpretation as much about the interpreter as about the text. As Fromm in 1950, p. 56, quotes Spinoza, "What Paul says about Peter tells us more about Paul then about Peter"—a maxim that psychoanalysts would do well to keep in mind.) But even among his contemporaries, Fromm was criticized on these grounds. As far back as 1961, Walter Kaufman was critical of Fromm's polarization of authoritarian and humanistic religion, and he objected to Fromm's tendency to see an evolution from the former to the latter (cited in Hartman, 1997). Also in 1961, Fromm was criticized by John Schaar for his belief that ethical standards, value judgments, and the norms of conduct can and must be derived from the individual him- or herself, rather than from authority (see the review of Schaar's book by Calef, 1964). We will soon turn to a contemporary of Fromm who endorses a very different value system.

Fromm's reading of the Eden story, however, has some characteristically Jewish elements, in that he views the outcome not as a fall but as a necessary and creative leap forward. "This is not the story of the 'fall' of man but of his awakening, and thus, of the beginning of his rise" (1966, p. 71). For Fromm, humans' independence, rebellion, and capacity for sexuality are all good. Fromm goes so far here as to even champion the snake. Far from being demonic, for him the snake symbolizes wisdom and rebellion—obviously two prized values. He leaves us with the haunting notion that maybe God wanted the whole drama to run its course just as it did. He set the tree in the garden, issued a prohibition, sent the snake, and got humanity to assert itself, take a stand, and say no, thus establishing freedom and autonomy, and in leaving childhood innocence behind, accepting self-consciousness, sex, work, and death.

Fromm's is a powerful interpretation, and there is much in it that I admire and with which I identify, but to me, his reading consists of a simple reversal. Where the snake was bad, now it's good. Where there was sin, now there is evolution and development. Where there was a trip up, now there is uprising. Rebellion, saying no, becomes valued for its own sake. I like it that Fromm champions the snake, but his assertive, agentic values need to be complemented by other ideals and considerations. Where Fromm understands the covenant as leading to freedom and independence, I understand it as leading to mutuality and interdependence. But of course, unlike Fromm, I have the benefit of writing postfeminism and in a more interconnected and interdependent world. But let's compare Fromm's reading to that of one of his contemporaries, who (I will show) read Genesis as a story of the establishment and disruption of intersubjectivity and interdependence.

Rabbi Joseph B. Soloveitchik, known as "the Rav" because of his authority, was one of the 20th century's preeminent and influential Jewish scholars. Born in 1903 in Belarus, Russia, to a family renowned for its talmudic genius, he graduated from the University of Berlin with a doctorate in philosophy with an emphasis on the study of Herman Cohen, the very same 19th-century Jewish philosopher who was such an influence on Fromm. Soloveitchik represented traditional orthodoxy engaged with the secular world. I turn to Soloveitchik because some of his ideas resonate for me with my understanding of our most current relational and intersubjective psychoanalytic theories.[5]

Soloveitchik begins with the two versions of the creation story found in Genesis 1 and 2. Recall that, in Genesis 1, God creates the human on the sixth day, only after God has created all other creatures:

> And God created the human in his image, in the image of God He created him, male and female he created them [Genesis: 1:27][6]

In this version, man and woman are created last and together.[7]

---

[5] Soloveitchik's various writings frequently refer to Adam and Eve, much more so than I think is common in contemporary rabbinic literature. Among his masterworks, *The Lonely Man of Faith* (1997, originally published in 1965) is organized around the Adam and Eve narrative, although in this work he does not refer to the sin or the serpent but only to the typology of Adam I and Adam II. Soloveitchik's references to Adam and Eve are spread throughout his recorded lectures and not gathered together in one text, so I will be drawing from a wide range of sources as well as from the secondary literature (Hartman, 2001). The Rav's use of the Genesis narrative varies from text to text in his work, depending on his objectives. For my purposes here, I do not examine or present his ideas systematically, but rather I draw from a wide range of his texts, freely mixing and blending his ideas in order to provide a broad overview of his approach so that I can compare it with the more familiar views of Fromm.

[6] All quotes from the Hebrew Bible are from the translation by R. Alter (2004).

[7] Or perhaps they are created as androgynous as they are sometimes depicted in the *midrash*, but Soloveitchik's interpretation assumes that they are two individuals.

Genesis 2 states, by contrast,

On the day the Lord God made earth and heavens, no shrub of
the field being yet on the earth and no plant of the field yet
sprouted, for the Lord God had not caused rain to fall on the
earth and there was no human to till the soil, and wetness would
well from the earth to water all the surface of the soil, then the
Lord God fashioned the human, humus from the soil, and blew
into his nostrils the breath of life, and the human became a living
creature [Genesis 2:5–7].

Animals are created only after the human, and of course the woman
is created from man's side or rib while he is asleep.

Biblical scholars of all traditions, going back to antiquity, have noted
these two versions of creation and have dealt with this problem in a
variety of ways. Traditional interpretation generally harmonized the
two narratives by suggesting that one version was a more detailed and
elaborate version of the other. Modern Bible scholars attribute the
differences in these two versions of the story to different authors,
communities, historical eras, and geographic origins. Dennis Shulman
(2003) persuasively argues that each version depicts a partial view of
God and humanity and so he argues that we need both versions as
dialectic counterparts, nevertheless Shulman's reading of the text is
closely influenced by Fromm's interpretation.[8] Soloveicthik's approach
is also dialectical and reads the two versions in relation to each other
as he examines each narrative to reflect on distinct existential
categories, but his interpretation is strikingly opposed to that of Fromm's.

Soloveitchik speaks of Adam the first and of Adam the second as
two ideal-types, not ideal in the sense of admirable but rather as pure
types, archetypes. It must be understood that Soloveitchik's
presentation is dialectical throughout. Each of us has an Adam I and
an Adam II. Each side, as Ogden (1989) eloquently wrote, "creates,
informs, preserves, and negates the other" (p. 208). While the two
sides are complementary and Adam I never disappears to be superseded
by Adam II, nevertheless it remains clear that Soloveitchik expects us
to aspire to the values represented by Adam II.

---

[8] In fact, it was reading Fromm's (1966) *You Shall Be as Gods* that inspired Shulman
to become a rabbi (October 19, 2004, personal communication).

The first chapter of Genesis describes the primal human surrounded by the cosmos. Here Adam I is part of nature, part and parcel of the environment, set against the backdrop of God's general creation of the world. In this first tale of creation, the name used for God is *Elohim*. According to the Rav,[9] *Elohim* connotes enormous power as depicted in the grandeur and might of the cosmic drama. Adam I lives a nonreflective, instinctive existence, an earth creature in nature, generic, an object among objects rather than a full individual person, viewing the world as an object to be manipulated and controlled in order to advance himself and obtain dignity (Soloveitchik, 2000, p. 8). Surrounded by the majesty of the cosmos, "his significance equals zero" (p. 9). Soloveitchik quotes Psalm 8:3–4. "When I see Thy heavens, Thy handiwork, the moon and stars that Thou has established, what is man that Thou rememberest him, and what is the son of man that Thou thinkest of him?"

Adam II, by contrast, takes a huge ontological leap from natural uniformity to existential complexity, from a nonreflective life to a meditative existence. Adam II is a human person, a subject, a dreamer; he has fantasy and imagination; he is a daring adventurer yearning for beauty and pleasure, for true happiness. In this second text, the name for the Lord God is *Adonai Elohim*. Adam II, human-as-subject, is not satisfied with a generic God of nature but wants a personal relationship with a God who has a personal name—the Tetragrammaton, the four letter unpronounceable, personal name of God. Adam II has emerged as a unique individual subject, an I, a subject relating to a personal God. Human dignity now entails the quest for purpose, meaning, and relationship. Adam II meets God in an intimate relational framework. No longer asking only functional questions, Adam II moves beyond relating to the world as only an object. Where Adam I tries to gain control over his surroundings to move forward and obtain dignity, Adam II tries to gain control over himself, to surrender to God in order to achieve redemption. Adam II is inherently lonely and needs an intersubjective relation. "And the Lord God said, it is not good for the human to be alone" (Genesis 2:18). God's statement about the human condition becomes the fundamental basis of Soloveitchik's existential, relational theology.

---

[9] Soloveitchik attributes this understanding of the names of God to Judah Halevi, the philosopher-poet of 12th-century Spain.

Soloveitchik is portraying a typology that captures two aspects of humanity. The first human feels insignificant, a speck in a vast world, an object among objects, trying to control his object world and achieve dignity and fame. Adam I is a social being, created with Eve; he is never alone, but his need for other people, his sociability, is in the interest of achievement and mastery. Others are used by Adam I as partners to work with, to achieve mastery and dominance. Adam I is not capable of loneliness, even when alone. The second human lives in a relational framework requiring passion, love, and companionship. Adam II is the lonely man of faith. Now another person is needed to complete the man's existence; a friend—a new woman—had to be created. This woman, like the man, had to change from an object into a person capable of being an intersubjective partner.

What transformed Adam I into Adam II? For Soloveitchik the answer is that having been addressed and commanded by God's speech and confronted by law and by limits, Adam becomes an independent subject with the newfound capacity for subjectivity and self-reflexivity. Now Adam II needs a friend, and this new closeness is attained through retreat, sacrifice, and surrender of self. An overpowering sleep falls upon Adam, and he must give away a part of himself to find his companion.

Adam II struggles with two drives and two sets of fears: the fear of death and the fear of ignorance. In this interpretation, Soloveitchik seems to take for granted that death had already entered the world. "Man wants to live and to know. He is curious and eager to live an intelligent, enlightened, inextinguishable existence. His greatest aspiration, his most fascinating dream, is to defeat death and to grasp the *Mysterium magnum*, the great mystery of creation" (2000, p. 11). God plants two trees in the garden for Adam, two great urges (dual-drives): "to desire, to quest, to long for and be fascinated by something great and wonderful—immortality and omniscience" (p. 11).

Soloveitchik, following traditional midrashic interpretation, assumes that Adam and Eve had an erotic life and were intersubjective, self-reflective individuals and involved in a mutual, sexual partnership prior to eating the fruit of the tree of knowledge. Soloveitchik attends to the nuances of the text toward the end of Genesis 1: "And God blessed them, and God said to them, be fruitful and multiply and fill the earth and conquer it" (Genesis 1:28). Why does the text bother saying "and God said to them" after it has already said that God blessed them, Soloveitchik asks (pp. 98–101)? This redundancy of language is not used in regard to God's blessing the animals. Soloveitchik infers that the text highlights the impact of God's direct speech. It is through speech that the earth creature becomes an individual self, a human subject. Notice how sexuality and power become connected in this command. Similarly, in God's speech to Eve after the sin, God said, "And for your man shall be your longings, and he shall rule over you" (Genesis 26:16), thus again interweaving desire and power.

It is immediately after God commands the human not to eat of "the tree of knowledge, good and evil"[10] that God pronounces that it is not good for the human to be alone. The earth creature is transformed into a human subject in need of intersubjectivity only after he has been confronted by divine speech and commanded by God's prohibition. In Soloveitchik's conception, sexuality did not enter the scene only with the snake or the forbidden fruit. Sexuality had been there in the form of biological instinct and drive discharge. The critical change occurs when the human meets up with the command of law with rules and regulations. We become aware of the self and the other simultaneously when we are confronted by and placed in the context of a wider system of language and norms. The decisive turning point for Adam was the moment in which he confronted God's moral will. On the one hand, it is precisely the imposition of this prohibition that transforms the human into a willful, autonomous agent. On the other hand, the urge for unlimited vastness and boundlessness, omniscience and eternity, must to some extent be overcome or transformed. What happens next is not the introduction of sexuality, but rather the disruption of intersubjectivity and the loss of mutuality. The question then becomes, What change took place after Adam and Eve disobeyed God's command? Why did they then feel ashamed of their nakedness?

Soloveitchik (2000) writes, "Man and demon met, they confronted each other, struggled—and the demon won. Who is the demon? The serpent! The demonic personality expresses itself in its desire not for common enjoyment but for exploitation. . . . The lack of reciprocity is the most basic trait of the demon. The other self fades into oblivion. The demon deals with an it" (p. 101). When the law is broken, intersubjectivity is lost. For Soloveitchik, the snake represents the will to dominate, especially through sexuality and seduction. That is also why the snake can only imagine God as power hungry, possessive, jealous, and dominating. In extending beyond their reach, in breaking the law, Adam and Eve have disrupted the intersubjective relation by

---

[10] I am using Alter's (2004, p. 21) translation of this phrase.

treating each other as instinctual, instrumental objects. Their quest for knowledge and power extended beyond their proper limits, and the drive for power, dominance and control complicated human sexuality. Soloveitchik coined the felicitous expression "unredeemed sex" to convey that it is not sexual desire itself that is the problem, but rather perversion—sex in the service of exploitation and objectification of the other (Soloveitchik, 2000, p. 73). They were embarrassed because of their nakedness, not because sex is sinful or the body degraded, but because they now desired each other for the sheer delight of possession. This is the shame of depersonalization and ruthless exploitation, where sexuality is imbued with the quest for power. As Jessica Benjamin (1988, 1995, 1998, 2004) has so beautifully described, where intersubjectivity breaks down we are left with sadomasochism, the seesaw of reversible complementarity, of doer–done to relations.

Intersubjectivity requires a Third, in Lacanian terms, symbolic castration. *Le nom du pere* refers not only to the *name* of the father or paternal metaphor but also suggests, through the pun of *nom* and *non*, the *no* of the father. The name/no of the father prohibits incest and establishes one's place in the social world. For Lacan, our capacity to symbolize is dependent on our capacity to accept a loss, submission, symbolic castration (Dor, 1997). In order for the imaginary dyadic structure to give way to the symbolic order, one needs symbolic regulation, representing law and order, lawfulness, and willing submission to the social order. It is the no of the symbolic father that creates individual autonomy and identity. For Lacan, the law/name/no of the father creates the threshold between the kingdom of culture and that of nature abandoned to the law of copulation. It is through speech that the person becomes an "I" and a sexed subject (Grosz, 1990). For Soloveitchik, Adam I and Eve are a dyad—they are two individuals who work together. But, by way of contrast, Adam II and Eve are joined together in a community with God, who, as the Third, changes their dyadic partnership into an existential community of commitment. When God joins the human community, the miracle of revelation takes place on both the transcendental and human levels. People can then relate to each other, and to God, with the existential fullness and depth of their being.

Ruth Stein (1998) describes the transgressive potential of sexuality and, drawing on Bataille, she links eroticism, prohibitions, transgression, and death. She would view Adam and Eve as apprehending and sensing in their bodies that sexuality is dark and painful, even deathly. Indeed, she points out that sexuality, work, and death are conjugated in God's enunciation when he drives them out of Eden (Stein, October 17, 2004, personal communication). Soloveitchik has a similarly dark view of the excesses of sexuality, but for him, this is not what has to be; rather, it is the perverse result of what happens when the desire for companionship is completely replaced by the lust for union that absorbs the other into the self, when power and pleasure and the will to dominate the other replace metaphysical longing, when sex is unredeemed.

For Soloveitchik, the human personality is split, scattered, dissociated through sin. Since God is one and there is an ethical imperative to maintain the image of God, Judaism desires the unity of the individual (as an impossible ideal). Links need to be made between otherwise dissociated parts of the personality. The *mitzvot* or commandments serve to unite the personality, whereas sin splits the personality apart; sin has a traumatic impact on the soul. On the metaphysical level, God can be conceptualized as a subject in the most absolute sense. A human, too, in imitating God, in following in his ways, must attempt to be a subject relating to other subjects. Sinfulness occurs when people treat each other or themselves as objects. Indeed, for Soloveitchik, the Fall consisted precisely of such a sin whereby man and woman treated each other as objects rather than as independent and interdependent subjects (Lustiger, 1998).

What better illustration could there be of dissociation than Adam's hiding both from God and from himself? "When *Elohim* confronts him, he attempts to dissociate himself from the consequences of his behavior and so lies to himself" (Fishbane, 1998, p. 21). Philip Bromberg (1998), in his introduction to *Standing in the Spaces*, hints at the spiritual function of linking together dissociated self-states. Dissociation protects one aspect of the self at the expense of another. For Soloveitchik, dissociation, while resulting from trauma/sin, also serves a useful purpose in that it protects the pure parts of the personality. Just as Bromberg speaks of normal and pathological dissociation, for Soloveitchik some dissociation must accompany the inevitability of sin in human life, and this splitting serves to protect the pure, healthier aspects of the person from corruption. I conjecture that, just as for Bromberg, a unitary self is an adaptive illusion that, from a theological perspective, wholeness is always an ideal state, because only God could be completely one. From Soloveitchik's perspective, Adam and Eve's sin leads to the disruption of intersubjectivity and the loss of wholeness and holiness.

Throughout his work, Soloveitchik is concerned with humans' tendency to alternate between the overinflated self (the exhilarated subjectivity in which they are at the center of the universe—the world created just for them) and the deflated view of themselves as objects among other objects: "For dust you are and to dust shall you return."[11] His philosophy is thoroughly dialectical, encompassing the duality of human existence as including the polarities that psychoanalyst Shelly Bach (1994) has called "subjective self-awareness" and "objective self-awareness" (p. 46). For Soloveitchik, humanity oscillates between self-negation and absolute pride, psychic ascent and descent, affirmation and negation. "[W]hat is man, that Thou art mindful of him?" alternates with "Yet, Thou has made him but a little lower than the angels" (quoted in Soloveitchik, 1983, p. 68). For Soloveitchik, each emotional experience extends to the antithetic state of mind. "The 'pauper' and 'king' frames of mind are not just two alternating emotional states, but an all-inclusive experience stretching from feeling the utter wretchedness and helplessness of a beggar to the self-assurance and confidence of a king" (2003a, p. 187). For Soloveitchik, the individual's spiritual crisis is constituted by this contradictory, split psychic condition. Indeed, a contemporary psychoanalyst will recognize the depth crisis of trauma and dissociation, the split self, in a beautiful, haunting prayer pushed into the margins of his footnotes, where Soloveitchik wrote:

> "Out of the straits have I called, O Lord" (Ps. 118:5). "Out of the depths I have called unto Thee, O Lord." (Ps. 130:1). Out of the straits of inner oppositions and incongruities, spiritual doubts and uncertainties, out of the depths of a psyche rent with antinomies and contradictions, out of the bottomless pit of a soul that struggles with its own torments I have called, I have called unto Thee, O Lord [1983, p. 142, note].

Each of us oscillates between subjective and objective self-awareness, the exhilaration of omnipotence and omniscience and the

---

[11] I am alluding here to the Chasidic story made famous by Martin Buber, about Rabbi Simha Bunam of Pzhysha (see Shulman, 2003, p. 57). Rabbi Simha Bunam, one of the early Hasidic masters, would carry two notes with him on which to meditate, one in each pocket. On one was written "I am dust and ashes" and on the other was written the Talmudic saying "For my sake was the world created."

despair of inconsequentiality. We oscillate between thinking that the world was created just for us and thinking that we are but dust and ashes. Maintaining self-awareness, reflexivity entails being able to smoothly shift back and forth among these experiences, standing in the spaces (Bach, 1994; Bromberg, 1998; Aron, 2000). To do that requires perspective, a self-awareness that can only exist within the context of a wider system of rules and regulations, an order of creation. Intersubjectivity cannot exist without mourning and surrender to a higher symbolic law. Our job is to return to God and be redeemed, overcome our dissociated split state, and once again become or at least aim to become whole, wholesome, and holy. Neither intersubjectivity nor holiness can ever be achieved as an ongoing steady state, because both are regularly ruptured and repaired, found and lost (Beebe and Lachman, 2002).

Let's now compare Soloveitchik's reading of the garden narrative with Fromm's interpretation. A reading of Fromm, from the perspective of Soloveitchik, would indicate that Fromm has been taken in by the demonic. The Rav writes that, for the demon, "God wanted man for the sole purpose of keeping him eternally in bondage and rejoicing in his ignorance and vulgarity. God is fearful of man the competitor, of man who may find out how to master his own destiny" (Soloveitchik, 2000, p. 102). This is precisely how Fromm (1950) depicts God in his own reading of the text: "The text makes very clear what man's sin is: it is rebellion against God's command; it is disobedience and not any inherent sinfulness in the act of eating from the tree of knowledge. . . . The text also makes it plain what God's motive is: it is concern with his own superior role, the jealous fear of man's claim to become his equal" (p. 43).

Fromm contrasts Adam and Eve—whom he describes as cowardly, meek supplicants who challenge God only through their act of disobedience—with Abraham, who proudly challenges God to uphold the principles of justice with regard to Sodom and Gomorrah, to which God has to yield. Fromm (1966) describes a linear development in which God begins as an authoritarian, absolute monarch and through a series of covenants is transformed into a constitutional monarch, "a step which prepares the way to the concept of the complete freedom of man, even freedom from God" (p. 25). Fromm's hero is certainly not the cowardly Adam, but instead is the proud, independent, challenging Abraham.

On the surface, Fromm's interpretation of Eden looks much more prototypically Jewish. He denies that there was a fall; he does not take sex as the central problem of the narrative; he sees the change in humanity as basically a good thing, even valorizing the snake. He views the expulsion from Eden as the necessary emergence from embeddedness and expects humanity to attempt to return in order to escape from freedom. He champions freedom, individuality, independence, and even a certain rebelliousness, as Jewish values.[12] Soloveitchik's interpretation, by contrast, like much of the Christian literature, views the snake as the devil, speaks of sin and the Fall, and focuses on nakedness and sexuality as deeply embedded in the story. Soloveitchik makes use of an allegorical model much in the style of the Jewish Hellenistic Philo and later Christian tradition.

As we dig deeper we see that the differences between Soloveitchik and Fromm have to do with their attitudes toward authority, law, submission, and rebellion. Fromm champions freedom and valorizes rebellion. He views the covenant as implying a mutuality between God and humanity that frees us from dependence and submission to God as the absolute ruler. Soloveitchik, by contrast, views submission to law as the basis for intersubjectivity and mutuality in human relations and in relations between humanity and God. Fromm characteristically sides with post-Enlightenment narratives privileging emancipation, reason, rationality, freedom, independence, rebellion, and revolution. For the Rav, the *akeda*—Abraham's willingness to sacrifice his son to obey God's command—is the dominant paradigm of religious life and thought (Hartman, 1999). While drawing on an awesome wealth of world literature and philosophy, Soloveitchik puts his emphasis on Halacha (the law) and submission to God. From Fromm's perspective, this abject submission to God's absolute authority is a regressive step from humanistic to authoritarian religion (Fromm, 1950). It reflects humanity's attempt to escape from freedom and existential aloneness and is thus masochistic, self-destructive, and self-degrading.

---

[12] A question worth pondering is whether anyone would read the story of Cain and Abel in such a positive light? The Cain and Abel story is essentially a variation on the Garden of Eden story, as numerous commentators have pointed out (Fishbane, 1998). Yet it is much more difficult to imagine reading Cain's murder of his brother in such a positive light as is commonly done with the eating of the forbidden fruit.

If the story of Abraham standing up to God in regard to Sodom illustrates the mutuality[13] of their relationship, then the *akeda*—the binding of Isaac depicting Abraham's silent submission to God's will— is perhaps the quintessential exemplar of asymmetry.[14] The asymmetry is inherent in our transience and nothingness in relation to the Creator; the mutuality derives from our dignity as human beings who are created in the image of the divine allowing us to commune with God. In the words of Rabbi Soloveitchik,

> In God, man finds both affirmation of himself as a great being, and a ruthless, inconsiderate negation of himself as nothing. This is the main, the dominant theme of Judaism. . . . Finding God is, on the one hand, the greatest victory which man may obtain and, on the other hand, the most humiliating, tormenting defeat which the human being experiences. . . . In a word, the dialectical movement of surging forward and falling back is the way of life ordained by God [2003a, p. 108].

Where Fromm understands submission as masochism and self-denigration, Soloveitchik sees submission as surrender in the service of communion with the source of being. For the Rav, it is *tzarah*, the crisis of falling into the existential depths that underlies prayer. Soloveitchik (2003b) quotes *Avot* 4:29: "Against your will were you born, against your will do you live, and against your will will you die," (p. 35); "man always loses the final battle" (p. 34); and "it is the hounded and entrapped creature, the tormented being, who cries out to God" (p. 175).

Fromm (1950) writes that, in humanistic religion, "the prevailing mood is that of joy, while the prevailing mood in authoritarian religion is that of sorrow and of guilt" (p. 37). Soloveitchik's emphasis on dread, submission, and dependency might seem to confirm Fromm's opinion regarding spiritual experience within authoritarian religion. However, this would neglect that for Soloveitchik, surrender is the necessary route to joy. In his discussion of the *amidah*, the central, "standing" prayer, Soloveitchik (2003b) comments:

---

[13] Mutuality, but not symmetry or equality (see Aron, 1996).

[14] For a detailed study of mutuality and asymmetry in psychoanalysis, see Aron, 1996; for an examination of mutuality and asymmetry in the relations between humanity and God, see Aron, 2004.

> After all the transformations and oscillations from love and mercy to the experience of dread and human helplessness, after man comes crashing down from the heights of yearning and aspiration to the depths of confusion and terror, after self-negation and self-recovery, after the sacrifice, the binding, and the offering on the altar, and after the return to existence—comes again the delightful, joyous and confident experience: God appears as a safe haven and secure abode. The praying individual lies down in green pastures [Psalm 23:2], cleansing himself before God like a son before his father. His tempest-tossed, riven soul finds happiness and serenity, all fear being forgotten. Dread has disappeared; the awesome mystery is past. In their place is a welling up of joy and a yearning for communion with the source of being [p. 181].

In his now classic study, Emmanuel Ghent (1990) clarified the difference between submission and surrender and elucidated that surrender implies not defeat and masochism, but a quality of liberation and of letting go. He shows how this kind of surrender is essential to growth and especially to healing. However, submission or surrender, healing or self-degradation, may be in the eye of the beholder. What to Fromm looks like masochistic submission with the preponderance of sorrow and guilt that characterizes authoritarian religion, is for Soloveitchik healing and joyous surrender and communion.

The two readings of the garden narrative by Fromm and Soloveitchik reflect their different visions and perspectives, and each seems to me a genuine expression of the religious experience. Fromm's reading posits an oversimplified, linear development from submission to independence. Nevertheless, I sympathize with Fromm's championing some measure of insurgence as healthy and constructive and to his vindication of the snake as an affirmative symbol of wisdom, rebellion, and phallic narcissism. There needs to be some room for rebellion in order for submission to be meaningful, some uprising along with the fall. In my view, while Soloveitchik continually attempts a dialectical approach, his own tendency is to valorize submission, as depicted in the binding of Isaac, over humanity's challenging of God, as depicted in Abraham's direct confrontation of God in regard to Sodom, "Far be it from you! Will not the judge of all the earth do justice?" (Genesis 18:25). So Soloveitchik's emphasis on submission and dependence may be balanced by taking into consideration Fromm's preference for independence and protest.

It is of interest, that in Fromm's later writings, as he became increasingly interested in Buddhism, he understood the necessity of giving up one's will to be open, responsive, alive, and awake. He associated this with the Christian idea that one has to "slay oneself and to accept the will of God" (1960, p. 95). A number of questions remain unresolved for me. Why would Fromm, with his intimate knowledge of Jewish literature, portray this as a Christian idea and not also as a Jewish one? *Bittul ha'yesh* (self-negation, or the dissolution of the self) is a significant theme within Judaism, and the theme of prayer as self-sacrifice is a dominant theme in Soloveitchik's writings (see Hartman's 2001 description of this interpretation of prayer, as well as his critique, pp. 190–191.) Finally, Fromm (1960) concludes, "To follow God's will in the sense of true surrender of egoism is best done if there is no concept of God" (p. 95). For Fromm, as far as I can deduce from a careful study of his work, submission to God inevitably evoked the image of the authoritarian father. I can only conclude that Fromm was able to appreciate surrender solely when it was surrender of self from one's own control, but not surrender to anyone or anything outside of the self.

For psychoanalysts, it is worth considering that Fromm's attitudes toward submission and authority had direct consequences on his clinical practice. Maccoby (1996) identified two voices in Fromm and argued that his prophetic voice sometimes eclipsed his analytic voice. Fromm could assertively confront and even aggressively challenge his patients in his attempt to unmask their illusions. Burston (1991) noted the irony that, in his very attempt to combat conformism, Fromm may have compelled submission to his own influence. In his effort to free his patients from authority, Fromm likely reenacted the very dynamic he was trying to analyze, thus dominating his patients with his interpretations of their resistances. In my view, this critique of Fromm's clinical practice is consistent with my interpretation of his simple reversal of the religious value of submission with that of dominance. Rather than working through these dynamics and learning to contain both sides of the split, Fromm valorized assertiveness and devalued surrender and self-sacrifice.

In contrast, for Soloveitchik, who so emphasized self-sacrifice, paradoxically, surrender to God's will did *not* feel like submission at all; rather, surrender to God was experienced as profoundly natural and free. One person's submission is another person's surrender! Thus, Soloveitchik (1983) wrote "halakhic man does not experience any consciousness of compulsion accompanying the norm. Rather, it seems to him as though he discovered the norm in his innermost self, as though it was not just a commandment that had been imposed upon him, but an existential law of his very being" (p. 65). It is essential to keep in mind that the Soloveitchik who advocates submission and self-sacrifice in his relation to God is the very same Soloveitchik who bows to no one when it comes to asserting his daring interpretations, and surrenders before no one in arguing his *halachic* rulings (Hartman, 1997, 2001). My point here is that Soloveitchik is not submitting to a law imposed only from above, beyond, or outside himself, but rather he is surrendering to God's law that he himself (and his own rabbinic tradition) has had a significant part in creating through the powers of human interpretation.[15]

These two interpretations of the story of the Garden of Eden are irreconcilable. Each explains some aspects of the story meaningfully and leaves other aspects less well explained. Each puts some features into the foreground and leaves other aspects of the story in the background. Each author selects and highlights certain elements, words, phrases, characters, and actions. In each case, the overall interpretation is an expression of the author's subjectivity. Neither Fromm nor Soloveitchik wrote as a literary critic; neither was analyzing this story predominantly to weave a tight literary analysis. They were using the story to elaborate their view of the world, their conception of what God expects of humanity.

As psychoanalysts we might think of how differently each of us might interpret this story if we heard it as the dream of one of our patients. Buber (1968) demonstrates how dreamlike is the scene in which Eve and then Adam eat the forbidden fruit. How would we interpret this dream? Interpretations inevitably reflect the subjective world of the interpreter, of the analyst. These two interpretations express different value systems, different images of humanity of God and of their relations, different worldviews. Interpretations can never be neutral. With each interpretation we not only express our own standards and ideals but at least implicitly influence our patients toward our own values and goals. Construction in analysis creates worlds, and in creating worlds we imitate God's work.

---

[15] My analysis of Soloveitchik's relation to authority (submission versus surrender) is rooted in Benjamin (2004).

Soloveitchik's reading is not meant to be a simple (*peshat*) point-by-point elucidation of the text. In fact, in my view, there are moments in his exegesis where he spins the text on its head, turning it into its opposite in order to make his point. He is not a fundamentalist, and his commentary reflects the boldness of rabbinic creative interpretation. Consider as one glaring example how he handles the final act of the story, the last verse of Genesis 3: "And He drove out the human and set up east of the garden of Eden the cherubim and the flame of the whirling sword to guard the way to the tree of life." Now, these symbols of awesome winged beasts, a swirling sword that flashes a flame to frighten the human, according to the plain definition of Rashi (the most outstanding Biblical commentator of the Middle Ages), are clearly intended to frighten and keep the human away from the tree of life. How does Soloveitchik deal with these symbols? Astonishingly, audaciously, the Rav claims that what the cherubim mean is *simple* to him (Soloveitchik, 2002). These symbols were used to adorn the Ark of the Covenant containing the Torah scroll and therefore, through a form of catachresis based on their contiguity, the cherubim symbolize the Torah or the book. For Soloveitchik, there are two roads to power: the sword and the book. There is military, economic, political power and there is the power of the original and imaginative interpretation: creativity. The snake uses both tools, sometimes raw power and sometimes the book, to deceive and seduce. Adam had overreached in an attempt to grab too much power, and so God punished him with stronger power. God put before humanity both the sword and the book, material power and the force of inspiration, in a sort of carrot-and-stick form of persuasion. According to the Rav, the sword threatens and the book creates worlds. Soloveitchik daringly creates a new world by interpreting a symbol of trepidation as a representation of the book. God threatens humanity with the sword but protects humanity with the Torah, the book of books, the creative spirit.

Soloveitchik's construal may be harder for some of us to see as compatible with the plain meaning of the text. But ask yourself, isn't it possible that our resistance to his interpretation is due to the fact that in our culture, in our time, we tend to value freedom, autonomy, assertiveness, and independence? We may be much less comfortable idealizing submission and surrender, bowing before a more powerful force, yielding and acknowledging our insignificance and abject dependence. Could this explain why Fromm's explanation of the garden story is more acceptable and satisfying to many of us?

Furthermore, Fromm's advocacy of rebelliousness and boldness are consistent with Western cultural gender stereotypes of masculinity, and he thus appears masculine and gender congruent, whereas Soloveitchik's ideal of surrender lines up with the culture's labeling of passivity as a feminine characteristic and so appears gender incongruent. Boyarin (1997) has described the classic rabbinic, pre-modern, Jewish "Yeshiva-Bokhur" ideal as counter to the dominant heterosexual culture. The traditional rabbinic male ideal was not aggressive and independent, but sensitive, gentle, passive, and submissive. Feldman (1993) persuasively argued that the Binding of Isaac, depicting the negative Oedipus complex with its bisexual and homosexual implications, was emblematic of the Hebrew Bible and Jewish culture. From this perspective, Soloveitchik's position rather than Fromm's is the more traditionally Jewish interpretation, whereas Fromm's analysis is more in the mainstream of the Western tradition.

I have come to think of the tree of knowledge, good and evil as being not only at the center of the garden, but also at the center of the narrative. This phrase has been explained in many ways, sometimes implying knowledge of all things, from good to bad, and at other times meaning moral knowledge of what is good and what is bad—and of course, in terms of carnal knowledge, placing sexuality at the center of the garden. As Neil Gillman (1997) writes, the meaning of this single enigmatic phrase, knowledge of good and bad, could fill a library.[16]

To me, the tree also represents knowledge that is radically ambiguous, the tree of knowledge, good and evil, meaning it may be good, it may be evil, it is both good and bad. I am developing here Buber's (1968) interpretation that knowledge of good and evil "means

---

[16] In Gillman's (1997) study of the origins of death in the Bible, he draws on James Barr's thesis to interpret death as the inevitable trade-off for the emergence of our distinctive humanity. Barr's thesis is close to Fromm's, and as Gillman points out, close to Martin Buber's (1968). This explanation has the advantage of linking our awareness of death directly to eating from the tree of knowledge and thus to our capacity for self-awareness. Within Soloveitchik's framework, it seems to me that it is not death as a brute fact that is new, but rather with the loss of intersubjectivity, death is bad because one is faced with the existential horror that not only does one inescapably die, but one inevitably dies alone.

nothing else than: cognizance of opposites . . . awareness of the opposites inherent in all being within the world" (p. 17). The tree of knowledge, good and evil is not only at the center of the garden but at the center of our story. The story itself may be read as a positive development for humanity, as Fromm reads it. It was essential that Adam and Eve ultimately disobey and thus grow up; emerge from embeddedness; and achieve self-reflexivity, morality, civilization and its discontents. Or the story depicts sinfulness, a fall, a slip, a loss of intersubjectivity, mutual respect and reciprocity.[17] From this latter point of view, desire itself can be good—longing for knowledge and wishing for immortality, the ego instincts and the sexual instincts are part of our nature. But there are limits that must be respected, for without limits we become fragmented or lose the precarious equilibrium between our insignificance and our grandiosity; we fall. The tree of knowledge, good and evil, at the center of the garden, may be understood to indicate that all of the symbols in the story may be viewed as *both* good *and* bad. Knowledge can be used for both good and evil; sexuality, both good and evil; self-awareness, both good and bad; leaving Eden, both good and bad; even death and our awareness of death, both good and bad.

Ultimately both Fromm and the Rav agree that Torah teaches living fully, joyfully, and creatively, in the image of God, as the ultimate ethical value. For Fromm (1966) quoting Psalms, "My soul thirsts for God, for *the living* God" (p. 44), what characterizes idolatry is that the idol is an object, a thing, lifeless, whereas God is the living God. The primary ethical imperative as interpreted by both Soloveitchik and Fromm is that we choose life. "Life and death I set before you, the blessing and the curse, and you shall choose life" (Deuteronomy 30:19). Clashingly at odds, diametrically opposed, both the views of the Rav and those of Fromm may be regarded as the words of the living God.

---

[17] Interestingly, in my view, Buber (1968) holds the tension of these opposite readings much better than does Fromm. Buber recognizes, as Fromm did not, that while the biblical narrator may have taken the theme from ancient myths that depict God as envious and vengeful, that for the biblical narrator this theme has been fundamentally transformed. For the biblical narrator, the human is clearly no match and no threat to God. For Buber, each element in the story contains its opposite, even the knowledge of death having its positive, limit setting and comforting side. While Adam and Eve sin and are sentenced, nevertheless the very punishment is also the beginning of human history.

REFERENCES

Alter, R. (2004), *The Five Books of Moses*. New York: W. W. Norton.

Aron, L. (1996), *A Meeting of Minds*. Hillsdale, NJ: The Analytic Press.

———— (2000), Self-Reflexivity and the Therapeutic Action of Psychoanalysis. *Psychoanal. Psychol.*, 17:667–690.

———— (2004), God's influence on my psychoanalytic vision and values. *Psychoanal. Psychol.*, 21:442–451.

Bach, S. (1994), *The Language of Perversion and the Language of Love*. Northvale, NJ: Aronson.

Bakan, D. (1958), *Sigmund Freud and the Jewish Mystical Tradition*. Princeton, NJ: van Nostrand.

Beebe, B. & Lachmann, F. (2002), *Infant Research and Adult Treatment*. Hillsdale, NJ: The Analytic Press.

Benjamin, J. (1988), *The Bonds of Love: Psychoanalysis, Feminism, and the Problem of Domination*. New York: Pantheon.

———— (1995), *Like Subjects, Love Objects: Recognition and Sexual Difference*. New Haven, CT: Yale University Press.

———— (1998), *Shadow of the Other: Intersubjectivity and Gender in Psychoanalysis*. New York: Routledge.

———— (2004), Beyond doer and done to: An intersubjective view of thirdness. *Psychoanal. Quart.*, 73:5–46.

Bloom, H. (1987), *The strong light of the canonical. The City College Papers*, 20:1–77. New York: H. Bloom.

Boyarin, D. (1993), *Carnal Israel*. Berkeley, CA: University of California Press.

———— (1997), *Unheroic Conduct*. Berkeley, CA: University of California Press.

Bromberg, P. (1998), *Standing in the Spaces*. Hillsdale, NJ: The Analytic Press.

Buber, M. (1968), *On the Bible: Eighteen Studies*. New York: Schocken Books.

Burston, D. (1991), *The Legacy of Erich Fromm*. Cambridge, MA: Harvard University Press.

Calef, V. (1964), "Escape from authority: The perspectives of Erich Fromm." *Psychoanal. Quart.*, 33:291–293.

Dor, J. (1997), *The Clinical Lacan*. Northvale, NJ: Aronson.

Feldman, Y. S. (1993), "And Rebecca loved Jacob," but Freud did not. *Jewish Studies Quarterly*, 1:72–88.

Fishbane, M. (1998), *Biblical Text and Texture*. Oxford, UK: Oneworld.

Fromm, E. (1941), *Escape from Freedom*. New York: Holt, Rinehart & Winston.

———— (1947), *Man for Himself*. New York: Holt, Rinehart & Winston.

———— (1950), *Psychoanalysis and Religion*. New Haven, CT: Yale University Press.

———— (1951) *The Forgotten Language*. New York: Grove Press.

———— (1955), *The Sane Society*. New York: Holt, Rinehart & Winston.

———— (1956), *The Art of Loving*. New York: Holt, Rinehart & Winston.

———— (1960), Psychoanalysis and Zen Buddhism. In: *Zen Buddhism and Psychoanalysis*, ed. D. T. Suzuki, E. Fromm & R. de Martino. New York: Harper & Row, pp. 77–141.

—— (1966), *You Shall Be as Gods*. New York: Holt, Rinehart & Winston.

Ghent, E. (1990), Masochism, submission, surrender: Masochism as a perversion of surrender. *Contemp. Psychoanal.*, 26:108–135.

Gillman, N. (1997), *The Death of Death*. Woodstock, VT: Jewish Lights.

Grosz, E. (1990), *Jacques Lacan: A Feminist Introduction*. London: Routledge.

Hartman, D. (1998), *A Living Covenant: The Innovative Spirit in Traditional Judaism*. Woodstock, VT: Jewish Lights.

—— (1999), *A Heart of Many Rooms*. Woodstock, VT: Jewish Lights.

—— (2001), *Love and Terror in the God Encounter*. Woodstock, VT: Jewish Lights.

Hornstein, G. A. (2000), *To Redeem One Person Is to Redeem the World*. New York: Free Press.

Kvam, K. E., Schearing, L. S. & Ziegler, V. H., eds. (1999), *Eve and Adam: Jewish, Christian, and Muslim Readings of Genesis and Gender*. Bloomington and Indianapolis: Indiana University Press.

Lustiger, A., ed. (1998), *Before Hashem You Shall Be Purified: Rabbi Joseph Soloveitchik on the Days of Awe*. Edison, NJ: Ohr Publishing.

Maccoby, M. (1996), The two voices of Erich Fromm: The prophetic and the analytic. In: *A Prophetic Analyst: Erich Fromm's Contributions to Psychoanalysis*, ed. M. Cortina & M. Maccoby. Northvale, NJ: Aronson, pp. 61–93.

Ogden, T. H. (1989), *The Matrix of the Mind*. Northvale, NJ: Aronson.

Shulman, D. G. (2003), *The Genius of Genesis*. New York: iUniverse.

Soloveitchik, J. B. (1965), *The Lonely Man of Faith*. Northvale, NJ: Aronson, 1997.

—— (1983), *Halakhic Man*. Philadelphia: Jewish Publication Society.

—— (2000), *Family Redeemed*. New York: Ktav Publishing.

—— (2002), *The Rav Speaks*. New York: Toras Harav Foundation.

—— (2003a), *Out of the Whirlwind*. New York: Ktav Publishing.

—— (2003b), *Worship of the Heart*. New York: Ktav Publishing.

Stein, R. (1998), The poignant, the excessive, and the enigmatic in sexuality. *Internat. J. Psychoanal.*, 79:253–268.

2

Uneasy Intimacy, a Siren's Call*

Margaret Crastnopol

▼   ▼   ▼   ▼   ▼

"This is Just to Say," a poem by the poet/physician William Carlos Williams (1968), nicely sets the tone for a discussion of what I call "uneasy intimacy."

This is Just to Say

I have eaten
the plums
that were in
the icebox

you were probably
saving
for breakfast

Forgive me
they were delicious
so sweet
and so cold

*My deep appreciation goes to those who offered invaluable suggestions on earlier versions of this chapter, namely Glen Gabbard, Dodi Goldman, and Joyce Slochower. Also extremely helpful were the comments of Raelene Gold, Ladson Hinton, Michael Horne, and Malcolm Slavin.

This is a poem to be savored for its straightforwardness, homey cadence, and ostensibly considerate message. It begins unceremoniously and familiarly as a memo without salutation, the title sinuously winding itself into the body of the poem itself. The writer apologizes for his infraction in one swift "forgive me," but quickly moves into the sensuality of those ripe fruits. He knows the intended recipient well enough to imagine that she—his wife?— was anticipating having the plums for a refreshing meal, on what was perhaps an already hot summer's morning. He begs her pardon, and in the face of his disarming apology, she can scarcely withhold it from him, even if it undermines her righteous anger at the loss she's incurred.

The poem captivates the listener because as we inhabit the space of the fictional reader to whom the note is addressed, we are drawn in by the writer's simplicity of expression, confidential tone, and winning self-assuredness. We are happy to be his "intimates," to share vicariously in the sensual experience of eating sweet, dripping plums—plums that weren't quite his to eat. The poet has charmingly won us over, and we'll forgive him anything … at least for the foreseeable future. It's easy to forget that his wife has been stripped of her "plums" (sexual reference intended), that someone has been ever so slightly betrayed. So it is with what I call "uneasy intimacy." There is the painfully delicious and deliciously painful experience of being "sweet-talked" into a psychic gain that houses within it a psychic loss.

Uneasy Intimacy: Its Phenomenology

Intimacy proper has many faces. It embraces a sense of one person knowing another's internal world; of recognizing how the other thinks, feels, and reacts to things; of familiarity with the other's strengths and weaknesses or vulnerabilities; of knowing his or her idiosyncrasies and preferences. Intimacy can imply a mysterious quality of warmth and the intensity, privacy, and exclusivity of mutual closeness. What I consider to be "uneasy intimacy" belongs to the darker underbelly of intimacy proper. It refers to the unconscious use of one's capacity for psychic resonance to co-opt the other into an emotional embrace that is equally or more toxic (Eigen, 1999) than nourishing. I stop short of calling it emotional seduction—though an element of seduction may be present—to avoid the implication of its being a conscious manipulation, which is not what I have in mind. Uneasy intimacy often begins and evolves differently than healthier types do, in that the two individuals become privy to each other's inner world to an excessive degree and at an artificially heightened rate. This intensity of degree and rate often fails to take into account other features of the two individuals' roles vis-à-vis each other. These are the features—like age discrepancy, role asymmetry, conflicting ties, value differences, and so forth—that under other circumstances would have modulated their close-ness.[1] While one of them is usually the primary driver, both of the intimates can get carried away in their involvement almost without being aware of it. Uneasy intimacy is a kind of siren's call, tantalizing and nearly impossible to forestall when within its range.

One reason intimacy is so potentially problematic is that human beings are many-sided, that selfhood is by its nature multiplicitous. So we may be intimate with one another vis-à-vis *certain* aspects of internal life, and yet be unconsciously masking, bracketing, or withholding *other* facets. When we are unaware of the internal parameters of intimacy we're acting under, we may give false or disingenuous cues that "everything's out on the table." If this prompts a similar openness from the other, one or both individuals are likely to end up feeling at best, disoriented and at worst, betrayed, once the discrepancy becomes apparent.

When the bond becomes laced with explicitly erotic overtones, it becomes that much harder for either person to disengage from the emotional knot. The chronic, everyday variants of uneasy intimacy can be just as damaging as more flagrant forms of the "fatal attraction" ilk, if only because they are look-alikes (Ghent, 1990) for normal behavior. They lie on the same continuum as the more acute, severe versions of destructive attachment.

Uneasy intimacy should be clearly distinguished from ethical or moral boundary violations per se. With its strong allure, such intimacy may sometimes be a *prelude* to boundary transgression, but more often it stops short of this.[2] Disciples may be under the excessive sway of a particularly compelling leader, children under the undue psychic press of their parents, analytic candidates under the collusive influence of a certain supervisor, without its necessarily evolving into an explicit transgression of psychosocial limits. Role boundaries are more like regions than sharp edges, and within such a region there is much room for the push and pull of confidence-sharing, attitude-influencing, overidentification with another's internal objects, and so on. Up to a certain point, then, there can be emotional bending without clear breakage of an "I–thou" social compact. Many role relationships permit considerable latitude in the personal di-

---

[1]Ann Patchett's *Bel Canto* (2002), about a fictionalized Latin American embassy take-over, offers a beautifully elaborated example of how such discrepancies could result in precipitous or unlikely intimacies that are not necessarily uneasy or otherwise corrupt. Patchett depicts (with fictional license) captives and captors developing personal bonds not only among themselves but across their adversarial divide. External coercive circumstance may sometimes engender intimacy and this intimacy is not necessarily toxic but in fact can be healing, if Patchett is to be believed.

[2]For situations in which uneasy intimacy did in fact evolve into flagrant sexual boundary violation within our field, see Gabbard and Lester, 1995; Gabbard, 1996; Celenza and Gabbard, 2003.

mension, and becoming more personal than a given role relationship explicitly calls for can be extremely productive. It sometimes becomes evident only in retrospect that one has gone farther into the private sphere of self or other than might be optimal.

In fact, one additional hallmark of uneasy intimacy is that it tends to fall below the legal or ethical radar, which makes it potentially insidious. Another is that it can lead to a kind of emotional exploitation in which one or both participants can neither leave nor thrive within the relationship. This effect—the curtailment of thriving as opposed to outright emotional/physical abuse—significantly differentiates uneasy intimacy from a boundary-violating relationship.[3]

The experience of an infatuation or, for that matter, falling in love, can set the stage for uneasy intimacy, but under optimal conditions it does not do so. Both the suitor and the object of affection can often withstand the temptation to overexpose oneself to the other prematurely, as they self-protectively intuit the value of letting closeness build only gradually on the proving ground of mutual trust. Where there is a differentiated and yet coherent enough sense of self on each one's part, both partners are more likely to hold their own in this force field of psychic attraction.

Theoretical Considerations in Uneasily Intimate Relatedness

Fairbairn's (1952) view of schizoid factors in endopsychic structuralization offers a perspective from which to view the troublesome phenomena under discussion. Fairbairn argues that ego (or self) is comprised of splits that occur by virtue of its efforts to cope with traumatizing relationships external objects. The trauma specifically cited is that of living with a mother who "fails to convince her child by spontaneous and genuine expressions of affection that she herself loves him as a person (Fairbairn 1952, p. 13)." (Singled out as "worst of all" is the mother who is both "possessive and indifferent," a constellation reminiscent of the clinical example to be discussed later.) The child's solution is to regress to a simpler form of relationship and concentrate on the mother's breast as a part object. The regression entails a depersonalization of the object and a "de-emotionalization" of the object-relationship. (p. 14), so that affect is repressed and thinking becomes overvalued. In this way the real external other can become a part-object "thing" to

---

[3]The foregoing idea and much else in this paper benefited from the rich theoretical contributions and editorial ministrations of Dodi Goldman (also named earlier in the acknowledgments).

be dealt with rather than a full-bodied other to be related to. This "dealing with" the other is a facet of the uneasy intimacy under discussion.

In Fairbairn's later theorizing, the ego responds to trauma by internalizing the bad object, which splits into exciting and rejecting internal objects, and the "central" ego itself develops split subsidiary internalizations, the libidinal ego and internal saboteur. An individual with such a developmental history and the excessively strong internalized objects Fairbairn describes might, I would argue, project the exciting object into the outside world and seek to woo and win the projected-on external other in order to assuage the inner rejecting object. Uneasy intimacy would be a strategy for doing so.

Applying this theory from another vantage point, someone who is inherently intuitive, empathic, and sensitive—or particularly intense—is more likely to evoke an "exciting object" projection from others. This in turn might call forth an overcloseness that is sterile and relatively counterproductive. A person whose internal saboteur (or rejected ego) is more profoundly wounded from the beginning is more likely to attach to someone who, because of his or her own narcissistic needs, implicitly invites being treated as an exciting object. Moreover, the person functioning as an exciting object may *seem* to be in a "central object" position— that is, the self "feels" that the other is a healthy, balanced influence, and can't discern the problematic qualities of their closeness. Someone unaccustomed to constructive closeness will likely be impaired in his or her capacity to tell the difference between a hug and a clench, or connectedness and suction.

Khan (1979) also elaborated on distortions in the healthy capacity for intimacy based on disturbances in early mother–child attachment. In his view, some individuals with this sort of history (he singled out schizoid individuals and "perverts") engage in the "technique of intimacy." He described the latter as "the attempt to establish a make-believe situation involving in most cases the willing seduced co-operation of an external object" (p. 22). This is an interpersonal game that dramatizes, but offers no real object relatedness and hence, no psychic nourishment. The individual uses confession and self-disclosure as a strategy to engage the other more closely. Khan emphasizes that such a person "tries to use the technique of intimacy as a therapeutic device and all he accomplishes is more expertise in the technique itself (p. 24)." He adds sympathetically that "This failure to achieve any form of ego-satisfaction is then compensated by idealization of instinctual discharge processes, which in turn lead to a sense of depletion, exhaustion and paranoid turning away from or against" (p. 24). It is a process bound to engender despair in the perpetrator, as his or her deepest wishes for authentic intimacy are self-thwarted. (Of course, Khan's emphasis was on those at the most disturbed end of the spectrum, whereas I'm describing a subtler and less pernicious version of this tendency.)

In a look at the clinical interchange likely to develop with such individuals, O'Shaughnessy (1992) describes a state of uneasy intimacy between her and a patient. She calls the situation an "enclave," her term for a kind of constricted relatedness characterized by feeling tones of closeness, in which the relatedness is primarily designed as a "refuge" from unbearable anxiety and disturbance. O'Shaughnessy describes this graphically:

> Reflecting on this analytic situation, I saw that I had mistaken, just as Miss A herself does, over-closeness for closeness, and mistaken, too, a restrictive and restricting part object relationship for full contact between whole persons. My dissatisfaction with the 'you-me' interpretations that I had been making was now clearer. These interpretations were not part of a full interpretation, which in principle could eventually be completed, and involve internal objects, the interplay between unconscious phantasy and reality, and the reliving of the past. These interpretations were intrinsically denuded of such connexions. They were part of the opening interaction between Miss A and myself, which both constituted and facilitated the emergence of Miss A's characteristic relations to her objects. (p. 602)

O'Shaughnessy goes on to warn us that "some degree of acting out by the analyst inevitably occurs as a relationship like Miss A.'s with her objects emerges in the analysis" (p. 602). Later she cautions even more urgently, "As important as not enacting an enclave with a patient is not pushing and forcing a patient out of his refuge" (p. 603). She describes her temptation to forge "there and then" transferential interpretations of the patient's over-closeness with her as a *continuation* of the enclave, in that it allowed her to avoid the anxious recognition that she did not truly understand who she was in the transference for the patient.

Key implications for our clinical methodology, as I understand the author, are (a) that the analyst probably cannot entirely avoid this type of enactment when the patient "needs" an enclave; (b) that the analyst's willingness to recognize the constrictedness of the enclave is a critical way-station in his or her ability to understand the patient's subjectivity; and (c) that there is no one right way for the dyad to work its way out of such a bind, though ultimately doing so is essential to the success of the analysis. Neither interpreting within the transference nor extra-transferentially will necessarily release the patient from the need to establish an illusion of perfect symbiotic resonance with the other.

Michael Eigen (1999) uses a feeding metaphor to get at the miscarriage of closeness associated with uneasy intimacy. He says,

> Emotional toxins and nourishment often are so mixed as to be indistinguishable. Even if they can be distinguished, it may be impossible for an individual

to get one without the other. In order to get emotional nourishment, one may have to take in emotional toxins.... A life can so sour, and a person so accommodate to high levels of toxins, that he or she may develop aversive reactions to less polluted opportunities for nourishment. Life may not feel real without large doses of emotional toxins. Some people cannot take nourishment that is not embedded in psychic poisons. (p. 1)

Uneasy Intimacy in Childhood Development

Nancy Chodorow (1978) notes that a parent whose emotional needs are not met within the marital bond will often seek to meet them through the relationship with her or his child. In making this point Chodorow focuses on the mother–daughter dyad, but I believe this can happen quite readily in other dyads as well, depending (paradoxically) on which family members have the greatest propensity for emotional sensitivity and relatedness. When the parent inaugurates this type of special relationship, the child is gratified by the singling-out and, I argue, may actually benefit from certain emotional lessons precociously learned through the situation. However, the younger person is at the same time also constricted by the growing emotional resonance with the parent, one that often creates a sense of inordinate responsibility for the parent's psychic well-being. The advantages and disadvantages of this dicey mutual involvement can seem so evenly matched that even the most perceptive child can become ensnared in it—as can the most well-meaning parent. What amounts to an arrest at a symbiotic-like stage of separation/individuation (Mahler, Pine, & Bergman, 1975) eventually takes its toll on both parties (Crastnopol, 1980). I have seen this more often between a child and his or her mother, but it can occur as well with the father when the latter has pressing unmet wishes and a strong capacity for emotional relatedness. As in the case with romantic adult partners, neither parent nor child is a villain (or *the* villain) in this scenario, though of course the parent implicitly bears primary responsibility for its consequences.

The bond thickens when uneasy intimacy becomes sensually tinged. Both the thirst for and the capacity to provide emotional intimacy become inscribed in each person's psychesoma through biophysiological pathways and circadian rhythms. A 10-year-old girl goes to visit her aunt in a distant part of the country, and for several weeks the aunt showers her with concentrated attention and verbal caresses—"darling, my sweetheart, you're the smartest thing that ever lived, come, let's take you shopping," and so on. There is constant affectionate snuggling or stroking. The girl reels with the extravagant involvement. When it's time to return home, she's in agony at having to part with the aunt she believes she's finally gotten close with after so many years. Once they're no longer together, her aunt emotionally disappears: few phone calls, no e-mails, not even a birthday present when the time comes. The girl misses her aunt with an almost physical ache. Thinking back on it in later years, she realizes that what the aunt had offered was only a forced, condensed *show* of involvement, one that was perhaps driven by a desperate wish to carve a place for herself in the 10-year-old's heart. The aunt's engulfing, momentary, sensual intimacy certainly had an authentic germ in it ("germ" in perhaps both senses)—but it offered promises that wouldn't be kept, and left the girl with a painful yearning not easily quelled.

A Gift for Intimacy Within the Sociocultural Milieu

Does the writer of Williams' "message as poem" *intend* a benign con, trading on intimacy to get what he wants with impunity? To the contrary— the speaker's motives and tone register as unpremeditated and quite sincere. He automatically without forethought draws the other in—he can't help but use this capacity that is so intuitively his. The ability to establish a sense of intimacy with another is a true gift, one we celebrate when we find it in poets and artists. But like any highly developed competency it can take on a life of its own, with complicated and consciously unintended consequences. Emotional closeness is at one time a one-person and a two-person phenomenon, with intrapersonal and interpersonal effects. And underlying this is the larger sociocultural trope of Western society (and perhaps others as well), in which establishing a sense of privileged knowledge and access to the other's private life has become common currency. A craving for closeness might indeed be a by-product of the anxieties and terrors of the current era. Facing ever intensifying threat, we naturally seek solace in the form of real or illusory closeness with others we invest with special and/or reassuring properties. From another angle, the social tendency to establish a sense of "hollow intimacy"—based on relating false self to false self—might be an adaptive/defensive undoing in response to the alienation engendered by the narcissistic challenges pitting us against one another in this competitive society.

Uneasy Intimacy in Romantic Pairing: A Case Illustration

Against this backdrop I now concentrate on the romantic partnership between a sensitive man and his female lover, though other manifestations of uneasy intimacy are certainly worthy of attention and will be touched on subsequently.

James was a 35-year-old public relations director in a midsized high-tech company. Tall, slender, almost wiry, he was a gentle man and a gentleman, with a ready smile and an unassuming manner that belied his high-powered position and economic stature. James came to treatment with a history of intensive, sequential romantic relationships that somehow always ended in a state of painful rupture and loss, though the endings were at his behest. He was excruciatingly lonely in between relationships, which caused him compulsively to call or e-mail friends to fill in the gap when alone for even just an hour or two. We determined that this was in part to compensate for the fact that he was noxious company for himself. In his internal world, he relentlessly second-guessed his actions at work, worrying about whether he'd handled each decision optimally, then arguing with himself about what "optimal" meant and whether he really had to function optimally or whether he was being too stern with himself, and so on. James would obsess about the most moral way to handle his underlings or whoever else crossed his path. These struggles took on a philosophical cast and he would indignantly insist on inwardly hashing out each action or choice for its intrinsic value as well as its repercussions on others. The result, of course, was painful paralysis and a sense of inefficacy, much psychic energy draining away in the process.

James was in addition neurotically genial. This was no doubt a function of his desire for others' approval, itself a substitute for his parents' and ultimately his own. It was an adaptation he'd developed in order to glean rewards for capacities he did have (empathy, attunement, generosity, concern) rather than relying on those he felt were in insufficient supply (personal ambition, steadfast goal pursuit, intellectual drive, etc.).

Particularly important was the way this played out in James' romantic life. With his nonthreatening, warm affability, James easily attracted women. Soon one of these bonds would intensify, as James and the woman spent hour after hour in heart-to-heart talks about their life goals and concerns, eventually revealing their anxieties and vulnerabilities to each other. James would feel listened to and accepted by the woman, which was of course soothing. Just as importantly, he would feel needed. He would begin caretaking, bending over backward to resolve her problems, lending or giving her money, licking whatever wounds life had inflicted, inadvertently courting her dependency on him. James was thrilled by the woman's admiration and gratified by her dependency. Yet he hesitated to seal the pact and make it permanent, and he himself did not quite know why. It took several extended iterations of the patterning before James could see that he'd been choosing women who were notably insecure about their own competency and/or position in life, and that this set the stage for his becoming ensnared in an uneasily intimate dynamic. The woman was usually someone who needed more a paternal figure than a romantic equal, which James both loved and hated to oblige.

A central point here and in many cases of uneasy intimacy is that James himself was largely unconscious of the sources of his ambivalence, of why he had difficulty making an ultimate commitment to the woman. He was unaware that being *needed* by the woman had become a substitute for being respected and loved by someone he himself respected and loved. Soon James was consumed with guilt at the tenuousness of his attachment to the woman. He berated himself for his doubt, and was acutely uncomfortable with his dawning analytic realization of the disapproval and disdain he unconsciously harbored toward her.

James did indeed genuinely appreciate a woman's individuality; he sincerely relished her softness and other maternal qualities. He turned his attentive psyche to hers and cared about what he found there. But only to a point, and that limit was his dirty little secret, a secret kept not only from the woman but from himself. In a kind of emotional "Don Juanism," James effectively dissociated his own assertive, critical, striving aspects, in the service of enjoying the warm "playtime" of his involvement with the woman. The judgmental side of him, however, could not remain fully buried. What finally emerged—the critical, self-important internal voice—felt monstrous to him, so he tried repeatedly to squelch and deny it. The woman was left feeling strongly attached but hanging as to the likelihood of a future together. James was recurrently writing the note, "This is just to say that you're a lovely person, but I can't stay with you and I can't explain why."

The youngest of three children in a lower middle-class family, James decided early on that he did not wish to compete in the same arenas as his elder sister and brother. He would not enslave himself in order to reap the academic or athletic accolades that pleased his always striving father. Instead he became the playful rebel, marshaling his considerable intellectual and verbal skills to challenge his parents' values and expectations of him. James' surcease and pleasure came from long, late-night talks with his mother, who offered time, attention, and seemingly warm understanding. He would try to convince her that he should be allowed greater freedoms in the household, more flexible standards, and so on, and she would listen carefully. However in the end she would always side with the father's categorical, authoritarian prohibition. James never, to the best of his recollection, won one of these arguments. Yet up until the middle of his analysis he was under the illusion that they were intimate, satisfying contacts. This was simply his family's version of intimacy—and as such, the best he could imagine, in keeping with Eigen's description of toxic nourishment. James had developed his taste—or craving—for female approval and comforting from this childhood closeness with his mother, such as it was. This situation echoes Chodorow's description of the mother pulling for emotional overinvolvement with her child, in the absence of having a full relatedness with a detached husband.

James transferred much of the earlier mother–son scenario to his courting behavior. He would sway the woman with his warmth and piercing attention, thereby winning her over to his side (and away from the oedipal father's). And if by chance she sensed his underlying disdain or otherwise recognized that they were not a good match and pulled back, he would pursue her all the more ardently, offering understanding and sensitivity to overcome her qualms. This unfulfilling, precarious engagement would feel to him like "good intimacy," because it resembled the aborted recognition he had experienced so often with his mother. In the end, the woman—being weak herself—could never give him the ultimate affirmation he'd craved from his own mother and of course, his father. She was trapped but so was he—stuck being the father/lover, never the full-bodied equal mate and partner.

As I noted earlier, adding sexual attraction to a situation of uneasy intimacy is like applying epoxy to an ill-fitting joint. The damaging position becomes fixed in space and time. James' untoward impulses toward emotional intimacy with an inappropriate woman became exponentially heightened when he found her particularly soft and feminine. His innate warmth and charm would simply go on overdrive, and before he knew it they were lovers. Weeks or months would be lost in the backtracking. Whether the passion precedes the emotional intimacy or vice versa, it tends to trump the individuals' ability to recognize the "uneasiness" of their closeness and to take steps to test and perhaps withdraw from it. So while the woman might be hurt or betrayed by it, James himself would too. This is "uneasy intimacy" par excellence.

The following process material comes from an hour about 3 years into this 4-times-a-week analysis. I include some contextual clarifications and also a sense of the transferential/countertransferential forces that seemed at play. James wrestles with himself and with me, as he tries to judge whether building intimacy in a dating context by being overly attentive and generous is at all problematic. In the meantime he's playing out another incarnation of "uneasily intimate" relating in which he tries to evoke maternal nurturance in me by presenting himself as exceedingly and appealingly weak. He further tries to convince me that he *deserves* to be fed—after all, he's worked hard to be a good boy who remembers and follows his psychoanalytic lessons. And I do find James both appealing and very likable, but more in spite than because of his efforts to endear himself.

J [James]: So I'm in the throes of thinking about my search for "a better mother" thing. I realize it'll never be satisfying. I know that I'm doing this again with H. I understand the problem intellectually but obviously not at the emotional level.

A
[analyst]: Somehow I feel that in your saying this, there's a plea for me to supply the answer, for me to mother you.

J: Yeah, [said jovially] if I could do it myself, I wouldn't be here!

A: Ah, and *that* feels like an angry, *insistent* plea for mothering.

J: I'm angry at *myself* for playing out the same dance … I've corresponded with three or four new women lately.… I didn't tell S. [another potential girlfriend] that I didn't want to have a relationship with her. I'm struggling with it—don't want to have that difficult conversation. Since I don't know what a healthy relationship is, it's difficult for me to make these kinds of judgments [about who to continue dating and who to let go].

During this discussion, James alternately courts my approval, confesses his weakness, and attempts to persuade me that certain suspect actions were actually healthy. His last comment in particular strikes me as self-diminishing and help-seeking, and rather worrisome after all his work in our analysis and the two treatments preceding it. I find myself fighting not to succumb to my frustration. I know that I'm in O'Shaughnessy's "enclave" for better and worse. If I give James the guidance he seeks, I reinforce the fantasied scenario of a needy, ingenuous little boy who can sway the powerful mother. I know that by instead *resisting* the guiding role and interpreting his wish, I reenact the victimized son–withholding mother scenario. Either of these can arouse affects that will constrict his analytic growth. Apparently I have no choice but to hunker down in the enclave and wait for what may come.

Coming back to the interchange:

A: I'm not sure how you mean [that you don't know what a healthy relationship is]?

J: I know I'm drawn to unhealthy relationships, ones that are unhealthy because they make me replicate unhealthy behaviors I've had. So if I'm drawn to somebody, then they'll inevitably evoke unhealthy behavior in me!

This strikes me as sophist reasoning, but quite typical of how he envisions himself as inadequate in order to evoke the actively caretaking, maternal me. Once again, I experience the pull of those early mother–son talks, so hard to resist getting sucked into.

J: … I have a good reason not to trust my sense of chemistry. I feel this because I can't tell what's healthy and what isn't. Unless the goal is to accept that I have these kinds of unhealthy relationships and I should stop worrying about it—which I don't think it is, seriously.

Out again comes the hope that he can just have unhealthy fun and that the problem is merely his being too self-critical about that. He's baiting me in that he knows I'm dubious, but at the same time he partially accepts my view of these relationships as bankrupt. So he retracts what he's said and makes reparation by saying, "I don't think that's the goal of therapy."

At this juncture I suggest that James has painted himself into a corner and then magically leapt out of it. He is hopelessly conflicted and there is no "best" answer, which seemingly gives him implicit permission to "luxuriously" give up and do whatever feels best in the moment. (I don't have to add that we both know this ultimately won't wash.)

> J: [Well, I'm coming to understand that....] a mutuality of seeking out (her wanting him as much as him wanting her, and vice versa) is a good indicator of healthy relationships. So if it's one-sided, me doing all the calling, it's not healthy.
>
> A: umhm.

My conscious intent with this nonverbal approval was to try to differentiate between being a "caring person" and being emotionally seductive in his over-solicitousness to women. Clearly I couldn't resist the overall transference/ countertransference pull to set him on the supposedly "right" emotional pathway.

Diligently James tries another angle:

> J: I have a hard time figuring out if I'm an introvert or an extrovert. ... I'm probably both, which creates problems being with somebody who's predominantly one or the other. It's hard to know how to get myself to let go of unhealthy relationships.... the trouble breaking the pattern, what drives me, is the feeling of loneliness ... [describes some constructive things he did, involving solo attendances at cultural and sports events]. I do feel my aloneness when I go to these things.... Yesterday morning and today I went to a tai chi class [something he'd been blocked about doing for months]. It was good for me, but [this next said with apparent shame and self-disappointment] I'm always looking for the breast.... I notice it when I'm alone, that I notice women and my attention is particularly pulled to their breasts ... I'm fixated on them [he borrows analytic lingo].[4]

---

[4]This preoccupation calls to mind Fairbairn's (1952, p. 11ff.) view of schizoid elements in which the child's libidinal interest focuses on the breast as a partial *(continued)*

A: What's going on in the "fixation"?

J: I'm noticing their breasts, which I associate with wanting to get close, be comforted, the feeling of being taken care of. A deep part of me really wanted to follow H. (last girlfriend) around. I so wanted to be taken care of, I wanted to be told what to do. Because I don't know what I want to do a lot of the time, I don't really care, ... I have no firm sense of my own direction. So I want someone to keep me oriented, comfort me, guide me.

A: So the woman knows what to do and can guide you, but you *don't* know? (Of course I'm "leading the witness" in my exchange with him, itself an evoked enactment of the hungry son/bosomy mother scenario.)

J: Right.... or more that, nobody knows what to do, but I want [her] acceptance for that being the case. "Nobody knows [for sure the best thing to do], but it's okay, you'll figure it out, give it time" [or so he wants to hear from the woman].... "you have to have confidence that it'll work...."

Now James' associations take a new direction:

J: You know, the tendency for me is to *not* be fully engaged in things. When my father had his open heart surgery, the whole family just sat there in the waiting room, as if each of us were completely separate from the other.... and ya know, my dad had the same issue.... He wouldn't articulate those things [tender, vulnerable emotions]. He'd give someone the shirt off his back, anyone needy in his office, especially some of the retired women, but you'd never hear that he'd done it, or why.... I could never tell what his feelings were 'til some anger fell out. But his reserve was typical of men of his generation ... and for men in general, not to be transparent about one's emotions. Where it's gotten dicey is that just because you're not expressing them, then you're not in touch with them. But it often runs together. The ideal is to be in touch and be able to express one's feelings, but not to need [or be compelled] to.

As the session ends James comments further on the meaning of his feeling of relative "noninvolvement" with his staff at work, as he perceives it. In

---

[4]*(continued)*   libidinal object instead of connecting to the mother as a whole person. The libidinal attitude that develops is characterized by "taking" as opposed to "giving," by tendencies to incorporate and internalize, and by feelings of emptiness and deprivation as opposed to fullness. These echo some of James' own psychic tendencies and complaints, both formulated and unformulated.

this he is accessing the deeper schism between himself and others. I'm sure he seems from outward appearances much *more* personally involved with his employees than is customary. I wonder privately if he attempts to seduce his staff with intimacy as part of competing with a lateral manager, but even more importantly, as a reaction formation to his recognition that he is actually at a deeper level detached.

Discussion of the Analytic Material

We knew that James had invested women with the power to heal him, and we learn in this session that he perhaps learned the trappings of how to do so from the father, who would engage in "random acts of kindness" or humanitarianism for no apparent benefit to himself. (These actions took his family by surprise … they didn't accord with his gruff exterior, and left his tender aspects unarticulated or unrevealed.) His son James picked up this beneficence, often a constructive, genuine aspect of his functioning—when he wasn't using it to extract emotional sustenance from his romantic partners. The unconscious fantasy was probably that one day he might match his father and woo away the mother/lover who handed out the laurels. From another standpoint we can see the intensification in James of a sensitive, generous attitude toward women as a counteridentification with his father's more customary brusqueness.

The analytic process as well as the content of James' case material illustrate several other frequent elements in the "uneasy intimacy" scenario. The first is the attunement, the genuine sensitivity, and the desire to gratify the other often found in the "courting" individual. James was unfailingly considerate of me, alluded with professed respect to what he understood to be my opinion, gave me great "daily life" recommendations (which he knew I enjoyed, if against my better judgment), and so forth. This solicitousness was constructive in many ways but also acted as a vehicle for ingratiation that could lead to a confining closeness.

The tendency to present oneself as emotionally weak and therefore meriting help is another striking element in this material. It creates a pressure in the other to offer the "weak" one nurturance and support, which oddly enough tends to feel like affection and again creates a semblance of closeness. The overall trajectory of this facet of uneasy intimacy is a state of instability in which the closeness is thin and unreliable. I felt this frequently in my work with James, where playing out the "strong, nurturant one" to his "weak, needy self" seemed like a *sine qua non* to the deepening of our bond, while at the same time it felt like it was getting us nowhere.

Another feature of this constellation is that the courted one is kept on tenterhooks, never knowing if *this* will be the time the other's hidden, dissociated subjectivity will emerge from its cave, causing a precipitous loss of the courted one's desirability. All of a sudden, an e-mail will go unreturned, a planned date will be forgotten, a criticism will shoot out from left field, or something equally wounding will happen, undermining the whole fabric of their mutual involvement. The courting one (or sometimes the object of attention) will have rebelled against the masochistic self-subordination involved. One or both parties ultimately end up damaged, dropped, or betrayed.

This played out in the tense, combative undertones of the seemingly decent patient–analyst exchanges I've reported. While James in general seemed to keep me close vis-à-vis factual knowledge of his daily life and stream of thoughts, I was in actuality often in the dark as to their deeper emotional significance. At times like in the session just discussed, James was caught in obsessive ruminating, absorbed in his internal self-arguments. If I challenged any one perspective, he responded with a knee-jerk contradiction. If we came to some shared understanding, it soon vanished into thin air. In this aspect of our relationship, it was as if we were engaged in a paradoxical dance, with James enacting the seductive, domineering masochist, and I the courted, submissive sadist. He felt hopeless and depressed due to the ongoing internal self-attack, and "meekly" but powerfully demanded that I guide him, only to balk at the guiding—and it was in this opposition that he found a semblance of autonomy, a modicum of self-respect. Returning again to the paradoxical enclave, my guidance was a countertransferential element that played into that defensive dynamic; but not guiding him ran the risk of a fatal blockage in analytic progress, as the absence of such direction left him spinning his wheels. (See Benjamin, 2004, on the doer/done to dichotomy). Together we were trying to engage in the natural rhythms of intimacy between the "averagely needful patient" and the "averagely helpful analyst," but it turned into a tangled knot of thwarted intentions.

Notwithstanding the enclaves and knots, however, there was a steady accretion over the course of the analysis in James' ability to recognize and withstand his own deeper needs and urges, particularly the ones that ruffled his moral sensibility. I attribute this to our persistent holding the mirror up to his (unconscious) nature, and to his own remarkable need to reach the authentic within himself and others. James could feel my genuine affection for him, and as his trust grew he could eventually metabolize my confronting his misapplication of the capacity for emotional attunement. His relationship with himself, not to mention his ties with others, took on a much more substantial quality, encompassing the bitter along with the sweet, the hostile and aggressive along with the loving and cooperative.

The Perils of Intimacy Gone Awry
in Professional Life

We mental health clinicians are a select group that gravitated to this sort of work because of our natural propensities—and needs—for deep emotional contact with others. Being psychoanalytically oriented, we've then gone through intensive trainings to hone those innate tendencies, so we can harness them in the service of our therapeutic aims. What we're left with—an even more profound capacity for evoking and sustaining psychological closeness—is a potent gift that (ideally) becomes more finely tuned with every passing year of practice. Ironically enough, as our capacity for sustained, meaningful relating grows, the number of outlets we have for fulfilling our needs for personal intimacy often shrinks (see Rucker, 1993). The more involved we get in our practice, with an agency, or as part of an institute, the less time we have for pursuing our emotional needs in the private sphere. For many of us, there's a blurring of professional and private spheres, with consultants becoming friends, and so forth, that makes it unclear who can be told what and to what depth we can discuss a confidential matter. It is natural and beneficial that we turn to individuals within our professional context—even patients—to engage in some degree of emotional sharing, mutual recognition, the fellow-feeling of jointly appreciating how the psyche works.

To complicate matters, some of the most immediate, most profound analytic work can only be done within the therapeutic relationship itself, with its web of transferential and idiosyncratically personal currents criss-crossing between analyst and patient. It's the perfect medium for cultivating healthy intimacy, but destructive forms as well. And we cannot always distinguish the two, because much of the work is done in a transitional space between the "real" real and the "psychically" real, and is dependent on both participants' agreement as to that distinction. If one person tacitly disagrees with the other about what is the "real" reality of his or her closeness to the other, we have uneasy intimacy in the making. There may be no chink in the walls of the cocoon of therapeutic confidentiality through which a third person could offer a salutary perspective on the proceedings.

This situation can readily lead to an "unholy emotional alliance" between patient and analyst in which one or both lose sight that the purpose of the developing intimacy is the patient's psychic maturation. They instead begin to pursue the emotional closeness as an end in itself, or they seek to reinstate a gratifying sense of being "the seeker" or "the one sought" (and either person can play either role). This ultimately results in one or both feeling the delighted horror (and horrified delight) of being drawn into closer closeness than they'd originally bargained for. It's helpful, I think, to temporarily remove this scenario from the charged context of professional ethics per se. We gain better perspective by viewing it as a manifestation of the wider-spread tendency for emotionally attuned people to sometimes use their powers to engage others in ways that can turn harmful.

The "uneasily intimate" moment is not restricted to our consulting rooms. In our professional meetings, our one-on-one lunches, our hallway conversations at conferences, and so on, we analytically trained practitioners sometimes show too much of our own vulnerabilities to or elicit too many confidences from our colleagues. Later, we wonder what we were caught up in, what we were really doing. Being richly conversant in this economy, we can't resist reveling in it—sometimes getting carried away or even trading on it. How often does the analytic writer establish an air of cozy familiarity with the reader, thus undermining any misgivings about the presenter's position? How often does an analytic speaker offer a clinical example with questionable ethics, but in such an engaging way that the audience forgets to raise the obvious concern about boundary-crossing? Would that we could turn up the lights and be less afraid of what we'll find there. As Harry Stack Sullivan reminded us, we're all "more simply human than otherwise," and often errors in intimacy modulation can be rectified and forgiven when they're deeply understood.

Conclusion

Uneasy intimacy strengthens and weakens its participants at the same time. Siren-like and habit-forming, it provides a kind of "intermittent reinforcement" that can make the problem-fraught bond even tighter. What makes us feel powerful at the moment does not necessarily strengthen us; when we're caught in the grip of a vexed closeness, this bit of commonsense slips away. No theory can fully express the pang, the bittersweet agony of this type of intimacy, that perhaps we've all experienced at one time or another. Balladeers, opera librettists and composers, flamenco "cantaores," rock musicians, and other songwriters probably come closest to conveying its flavor.

To draw on a last metaphor, emotional intimacy with all its variants is like sugar, providing the energy and the sweetness we humans need to fuel our psychic and physical life. But like certain types of sugary foods it can also be "too much," leading to the development of a psychic "sweet tooth" that creates "cavities" one will live to regret. I argue that developing such a sweet tooth for uneasy intimacy can disrupt or thwart our efforts at a fuller, more substantial psychic nourishment.

References

Benjamin, J. (2004), Beyond doer and done to: An intersubjective view of thirdness. *Psychoanal. Quarterly,* 73:5–46.

Celenza, A., & Gabbard, G. (2003), Analysts and sexual boundary violations. *J. Amer. Psychoanal. Assoc.* 51:617–636.

Chodorow, N. (1978), *The Reproduction of Mothering: Psychoanalysis and the Sociology of Gender.* Berkeley: University of California Press.

Crastnopol, M. (1980). Separation-Individuation in a Woman's Identity Vis-à-Vis Mother. Unpublished dissertation.

Eigen, M. (1999), *Toxic nourishment.* London: Karnac Books.

Fairbairn, W. R. D. (1952), *Psychoanalytic studies of the personality.* London: Routledge & Kegan Paul.

Gabbard, G. (1996), *Love and Hate in the Analytic Relationship.* Northvale, NJ: Aronson.

Gabbard, G., & Lester, E. (1995), *Boundaries and Boundary Violations in Psychoanalysis.* New York: Basic Books.

Ghent, E. (1990), Masochism, submission, surrender: Masochism as a perversion of surrender. *Contemporary Psychoanal.* 26:108–136.

Khan, M. M. R. (1979), *Alienation in perversions.* New York: International Universities Press.

Mahler, M., Pine, F., & Bergman, A. (1975), *The Psychological Birth of the Human Infant.* New York: Basic Books.

O'Shaughnessy, E. (1992), Enclaves and excursions. *Int. J. Psa.* 73:603–611.

Patchett, A. (2002), *Bel canto.* New York: Perennial (HarperCollins).

Rucker, N. (1993), Cupid's misses: Relational vicissitudes in the analyses of single women. *Psychoanal Psychol.* 10:377–391.

Williams, W. C. (1968), *The Selected Poems of William Carlos Williams.* New York: New Directions.

3

Ma Vie En Rose: A Meditation

Muriel Dimen

▼   ▼   ▼   ▼   ▼

"Sometimes you just have to be yourself." (Ludo)

"We have no idea what goes on in his mind." (Hanna)

The apparent earnestness of *Ma vie en rose*, a Belgian film (1997), is finished with dark music, which brought to my mind the song, "Fairy tales can come true ..." (That's the way Martin Ritt's *The Front* [1976] ends.) A disjuncture expressing a familiar unease, the juxtaposition of earnestness and irony: You want equality and justice for all, sexual freedom, self-realization? As if.

Directed by Alain Berliner, *Ma vie en rose* tells of an 8-year-old boy, Ludo, who wears his mother's clothes and makeup, falls in love with the boy next door, believes he is or ought to be a girl. The film also portrays his adoring parents who enjoy his fantasies until troubles with neighbors and his dad's boss ruin everything. We also learn about Ludo's wild and sexy grandma who guides him through this terribly rough passage until—well, we shall see whether it's a happy ending.

I read this film subjectively, through my own responses to it, and along the way offer a musing or two about psychosexuality and cultural sexuality. So I should say that I was very angry at Ludo throughout most of the film. But I was also conscious that my anger was connected to his lack of shame about his sexual desire. These emotions hook up: Ludo's refusal to be shamed into changing his desire occasions my anger. Now if he were my patient, I would diagnose my response as countertransference anger. However, because he isn't, I prefer not to analyze him or his family (after all, they can't talk back to me). Instead, I want to explore my own reaction as a way to probe the fascinating intersection of mind and culture.

My anger at Ludo is produced by many things. And I want to say here that I am aware that anger is not the most popular emotional response to *Ma vie en rose*. Certainly it's not politically correct. Eve Sedgwick (2001), for example, envies, not to mention loves, Ludo; surely it's better to envy and love than simply be angry at this little boy. Indeed my anger probably has quite a bit to do with my envy of Ludo's freedom to love where he loves.

But I am very interested in my anger because, in the context of a film that challenges conventional heterosexual mores, it's such a normal, conservative, suburban feeling that it's almost transgressive. In my anger, I join the other grown-ups—not only the neighbors, but Pierre, Ludo's dad, and, for a while, Hanna, Ludo's mom: I too am an agent of shame: Shame and sexuality constructs and polices sexuality, and adults' anger at sexual transgression, like their pleasure at sexual compliance, transmits sanctioned sexual structure. However, I also like to think the film meant me to be angry so that, like Ludo's parents, I too could be transformed. But maybe it's just my pettiness. We'll see. Or maybe you will.

As I say, many things produce the anger. Most relevant here is the contagion of sexuality and of shame. Sexuality is one of those affects that, like shame, is infectious. These emotions do not really exist within the individual. Or, insofar as they do, it is because they also live between individuals— in dyadic relationships, in social form, in representation. "On the deepest level," writes Steve Mitchell (2000), "affective states are transpersonal" (p. 61). Recent theory (e.g., Stein, 1991) emphasizes affect's central place in the primal swirl holding and creating infant and caretaker. Feelings come to us at once corporeally and psychically, but corporeality is, Fairbairn (1954) observed, as much a two-body as a one-body phenomenon, standing, as we know, for both psychic and interpersonal reality. To quote Mitchell (2000) again: "Questions like 'who started it? And who did what to whom?' tend to be meaningless when intense affective connections are involved, as in strong sexual attraction, terror, murderous rage, or joyous exhilaration" (p. 118).

Sex and shame inhabit intersubjective space: they originate from shared, primal states of relatedness that get relived in subsequent relationships. Together the two, sex and shame, are combustible. So Ludo's following of his own desire the sexual paths his parents kept themselves from following. Maybe it recalls the viewer's loss too or, perhaps, the paths followed despite the shame they produced. Ludo's unashamed embrace of his desire reminds us that we are supposed to distance ourselves from the forbidden through shame, the shaming that, directed toward us, we internalize and represent in disgust.[1]

Here are two moments when my anger at him surged: When a neighbor, Lisette, faints after Ludo puts on her dead daughter's dress to impress Lisette's son, Jerome, whom Ludo wants to marry; and when Ludo is betrayed by his brothers and Jerome in the locker room. "It's his fault," I feel (and I mean "feel," not think, because of course if I "think" about it, I "know" it's not his fault, indeed, that fault isn't the point). He brought it on himself, I fulminate; he's to blame because he didn't give in. I am angry at him when he seems not to understand why people are inflamed by him, why they think there's something wrong. He just refuses to get it! "I don't want to change," he states, "but I want them to love me." "Well," I rage, "who doesn't? Just change." I flare (and surely this must be from envy) when he retorts, to Granny's observation that they want the best for him, "It's not the best for ME!"

However, this last scene with Granny is also an example of Ludo's will, of his strength and pride. This brings us to the second emotion that I think is important in this film—shame—which Ludo lacks and all the grown-ups except for Granny (and, I suppose, his therapist, though of course we know her only as a professional), at least, possess in spades. Ludo is sorry, confused, startled, angry, stubborn, despairing, even embarrassed. But he's never ashamed. (Yes, I do envy this.)

Let me stop briefly to distinguish between shame and embarrassment. Embarrassment, says Morrison (1989), is a mild form of shame. In embarrassment, you feel exposed for some feeling or act which is transgressive against interpersonal or social morality but which allows you to remain within the human pale. It's as though preconsciousness suddenly bursts into consciousness and, without much preparation, you and someone else see what you prefer to keep hidden from self and others.

Embarrassment may or may not snowball into shame, in which, in contrast, you feel that your core is corroded and that you should be excommunicated. The religious terminology is no accident, and not only because religious beliefs and family values associate sex with shame. In Morrison's persuasive view, shame, the other side of self-regard, is a problem of narcissism. Like other affects, shame is infectious, but, in my view, it always feels more virulent than others. One patient refers to his experience of this as "wildfire." Someone demeans him or fails to deliver a promised ser-

---

[1] Freud would have agreed: it is through feelings of disgust, he says, that children learn to recoil from fecal and other groinal aromas, tabooing the genitalia (Freud, 1930, pp. 99–100, n. 1; p. 106, n. 3)—even if he also contradicts himself and says that such disgust arose when *Home sapiens* stood upright and assumed bipedal locomotion (Freud, 1930, p. 99, n. 1).

vice or even, merely, disappoints him, and he burns with humiliation and anger. And as he reviews the burn, he distills it into pure form and relives it repeatedly, and quickly it fuses to other times he has been burned. And, before you know it, he will have recited to himself and me the story of every insult to his being that he remembers. Perhaps this virulence derives from shame's utilization of narcissism's primary defenses, splitting and projection. When the other becomes all bad in contrast to one's perfect goodness, and is thereby destroyed, one faces a tidal wave of shame, and so the expulsion of one's own badness redoubles in necessity, frequency, and intensity.

When someone with narcissistic difficulties feels shame about one thing, soon they feel it about other things until, finally, they feel shame in their entirety. Eve Sedgwick (1993) has referred to shame's replication of itself as its performativity: if you near the shame feelings of a patient—or a friend—suffering a narcissistic wound, you find that the patient feels, lo and behold, ashamed. Shame also oozes into intersubjective space, which in psychotherapy makes countertransference errors very easy. "The shame of patients is contagious," Morrison (1989) explains, "often resonating with the clinician's own shame experiences—the therapist's own sense of failure, self-deficiency, and life disappointments" (p. 6). Shame is, in its own way, as infectious as sexuality, if not more so, and when the two show up together in the consulting room, it's a tinderbox.

Sex and shame, shame and narcissism, narcissism and sex—at issue is self-regard, which, Morrison (1989, p. 42) suggests, is the other side of shame. Sex, in turn, bears directly on self-regard, the maintenance of which is, in turn, narcissism's problem and project. These issues indicate one of the important problematics now emerging in postclassical psychoanalytic times (Dimen, 2003; Green, 1996; Stein, 1998): the relation between sex and narcissism. Sexuality, albeit classically analyzed in oedipal terms, in fact draws deeply on narcissistic experiences in ways we are only just beginning to theorize.

So, to return to *Ma vie en rose*, Ludo is embarrassed but not, I think, ashamed. Not even in the end, when he tries to conform: Instead of letting shame reform him, he allows his desire to live in fantasy. He speaks to Granny of a time "when I'm not a boy," and she, ever the seductive hipster, replies, "You have a lot to teach me." He dreams up a story about the "missing X," the X chromosome he was supposed to have received from God, from which he concludes that he is a "*garçonfille*." Not an ironic girly-boy, a plain, earnest, sincere "boygirl." Nor when he goes into the dead girl's room, does he succumb. He's completely in charge. Femininity is not weak; as we see, his desire dominates—wearing the dead girl's dress, he and Jerome marry before the Teddy-Bear minister. He's not ashamed even when Lisette and his mother discover their forbidden play.

But shame lives in the adults. Look at its build-up in his mother, his stalwart champion, initially charmed by his experiments in dress and make-up. But then comes the Snow White trick: at the school play, Ludo locks Sophie in the bathroom so he can take her place in the coffin and be kissed awake by Prince Jerome. As they leave the school, you can see that he and his entire family are about to be shunned by everyone else in the neighborhood. Then he's expelled from school and Hanna is annoyed and impatient with him because she has to get up earlier and walk him to the bus stop for his 1-hour commute. Then, when his father loses his job, she really begins to turn on Ludo. "People are shit," says Pierre in despairing response to Ludo's blaming himself for the firing. But in fact Hanna agrees and screams at Ludo, "It's your fault." When, as his next move, Ludo stops talking to his therapist, his mother becomes furious and despairing.

And finally there arrives his father's humiliation over the graffito painted on the garage door: "Bent boys out." Ludo's mom responds with rage and, finally, shaming: While the whole family watches, Ludo's mother cries and cuts his long hair off, and "crucifies" him, to use the language she used when Pierre, in an earlier scene, had insisted she take Ludo to the barber for a shearing. I suppose here we might consider the oedipal dimensions: Hanna performs the castration Pierre is too weak to do (and indeed the film notes this conventional account of the problem in the voice of Pierre's boss Albert—husband to Lisette—who says, "Hanna has too much control over your boys").

I am, however, more focused on the narcissistic, pre-oedipal dimension. Shorn, Ludo looks at Hanna first with dignity, later with hatred, and then insists on going to live with wild, crazy, sexy, and feminist ("Having a pecker is no excuse not to lay the table!") Granny. (And even in the midst of all this shame and turmoil, he imagines he's getting his period, just like his older sister.)

Ludo, as it turns out in this fairy tale, is rescued by his father's fall from grace. When Pierre gets a new job, they move from their very cushy suburb to a more blue-collar community. There the neighbors seem to be more accepting of Ludo's idiosyncrasy (I don't know whether the film intends such a class-analytical point, but it's hard not to draw it). The move's downward mobility shows Ludo that he's shamed his parents. Loving them, he feels responsible and so he behaves. He doesn't cross-dress or put on make-up or act as though he has a female body. Rather he contents himself with his fantasy of Pam, the Barbie-like resident of the advertising world. When sad, he sits on a bench along the main road and, gazing up at the billboard Pam inhabits, joins her in her world of feminine excess, of, one would have to say, *jouissance*.

But then Ludo meets his match: Chris, a.k.a. Christine, a *fillegarçon*, perhaps, through whom he finds a reprieve from his condemnation to the world of drag. "It's just a dress," say the other mothers to a maddened Hanna, who slaps Ludo upside the head when Christine has, at her birthday party, forced Ludo to trade her his masculine costume for the gown she abjures. He flees. Hanna, frightened that he has once again tried suicide (as he did after his locker-room humiliation by locking himself in the big horizontal freezer in the garage), runs wildly around the neighborhood looking for him, climbs the ladder she finds leaning on the billboard, and dives into Pam's, that is to say, Ludo's, world.

And there, in her empathy, she recovers her love for her son, and puts behind her her own shame, humiliation, and hatred. She is able to do what the therapist does, she is able to accept that, as the therapist says, there are things about her son she will never understand. Is it this mystery—the other's otherness—that made the grown-ups (the parents, the neighbors, me) so angry? Hanna now accepts Ludo in all his mystery. "Do whatever feels best," she says to him in the end, "you'll always be my child." "Our child," says Pierre. "Our child," says Hanna, "you'll always be our child."

Don't you want to cry? I do. He can be whatever he wants. He doesn't have to be a drag queen if he doesn't want to. He can be a *garçonfille*. Put your gender and your sexuality together however you want to. Be your own person. Your own mystery. Fairy tales can come true? The film doesn't think so and, as analysts, we don't either. Shame inevitably attaches to sexuality; there is an intimate link between sex and shame which has not yet been decoded; and sexuality is always a place of otherness, and therefore of struggle, anyway. But if, for the Ludo in each of us, there were a Chris in the next county, life would perhaps be a little more bearable, a little richer in *jouissance*.

Afterword

An odd, interesting note of cultural criticism sounds throughout the film. I have observed that Ludo's salvation takes place in a working-class community. And we need to notice that Ludo's—and his parents'—problem becomes a public, community matter in the upper middle-class suburb they eventually leave behind. But, although they are driven to leave, that community's condemnation of Ludo's unorthodox sexuality is not unmitigated. Open discussion of it takes place. People are impolite, errors of tact are made—the disastrous life of a gay child is told by one woman to all the others in front of Hanna—and forgiven. When Jerome insists on wearing a skirt to Sophie's birthday party, even Lisette, the mother of the dead girl, tries to save the situation by saying that it's a costume party and putting a lampshade on her head to show that she's in costume.

I don't, as I say, know whether the film, by situating tragedy among the *petit bourgeois* and salvation in the blue-collar community, is making a class analysis. But I do believe it is conveying a lesson about a cross-class, cultural hypocrisy: It points at French *mores*, at the standard acceptance of personal eccentricity—look at Granny—and then asks why no such leeway is given for variations on gender and sexual desire. Ludo's shame-free certainty of his own desire stands as a utopian image, of course, but the film, in also representing a *fillegarçon*, universalizes, representing a common hope to re-find the part of us that could feel free of sexual shame. The acceptance of the other's otherness, a stance taken by the boy's therapist and grandmother, and, in the end, adopted by the parents, suggests how such utopian moments of *jouissance* might be realized.

References

Dimen, M. (2003), *Sexuality, Intimacy, Power*. Hillsdale, NJ: The Analytic Press.

Fairbairn, W. R. D. (1954), Observations on the nature of hysterical states. *Br. J. Med. Psychol.* 27:105–125.

Freud, S. (1930), Civilization and its discontents. *Standard Edition,* 21:64–146. London: Hogarth Press, 1961.

"The Front." 1976. Directed by Martin Ritt, USA, 95 minutes.

Green, A. (1996), Has sexuality anything to do with psychoanalysis? *Internat. J. Psycho-Anal.,* 76:871–883.

"Ma Vie En Rose." 1977, Directed by Alain Berliner, France, 88 minutes.

Mitchell, S. (2000), *Relationality*. Hillsdale, NJ: The Analytic Press.

Morrison, A. (1989), *Shame: The Underside of Narcissism*. Hillsdale, NJ: The Analytic Press.

Sedgwick, E. K. (1993), Queer performativity: Henry James's *The art of the novel. GLQ: The Journal of Lesbian and Gay Studies,* 1:1–16.

——— (2001, October 13), Commentary on *Ma vie en rose*. Bank Street College of Education lecture.

Stein, R. E. (1991), *Psychoanalytic Theories of Affect*. New York: Praeger.

——— (1998), The poignant, the excessive and the enigmatic in sexuality. *Internat. J. Psycho-Anal.* 79:253–267.

4

Unsexed and Ungendered Bodies: The Violated Self

Sue Grand

▼   ▼   ▼   ▼   ▼

When Rosa came to me, I felt I already knew her. Our memories were drawn from the same landscape. Postwar Brooklyn, the row houses of Brownsville. Stickball in the streets. Delicatessen floors covered with sawdust, barrels full with pickles that were floating in their own brine. Grocers selling homemade pasta. The smells of mandlebrot, hot bread, sweet cannoli. Prices were always negotiable for a well-told story. And in Brooklyn, there were stories. In Russian and Polish and Yiddish. In Italian and broken English. The streets were rich with gossip, with the exchange of food and solace and unwanted advice. Couples courted and quarreled and scolded their children. Children ran free in a new world. Everything was loud and public and impassioned. Voices quieted by nightfall, erupting again as dawn struck the street.

Inside the row houses, there was a dimmer universe. There were yellowed pictures, silver candlesticks salvaged from the old country. Old things, sacred objects, heavy with grief. There were wall-to-wall carpets, furniture sealed in clear plastic, pristine rooms that could not be entered. To be impoverished and to labor, to acquire a home, and at last to buy furniture. To seal that furniture in plastic for all perpetuity: This was discipline and hope and fatigue and sadness. It was a mimicry of America and a reverence for America, a longing for assimilation and a dread of dislocation. Outside on the street, children were simply children. But within these interiors, the full weight of history was fixed on their backs. Expansive bodies shrank in upon themselves. Children moved with caution and sobriety through dark hallways, through the narrow confines of parental memory. At every opportunity, they fled to the streets. In spring, in summer, in fall. Then winter came, and ice would descend on Brooklyn. Exuberance would be pressed into dim quarters.

When I met Rosa, I knew she was from Brooklyn. I recognized her in the way she told a story: straight shooting, quick witted, dark-humored, and absurd. She would have us roaring with laughter while pain sat on our chests. Impassioned by the truth and resolute in her intentions, she looked back into the past and forward into the future. She seized life amidst dark places; she retrieved knowledge from obscurity. She could change the endings of her stories before she had even finished telling them. She had that kind of discipline and mobility and courage. She suffered. But she always did the right thing. From the first, she looked me in the eye, and she registered me as human. There would always be something simple and warm and authentic between us, a basic human decency and a basic human trust. It would take her years to offer that kindness to herself. She hated her body. She was depressed. She was always alone. She was not really lonely, but coveted her isolation. There was a dread of invasion, an exhaustion at the prospect of any intimate contact.

She lived the changing seasons of Brownsville. Professional life was the summer street: At work, she was sharp and real and really herself. Bold and independent, confident, risk-taking. She was hard driving and hard working, ethical and generous in her business encounters. There were 'work friends.' But evenings and weekends found her in a wintry row house. There was deadness and panic, and an episodic blankness which transpired without memory. A desire to drink, and a struggle to avoid drinking. And a body she never looked at, or allowed to be seen. She despised her orifices, her curves and the places she thought she was lacking in curves. To Rosa, her body was nothing but a conglomorate of deformities: small breasts, sagging belly, fat hips, legs, arms. Attractive, she moved with grace, but she could not feel herself moving. For me, there was an appealing quickness to her physicality; I thought her shape made interesting shifts between the angular and the round. I was arrested by the immediacy of her eyes. Face, body, mind: I responded to her as an evocative whole. But to Rosa, her body was in pieces; it was loosely linked fragments united by blunt hatred. She ate compulsively and she vomited, she gained and lost weight. And she joked about aspiring to anorexia.

In the years of her alcoholic youth, there were sexual encounters. Stone drunk, she still insisted on dim lighting, heavy blankets, the concealment of clothes. There was little pleasure. But there were beatings by a drunken man who made use of her. She left him. She stopped drinking, alone, without any help or intervention. She was never beaten again. Now she lives a life in which there is no female body. Insofar as she is female, she is inspired with self-hatred. Insofar as there is no self-hatred, there is no body. Below her neck is a neutered edifice, moving parts in service to mental function. Feet transact pavement; hands operate telephones, keyboards. There is nothing much in between. She has lived most of her life in an unconflicted celibacy. She always *knew* she was female. But in disembodied states, her body did not have genitals, or any gender marker. Indeed, her body was often entirely without existence or sensation. Twice she had almost died because she could not experience an encroaching illness.

Still, she was exceptionally clear and cogent and related in our sessions. She knew that her childhood history was undoing her. Rosa was unsure whether she had been adopted as an infant. There were indications that she was adopted, and lies about that adoption, and no information about biological parents. She didn't know if her roots were in Italy or in Russia, or even whether "her people" were really Jewish or Catholic. She grew up with her older brother, her younger sister, her mother, her father. She did not look like them. In this house, there was real warmth with her Russian Jewish father, and strict propriety from her Italian mother. There was a brother disabled by some cognitive defect, who depleted what there was of maternal attention. There was a little sister who required Rosa's nurturant attention. If Rosa was unsure of her own origins, the mother's origins were obscured by dislocations, separations, abandonments. There were relatives missing in Turin who were subsequently restored. There were relatives missing who were never restored. There were years when the mother was missing from her own family. In the mother's own childhood, there was a "home" she was taken from, and a "home" she was returned to, without knowing that she had ever been missing from home. There was an adoptive family she was left with and removed from. There was a biological family where relations were ill-defined. There were brothers who were not real brothers, and real sisters who were unknown to each other until their own adulthood. There were no grandparents left alive, but there was a great uncle who seems to have been her mother's actual father. All of this was dimly connected to the disappearance of Rosa's "real" mother, her maternal grandmother, and the great uncle's wife.

With regards to these figures, there were false explanations and no explanations, and stories that cracked under the slightest scrutiny. And there was a seamless disregard for all contradiction: They were long dead, and they were not dead. Grandmother was in an Italian sanatorium, she was in an American psychiatric institution, she was mad, she had never been mad, she had died many years ago, she had only recently died. The great aunt was dead of a brain tumor, she had died in childbirth, she never got out of Italy, she died while emigrating to America, she had been arrested by Brownshirts. No one seemed to know who or where these women were, or when or where they had last been seen, or precisely where they had been lost.

With regards to Rosa's "real" mother, there was no disappearance. Rosa's mother *was* her real mother. But somehow, Rosa never believed it. In this family, there are lost attachments and no attachments, and people who do not know where they come from or to whom they belong. Some relatives are Russian and some relatives are Italian. Some aunts cook with garlic, and some aunts cook with "schmalz." There are Catholics who turn out to be converted Jews. There were no religious rituals, and there were peculiar religious rituals, and there were Catholics discovered crying in synagogue. Rosa identifies as Italian, and as a Brooklyn Jew. She speaks some Yiddish and some Italian, and has an affinity for Easter and Christmas. Although the father's family was more cohesive and intact, still, there were numerous gaps and lost relatives. Throughout all of this familial confusion, there is never any talk about what mobilized such ambiguity and dislocation: there are no Cossacks or Nazis, or Fascist assassins.

The only relative left from the grandparent generation was the mother's "widowed" great uncle. There are a few family stories about him from the old country: he seemed garrulous, elegant, irreligious, irreverent. Then, in America, he was absent of his wife, and mute about her absence. Family gatherings found him silent. He could not, or would not tell his story. He did not sit with the other immigrants. He would not raise his own voice in their communal joy and lament. He refused speech and grief and all possibility of comfort. In his silence, succeeding generations were denied the privilege of remembering. Stiff moving, remote, he passed his days in the living room. That sacred space of old photos and new furniture. He alone was permitted access to the radio, and later, the television. Sometimes, Rosa would slip in. She was curious: the forbidden furniture, the stories on the radio, the allure of the moving image. He would not speak, meet her gaze or shift his body; he never seemed to know that she was there. There was no evidence of life on his face. The radio, the television, the newspaper, the drone of sound, the shifting image, the black and white "snow" on the screen after programming had ceased: these were his hypnotic. Silently, she watched him listen and she watched him watching. She would slip out again, unseen. In this silence, there was a universe of untold stories. This man was the locus of familial sadness and confusion. He was pitied for a solitude that could never find its name. And so, his acts of sexual predation fell outside the family register. Rosa and her sister, all of their cousins: these children knew this man as their molester. But they obeyed the prescription about the secrecy of grief. They spoke of these violations only to one another. To the adults, they spoke of nothing. Each child had a story of being molested as she "slept." Each one had pretended to be sleeping. As adults, they discovered that none of them could sleep.

Rosa knew that incest informed the hatred of her body. Our treatment explored family mysteries and stories and violations and lies. We wondered who belonged to whom, who was missing and who was there, and she tried (and often failed) to locate family history. We continued the investigation Rosa had begun in childhood. At 10, she discovered concealed documents. The "dead" grandmother was alive in an American psychiatric institution. She had been there for more than 20 years. In this family, there was a "dead" person who was both mad and left alive. There was an alive person who was "dead" and disappeared. Exposed documents had no impact on the family story. There was an insistence that the grandmother was long dead, until the day when this grandmother actually died. Rosa was 18. There was a recognition of familial loss and a denial of familial loss. Somehow, the grandmother's recent *real* death was conflated with her old, *fictitious* death. Truth was absorbed into falsehood. Rosa's mother did not want any real maternal story. Fiction was her constant, soothing object; it occupied the space where disintegration might have been. Despite familial collusion and resistance, Rosa kept looking and she kept asking. During her treatment, Rosa discovered the conversion of Jews into Catholics, her mother's early adoption by a foster family, her subsequent return to a biological family which was mysteriously absent of a mother.

In the context of this family, we explored the incestuous experience. I wondered why none of the children had exposed him. She said that they had pitied him for his grief and loneliness. They knew he needed something he could not have with a wife. He had aroused Rosa and he had soiled her, and she had sheltered him through her compliance. If she pitied him, so she pitied her mother. This man was her mother's only parental object. Rosa sensed that the revelation of incest would orphan a woman who had already been an abandoned child. And if Rosa *was* adopted, who would the mother choose? And in telling, would she expose the mother's own memory of being molested by the man who was molesting the mother's children?

Rosa's mother was decent and responsible, and competent in the provision of basic care. But there was something strict and dour about her, an absence of tenderness, intimacy, play, and understanding. She was peculiarly withholding and dictatorial about food consumption, inducing a sense of subtle starvation. This coldness may have led Rosa to believe that she was adopted. Perhaps the image of a missing mother was a fantasy of another, more intimate attachment. A mirror for the mother's missing mother. We would never know. But certainly, there was little strength in the mother for Rosa to rely on. The mother saw my patient's independence, and decided that Rosa did not need. She saw her son's inadequacy and dependence, and decided that he needed. She saw Rosa mothering the younger sister, and deferred that sister to Rosa's care. When she did mother Rosa, she was cloying and anxious, controlling and intrusive, full of predictions of doom. Rosa learned not to need, and she learned not to ask. To the mother, it was Rosa herself who had repudiated all mothering.

Injured, rejected, bewildered, she gave less, but she did not cease her intrusive commentary. Ultimately, my patient knew that there was no
mother there to tell. With Rosa's father, there was a steadiness of warmth
and affection. He seemed solid as a rock, and just as enduring. There was
shared laughter between them, and an easy support for her competence
and independence. But he was overworked and overtired, rarely home.
One did not burden him with family matters, although undoubtedly, he
would have intervened about the incest. And so, for Rosa, home meant the
great uncle, the mother, the gentle but weak older brother, the dependent
younger sister. It meant invasion and compliance and isolation, the defer-
ment of her own need, and the derailment of her own feelings. Self-isola-
tion was her first, and only, effort at self-regulation.

   She feared that, like her mother, I would retaliate for her isolating ma-
neuvers. But it was so clear that we were attached. The simplicity of our
bonding seemed transacted through the father. And through the shared
memory of those Brooklyn streets. I was at ease with her movement in and
out of connection. And so, she rarely moved out of connection. We developed a relation rooted in an understanding of her need for solitude. We
knew it as a healing retreat, the first of many movements towards self-regulation. With this reframing, she embarked on the project of experiencing
her own needs and feelings. And I never left her. In experiencing self-regulation in the transference, it became possible for her to read her own sensations and affects. At last, she became linked to the somatic. Suddenly,
there were bodily complaints about pain and illness and hunger and over-
fullness. She exercised, had massages, sought out doctors and dentists.
She lost weight naturally as she engaged in conscious, healthy eating. She
began to speak about feelings that were rooted in sensation, about sensations that were rooted in feelings. Where there was deadness, now, in her
solitude, she alternated between quiescence and felt pain. She spoke of
some desire for intimate human contact, and a dread of relinquishing her
solitude. She even imagined a renewal of sexuality. Still, she felt too ugly to
allow herself to be seen. In her feminine body self, hatred had softened
into dislike, and into a more realistic appraisal. But there was a persistent
dual body experience: the maligned feminine self, and the unsexed, disembodied self.

   Two years passed. Suddenly, she was offered a high-level executive position in the fashion industry, which required her to travel throughout Europe. She realized that travel would interfere with her treatment, rupturing
our attachment, evoking some of the depression and anxiety that comes
with displacement and homelessness. And of course, the fashion industry
would exacerbate the devaluation of her body. But she was very excited
about traveling, about the enhancement of her career. She felt ready to ter-
minate "for now," knowing that more work would be needed if she wanted

to pursue intimacy. In the weeks before her termination, she remembered childhood adventures disrupted by mother's anxiety. She needed to share both excitement and realistic concern. We knew that we would miss one another. It was a sad but fulfilled parting.

A year passes. I receive a call. She is in trouble, depressed, professionally mute and frozen. She arranges telephone sessions while she is traveling throughout Europe. She calls me, and in these phone calls, we enter a strange new phase of treatment. I cannot see her embodied. Her missing image begins to play on me with a kind of hallucinogenic action. Her voice seems cast in strange textures. I cannot see Rosa. But I can see the telephone cable traversing frigid waters, emergent in strange cities, buried under continents, ruthless in its progress. I feel my voice emerging from my own mouth. It is like a substance poured into plastic, poured from plastic into wire, from wire into that cable which is a conduit for her fear. I wonder if she can hear me speaking. I ask if she is feeling unreal. She says yes. I ask if she can see her body. She says no. Her mind is located somewhere outside of her head. She has no head. I tell her that she seems to be imploding, not with depression, but with fear. She says that she did not know it was fear. And then she says that she has known anxiety, even panic, but this is something beyond those states. It is something crackling, unraveled, avoidant of light and sound. The warm sun of Cannes has become a terrible illumination. Objects are growing in size and in dimension. Desk tops, table tops, the cushions of chairs: the inert becomes mobile and the mobile, inert. Voices are obscured in a tinnitus of sound. There has been an alteration in the lens of her sight; a tactile shift in her relation to the ground. Her universe is electrified by the uncanny significance of things. There has been no access to words, no proximity to the symbolic. She is mute in all the places where she has always been able to speak. And she cannot speak to me in our familiar language.

There is a visual acuity to my listening that I have rarely experienced. I see her landscape, and yet, I cannot see her. My words seem to grasp the shape of persecutory scenes. Shared remoteness begins to dissolve into the mirroring of fear. Still, we are mystified by the quality of her dread. She tells me what she can. For a year, she has been an executive purveyor of the young and the beautiful. Her world is peopled by idealized constructions: men, women, tall, sculpted, thin, impeccable in every feature. I anticipate the self-hatred aroused in her by their perfection. But where there has always been self-hatred, now hatred is absent, *because there is no body to hate.* And then she tells me this. As her work cycles through the fashion capitals, she re-encounters figures who look as if they are themselves, and yet, they are not themselves. Alien, yet recognizable, their brown eyes have become green, become blue, become brown again. Brown hair becomes red, becomes blonde. Plastic surgery erases all evidence of human frailty. What might have become real is 'beautified' and obscured. Bodies are disassembled, parts reconstructed, cut, burned, inflated. Skin is peeled and shrunk and stretched, as if human skin was malleable stuff. Faces 'lift' into masks. Silicone is implanted in muscle, supplanting real muscle and flesh. Souls evaporate as fat is suctioned out. Lives are lived by false copies of the real, so that there is an appearance of humanity *without being human*.

I think about the continuous rupture in object constancy, about the absence of any attachment. The reawakened mystery of who is where and who is missing. These are familiar conditions for her pain, but they are not the terror itself. The terror seems to reside in these peculiar bodies. As I listen, my mind seems crowded with hallucinatory scenes. I see fashion models seated in identical repose. Rosa's hand unscrewing plastic heads. Revealing mechanical works where human brains should have been. Row upon row of plastic heads filled with plastic works. Torsos severed, bloodless and immaculate. Wires, screws, computer chips, plugs emerging from white necks. Heads screwed back on and a simulation of movement. Everything but the eyes. The eyes are fixed, slow-moving glass. The eyes of dolls, the eyes of the dead. I am staring at the telephone receiver in my hand. Riveted by the surface of hard plastic, by its alien internal mechanisms. I need to unscrew the casing of the receiver and expose that interior. To find the cable which is the conduit for our voices. Perhaps this is not Rosa's living voice, but some technological improvement on the human voice. A simulation of thought and a simulation of sound. Or her voice has been pre-recorded prior to her disappearance. This voice is really the voice of a prior transmission. I have been speaking to someone who was never present. I need to see her. I cannot locate her. She is the cable, buried under continents, buried under the sea. She is inside of my receiver. Trying to get out. Embalmed in plastic and wire and cable and transmitters, no longer trying to get out.

I re-awaken to a considerable silence. She has stopped speaking, when, I cannot remember. Finally I speak, and she tells me that she was afraid that I was dead. I tell her about the unscrewed heads, the bloodless torsos and the mechanical works. I say that humanity seems to have been replaced by the robotic. Humans are eradicated, and the natural world has no living matter. The landscape of Cannes is an artificial rendering. Light is the residue of nuclear radiation. The earth is populated by the mutant and the dead. When she calls me, she is calling out to some remembered universe of the human, in which there is a possibility of a living human bond. She calls in the possibility that she can be alive. She says *yes*. There is a flood of talk about the nuclear landscape, about the humanoids which surround her. It is not *as if* they were robotic, *they are robots. And she was the only one who knew it, until I saw their unscrewed heads.* Of course, she "knows" that they are not robots. She is no more paranoid or psychotic than I am myself.

She is sane and strong and rooted in reality. But there is an alternate universe which is *really populated by the mutant and the robotic.* We see them and we know them. In that clarity, we feel exceptionally sane and exceptionally mad.

Some truth is emergent in this sharing of delusion. Knowledge seems to require a breakdown into symbolic equation. There is an elasticity to our minds which anchors us in "reality," and yet, it allows us to play with a contained madness. She has opened this gateway to knowledge, and will not retreat from it. Once again, she is fierce in her desire for the truth. At last, I deeply recognize her, and I almost see her as I saw her last, sitting on my couch. Human, alive, embodied. She is Rosa, who tells her story "walking." In this measured disintegration, she is telling her story and rewriting her story while she tells it. I have rarely known someone to risk this path. I comment on her courage. She sighs. She doesn't think it is courage. But I know her to possess a remarkable curiosity and fortitude. Within a week of speaking about the robots, there is a coherence of her terror and an abatement of that terror. Over the next 2 weeks, she speaks about the "humanoids," and rapidly recovers her capacity for speech in professional meetings. Still, she covets human contact and cannot locate anyone who is human. The world retains its peculiar cast. Fearful of light, and of "robotic" encounter, she stays in her hotel room at every opportunity.

Now I realize that her great uncle was the original humanoid. Incest did not just happen as she slept. There was another story. Every Sunday, the uncle would leave the house and not return until many hours later. Rosa discovered that he was going to the movies. She longed to see a movie, to make contact with this man who did not see her. She was about 8 years old, and even then, she was resourceful. She got the money for the ticket, and she followed him. She pleaded with him, and she pestered him, and he moved forward in his silence. At the ticket window, they buy their tickets. He seems to accept her presence. They take their seats, and the movie starts. Together, they fix their eyes upon the screen. She is excited. He is blank. Not a word has been spoken to her. He is oblivious to her presence. He masturbates her in the dark. He is without arousal or aggression or sadism. He makes no plea for the "tender" relief of his hunger. There are no threats, no coercion of lies. There is not any kind of human regard. He never turns his head to look at her. He does not laugh at the cartoons, or respond to the film. There is only sound, flickering image, fingers moving in her vagina. Infinite hours, as the film begins and ends and begins again, a continuous cycle, at which he stares unblinking. He does not register that the film is *over.* His fingers move, they stop moving, they move again. For Rosa, the first moments of excitement and arousal—the stimulation of the film, the stimulation of her genitals—become deadness and imprisonment and dread. She is lost, and does not know her own way home. She is too frightened to leave without him. She is hungry. She needs to urinate. She needs this thing to stop in her vagina. She tries to tell him. She tries to shake him. He is unmoving and unresponsive. She becomes mute and unmoving. At last, the last show ends, an usher makes him leave the theater. She follows her uncle home. She goes to bed, mortified in her body, and stripped of all embodiment.

We have spoken of this incident before. But not in so much detail. And we have never explored the impact of his deadness. Now, we realize that she was molested by a corpse. He was a rapist who didn't even seem to know that he was raping her; he didn't know she was there even while she was being raped. Her first passions—degradation, anxiety, anger, arousal—were inspired by a severed hand. There was no whole, living human rapist imbued with the quality of malevolence. There wasn't even a whole, *dead* human rapist, possessed of essential bodily coherence. There was a dismembered body part autonomous in its movements. Fingers still moving after rigor mortis had consumed the rest of the corpse. Or perhaps they were *not his own fingers,* but those of other, remembered hands. Moving with violence and hunger and abject supplication. The twitching of his hand inside her: did this mean that someone is still alive, and that she must save them? Could her arousal be the stuff that could animate the dead? Or would rigor mortis simply trap stiffening fingers inside of her?

The cold cave of her vagina. A vagina filled with bloody body parts. A vagina filled with bloodless things. As we speak of these images, we have reached the core of her disintegration. There are pieces of dismembered corpses deposited inside of her. And there is nothingness deposited inside of her, and there is no inside of her vagina in which to deposit that nothingness. There is a vagina which is a repository for corpses. There is a warm human vagina which is the repository for human grief. And there is a thing vagina, a crypt constructed of mortar and stone. And there is an evacuated no-self vagina, a blankness where a vagina should have been. An absence mirroring a series of absent female bodies: mother, grandmother, great aunt. Through this act of incest, bodies have been registered as whole corpses and fragmented corpses, as thing-like and nonhuman, as empty caskets and whole cemeteries, as the body parts of unwanted memory. Insofar as she was raped by a dead *thing, bodies were not bodies, and they had no sex and no gender. Genitals were absent because incest was transacted between nonhuman things. Incest was sexed and yet, it was unsexed; it erased the very genital which it penetrated.*

In the analysis of these fantasies, in the excavation of memory, she mentions that the fashion "humanoids" are without sensuality or erotic. Beautiful, they do not possess, or evoke, desire. I ask if they have genitals, and she realizes that it is as if they do not. Big breasts, broad chests, nothing between their legs. It is true that she defensively subtracts people's genitals, for in the absence of genitals, genitals can neither violate nor be violated. This is how we had initially understood her unsexed and ungendered self, in the first phase of her treatment. As a defense against rape, against the degradation of her own incestuous arousal. This was an understanding cast in terms of human malignance and human mortification. It was a half-truth which did not reach into her disembodied self. For Rosa, there would be no half-truths. She must have sensed that bodies lacked genitalia because *they were not human*. But this was a memory which could not be spoken in our human encounter. And so, she took a job devoid of real human bodies. She contrived a telephone treatment in which there was a missing human image. The absent image, the absent body: these opened into traumas in which the human were not human.

After we worked with the scene in the movie theater, our conversations lost their edge of primitive disorder. When she calls, we are simply speaking. The telephone retreats into an invisibility. Strong and no longer fearful, she transacts the "humanoids" with her old humor and vitality. She inspires respect at work for her dedication and creativity. She refuses the ruthlessness which pervades her profession. She facilitates and supports subordinates, and finds some friends who are related and authentic. She speaks of transferring to a position where she can settle in either London or Paris. Then there is an extraordinary dream. She finds herself looking at her naked body in a mirror, knowing she has never looked at it before. It is attractive, slender, voluptuous. She has the larger breasts she has always desired, the long limbs, the slender waist. And she discovers that she has a penis as well as a vagina. The penis is erect, and she masturbates it, not with arousal, but with a delighted astonishment. She feels beautiful and sufficient unto herself. We speak of her having an inviolate body, a new body, unmolested, emergent from within her own mind.

This is not a body conferred on her by rape. And it is not conferred on her by any form of erotic affirmation. It is an imaginary body, an undoing of time. It is postwar Brooklyn. There is sun and light and air. There are no missing relatives, no stories that cannot be told. Front stoops are rowdy with immigrant speech. Open fire hydrants spray water on hot, loose-bodied children. The great uncle joins in the clamor of humanity. Rosa has the body of an unmolested child. Moving outside to the streets, inside to the row house, she is alive amidst others who are embodied and alive. With this imaginary body, she meets a man outside of her work, and has an affair. He is warm and kind and passionate. She is sexually alive, naked, and unashamed. She is altered. Nonetheless, she will always need to move in and out of solitude. From this solitude, her body emerges, collapses, disappears, mutates, transforms. These shifts are no longer an occasion for dread. Rather, there are bodiless states infused with a sense of oceanic rest. Still, she can be lonely, and ambivalent in her desire for intimacy with another.

Discussion

Incestuous Perpetrators and the Thingness of Sex

> The woman is perfected.
> Her dead
> Body wears the smile of accomplishment …
> Her bare
>
> Feet seem to be saying:
> We have come so far, it is over …
>
> Each dead child coiled, a white serpent,
> One at each little
>
> Pitcher of milk, now empty,
> She has folded
>
> Them back in her body as petals
> Of a rose close when the garden
>
> stiffens and odors bleed
> From the sweet, deep throats of the night flower.
>
> —Plath (1981)

Incest and rape are the unsexing of sex. They transmute violated genitals into no-genitals; they subtract penis or vagina from the violated body. Rosa's body was a *she* insofar as she was penetrated. But she was neutered insofar as he used her as an "it." To be molested and to be undifferentiated from movies, television, radios. To have your genitals merge with repetitive cartoons. This was the reservoir of her disintegration. And so, Rosa tried to humanize memory. She tried to remember that she got hot. Or she imagined that she got hot. She humiliated herself with her own arousal. Humiliated, aroused, filled with anxiety and self-hatred, she was almost embodied. And if he could be filled with sadness and longing and emptiness, he was almost human. But she could not escape his deadness. Then she tries to imagine him as a cohesive human corpse. Once human, once a man, once able to register her as a living girl. But what she felt was existential erasure, the fragmentation which inheres in the thingness of sex. The human hand had become a mere "object of horror" (McDougall, 1989). The disappearance of bodies and gender and genitals, the equation of her vagina with absolute nothingness: this was her testimonial to sexual trauma. If Rosa's perpetra-

tor registered her as warm surfaces and open holes, she inevitably registered him as the dead and as the prehuman. The accuracy of this perception
made the "humanoid delusion" more real to her than any other human reality. Rosa could sense that the trespass on her body was not the omnipotent
fusion gained through narcissistic relatedness: it contained neither sadism
nor blissful arousal. She knows that in his psychic condition, she did not
even function for him as a narcissistic *human* object. He appeared to be that
pre-narcissistic, "autistic-contiguous" perpetrator (see Grand, 2000) for
whom the first order of human existence is always arriving but never arrives. For both herself and her perpetrator, incest negated the human self
and the human object. In this incestuous coupling, there was only an
impenetrable "line of demarcation—on the one side, nobody, on the other,
all the others, those who understand, care, live and understand" (Blanchot,
1973, p. 115).

The Disembodiment of Survival

Through this case study, I am proposing that rape potentiates a dual rendering of its history. There is a narrative cast in gendered/sexual states and enactments. And there is a thing narrative told by an unsexed and ungendered
self. The former seeks an audience with a human recipient; but the latter is
in search of disembodied witnessing. In all of its forms, rape locates and
mortifies the genitals which it violates. In the aftermath of sexual violation,
there will be a labyrinth of masculinities and feminities inscribed on the survivor's body, each of which is a commentary on the history, and the experience, of rape (Grand, 1997). This complex gendered embodiment is
imbued with what Sekoff (1999) calls the "abject triad" of fear, fascination,
and bodily horror. Here, "sensuous, but often repellant, textures of bodily
experience are drawn upon to establish the boundaries and limits of psychic space." (Sekoff, 1999, p. 116). In this abject triad, *living bodily experience* is linked to internal persecution, and gendering often becomes
inseparable from self-hatred (see also Gartner, 1999). Toxic in all of its dimensions, this is a self-hate which nonetheless insists upon the possibility
of human-to-human dialogue.

But if sexual violation is a perverse rendering of human embodiment, it
is also negates the existence of the sexed and gendered body. Rape (and incest) seems inspired by some urgent desire. But there is a moment during
rape when rape undergoes conversion. It reverts to its origins in the perpetrator's own extinction, in his or her dead-child self (Bollas, 1995; Grand,
2000). In these moments, there is always an it–it encounter. This encounter
is void of *subject–object* desire. Perpetrator and victim are united in what
Bollas (1995) calls the companionship of the dead. Corpses are devoid of

all human passion. They do not hate; neither do they lust. This absence of desire often produces a nonliving *thingness of sex.* Here, genitals are erased even as they are violated. Because rape and incest carry the itness of self and the deadness of self, the human lexicon of masculinities and feminities will be inadequate descriptors for the story of rape/incest (for a discussion on the gendering of traumatic dissociation, see Grand, 1997). And sexed enactments will be insufficient to it as well. As Corbett (2000) suggests, gender does render the inexplicable; it is a slippery silence, a "hole in relationality ... (which) jibes with the myriad failures in reason and empathy" (p. 777). Still, gender is defined by "a sheer lack of it-ness" (Corbett, 2000, p. 775). Where there is an it–it relationship, an unsexed thing-self emerges to tell the rest of the story.

The thing-self (or what I refer to as the *nonhuman* or *disembodied self*) can emerge in a multitude of forms—as a living neutered body, absent of all sex and gender marker; as a deadened sexed body absent of all sensation (not just sexual sensation); as projective dread about the thingness of others who only appear to be human; or as an identification with some nonhuman form (Searles 1960). All of these manifestations were evident in the treatment of Rosa. Although they can differ significantly from each other (the dead body with genitals but without sensation; the living body with sensation but without genitals), and encode different meanings, they share a common thrust: the attempt to tell a story about the it–it relation. In our clinical work, the thing-self can surface through gross symptomatology or through subtle derivatives. Thus, the patient who says, "I'm as big as a house" or "I look like an eggplant" may be attempting a dual narration. She communicates hate for an existent sexed and gendered body. And she communicates the thing-self, a nonhuman identification that subverts her human form.

But regardless of its particular shape, I am proposing that the thing-self will seek, and defy, human recognition. As I have suggested elsewhere (Grand, 2000), the solitude of memory is a defining marker of traumatized history and subjectivity. To escape from that loneliness is an imperative for the survivor in search of healing. But any escape from that loneliness is also an act of self-evisceration: it is a loss of identity, a false testament to history. There are a multitude of pathways through which survivors attempt an escape from loneliness. And there are a multitude of ways in which survivors undo that attempted escape. In the aftermath of rape, the survivor longs for, and fears, her own human embodiment. Embodiment would make her visible to human recognition; she might heal in the comfort of empathic witnessing. Without embodiment and human recognition, the survivor is raped in perpetuity by the foreclosure of her human subjectivity. But for the survivor of incest/rape, embodiment and human recognition can also renew the threat of annihilation. First, because embodiment is an invitation to rape. But more importantly for my present purposes, embodiment and embodied recognition can function as a *false self interaction that rapes the raped thing-self by eviscerating its true identity and history: its essential nature as a thing*.

What empathic human witness can recognize the thing-self? The *human* witness is locked into the language of psychosomatic parameters (not just sexual/gender parameters); such a witness cannot see or hear those truths carried by the thing-self. For survivors like Rosa, life (within the analysis; before, and outside the analysis) often becomes a series of true and false gestures in the arena of sex and gender. In this way, catastrophic loneliness is searching for its corporeal register so that it can be seen and known by a living human other. Cloaked in sex acts, and in displays of masculinity and femininity, the thing-self appears to enter into somatic existence. Now there is the hope of being recognized by a human witness. But there is an inevitable despair about that recognition because that recognition is false.

The assumption of sex and gender will have obscured the very testimony which requires witnessing. Whatever will be recognized by an empathic human other is not the truth of the "it–it" experience, but something else, some embodied category of traumatic experience. Fraudulent, renewed in human violation, the unsexed and ungendered self protests through the resurrection of its own disembodiment. It unsexes and ungenders "itself" as an assertion of true self-experience. For such a patient, as Laing (1960) would suggest, the true self is radically disembodied, and is more true than the false self which resides in the body. But just as the thing-self reclaims its disembodiment, it will also dread the absence of any somatic parameter. For in that absence lies invisibility, the loss of all possibility of being known as a human being. Thus traumatized selves are in continual movement: they are the once-embodied, the almost embodied, the never embodied, the disembodied, the dead, the disappeared. They are almost seen and never seen, moving in and out of hope, time and existence.

If we are to begin an understanding of the thing-self, we must grasp that "it" is not just defensive in its function. Disembodiment is not a straightforward dissociative function in which the disappearance of body prevents the body from being violated. To be ungendered and unsexed (or to be entirely without a human form) is more than an emptying out of experience by becoming insensate and inanimate (see Eigen, 1986). The unsexed, nonhuman self appears as a quasi-delusional imago which tells a story about a moment of traumatic "de-animation," in which an annihilated self comes into being *without a body*. I wish to entertain, in a moment of creative speculation, an unsubstantiated and controversial notion: Just as culture can give birth to, and organize the psyche-soma, so culture can give birth to, and define a disembodied, nonhuman thing-self.

If the psyche comes into being in relation to human others, so it comes into being in relation to the nonhuman world (see Searles, 1960). Perhaps we all have a nascent thing-self articulated in the nonhuman environment; but we foreground our human transactions and bodily identifications. In the ordinary course of things, we are virtually unconscious of thing-self states and identifications, although they contribute to the richness of life experience (through an appreciation of nature, aesthetics, etc). Perhaps the thing-self (marginalized and largely unconscious) operates on a separate developmental track from sexed/gendered/embodied selves. These tracks would be coexistent, covertly interactive, but largely out of our awareness. But during sexual violation the thing-self would be writ large in abasement (even while the body self is also fractured). Now, the wall isolating the thing-self cracks open, so that there is actually *less* dissociation surrounding this self, rather than *more*. This revelation of the thing-self occurs because rape involves a "loss of distinction between the animate and the inanimate" (Searles, 1960, p. 147), in which the body is not a "living corporeal self, but rather, an inanimate object which has been irreparably damaged" (Searles, 1960, p. 149). Thus, what appears as a quasi-delusional imago of nonhumanness might actually be a self-state which has always existed, but which is newly roused (and defined) by trauma. In survival, the voice of the thing-self becomes a heroic, asserting the fullness of traumatic memory.

But this heroic inevitably seems "crazy" in its emergence. We have previously silenced the thing-self in deference to the embodied self; we tend to meet only the traumatized version of the disembodied self. Naturally, it will be imbued with the darkest affects, and appear as an intrapsychic (or interpersonal) assault. But rather than being a form of madness, it is a "carbon dating, a freezing of certain physical states and stances that appear relatively unelaborated and unaltered" (Harris, 1998, p. 53). In its hallucinatory aspect there "may be read the remnants of a broken history" (Eigen, 1986, p. 47). The missing image in the mirror, the physical disorientation of self, the lack of somatic boundedness, the lack of skin, the numbing of sensation and of all physical fear, the seamless pelvic skin uninterrupted by any genital: This is an encryption of death's nothingness (for an interesting case example, see Williams, 1998) and the "it–it" relation. Symptoms that are pathogmonic of dissociation (Herman, 1992) and of alexithymia (Krystal, 1988; McDougall, 1989) are speaking here in a somewhat different register. Unlike alexithymia, the nonhuman self is not psychosomatic, but *antisomatic,* notable for its complete elision of the human soma. Once psychosomatics are manifest, the patient is linked to a human body, even if that bodily communication is divorced from appropriate affect.

The Disembodied Self and the Disembodied Analyst

When the raped self is speaking, the patient needs an analyst who is human, and who affirms the patient's human subjectivity. But she also needs an analysis that is not constrained by bodily parameters. In the analysis of disembodiment, the analyst investigates through the usual lens of dissociation and defense, developmental arrest, fantasy, conflict, and desire, affect and symbolization. This will have a curative effect. Nonetheless, there may be an impasse. We may find ourselves analyzing a patient whose human form cannot be seen, or who cannot see us in our human form. In this encounter, our presence and our words must shift in their function. They must become a bridge between the human and the nonhuman; they must, in Bromberg's (1998) words, "stand in the spaces" of the it–it encounter. Not interpretive but holding (Slochower,1996; Winnicott), there is a meeting with the body-as-thing, and the body-as-no-thing. There is a recognition of the absent body, the unsexed and ungendered body, the nonhuman form or the dead human body. In this effort, we will be recognizing that, "the intensity of belief attached to delusions indicates that the individual is trying to hold fast to a terrifyingly important dimension of his own story" (Eigen, 1986, p. 10).

We are only able to offer ourselves as witnesses for the nonhuman insofar as we have fairly comfortable access to our own nonhuman selves. The patient needs to be able to reach the analyst's nonhuman self in the context of a reliable, human empathic relationship *and in the context of a disembodied relationship*. She needs to be restored in her humanity even as she is known as an experiencing *nonhuman subject and as an evacuated nonhuman object*. To live in the nonhuman aspects of human experience: this requires the analyst to open her mind to what may feel like "hallucinatory chasms" (Eigen, 1986). Now, the analyst and patient share in a schizoid transference-countertransference enactment described by Akhtar (1999) as "inanimate." And because this is an encounter with a *traumatized* thing-self, this inanimate dyad will be imbued with dread. Here, patient and analyst become inanimate objects who have lost their humanity because the patient has been treated like a thing. Relinquishing metaphor, and deferring to symbolic equation, the analyst allows reality to be defined by the disappearance of body and by the thingness of self. There may be a tandem disembodiment, or a tandem merger with things. The interactive field may seem filled with dead body parts, or with physical properties that are not human. The analyst may feel provoked to treat the patient like a thing, or may feel treated like a thing. If the analyst can remain connected with the benign aspects of her own thing-self experience, there may also be a sense of coherence as nonhuman things, even an oceanic merger with cosmic experience. Throughout, there will be both the terror, *and the solace,* of being unsexed, ungendered, or completely disembodied.

This type of state can feel endangering to the analyst. It may feel psychotic if we assume that sanity and existence is associated with *being sexed and gendered, even if that gendering is conflictual or complex.* In psychoanalysis, we have made the assumption that the consolidation of body ego precedes the consolidation of mental ego. This body ego quickly moves into gendering. From this perspective, the removal of sex, gender, and body would imply the absence of mental ego; there would only be a psychotic process. In equating body with sanity, it is as if we have accepted the body as bedrock in its reality, whereas in fact, it "is constructed, as it were, with a false history. It comes into psychic being and then comes to have the characteristics or features of 'always there'" (Harris, 1998, p. 43). But it is not always there. As Federn (1957) suggested, the mental ego may precede the body ego but is not coextensive with it. Perhaps the "I" feeling can contract and expand to include or exclude the body, so that it is not simply derived from bodily states. Perhaps we have something like a nonhuman mental ego, constructed in relation to nonhuman "culture," and generative of both anxiety *and* "centeredness."

Like Searles (1960), I believe that there is a nonhuman stratum to early self-experience. He has suggested that there is a moment in development when we are undifferentiated not merely from the human other, but from the nonhuman environment. Thus, the self can accrue a nonhuman physical form. There is a merger with, (and later, an identification with), nonliving objects as constant and beneficent sources of nourishment and attachment. When human environmental contact is barren, cruel, or depriving, Searles suggests that there may be a failure to differentiate from the nonhuman, or there may be a regressive retreat into merger with thingness. Whether the human environment is traumatic or benign, there is always an unconscious residue of the nonhuman self. At various times, this nonhuman self emerges into our lives, both in and outside of analytic practice.

If this nonhuman self sometimes threatens us with chaos, it also guarantees us vital aspects of our sanity. As a layer of pre-human ontological security, the nonhuman self operates as an omniscient barrier to extinction. As such, it is generative of solidity and invulnerability. As a regressive retreat from the human, the nonhuman self also signifies the annihilation of the human self, articulating the *failure* of ontological security. Now the nonhuman self is associated with dread and imminent disintegration. Depending on the precipitant, on the availability of nonhuman supplies (as in the autistic-contiguous modality), either affective state can predominate, or they can alternate in rapid oscillation. As the analyst opens herself to nonhuman self states, a sense of potency will countermand experiences of dread. In the encounter with the patient's traumatized nonhuman self, there is only an *apparent descent into madness*. And even that appearance is attended by an increment in sanity. As Federn notes, human body ego feeling can be lost prior to mental ego feeling; it may seem like the precursor to psychosis, but it is not psychosis itself. And as Winnicott (1972) might have reassured us, the breakdown which the analyst is anticipating has already occurred during the patient's trauma: It is the disembodiment of the no-self which the patient has already been survived.

References

Akhtar, S. (1999), *Inner Torment*. Northvale, NJ: Aronson.

Bollas, C. (1995), The Structure of Evil. In: *Cracking Up: The Work of Unconscious Experience*. NY: Hill and Wang.

Bromberg, P. M. (1998), *Standing in the Spaces: Essays on Clinical Process, Trauma and Dissociation*. Hillside, NJ: The Analytic Press.

Bion, W. R. (1965), *Transformation*. London: Tavistock.

Blanchott, M. (1973), *The Step not Beyond*. (L. Nelson, Trans.). Albany, NY: State University of NY Press.

Corbett, K. (2000), Toward the Coexistence of Effort and Lack: Commentary on Paper by Cynthia Dyess and Tim Dean. *Psychoanalytic Dialogues,* 10 (5):775–786.

Eigen (1986), *The Psychotic role*. Northvale, NJ: Aronson.

Federn, P. (1957), *Ego Psychology and the Psychoses*. London: Maresfield Reprints

Freud, S. (1920), Beyond the Pleasure Principle, *Standard Edition,* 14:237–260.

Gartner, R. (1999), *Betrayed as Boys*. NY: Guilford Press.

Grand, S. (1997). On the gendering of traumatic dissociation: A case of mother–son incest. *Gender and Psychoanal.,* 1:55–79.

Grand, S. (2000), *The Reproduction of Evil*. NJ: The Analytic Press.

Grotstein, J. S. (1990), Nothingness, meaninglessness, chaos and the "Black Hole" II. *Contemporary Psychoanal.,* 3:407–445.

Harris, A. (1998), Psychic envelopes and sonorous baths: Sitting the body in relational theory and clinical practice. In *Relational Perspectives on the Body*, eds: Aron, L. & Anderson F. S. NJ: The Analytic Press, 39–64.

Herman, J. L. (1992), *Trauma and Recovery*. NY: Basic Books.

Krystal, H. (1988), *Integration and Self-Healing: Affect, Trauma, Alexithymia*. Hillsdale, NJ: The Analytic Press.

Laing, R. D. (1960), *The Divided Self*. NY: Penguin Books.

McDougall, J. (1989). *Theaters of the Body: A Psychoanalytic Approach to Psychosomatic Illness*. NY: W.W. Norton.

Plath, S. (1981), Edge. In *Ariel*, NY: HarperCollins, pp. 93–94.

Searles, H. (1960), *The Nonhuman Environment*. Madison, CT: International Universities Press.

Sekoff, J. (1999). The undead: Necromancy and the inner World. In: *The Dead Mother: The Work of Andre Greene*, ed. G. Kohon. London: Routledge, pp. 000–000.

Slochower, J. (1996). *Holding and Psychoanalysis.* NJ: The Analytic Press.

Williams, A. H. (1998), Psychotic development in a sexually abused borderline patient. *Psychoanal. Dial.,* 4:459–493.

Winnicott, D. W. (1972), *Holding and Interpretation.* London: Hogarth Press

•

5

The House of Difference:*
Enactment, a Play in Three Scenes

Adrienne Harris, PhD

▼ ▼ ▼ ▼ ▼

In "The House of Difference," an essay of Audre Lorde's, she writes, "We came to realize that our place was the very house of difference rather than the security of any particular difference" (Lorde, 1984, p. 226). Lorde was exploring the insufficiency of many single points of difference—black, female, gay, dyke. Each form of identification yields up a unique constellation of experiences. At the same time, each subjectivity creates a complex dialogue with its alternatives; the result is a wonderful tapestry of variegated experience where difference and uniqueness and points of deep recognition could all coexist. Although she and others constructed a capacious house for black gay women, a space of multiple, complex shifting identities, expressed in distinct styles of speech and ways of being and doing, I would say that looking broadly at matters of race, gender, class, and culture, in a Western, North American context, our house of difference is still under construction. In this chapter I want to contribute to such a project.

Writing this chapter now in the fall of 2005, even the potential of a house of difference seems in jeopardy. Phobic dread dominates the political discourse, driving strategy, policy, and rhetoric. In a perhaps hyperbolic attempt to alter the larger social and political situation, progressives fear that we have rolled back the Enlightenment, overturned reason for raw fear and fanaticism. So I am writing about racism and racialized subjectivity in a particularly tense and contested social context.

*This chapter was developed from a paper presented at the 10th conference at the Institute for Contemporary Psychoanalysis and Psychotherapy. "Race as a Social Construction." Washington DC, April 17th, 2004.

I am also writing about race as a psychoanalyst within a particular intellectual history. Psychoanalytic accounts of cultural and social phenomena were initiated by Freud. From my perspective, the most interesting trajectory of that project is the writing that seeks to exploit and explore the intersect of Freud and Marx, a tradition we might see as reaching its highest form in the Frankfurt school (Jay, 1973). In the second half of the 20th century, the developments of poststructuralism and postmodernism put another spin on psychoanalytic theory's intersect with political theory and culture studies. Postmodernisms are both continuous with, and radically discontinuous with, the Freud–Marx explorations (which are perhaps best understood as projects developing under the umbrella of modernism). Certain aspects of postmodern methodology draw on the tools of psychoanalysis as a hermeneutics of suspicion (Ricouer, 1970). But, in particular through the influence of Foucault (1965, 1975, 1988), psychoanalysts have been required to conduct more scrutiny, self-consciousness, and vigilance in their own theorizing. The analytic instrument is a tool of the state *and* a device with the potential to undermine social regulation (Butler, 2004a, 2004b; Harris, 2005).

This chapter is a commitment to the value of psychoanalytic tools for work on racialized subjectivities and racism. Alongside political and cultural theory, literary theory, ethnography, social analysis, the method of psychoanalysis (a set of contaminated tools to be sure) is a commitment to looking at what is hidden in silence. Psychoanalysis, at its most unflinching and courageous, allows us to maintain curiosity at the strange, fuzzy, unreasoning moments in the psyche and in the culture. In this way, psychoanalysis has the potential to be, in part, a revolutionary practice. Or to put it more modestly, psychoanalysis can be part of a radical practice of social resistance.

In this chapter, I am going to approach the project of studying racialized subjectivities with the need to deconstruct "whiteness" from inside the category, an activity for which psychoanalysis is crucial. I would argue that a relational psychoanalysis in negotiation with various postmodernisms is a synergy with great potential. The substitution of indeterminacy, movement, and temporality for fixed structure and polarity is one way to understand the project of some intersubjectivity theorists. Here I am leaning a lot on Bhabha's (1994) particular interpretation of the "post" in postmodernism, as a signifier for hybridity, movement, restlessness, and revisioning.

As a relational analyst with a postmodern inflection, I want to explore racialized subjectivities as social constructions starting with countertransference.

I connect postmodern preoccupations with the relational interests in analytic subjectivity, which is not a refusal of meaning making but a decentering of it. If you accept ambiguities and indeterminacies, both in the subject and object of study, it is not that you are adrift in some sea of relativism but that you are suspicious of claims of exhaustive knowledge. These suspicions center around the worry that it is power that is often more at stake than reason. (Harris, 2005, p. 9)

The subtitle of this chapter, "Enactment, a Play in Three Scenes," draws on a term that has virtually replaced terms like *acting out* or *acting in* to describe the infusion of countertransference and transference interdependences into clinical dyadic life. This term *enactment* speaks to the inevitability that unconscious pressures on action and expression usefully haunt psychoanalytic or social processes.

Enactment, Scene One

In 2002, I was invited to be the keynote speaker at a conference organized by an analytic institute in Washington. The conference was to be called "Race as a Social Construction." I tried for several months to talk the organizers out of the invitation. Politely they persisted, making many adjustments in the schedule to enable me to participate. In the months after this invitation I maintained a strange, private, rather inchoate worry. I could tell myself that the invitation came on the basis of my work on gender and in relational theory, but I foundered on how little I had written about race, really only a discussion with Kim Leary published in *Psychoanalytic Dialogues* about the haunting of racialized identities (Harris, 2000; Leary, 2000)

This odd mixture of anxiety and shame coalesced in the following self-interrogation: Did I have anything to say? Had I really written enough on this topic? But then a second wave of questions began to assert themselves: Who was the interlocutor in this internal dialogue? To whom was I apologizing? To whom was I insisting that I had nothing to say? When had I ever behaved so modestly or prudently? I was *not* having the honest unvarnished thought that perhaps I had not done enough to merit this invitation. My psychic state was more primitive and anxiety-riddled. I had to recognize a bleak, unpleasant truth embedded in the question "What did I have to say about race or racism?" It is embarrassingly obvious, a truth in plain sight. For surely, there is no psychoanalyst, relational or otherwise, who could possibly justify having *nothing* to say about race and racism. That blanked-out silence is the first enactment. The rupture in agency or voice is, in itself, the problem. In a sense, I am trying to take Homi Bhahba's (1994) methodology for grounding or authorizing a postcolonial discourse, a multiply positioned subaltern[1] speaker, and turn this method toward "white" speech, and so to

---

[1]*Subaltern* is the term postmodern cultural critics like Bhabha and Spivack and others have coined to describe the particular position of a contemporary colonial subject, that is, a subject often fragmented by time (migration) and space, dislocated from tradition and community, and forced to speak and function in a distinctly hybrid form. Bhabha makes of this subaltern state both the occasion of alienation and for resistance.

wonder about the blank space and silences where agency and responsibility might be. I was blanked out, dissociated, primarily, I suspect, through fear. How could I understand this fear of talking? I who believe in and practice the talking cure was apparently out of words and thoughts.

This chapter, and the thinking that I have been able to do in preparing it, is very indebted to three intellectual traditions. First, the writing of Homi Bhaba (1994), bell hooks (1989, 1992), Tommy Lott (2000), Franz Fanon (1986), Cornel West (1993) and others took me into an encounter with a century of black scholarship on questions of identity. Second, I am writing from a relational and postmodern perspective, in which the co-construction of intersubjective experience, the historical contingency of unconscious process, and the need for self-reflection on the regulatory practices implicit in psychoanalysis, are all aspects of my thinking about social and intrapsychic phenomena (Mitchell & Harris, 2003). Third, I am indebted to the psychoanalytic study of racism (Apprey, 1996, 2003; Ainslie & Brabeck, 2003; Gump, 2004; Holmes, 1992; Kovel, 1983, 1994; Leary, 1994, 1997, 2000; Moss, 2003), but particularly to the contemporary work of Altman (2003), Suchet (2004a, 2004b), and Straker (2004), three psychoanalysts who have very courageously begun the task of thinking about the impact of racism on their own identity formation as a way to deconstruct racist thought in the wider culture.

Although Altman, Suchet, and Straker speak from within a relational perspective of carefully examined countertransference, none ignores the social, historical, economic or psychoanalytic analysis of racism, of the kind developed by Moss and Kovel, among others. They point to the racist use of the culture for intrapsychic ends, noting how shaky egos are propped up by the cultural formations that maintain a hegemonic status for "whiteness." Looking at the move from psyche to culture, these writers examine the way unconscious and intrapsychic instantiations of racism support the particular hegemonies of globalization. They look to the use of racist practices and ideology to undergird capitalism. They give amazingly acute readings of the perversion and fetishization in racism.

When you approach racism psychoanalytically, you can observe the terrible excitement in phobic hatred, the animations of disavowed desire, and of destructiveness covered over in guiltiness. You observe the cover of rationality that masks splitting and disavowal. This is the argument bell hooks (1989, 1992) approaches from another perspective, namely, that splitting not only alienates danger and destructiveness into others, it also uses the warmth and vitality of the Other to reappropriate humanity and feeling into a deadened and empty life. Treating a person of color as a fetish, in other words, can be used to export degradation and to import passion and energy. This perspective is very deeply in Fanon's (1986) analysis of the grip in which the colonial subject is held and used.

For Straker and Suchet, psychoanalytic tools are turned on their personal experiences forged in South Africa. In theorizing racism, Straker argues that by forcing the Other, particularly black otherness, to contain disavowed experience and disavowed knowledge, the Other is asked to function as a fetish, carrying badness, aggression, sexuality, and destructiveness.

What distinguishes Straker, Suchet, and Altman for me is that they have determined that an analysis of racism must begin at home and so must include an analysis of "whiteness." So they have undertaken a personalized excavation, seeing this as a necessary element in the larger project of "decolonization," a project described in bell hooks as "only complete when it is understood as a complex process that involves both the colonizer and the colonized" (hooks, 1992 p. 20). To turn to a deconstruction of whiteness is to make the unremarkable remarkable, to force unexamined assumptions, to open up to a set of questions. The goal, of course, is to see whiteness as a social construction, to see that whiteness is the unmarked category and in that particular way accrues and hoards power. This kind of analysis or deconstruction is intended to undermine both the category itself and the psychic and cultural work the category of whiteness does.

Enactment, Scene Two

So, in this tradition of interrogating whiteness, I begin to think of my own history. And this has taken me to the surprising recognition of a second enactment. Like Straker and Suchet, I am a British colonial subject, but because my world is Canada where, in the East, the aboriginal presence is completely erased, I grew up cocooned in whiteness. In the 1940s and 1950s Wasp Toronto was so ethnically managed that the most prominent exotic and forbidden alterity was Jewishness. Down the road in Montreal, the French Canadians were also construed as foreign creatures of excitement and danger, to which was added the Protestant prejudices against Catholic "primitivity." The particular stranglehood that Methodist and Presbyterian religious dogma had over English-speaking Canadian social formations makes a grim story. The common enemy was pleasure and individuality. Danger *and* delight had been evacuated into outsiders. Born in 1941, I was also a child steeped in wartime images where the significant frightening Other was Asian.

Examining the snowy whiteness of the Canadian landscape, elaborated as a terrifying devouring freeze in literary and aesthetic images, there seems to be nothing to talk about. Canadian novels of the early and mid-20th century are filled with murderous, silent, and deadly snowstorms, very quiet and very white, eerie and empty. A staple of educational reading in my adolescence was a Quebecois novel in which an innocent young girl falls in love with a dramatic, dark-sounding, dark-looking fur trapper, named (evocatively, I now see) François Paradis. Of course, the minute their eyes meet, and desire blazes up, the trapper is swallowed in a fatal blizzard. Many lessons here, but the intention surely was both to constitute desire for a dark Other and at the same time promote the orderly choice of safe banker husbands as suitable for a girl of the Anglo bourgeoisie.

One might reasonably ask what kind of snow job is going on. Landscape paintings, novels, and poetry whitens the Canadian landscape, creating a haunting, absent presence, all rendered opaque and without historical reference to the young and impressionable readers. Apprey argues that it is precisely through the management of these public discourses and products, that intergenerational trauma is reproduced and at the same time disguised (Apprey, 1996). Yet, despite the amnesia-inducing whiteness that Canada conjures up for me, Straker's use of the term *fetish* has caught my eye. My grandparents' house, I can see, was a museum of fetish objects. The Edwardian gents in my family had soldiered, prospected, and touristed around the world sending back roomfuls of artifacts, looted from the cultural and natural world. My grandfather had been a surveyor for Cecil Rhodes in Africa, so the rooms and hallways of his house were filled with tiger skins made into rugs, elephant feet transformed into umbrella stands, skulls of creatures large and small, shot and stuffed and set out in long rows along the front hall. As a small child I was mesmerized and entranced, following along hallways where each skull was, mounted, identified and dated. Emu, ibex, eland, even the names of these creatures were exotic.

Now, in retrospect, I notice the jumbling of animal parts, military trophies, and cultural artifacts. This is surely part of what Altman describes as an alienated rupture with the natural and the social world. There is the perverse equalizing of animal and tribal culture into one new category—the domesticated decoration—the bourgeois celebration of fetish, airbrushed into fashion and style. This style, we might see, made a chic of fetish objects, coinciding, all too neatly, with the imperial and capital expanding end of the 19th century.

Absorbed into personal domestic décor and private family space, these shields, spears, cannonballs, and carvings were the manifest content of a latent, greedy worldwide shopping or rather shoplifting binge, conducted over several generations. One might remember the critical discussion of the 1980s MOMA show on "Primitivism" in which the question was raised as to who exactly was "primitive," the Europeans who had kept living cultural material in museums or on walls or the tribal communities for whom these objects were tied to complex social practices and forms of life.

Flash forward to the 1990s when I was kayaking in the Queen Charlottes. These islands in the Pacific, west of British Columbia, are a region of enormous beauty, with the familiar gray, deep green, and black palette of my childhood memories of Northern Canada, a natural world that seems deeply homelike and familiar to me. We were paddling to the site of the Haida totems and lost villages and, as it turns out, one locale of my grandfather's prospecting and shopping tours.

A lost history, certainly never taught in eastern Canadian schools, comes into focus. Thirty years before my grandfather's visit, the destruction of the Haida, a fierce community with a world-class aesthetic and a Rabelesian mythology, occurred in the 1860s, probably via smallpox-infested blankets introduced by English traders. This destruction is tied to industrialization and capital development, *not* to the first contacts with the Haida. A proud and successful trading partner was transformed within months into a demoralized remnant of charity cases, placed under the wing of the Methodist Church. Over the next quarter century, that collapse occasioned the removal of totems, artifacts, and cultural materials to many collectors and museums.

By the 1990s, cultural, physical, and economic revivals are in full swing, but not without ironies. The Haida territory now looks lush and bounteous in comparison to the despoiled clear-cut forests owned by the timber companies and worked by a bitter white underclass. The village and its totems are administered by Parks Canada as a U.N. Heritage site, a process that can easily Disney-fy any historic setting. Giant tour boats cruise alongside the island, giving consumers an easy pleasant sighting of the ruins of the ancestral Haida village. We kayakers, more intrepid eco-tourists, are allowed to land and walk around—12 at a time—preserving the fragile ecosystem while offering the tourist the kinds of consumption and spectacle that, ironically, keeps that community economically viable.

Deep questions are being undertaken in the Haida community about the fetish nature of aboriginal objects: How will religious practice, globalization, the replacement of fishing and agriculture with a service economy, eco-tourism and eco-terrorism all coexist? We meet young Haida men and women who are sometimes postmodern multiples and sometimes reverential custodians of the past. Some are exuberantly planning to export carved abalone shell to markets in Europe and others are tending the ruined and august village of their ancestors. We listened to a young Parks Canada employee, the grandson of distinguished Haida carvers, confess he had been afraid to sleep alone among the totems. Later the same day, we eavesdropped on a young Haida man chatting up his art dealer in Berlin on his cell phone. At the tourist center, the guidebook's bland descriptions of the Haida story had been marked up and annotated in a way that would have made any postmodern theorist deeply happy. No simple unmediated Others here. Subalterns in possession of the "master's" tools. I felt at home and on another planet.

A year after my trip, I follow closely the accounts in the New York press of the Haida's negotiations with the American Museum of Natural History for the return of bones and artifacts. The story in the *Times* details the voyage of the Haida to the museum. They arrive. They sing to the bones and the other objects and they repatriate them to their island world. Meanwhile I, as time and death has dispersed some of my family possessions, sit in my New York apartment looking at a beautiful carved Haida bird with its elegant neck, a beaver with fierce teeth and a powerful tail, and a lovely carved spoon. I notice only when working on this chapter, that although I wept at the newspaper account of the repatriation, I have not and, more perversely, I do not want to give these objects back.

Now I feel the bite and grip of perversion in my psyche. My need for this fetish is quite outside reason and this makes me feel helpless, odd, and bad. I cannot claim to be remorseful in any way that would be honorable or authentic. The feelings I can detect around this experience are fear, anxiety, and shame, certainly, but, more acutely, for my analysis here, there is *guiltiness* rather than remorse.

Let me turn to the theoretical preoccupations Altman, Straker, and Suchet develop, as a way to interrogate my own perversions. For Altman, the project has been to use psychoanalysis and autobiography to look at racism within a liberal Jewish progressive stance. As in the work of Straker and Suchet, this has meant exploring both personal biography and an active history in antiracist, liberal work, a deconstruction that brings a particularly acute pain in giving up some of the illusions of progressive support for integration, civil rights, and anti-apartheid movements.

Straker's work emerged from her consultation and adjunctive work with the African National Congress, and draws on Lacan, Eng, and Han's work on racial melancholy and ultimately on the work of Butler on gender melancholy.. Eng, a cultural theorist, and Han, whose clinical work is located in the area of transnational adoption, propose that we see the disrupted mourning in someone whose ethnicity or racial identity marks them as degraded Other in a hegemonic society that idealizes whiteness. Straker, taking up this idea of blocked mourning, speaks of the "melancholy of the beneficiary," the anxiety in regard to emptiness and insufficiency in relation to the ideal of "whiteness" for white persons. She is looking both at the sense of lack and emptiness in the individual asked to represent whiteness as well as the perversions that arise in that individual in relation to alterity. What I find especially useful in her work is that she does not take this analysis of the deficits in "whiteness" into a request for empathy. Her concepts do not lead to a shift away from the moral questions in regard to racism. She is not talking of the white man's burden.

The state of alienation and brittle, covered emptiness leaves the person bearing "whiteness" in a double state of knowing and not knowing, depending on a polarized idea of racial identity and at the same time disavowing its falseness, its defensiveness, its empty dangers. The use of the term perversion is both rhetorically and conceptually deliberate, I believe.

Melanie Suchet's work is a reflection on her own childhood embedded in the society of apartheid, where racism both constituted and erased her primary attachments. In exploring her relationship with her beloved black nanny, she encounters the ironies and tragedies of ruptured attachments. This might extend to examining the ruptures in attachment of third-world women with their own children, a topic much under consideration at the moment. Social theorists are concerned with the impact of global economies on the "outsourcing" of maternal work. Taking this concern into the clinical situation, Gump (2004) has opened up thinking about disruptions in mother–child attachment processes as intergenerationally transmitted phenomena in her black patients. These ruptures and disturbances are sequelae, she suggests, of the impact of slavery on the maternal processes of bonding and relatedness.

Altman links progressive thought and clinical work informed by social theory and seeks to deconstruct the impact of racism on any American psyche. The falseness of the ideal of whiteness, its moral bankruptcy, needs to be mourned, he argues, the illusory claims embedded and hidden in whiteness need to be faced up to. This includes appreciating the rupture of the natural, material world, the alienation that comes with materialism, and consumption. white privilege masks the distortions of work, its impact on attachments and relatedness that crosses class and culture, the very issues currently being explored in the domain of childcare and maternal work. Work's invasion and deformation of bodily and psychic life affect the relational forms of all social classes. We might say that for all three writers, the illusions of white privilege must be exposed and the realities of white privilege owned and given up.

On a rhetorical level, this is relatively easy to propose. A psychoanalytic interrogation is required to discover why, in fact, both owning and relinquishing power is so difficult. Interrogating the perversion in my "owning" Haida objects, I need to examine how my identity, my history, and perhaps my sexuality, seem at risk without these fetish objects. I seem in possession of needs I cannot describe or account for, in the grips of unconscious forces. And most acutely, there is a feral, willful adhesion I feel in relation to these objects. I have a kind of hysteria and guiltiness, not guilt.

This brings me to an issue raised in the work of Altman, Suchet, and Straker that has to do with guilt, shame, and remorse as processes of work on racialized subjectivities, and healing racism. I think that this is a complex matter. We know this from the accounts of the work in South Africa at the Truth and Reconciliation Commission. Genuine remorse was considerably rarer than confession and there seem to be social and psychic consequences to this.

I suggest that certain forms of guilt—actually what Steve Mitchell (2000) called guiltiness—or perhaps what might be thought of as guilt in the paranoid schizoid position—are actually counterweights to both politics and identifications in working on racism and the massive consequences of segregation. Guiltiness is a complex and unstable basis for theory or politics, a kind of false consciousness. I am making a parallel between the alternatives surrender versus submission and guilt versus guiltiness, drawing on the work of Ghent (1990). Put another way, how to live in the depressive position with regard to responsibility and remorse? What will constitute guilt as an act of surrender? Guiltiness and tears, in the context of my "possession" of the Haida artifacts, are a kind of hysterical defense, disguising, even to me, the perverse reifications and delusions of ownership that are in play in me.

I am making an argument against what I want to call "melancholy politics," a big feature of the far left in the 1960s, I would argue, and certainly a surviving remnant in some analyses of racism. Guilty fears and a consciousness of white privilege can create another kind of fetishizing of alterity. Zwerman (1994) has explored the dynamics of guilt and masochism in extreme left groups in the 1960s and 1970s. In particular, she was struck by the lapse of gender politics and self-interest among women in these groups. Radical political practices and conservative gender politics were a lethal combination for many women, particularly looked at in the light of very long prison terms and ruptured families. In a guilty abjection in relation to people of color, I think there was a dissociation from self-interest, a romanticizing of violence and oppression. Masochism took the place of any real deconstruction of white privilege. Guiltiness is a kind of hysterical form of attachment and narcissism, not a break with colonizing gaze or structure. It makes for ruptured, anxious, and dissociated speech. Perhaps this is a reasonable first step from the seamless voice of authorized and naturalized identities, from keeping otherness in a fetishized state. But guiltiness too often includes a demand for maternal care, for forgiveness and solace. It has a sometimes hidden, sometimes explicit interlocutor, and it is primarily pre-reflective.

I am aware that one reaction to this revelation of enactment is to ask why this white girl is wringing her hands over a wooden bird. "Give it back, for heaven's sake, and let's get to the really serious aspects of racism, its pervasive hold on social and economic life." Fair enough. But I am drawn by the kind of thinking Fanon and Bhabha encourage, that is, an excavation of the affective and unconscious links in the strange hybrid worlds of postmodern life. Do these objects convey for me some illusion of power? Are they important as property or as art? The general point to make here is to ask the question: How is "white" identity built still on an imperial stance, even if it is an identification primarily lived in the unconscious?

Enactment, Scene Three

Beginning this process of looking at the disavowed elements of "whiteness" in my own psyche led me to an important essay in psychoanalysis and to find that there a racist construction at its very heart, which I discover I had both known and not known. The text—the site of the third enactment I am looking at—is one of the founding texts of contemporary postmodern analyses of femininity, Joan Riviere's (1929) "Womanliness as a masquerade." Note the date of its publication—1929. It is a text beloved of Lacanians, feminists, and postmoderns alike, as an early proto-theorizing account of the performative border-living, liminal aspects of identity. So this third enactment is ours, the field's, as well as mine.

In her essay, Riviere, somewhat anxiously and self-consciously, articulates a view of identity that is not naturally founded on body or psyche, nor rooted in essentialism. To illustrate her thesis about disavowed desire and aggression and its relation to female homosexuality, a patient's fantasy is presented, cast first in a daydream and then in a dream. A desirable woman seductively manipulates a man's sexual longings in order to trap and denounce him to the authorities. Actually these desires are projected into him. It is not clear he feels desire at all. The desiring man in the dream is described as an American Negro, the dreamer apparently an American Southerner.

Here is the text:

> This phantasy, it then appeared, had been very common in her childhood and youth, which had been spent in the Southern States of America; if a negro came to attack her, she planned to defend herself by making him kiss her and make love to her (ultimately so that she could then deliver him over to justice). But there was a further determinant of the obsessive behaviour. In a dream which had a rather similar content to this childhood phantasy, she was in terror alone in the house; then a negro came in and found her washing clothes, with her sleeves rolled up and arms exposed. She resisted him, with the secret intention of attracting him sexually, and he began to admire her arms and to caress them and her breasts. (Riviere, 1929, p. 309)

Riviere subjects this material to a quite conventional discussion of oedipal dynamics. The dream and the fantasies are stripped of context and history, viewed as the endogenous product of drive, anxiety, and conflict. Projection or projective identifications are ruled by intrapsychic, never interpersonal or historical needs. This is an exemple of what Gump, Apprey and others are talking about, the presence of trauma unconsciously transcribed and repressed. Abraham and Torok (1994) term this phenomena the presence of *encrypted* identities. A secret in plain sight, secret to its bearer and in the case of the Riviere text, remarkably opaquely secret, to 75 years of psychoanalytic and cultural theory readers.

When I first worked on this material I was interested in women's relation to envy and to each other. I read the dream as one in which the black man, that signifier of phallic hypersexuality envied and feared by men and women, stands in as homosexual desire for a woman. I was drawn by a critique of this essay by Butler, who kept wondering where in Riviere's essay on homosexual women one could locate homosexual desire. Here is what I wrote in 1995:

> Now an American woman in the 1920s dreaming of sending a black man to the authorities for the crime of sexual advances is a woman with lynching on her mind. In the dream the fate of a dangerous desire is to be degraded. It must be policed and destroyed. Heterosexual and homosexual longing is masked; masculinized, blackened, apprehended and headed for execution. (Harris, 1997, p. 305)

I can see now that I was appreciating the racial implications but I can also see that I recruited them for an understanding of the repression of femininity and female desire. Re-reading in the context of work on this chapter on race has forced me to look at how, in psychoanalysis, one kind of identity (white femininity) is founded on the destruction of another (black masculinity).

But even this reading is insufficient. I realize as I work on this chapter a year after the conference that I have been warding off thoughts that seemed too frightening and ominous at the time. Think of this situation for a minute, reported by Riviere as an interesting clinical fact in the service of understanding defensive and performative femininity. This Southern woman tells her English analyst in 1929 that she has repeated obsessional (we must also think masturbatory) fantasies of this scene of sexual assault by a black man that ends (and was always intended to end thus) with a call for arrest and the police. Think of this in the context of the 1920s in America, a peak period in the ghastly history of American lynching. By the 1920s, 90% of the lynchings occurred in southern states, as the studies of Morton Work at Tuskegee attest.[2] Remember also that a common pretext for lynching was an imagined sexual advance of a black man towards a white woman. Whose fantasy is this? Whose projections of disavowed desire might have led in repetitive forms to actual lynchings?

Riviere and all the later commentators, myself included, have stayed focused at the individual level, even where a social aspect is implicated. Why are we not hearing the unconscious, preconscious, but powerful intrapsychic braces for racial violence? What could the presence of this kind of projective identification of desire from white female psyche into black male

---

[2]Work estimated over 4,700 lynchings from the period of 1882–1968, with 2,500 occurring before 1900 (Zangrado, R. (1980)

body/mind mean at a social level? How much does a *racist* unconscious crossed with female anxiety about desire and agency contribute to actual racial violence? This is a historically constituted unconscious fantasy integrated with or perversely animated by white anxieties about vitality and desire.

This is a point central to relational thinking. We have here not just an individual fantasy but a reading of the collective, historically contingent fantasies, carried in the group and in the individual. These individual fantasies all so sinisterly and effectively support the other rationales for racial hatred and lynching: matters of employment, emancipation, and economic forces loose in the American culture in the early 20th century.

The scotoma in reading Riviere can only be part of the answer to my perverse relation to the Haida bird, spoon, and beaver. These objects are functioning both as commodity fetishes and fetish in the more usual psychoanalytic sense in that they incorporate disavowed loss and criminality, but also they contain and manage a determination to hold power. I feel the pull of the perverse in a quite distinct way. I feel inhabited. Something in my identity feels at stake and so I cannot fully appropriate these matters consciously into my psyche in a way that would organize aggression and identification into genuine ambivalence and remorse. I cannot undertake what Homi Bhabha describes as "thinking the unthought."

It may be that there is in "whiteness" a "psychose blanche" named by Andre Green for quite other purposes (Green, 1970). Deeper than depression, deeper than rage, there is a blankness, a place where there is not sufficient structure for mourning, where the psyche gives way. Perhaps this is what "whiteness" is: the disruption or erasure of mourning, a gap in the psyche though which "whiteness" functions like an imploding star, refusing signification. It is not trauma solely that is whitened out, but destructiveness and memory.

References

Abraham, N., & Torok, M. (1994), *The Shell and the Kernel*. Chicago: University of Chicago Press.

Ainslie, R., & Brabeck, K. (2003), Race murder and community trauma: Psychoanalysis and ethnography in exploring the impact of the killing of James Byrd in Jasper, Texas. *J Psychoanal. of Culture and Society*, 8:42–50.

Altman, N. (2003), How white people suffer from racism. *Psychotherapy and Politics International*, 1:93–106.

Apprey, M. (1996), *Phenomenology of Transgenerational Haunting: Subjects in Apposition, Subjects on Urgent/Voluntary Errands*. Ann Arbor, MI: UMI Research Collections.

——— (2003), Repairing history: Reworking transgenerational trauma. In: *Hating in the First Person Plural*, ed. D. Moss. New York: Other Press, pp. 3–28.

Bhabha, H. (1994), *The Location of Culture*. London: Routledge.

Butler, J. (2004a), *Precarious Life*. New York: Routledge.

——— (2004b), *Undoing Gender*. New York: Routledge.

Eng, D., & Han, S. (2001), A dialogue on racial melancholia. In: *Bringing the Plague,* eds. L. Layton, C. Stack, & S. Fairfield. New York: Other Press, pp. 233–268.

Fanon, F. (1986), *Black Skin, White Mask*. London: Pluto.

Foucault, M. (1965), *Madness and Civilization*. New York: Vintage Books.

——— (1975), Surveiller et punir: Naissance de la prison/Michel Foucault [Discipline and punish: Birth of the prison]. Paris: Gallimard.

——— (1988), On power. In: *Politics, Philosophy, Culture: Interviews and Other Writings 1977–1984,* ed. P. Rabinow. New York: Routledge, pp. 00–00.

Ghent, E. (1990), Masochism, submission, surrender. *Contemp. Psychoanal.,* 26:169–211.

Green, A. (1970), The dead mother. In: *On Private Madness*. London: Hogarth Press, pp. 142–173.

Gump, J. (2004, April), Paper at Conference "Race as Social Construction." Washington DC. Institute for Contemporary Psychoanalysis and Psychotherapy.

Harris, A. (1997), Envy and ambition: The circulating tensions in women's relation to aggression. *Gender & Psychoanal.,* 2:291–325.

——— (2000), Discussion of Leary's Racial enactments in dynamic treatment. *Psychoanal. Dial.,* 10:255–264.

——— (2005), *Gender as Soft Assembly*. Northvale, NJ: The Analytic Press.

Holmes, D. E. (1992), Race and transference in psychoanalysis and psychotherapy. *International Journal of Psychoanalysis,* 73:1–11.

hooks, b. (1992), *Black Looks*. Boston: Southend Press.

——— (1989), *Talking Back: Thinking Feminist, Thinking Black*. Boston: Southend Press.

Jay, M. (1973), *The Dialectical Imagination*. Boston: Little, Brown.

Kovel, J. (1983), *The Age of Desire*. New York: Random House.

——— (1994), *White Racism*. New York: Columbia University Press.

Leary, K. (1994), Psychoanalytic problems and postmodern solutions. *Psychoanal. Quart.,* 63:433–465

——— (1997), Race, self-disclosure and 'forbidden talk': Race and ethnicity in contemporary clinical practice. *Psychoanal. Quart.,* 66:163–189.

——— (2000), Racial enactments in dynamic treatment. *Psychoanal. Dial.,* 10:639–654.

Lorde, A. (1984), *Sister Outsider: Essays and Speeches*. New York: Crossing Press.

Lott, T. (1998), *Subjugation and Bondage. Critical essays on slavery and philosophy*. Oxford: Rowman and Littlefield.

———(2000), DuBois and Locke on the Scientific Study of the Negro. *Boundary,* 2(3):135–152.

Mitchell, S. (2000), *Relationality: From Attachment to Intersubjectivity*. Hillsdale, NJ: The Analytic Press.

——— & Harris, A. (2003), What's American about American psychoanalysis. *Psychoanal. Dial.,*

Moss, D. (2003). (Ed.), *Hating in the First Person Plural*. New York: Other Press.

Ricoeur, P. (1970), *Freud and Philosophy*. New Haven, CT: Yale University Press.

Riviere, J. (1929), Womanliness as a masquerade. *International Journal of Psychoanalysis,* 9:303–313

Suchet, M. (2004a), A celestial encounter with race. *Psychoanal. Dialog.,* 4:423–438.

———— (2004b), Paper presented at Division 39. Miami, Florida, April, 2004.

Straker, G. (2004), Race for Cover: Castrated whiteness, perverse consequences. *Psychoanal. Dialog.,* 4:405–422.

West, C. (1993), *Race Matters.* Boston: Beacon.

Zangrando, R. (1980), *The NAACP Crusade against lynchings: 1909–1950.* Philadelphia: Temple University Press.

Zwerman, G.(1994), Mothering on the lam. *Feminist Review,* 47:33–56.

6

Waystations
on a Psychoanalytic Journey*

Ruth Stein, PhD

▼   ▼   ▼   ▼   ▼

Multiplicity, Heterogeneity

Any attempt to spell out one's work, or rather, one's conception of one's work, in analysis, is Sisyphean and leaves one frustrated with an ever unfulfillable desire for transparency and nuance. The challenge comes not only from the fact that writing about how one works is infinitely complicated in itself—such articulation is even more difficult when one's training and the influences one absorbed came from many and disparate sources. Although this heterogeneity is part of the pluralism embraced by most psychoanalytic schools today; this has not always been the case.

The present tendency stands in marked contrast to the wishes and ambitions held until a decade or two ago, to find the "common ground" of the diverse theories and to extract the component shared by all so as to finally possess it (cf. Wallerstein, 1990). Such a program took too little account of both the power of diversity and the culturally specific worldview that informs each school. Some analysts (e.g., Schafer, 1990) soon realized that it would be a retrograde step to try to reduce the multiplicity of psychoana-

---

*An early version of this chapter was presented at a self-psychological conference in Dreieich, Germany, in June 2003. Paul Ornstein, Lew Aron, and I discussed our clinical affiliations as a self-psychologist, a relational analyst, and an object-relationist respectively. Because I had to define myself *a priori* as different from them, yet wishing to be in a dialectical-dialogic relation with them, I hardly included in this chapter other influences (e.g., the French perspective) on my clinical work.

lytic currents into an imaginary common denominator that would bind—
and dominate—them all. One of the factors that facilitated this shift toward
greater tolerance for multiplicity is the current *Zeitgeist* that effected a
downgrading of the concept of integration in favor of notions of mutually
incommensurate multiple accounts and heterogeneous kinds of knowledge. Although there is a Wittgensteinian family resemblance between the
different currents in self–object–relational theories, and to some extent
even between these theories and more classical ones, the heterogeneity I
am talking about has come to inhabit many parts of the analytic world.[1] It
seems that the Freudian, truly classical, model, that was the indelible proto-
type for analytic work and conduct, has substantially given way to object relational and neo-Kleinian models. The object relations (e.g., Fairbairn,
Guntrip), and what is called Independent (Winnicott, Balint, Khan, Bollas,
Coltart) theories, both influenced by and diverging from Melanie Klein,[2]
have come to have an enormous influence on analytic work throughout the
world. These currents were later joined by the influences of Kohut,
Loewald, Ogden, and Mitchell, to name but a few.

Some years ago, I[3] undertook a study (Stein, 2001) analyzing 20 years of
case presentations written by candidates at the Israel Psychoanalytic Institute, where I had trained. A candidate who terminated her training at this
Institute was required to write up the analysis of one of her control cases
to qualify as an associate member of the Israel Psychoanalytic Society. In
my research, I approached these presentations as texts that—because
they were geared to demonstrate their writers' analytic competence—
could be taken to reveal the implicit assumptions regarding who is considered a "good analyst," how a "good analysis" should proceed, what counts
as pathological, what is considered analytic and transformative, and so on.
Scrutinizing the "unconscious of the text" according to preset categories,
yielded illuminating results. The findings[4] showed an increasingly
phenomenological, experience-near and pluralistic turn of psychoanalytic practice in Israel, which coexisted with a more marked tendency to

---

[1]See, for instance, the IPAC in July 2004, and the International Relational Conference
in 2004, all dealing with interschool dialogues.

[2]Melanie Klein in Britain, like Lacan in France, cast a long shadow over all of psychoanalysis each in his/her respective country.

[3]I am grateful to Gila Horesh who collaborated with me on this research project.

[4]That this project stirred a scandal in the Society was not surprising, in view of its oedipal and parricidal implications (which is also one of the reasons I did not publish it [yet],
except in a very abbreviated from in the newsletter of the Israel Psychoanalytic Society
[2001]). As to the findings, we could show that a central trend in the evolution of psychoanalytic practice in this historical institution (it was founded in the early 1930s in Pales-
tine) was the increasingly phenomenological, self-psychological and existential turn of
psychoanalytic work over the years of the survey. The different, even contrasting opinion,
from the strong classical bent of earlier times was significant (see also Berman, 2005).

draw on the analyst's subjectivity and on improvised uses he made of himself and his emotional experience.

The diversity within psychoanalytic thinking and ways of doing analysis is of crucial importance. Without becoming superficially eclectic, and without losing sight of the need for persistence and consistency, I believe it is fruitful and rewarding to enter the "mind" of different theories in order to enrich ourselves with variegated resources for sustaining a creative analytic process. Panoramic involvements enable us to be free to receive and use heterogeneous means of intervening and reflecting when working with very different people, particularly at pivotal moments in such work.

Some Steps in the Evolution of my Training

My basic worldview about therapy and analysis was forged well before I entered analytic training. In the 1970s, during my internship and subsequent several-year-long work in a psychiatric hospital, I came upon the writings of authors such as Sullivan, Searles, Fromm-Reichmann, and Laing and Cooper. Reading them sustained me in my first encounters with psychotic (mostly chronic or acute schizophrenic) patients, who impressed me less with their bizarre behaviors or with their hypersymbolic speech than with their stunning indifference to other humans, which was occasionally coupled with indiscriminating cloying and insisting on something they wanted even if it was not going to happen, and even when they knew it was not going to be given to them. The psychoanalytic authors who interested me at the time spoke about intense and meaningful self–other relations, and they made sense to me in their descriptions of psychotic experiences. They showed how psychotics think and feel, and what agendas they may have regarding the other beyond their appearance of frozen withdrawal and obliviousness, and beyond their rage and violence. Immersing myself in these writings, I found I was avidly responding to what I perceived was their appeal to understand the intentions and suffering of psychotics. They allowed me almost boundaryless identification with my regressive longings. At the same time, I felt the (defensive) shock at witnessing the violent words and acts in which these people denuded themselves of responsibility for their own lives and the lives of others. But I also envied them these states of license and of being taken under someone's care. The books and the theories narrativized what may have caused these states, at the same time as they fueled my desires to weave what I later recognized were idealized accounts of what had happened in the past and what was happening in the present to the people I treated in the hospital. The gratification obtained by resonating with the embellished accounts of the patients and with my unconsciously self-idealizing rescue fantasies, coexisted with the passionate devotion to the therapeutic task, which I was allowed to fully take to heart in this setting that no longer exists today.

Classical Psychoanalysis

Then (on the advice of the hospital director, who was my supervisor) I went into psychoanalytic training. Before going into this phase, two facts stand out for me: (1) my fear of engulfing commitment, and (2) my powerful encounter, in the car on the way to be interviewed for this orthodox psychoanalytic institute, with Edgar Levenson's writings. I distinctly remember the electrifying encounter with Levenson's subversive and incisive critique of notions of (unconscious) fantasies in favor of the immediate semiotic relationship between patient and analyst. It would take some time before I returned to his ideas, but the impact of his message stayed with me. As to my first fear—I told myself (and others) that even if I now lawfully wed psychoanalytic training—I am still going to keep my mistresses …

When I began training, I found myself facing the enigma of Freudian solemnity, and the sense of rightness that was inculcated in the arduous classical analytic training. The Israel Institute for Psychoanalysis was named after Max Eitingon, Freud's most literal and ardent disciple. This institute was one of the oldest in the world, and during its first decades, beginning in the early 1930s, the language spoken there, as well as the language of the books in the library was German, as befitted an institute built by analysts from Freud's coterie, who were refugees from Germany. When I began my long training, in the late 1970s, we spoke, of course, Hebrew (and read English), but I was deeply impressed and awed by the Freudian still depths and by the grave seriousness with which practice was treated. One had to wait long enough, I surmised, to discern a meaningful pattern in the patient's speech for the necessary interpretation to form itself, and one had to deliver it at the right moment. There was a gap between the rhythm and intention of the patient's communications, and the meanings the analyst discerned that built up with time, which were based on, but not equivalent to, what the patient said. The patient, so I imagined, had somehow to learn about the disjunction between his ostensibly straightforward statements and the unconscious meaning that lay behind these statements. One of the central visual images circulating in my mind at that period was the youth from Schiller's *Das Verschleierte Bild zu Sais* (The Veiled Picture of Sais), who in his unquenchable thirst for knowledge, approaches the Holy Place in the Egyptian temple, and is told by the priests that what lies veiled there is the Truth, but the deity does not allow the veil to be lifted by human mortals.

The young man did lift the veil, but nobody knew what he saw; for they found his pale body on the floor the next day. The poem conveys the sure premonition that, at the moment the young man will lift the veil, the Truth will strike in all its blazing fullness, and the priest—as well as anyone who will attempt to expose it from now on—will die instantly. Truth is ultimate, powerful, and devastating enough to kill. Truth lies dormant in the depths of the psyche and can be touched only by approximations, in small bits, and very cautiously. I was therefore surprised, almost amused, when my first analysand told me after many years that what had saved her life was her spending the first year on the couch and being given the opportunity to weep and to feel her deep pain, padded and cushioned by my motherly patience. She called it "the patience of a good, even if not very bright, mother, who takes her child by the hand and walks her." I felt deeply gratified that she did perceive me as not very smart. At other times my silence must have been experienced by my analytic patients (and there were lots of them in the 1980s) as distant and detached which I must have been, in partial identification with my first analyst, although I never reached the level of his unabetting silence. The *gravitas* of Freudian theory and the art of listening for unconscious drive derivatives, hidden impulses, and oedipal themes which I was being taught, made me appreciate the power of analytic discipline and gave me a feeling of confidence in the sensibility of informed listening and good interpretations. I still deeply believe in some of these ideas and have serious respect for dreams and unconscious meaningfulness, but now I do not wait for large patterns to emerge, nor for the patient to arrive at a meaningful theme after prolonged periods of aloneness.[5] At that time, I was unaware of psychoanalytically living in two worlds: the object-relational world of damaged, victimized, violent, passionate people—the (inadequately medicated) psychotics living in the hospital, and the world where I did the Freudian work of deciphering the derivatives of the eternal Unconscious with patients who lay on the couch four times a week.

The Encounter With Kohut

At some point I discovered Kohut. I don't remember how,[6] for he was still not known in my Institute, but getting to read him was for me a shock and

---

[5]One analysand who had the two parts of his analysis separated by the years in which he went to live abroad, remarked on the difference in my approach.

[6]Just as I am writing these lines, it occurs to me for the first time that finding Kohut came simultaneously with my officially relinquishing religion as well as orthodox psychoanalysis.

a revelatory experience. Not only did his heavy, convoluted, clumsily an-glicized Germanic syntax resonate with my maternal German, but I sensed between the lines of his writings a deep contact with patients (and of course with the corresponding parts in myself) of a quality which I had never before found in any person, book, or theory. Something scandal-ously new and important radiated from the metapsychological concepts he used. Kohut was unabashedly saying things which I felt were not only connected to a different theory and a different philosophy of life; he un-covered and verbalized very private yet valid pieces of experience I had always felt inside. These were described by him most naturally and accep-tingly, page after page, and were explained by recourse to new sectors of the personality, and through ways of thinking totally different from what I had known before.

Kohut was an unparalleled master at in-depth painting the lonesome, empty, pining states in which the narcissistically starved person goes to amazing lengths to procure self stimulation, sensuous experience, per-verse pseudo-intimacy, even delusional constructions, to stabilize his sense of self. Smelling mother's lingerie, engaging in compulsive mastur-bation, cruising in the park, fantasizing glorious triumphs, were all seen as desperate attempts to collect poignantly sensuous and self-caressing bits and pieces in order to weave a self, rehabilitate a sense of a crumbling self-esteem, and connect to a "self-object" that will offer a presence that sustains without questions. Kohut's important idea of idealization, which Freud never made explicit (although Freud often confessed to experienc-ing, especially in his youth), was most valuable to work with. The idea of *overvaluation* inherent in narcissism, including healthy narcissism, was illuminating and merciful. The need to idealize and be idealized, the seamless self-object transferences, the nonreducibility of values and ideas to instincts, the attitude of understanding and receptiveness toward these easily repellent behaviors,[7] impressed me deeply and influenced my work. I remember asking my supervisors at our Institute to please read Kohut, or at least to look at the clear exposition Lawrence Friedman (1980) gave of his thinking. Vicariously introspective immersion and the idea of empathic failure resonated with my earlier readings of Guntrip and Searles. The importance of valorizing and validating the patient's subject-hood and his most idiosyncratic and rarified experiences as a way to strengthen or restore his sense of self—all were familiar and reverberated with my intuitions regarding psychotic experience—and all had been un-til then excluded from the training program as non-analytic. Now, these notions were spelled out and legitimized. Moreover, they came with the exhilarating idea that the analyst had better possess varieties of experien-

---

[7]Whether these behaviors were solipsistic and masturbatory, or grandiose and entitled.

tial descriptions and be able to elaborate them. I felt I was given powerful tools to understand, engage, and treat the wildest variety of people, including myself.

I asked one supervisor in particular to read Kohut because I hoped this would help him help me help a patient I had at that time who developed an idealizing and sexualized transference toward me. *A priori* diagnosing this transference as psychotic, as was sometimes done in classical psychoanalysis (Rappaport, 1956), which was also what my supervisor did, felt wrong to me. I thought my patient should be treated in a self-psychological way, that is, that he should be more empathized with. I therefore interpreted to him his longing for me and idealization of me as a developmental need and as a manifestation of his courage and ability to love. Inspired by Kohut's writing, I tried to convey to him my resonating understanding of his experience, but with no regard for the fact that his experience was poignantly directed at me. This of course did not prevent the situation from deteriorating: My patient kept insisting on my returning his love and threatened to commit suicide if I did not respond in kind to his feelings.

The situation got worse for various reasons, part of them having to do with the patient's past experience and trauma, but also with my own (countertransference) feelings toward him. Not only did this man resonate with many areas in myself, his taste, his desires, what he liked and disliked, the things he got passionate about, what mattered to him and what repelled him, were similar to mine in an uncanny way. To compound matters, I was at a point in my own life where radical changes (in great part promoted by my own analysis) swept me into a tumultuous and emotionally draining time. The changes I was undergoing created for me the freedom to embrace those things that he and I felt passionate about. The thought that returning his love would bring us both happiness passed through my mind more than once. After all, we had enormously much in common, and I was tempted by his depth of understanding and by the passions that we shared. At the same time I knew I would never be capable of acting on these feelings; I believed in psychoanalysis too much. Conscientious and well trained in Freudian analysis, I kept my countertransference to myself and made great efforts to function as a good (Freudian-Kohutian) analyst, that is, to hold him safely, to accept his idealizing transference, to empathize with what he felt towards me, and to interpret *his* experiences and motives.

I am in no way dismissing the role of my inexperience and my life situation in this failure (eventually he left, to embark on another analysis with an elderly male analyst, at that point still hoping to realize his long-range fantasy of approaching me later in life). Yet I believe that had I thought "relationally" at that time, I would have been enabled to accept my countertransference in a more benign, less anxious way. I would have understood that in order to be of help to my patient under these difficult circumstances,

I would have had to make use of my feelings toward him to help him—and myself—acknowledge and mourn this kind of love, and perceive the ambivalence and the hostility, the mutual narcissistic stakes we held for each other, and the intense rage (at me, at women) behind his passion. I knew I did not really want to ever have a relationship with him in reality, but had I known and absorbed relational, intersubjective thinking, I might have been freer to feel and work with what I felt and to present it to him in a more honest, even if mitigated and processed way. Such an attitude would have enabled us to open up further exploration,[8] possibly using humor and sublimated erotic feelings in the process (as I would do with a patient I treated some years later). My interpretations would have included not only transference analogies and pointing to his needs for idealization and merger experiences—they would have included as well the articulation on my part of what was going on between us. I would have worked through and worked out a highly processed version of my feelings toward him, of his defensive blindness, and of our aggression and coerciveness toward each other. I would have had to face the disavowed seduction, and the violent, manipulative parts not only in him, but also in myself. And I would have had to mourn a love that, even if it were true, was not possible. These intersubjective and interpersonal understandings and the psychic energy that needed to be spent in areas different from that of defenses and concealment would have helped move the analysis out of its impasse. I would have taken into account, as Lew Aron (1992) wrote, that "interpretation is the principal process by which analysts position and reposition themselves … in relation to their patients, and in this sense interpretations contain aspects of the analyst's subjectivity made available for use by the patient" (p. 118). I would have assumed a more dialogical stance, in which I would have placed myself not only within my patient's experience (as is proposed in self-psychology), but I would have judiciously expressed my understanding of both my patient's and my own experience, thereby creating a more mutual, intersubjective space, in which to articulate more of the here-and-now unfoldings. What was lacking in this analysis were intersubjective dialectics (Benjamin, 1988), that would hold the tension and eventually overcome splits and complementarities of doer and done-to. The manifest version was that he was the doer, I was the done-to: he loved me, I rejected him. Alternatively, there would have to be recognition, not only of his feelings toward me (which I was quite good at articulating), but also of my responsibility in what transpired between us. Instead, we had on our hands a false, because incomplete and truncated, version of an analysis, a version

---

[8]Such exploration would have included questioning his view of me as cold, addressing his aggression and defensive sadism, expressed through his emotional blackmail, and contacting our more accurate perceptions of each other.

which disavowed my love and his hostile rejection of my choices, as well as my active participation and his anxiety-propelled need to deny it. I did not possess the knowledge that would have set me free to work better and be of help (or to refer him to someone else); but neither did the two supervisors.[9] I turned to with the hope of getting help with this case.

My Encounter With Relational Thinking

The time was ripe indeed for discovering relational writing. One day, a dear friend gave me a copy of *Psychoanalytic Dialogues*. I was immediately impressed with its intellectual sophistication and a liberty and freshness I had never before encountered in psychoanalytic writing. The experience of reading *Dialogues* seemed generically similar to the discovery of Kohut, but it was also different. This time too, I came upon novel, bold,[10] and what I sensed as deeply truthful formulations of something that was bursting to be spelled out. But the experience this time was also different from that of encountering Kohut: Now, what was being touched and given words to were ideas. This approach engaged my thinking side, rather than the emotional side that was so powerfully touched by Kohut.[11]

There were many ideas in this rapidly developing new field. Perhaps the most pregnant and central for me was *the use of the analyst's subjectivity*. This was something new or, at least, a substantial expansion of earlier ideas. Excepting interpersonal psychoanalysis (which, at that time, was not deemed to be psychoanalysis proper in many quarters), the different ways in which the analyst's role has been conceived until the appearance of relational thinking to wit, the analyst's function as a transitional object, a subjective object, a breast-container, or a self object—all here subordinating the subjectivity of the analyst to the patient's manner of relating to him or her *as object*. Even when the use of countertransference experience was harnessed to detect the work of projective identification, or, even when the countertransference became more expressible, as in the work of Bollas

---

[9]In my desperation, as I later realized, I chose my two supervisors in the following way: one was the most conservative, patriarchal training analyst around, and the other, an *enfant terrible,* the black sheep of the Institute. At the same time, in my efforts to get help, I also consulted with my fellow-candidates in our carpool when commuting to attend classes out of town.

[10]Comparing Kohut's boldness with that of the relational school, I would say that whereas Kohut is bold regarding *inner* states, the relational boldness has to do with *interpersonal* awareness and expressiveness.

[11]Although I made both discoveries on my own, outside of what I was taught at the Psychoanalytic Institute, both self-psychology and relational theory later became part of the curriculum in the Institute, although not everyone adopted these approaches.

(1983), where the analyst's subjectivity is introduced in an indirect way through the notion that the analyst lends her inner resources to the patient, still, object relations approaches (e.g., Joseph, 1978; Winnicott 1947) tended to focus on the dynamic the patient created in the analyst as she or he (the patient) would *in any other person*. The classical idea that the patient would equally bring his or her inner world to bear on any other was preserved. In other words, the subjectivity of the analyst had been treated as the (almost impersonal) site for the creation of countertransference phenomena. This object-related stance is, from the perspective of the analyst, *subjective but not personal* (Cooper, 2000; see also Hoffman, 1998). For many years, I had indeed believed that this accommodating stance (whether by serving as selfobject, as holding environment, or as a "donor" of one's resources) was what was needed in all cases, whereas interpretations will be needed some of the time. Over time I have come to change my way of work, and I became deeply involved in the relational orientation and with the iconoclastic yet judicious thinking of this group. My earlier work on affects and my realization that intersubjective events, far from constituting an interference with the patient's production of material from his unconscious, were the very matrix where each subjectivity is born and shaped by another, made me wonder at analysts who do not work in this way. Thus, when I wrote about the shame experiences of the analyst (Stein, 1997), the manuscript was rejected by a mainstream psychoanalytic journal with the explanation that what I was describing was nothing more than a countertransference reaction that needed to be worked through rather than written about.

The Relational (Self–Object–Relational) Current

I am aware that the picture I am drawing here has become quite complicated in regard to what is an analytic identity and what are one's allegiances. The analytic identity I anm identifying with is obviously hybrid and the allegiances polygamous. Fortunately, what makes such multiply-hyphenated identities of contemporary analysts (I am not the only one to have such identities) easier to bear and to pronounce is the greater tolerance for multiplicity in contemporary psychoanalysis. Within this plurality, where some analysts realize that they are essentially putting together "toolkits" produced out of many theoretical ways of working, it seems useful to distinguish between inclusively "relational" currents *grosso modo*,[12] and Freudian drive theories. Relational theories, with a capital "R," encompass

---

[12]Charles Spezzano (1998) talks about the "American Middle School"; Steven Cooper (2000) juxtaposes the British relational and the American relational schools.

the Kleinian and object relations theories, including the British middle school, self-psychology, relational analysis, intersubjectivity theory, and attachment-derived mentalization theory. All these theories prioritize and centralize the relation with the Other—the object, the self-object, the other subject—relative to the drive and "the" (substansivized) Unconscious. These theories, particularly object relations theories, attribute the strangeness and foreignness of mental phenomena to relational sediments rather than to "endogenous stimulation."[13] I call them *self–object–relational theories.* These theories advocate a listening stance that is less intent on tracking disguised defended *contents,* as it seeks to know and to make known the patient's *experience,* and in particular, her emotional experience (cf. Mitchell, 1995), with the other and with the self. Limiting oneself to tracking associations (cf. Busch, 1994; Gray, 1990) may afford more continuity, because the grid one subjects the associations to is a thick line that stays on track. A great part of the contemporary Freudian approach, however, limits the scope of inventiveness and the license to own an acute awareness of indeterminacy is greatly limited. *Self–object–relational theories and their clinical implications may foster less continuity, but they allow for greater freedom* (Stein, 2003) *in clinical work* than do classical drive theories.

Furthermore, object relations theories are particularly intent on *the task of complexly containing affect* that is demanded of the analyst, whether it is hers or her patient's. Retrieving painful repetitive past experiences, processing them and looking after the emotional needs of the other, carry enormous value in themselves at the same time as they make possible self- and other-knowledge. The world of inner objects, differently described by various object relations theories, is "deep" in a metaphorical rather than concrete sense; it is dramatic, and it deals with primary process relations, of joining and separating, incorporating and ejecting (Stein, 1990), identifying and counteridentifying. An object-relations way of analyzing treats different symbolic meanings of fantasies as types of inner actions. Sometimes this world becomes a strange mythology, as in James Grotstein's writings; at other times it constitutes a detailed narrative whereby one part of the psyche is taken hostage by another part, as in Herbert Rosenfeld's descriptions; or it becomes absorbed in larger-than-life body zones, as in Donald Meltzer's visions. Quite often object-relations-inspired analysis concerns an inner citadel or a retreat, as in Harry Guntrip or John Steiner's accounts, and on other occasions it addresses a buried mythological, idealized "true self" as in Donald Winnicott's thinking. Some of us have a taste for all of these theories, some of us for some of them, some of us for none at all. In any event, this cluster of theories contains wise narratives that help articu-

---

[13]With the exception of Jean Laplanche (1999), who considers the drive as coming from the other.

late and give meaning to primitive and distressing affects felt by either patient or analyst or both. Object relations theory is also good in discerning role reversals, projections and identifications, relational perversions, seductions, and betrayals that are happening inside oneself and are then externalized at which point they offer the opportunity to be reflected upon.

Somewhat schematically, we could say that working as an object-relational analyst means putting great stock on unconscious fantasy, the intrapsychic, primary processes, and the transitions from primitive, somatic sensations to understandings of the other, and symbolization of experience. Being aware of the complexity of relations among internal objects—including their functioning as defenses against relations in the external world (as is the rule in schizoid functioning)—makes one aware of the varied ways in which these relations are played out in the transference. The transference itself is conceived as the present arena of interpersonal perceptions subtended by past events, yet at the same time as exquisitely sensitive (or exquisitely defended against) present happenings.

Working With Object Relations Theories

Very few analysts today would identify with one well-defined school; after all, the conceptual interrelations between different psychoanalytic currents have become unbelievably intense. This may be less visible in local clinical quarters, where analysts hold rather definite professional affiliations, and more so in cutting-edge thinking, published in the main psychoanalytic journals, which strongly tends in the direction of "comparative psychoanalysis" (Schafer, 1985). Authors such as classical-relational Steven Cooper, neo-Freudian Steve Ellman, intersubjectivist-intrapsychic Jessica Benjamin, object-relational Peter Fonagy, relational/neoclassical Jay Greenberg, or neo-Kleinian Charles Spezzano,[14] as the hyphenated appellations I use to describe them show, use different currents and conceptions in psychoanalytic theory and practice. Most of these clinical theoreticians do not attempt to integrate or abstract a common ground. Rather, they pay close attention to the *differences* among theories, and to the various ways of practicing analysis that these theories imply. On the other hand, common problems and overlapping areas of interest among analysts of different schools may not be visible because many clinicians do not publish aspects of their work that contradict their formal allegiances, or unwittingly ignore clinical material that they cannot explain according to those allegiances and beliefs, thereby avoiding the articulation of their "private theories," as Sandler

---

[14]I ask these authors for forgiveness for simplifying their complex positions.

(1983) called them.[15] Nevertheless, it is the relational current that must be credited with the sharp awareness of multiplicity.

Albeit we do not work according to this-or-that theory anymore, and the seasoned analyst is an analyst of all seasons, object relations theory has left its imprint on me as the origin of my learning to treat very sick people.[16] This mode of thinking is particularly poignant in shedding light on the primitive, the foreign, all that does not coincide with itself, what is different than what meets the eye. This approach is also rich in so-called theories of thinking beginning with Melanie Klein's epistemophilic instinct and anxiety as interfering with learning, through Bion's theory of thinking and emotional meaning-making, to Fonagy's models of mentalization as thinking about and understanding another mind and one's own. I utilize object relations thinking as a first step to teach candidates at Freudian institutes, often witnessing their moments of liberation from rigid postures and their opening to new, resourceful ways of working. I also use object relational thinking with students and supervisees in relational frames to supplement their interactive skills and their attention to conscious subjectivity, and to help them acquire the habit of thinking in terms of unconscious fantasies and internalized objects. It could be said that one of the main differences between "classical" theory, or rather its most prevalent descendant, ego psychology, and object relations theory has to do with different views of *what constitutes a "center of adjudication" in the personality:* is it the ego as an instrumental, rational center of synthesis and adaptation to reality, or is it rather an ego that is formed by strata of past internalized "objects,"[17] which, particularly when they are "bad objects," create, according to Fairbairn and Guntrip, abiding psychic *structure?*[18]

Object relations theories put forth a radical and profound idea, namely that *emotions create objects:*[19] that *our* hatred makes people feel hateful to us, *our* fear makes them persecutory, *our* fascination endows them with mystery and depth. This idea is valuable, in that it shows the power of feelings, and how enormously difficult it is to own our emotions. The emotions in which we bathe our "objects" become amplified and modified by the in-

---

[15]Pressed hard to identify my work, I would thus present myself as a "self–object–relational" analyst. Jokingly, I would say my relation-ship sails in many ports …

[16]Also, additionally, as the effect of the tight communication between British analysts, particularly Joseph and Anne-Marie Sandler, and the Israel Institute and the Freud Center at the Hebrew University in Jerusalem.

[17]The two differing conceptions spring from Freud's (1923) reasonable, calculating ego as center of reality testing and synthesis, and Freud's (1917) melancholic ego made of shadows of past objects, respectively.

[18]Ferenczi, a poignant and telling figure for me, who is considered the first relational or intersubjective analyst, has some affinity with Guntrip. Both talked about real traumata and real relationships.

[19]See Riviere (1936) and Stein (1990).

dividual contributions of those objects; the emotions then return from the objects to us and shape *our feelings toward ourselves*, these, in turn, color our self-representation and self-image. These representations include the parts we experience as alien (Fonagy) or "not-me" (Sullivan). These are the parts that were deprived of recognition and mirroring, and some of them include what I have come with time to see as carrying the core of mental illness, namely, self-loathing, internalized shame, and self-hatred. Joseph Sandler put it succinctly when he talked about "left-over" infantile parts that were once compatible with the person's self-image but later became shameful and embarrassing to the adult self and therefore need to be repressed or dissociated. But the shameful parts are not only infantile and developmentally anachronistic zones. A great part of therapeutic work has to do with helping patients embrace and re-admit these parts back into their conscious mind by making them thinkable, bearable, acceptable. Notably, the very process of embracing these parts is also the process that procures self- and other-understanding. Feeling understood engenders safety, which in turn encourages mental exploration, particularly the exploration of one's mind as it is held in the mind of the other (Bateman & Fonagy, 2005), and letting the other into one's mind (Benjamin, 2005).

The imagistic, emotional bent of this stance is a rich store of narratives and pictures to dress emotions in, and to carry out the basic task of clinical work: *forging conceptual linkages between emotions* (particularly emotions that call forth defenses) *and* (through thinking and articulation) generating sustaining internal or external *relations with others*. According to object relations theory, there is a constant juggling and contending that is carried out by different psychic representations in the psyche that cope with mental pain that generates rage, dread, and hatred, but also lust, excitement, paralyzed detachment, or any other excessive mental state. Further clashes may be set off between strategies for dealing with pain and the means of dealing with object loss and self loss—which ultimately threatens the self. Pain, if excessive, does not allow the processing of loss and its mourning; the self, in its efforts to defend against dangerous pain then spawns ways of relating that lead to rigidity and further vulnerability.

James Grotstein (2000) vivaciously portrays *internal objects* (whether they appear in dreams, in symptoms, or in delusions) as dramaturgically *encoding and describing unmentalizable psychic pain so as to render it thinkable*. Internal objects "pantomime the meaning of the pain in encoded terms for us first to experience and then to 'translate.' The Ineffable Subject continues pantomimically to present the analytic object (the unmentalized pain) until we 'get it'!" (Grotstein, 2000, p. 129). Grotstein describes the adaptive role of internal objects, but these objects have their darker side too, which is their power to hold us in thrall and enslave us. Scared of living in a vacant, meaningless world (Fairbairn), we desperately cling to harmful, exploitative, abusive inner objects; we even promote them and let them get away with (soul) murder and cruelty. The false reasonableness and security their protection offers make the assumption of guilt and badness upon oneself seem a just price. Guntrip gave this Fairbairnian idea a somewhat different cast when he proposed that it is not a question of gaining control by taking the badness of the objects upon oneself, but on the contrary (which is not the contrary at all): it is *the indigestibility of bad objects* that makes the person need to struggle to incorporate them so as to purportedly shred them into annihilation inside oneself. In the language of Bion, bad experiences cannot be metabolized, and are retained as foreign objects that the psyche seeks to project.[20] Going deeper into object-relations thinking leads us to places where we try to understand people struggling to make sense of their seemingly intractable self-destructive behaviors and to overcome them. With these understandings, we get windows into situations where the attempt to process trauma (which, at its core, has to do with the inability to come to terms with the badness of a trusted person who was supposed to be benevolent) results in attempts to destroy the other, thereby mutilating one's capacity to be loved, a capacity that is precisely what is so badly needed particularly by traumatized people. This is the point where *processing and destruction converge*. On this view, destructiveness is not necessarily a given, inborn aggressive drive; neither is it just a contorted developmental need for assertiveness. Destructiveness is rather a relation that aims at overcoming a bad object, attempting to come to terms with it with the most primitive means, such as taking in, trying to "eat up," to master, to dominate, to destroy, to love destructively. The words we use to describe such situations move between primitive love, perversely aimed empathy, and outright hate and malice.

I realize that, wishing to describe my psychoanalytic voyage thus far, I have registered it mostly in terms of theories. Although each theory encircles certain patients, or parts of certain patients and relations with them, it is important to note that these theories are not "really" theories after all. One cannot at this point adjudicate one such theory's truth over others,[21] and one can certainly not ascribe a greater predictive power to any one theory over another. Rather, these theories are metaphors for regenerating, amplifying, or modifying the *theories patients hold about themselves,* which, by having been woven by the patient alone (or with wrong others) are one-sided, limited and often truncated. From this perspective, a theory is a metaphor (and sometimes a "metaphor of metaphors") that resonates

---

[20]Peter Fonagy, a British attachment theorist, built a theory of borderline pathology based on this core idea plus his infant observations, where he talks about the *alien self* that in borderline pathology is constantly sought to be re-externalized and projected into other people.

[21]Therefore it is good for the analyst to have a "tool-kit" to assemble different theories.

with difficult situations and provides a narrative of how such situations came about in a person's life. *A clinical psychoanalytic theory is a possibility for resonance with a complex emotional configuration.* Although every theory can be used defensively and become an alibi for not engaging with the other and with oneself, these theories can also function as post-hoc justificatory systems for "practices we have found to be useful" (cf. Fonagy, 2003, **pp. 000–000**). And what we find useful and what furthers the effectiveness of treatment is what counts. Thus, if the analyst, in order to be clinically effective, needs to enable her patient to make free associations; needs to open him up to his pain-fighting unconscious fantasies; needs to empathize with him, needs to provide metaphors, reverie, and containers; needs to engage in intersubjective mutuality; needs to use her irreducible subjectivity; needs to teach her patient skills, whether semiotic, social, or living skills; needs to recognize and support being recognized by the patient; needs to surrender to the process transpiring between them or to the patient's challenges; needs to make her own psychic life a source of reflection and use; and needs to withstand toxic onslaughts and projections—she finds narratives, descriptors, and metaphors for these needs in the multitude of available psychoanalytic theories.

This brings me to another influence on my clinical work, which is that of French psychoanalysis, particularly some colleagues from the French Psychoanalytic Society (APF) with whom I used to communicate.[22] Reading such books as Michel Gribinski's (1996) *The Trouble of Reality* (1996), or Jean-Claude Lavie's *Love is a Perfect Crime* (1997), I used to wonder what these personal, literary, highly evocative texts had to do with psychoanalytic writing proper. But I could not get a direct and satisfying response to my queries from these people, and I was left to surmise that, because psychoanalytic theory is not a theory that derives from such "theory" properly speaking, there is no specific "technique." Hence, it is sensible to assume that the more literarily rich, wise, and perceptive writings analysts produce and share, the more adequately they enable their colleagues and themselves to craft and enrich their tool-kits.

I poignantly feel the impossibility of summarizing where I am now, although I could talk about it much more. I do know that something in me, which is personal no doubt, but also a distillate whose elements and influences have lost their distinctive particularity, makes me always foreground the emotions, which are the Ariadne thread, the markers, of what the Kleinians call "the point of urgency." Ultimately, the critical emotions are

---

[22]There are two IPA societies in France: the Paris Psychoanalytic (SPP) and the Psychoanalytic Association of France (APF). The latter have a different training structure than most psychoanalytic societies; they are more heavily influenced by Lacanian thought, but also by philosophical thinking in general.

the things that agglutinate around what I call the "kernel of unbearability," that crystallize out of pain, neglect, and other forms of emotional violence into a *structure* or several structures that come to dominate one's life. Whether we call this structure the bad object (Fairbairn), the bad breast (Klein), the alien self (Fonagy), the internalized phallic mother (Bak, Chasseguet-Smirgel), or the phallic father (Stein)—it is an internalized object, concocted and concretized out of noxious experiences, which is intended to deal with the unbearable parts of life that everyone ejects outside of one's conscious grasp. A tiny episode regarding what it feels like when one gets rid of such a "bad object" in terms of body and mood, closes my account.

The Case Of Walter

Walter is a successful businessman, happily married, who has been struggling with a self-representation as poor, needy, ostracized, and abject. His history is strewn with acute panic attacks and multiple somatic symptoms. Abused, seduced, and rejected by a self-absorbed and self-idealizing, charismatic, fragile, depressed mother and an abusive neglectful father, he needed many years of several analyses to put the fragments of his life together. His relations with women were marked by masochistic tendencies, such as falling in love and going after women who were seductive and either cold and callous, or superficially nice but deeply uncaring.

The incident I am about to recount, an event that must have been linked to his personal evolution in analysis, began in a bookstore. While he was looking around, he unexpectedly saw his (woman) boss, who had been indifferent and negligent in helping him get promoted at his job. He had felt shattered by the injustice of the deferral of his promotion. The rage and the hatred he felt toward her had been a frequent subject on the couch, and was all the more seething and searing because he could not express it to her. We spent many months trying to understand not only his extreme pain and utter humiliation, but his abject feelings of impotence and later, the total self-rejection and powerful self-mutilating wishes he had to struggle within the wake of his disappointment.

While greeting this woman in the store, he realized all of a sudden that she was *not* the horrible, malevolent person he had taken her to be. He could see that, far from harboring the Machiavellian intentions he had attributed to her, she was limited and too weak and lacking spine to stand up and defend his case. Suddenly, a feeling of liberation came over him: He felt, as he put it, that he was freed of his transference to her. But as he was leaving the store, he began to feel "weird." "You shrinks call it depersonalization," he says. He could identify this feeling from his past when it regularly overcame him before one of his panic attacks: the feeling of being sick, the shakiness, the heart palpitations. He struggles and strains to describe the experience to me: "I felt I was not coinciding with myself ... as if not being within my own outline ... looking kind of out of focus, my view slightly doubled, as in my [short-sighted] way of looking at things, like a TV with no good resolution...." He was gripped by anxiety that he had forgotten or lost his things somewhere, but most frightening was the lightness going through him. He felt he could just float away. To calm himself, he tried to talk sense to himself, reminding himself that he was now liberated, and he should feel good. He then went to the biofeedback treatment he had for his migraines. The trainer told him he was having unusual brain waves. He wondered to himself why he could not be happy, now that he was finally promoted, and now that he has relinquished an old, abusive sexual relationship he had with a woman. He realized that instead of being free to be expansive and exuberant and enjoy the creative project he was involved with, he was seized by a sense of lightness, feeling as substantial as a helium balloon. We came to understand that he required somebody who harmed or persecuted him—that he needed a "bad object" to stabilize him, like a ballast that anchored and grounded him and saved him from the unbearable lightness of being. This sent him thinking about what he saw as two parallel tracks of his life: in one he was happy, at work, where he felt more focused and aware, as well as in his love life, where his relationship deepened. The other track "constantly reminded ... [him] of the past, of things ... [he] had done that made ... [him] cringe and feel again and again a terrible abjection," as well as a sense of confusion and mystification about who he really was. "It is as if I want to be myself, but I don't know who that self is ... I'm undergoing this huge change ... and I don't know if I want to be myself, because there are parts I don't like, parts I want to get rid of, like being so compliant with other people." A feeling of vanishing into air with weightlessness signaled to him that to get rid of this "bad object" will throw him off balance and will make him lose his moorings and spin him off into space. He felt in his body how he had masochistically clung to abusive (or abusively constructed) objects, in order to feel weighty and worthy. To accept himself with his history and the shameful parts of this history and of himself without feeling self-loathing and abjection, that is, free of an inimical "alien self," and a self-abasing "bad object," as their relentless generator, was too difficult to contemplate and seemed to him more than he had bargained for ...

References

Aron, L. (1992), Interpretation as expression of the analyst's subjectivity. *Psychoanal. Dial.*, 2: 475–507.

——— (1996), *The Meeting of Minds: Mutuality in Psychoanalysis*. Hillsdale, NJ: The Analytic Press.

Bateman, A., & Fonagy, P. (2005), *Psychotherapy for Borderline Personality Disorder: Mentalization-Based Treatment*. London: Oxford.

Benjamin, J. (1988), *The Bonds of Love*. NY: Pantheon.

——— (2005), Creating an intersubjective reality: Commentary on paper by Arnold Rothstein. *Psychoanal. Dialogues*, 15:321–346.

Berman, E. (2005), *Impossible Training: A Relational View of Psychoanalytic Education*. Hillsdale, NJ: The Analytic Press.

Bollas, C. (1983), Expressive uses of the countertransference—Notes to the patient from oneself. *Contemp. Psychoanal.*, 19:1–33.

Busch, F. (1994), Some ambiguities in the method of free association and their implications for technique. *J. Am. Psychoanal. Assn.*, 42:363–384.

Cooper, S. H. (2000), *Objects of Hope: Exploring Possibility and Limit in Psychoanalysis*. Hillsdale, NJ: The Analytic Press.

Cooper, S. H., & Levitt, D. B. (1998), Old and new objects in Fairbairnian and American relational theory. *Psychoanal. Dial.*, 8:603–624.

Fonagy, P. (2003), Some complexities in the relationship of psychoanalytic theory to technique. *Psychoanal. Quarterly*, 72:13–48.

Freud, S. (1917), *Mourning and Melancholia*. SE 14, pp. 237–258.

Freud, S. (1923), *The Ego and the Id*. SE 19, pp. 1–59.

Friedman, L. (1980), Kohut: A book review essay. *Psychoanal. Q.*, 49:393–422.

Gray, P. (1990), The nature of therapeutic action in psychoanalysis. *J. Am. Psychoanal. Assn.*, 38:1083–1096.

Gribinski, M. (1996), *Le trouble de la réalité* [The trouble of reality]. Paris: Gallimard.

Grotstein, J. (2000), *Who is the Dreamer Who Dreams the Dream*. Hillsdale, NJ: The Analytic Press.

Hoffman, I. Z. (1998), *Ritual and Spontaneity in the Psychoanalytic Process: A Dialectical-Constructivist View*. Hillsdale, NJ: The Analytic Press.

Joseph, B. (1978), Different types of anxiety and their handling in the analytic situation. *Int. J. Psychoanal.*, 59:223–228.

Laplanche, J. (1999), *Essays on Otherness*. New York: Routledge.

Lavie, J.-C. (1997), *L'amour est un crime parfait* [Love is a perfect crime]. Paris: Gallimard.

Mitchell, S. A. (1995), *Hope and Dread in Psychoanalysis*. New York: Perseus.

Mitchell, S. (2001), No search or getting down to business. *Psychoanal. Q.*, 70:183–199.

Rappaport, E. (1956), The management of an erotized transference. *Psychoanal. Q.*, 25:515–529.

Riviere, J. (1936), On the genesis of psychical conflict in earliest infancy. *Int. J. Psycho-Anal.*, 17:395–422.

Sandler, J. (1983), Reflections on some relations between psychoanalytic concepts and psychoanalytic practice. *Int. J. Psycho-Anal.*, 64:35–45.

Schafer, R (1985), Wild analysis. *J. Amer. Psychoanal. Assn.*, 33:275–299.

Schafer, R. (1990), The search for common ground. *Int. J. Psychoanal.*, 71:49–52.

Schiller, F. (1795), *Das verschleierte Bild zu Sais* [The Veiled Picture in Sais]. Stuttgart: Teubner.

Spezzano, C. (1998), The triangle of clinical judgment. *J. Amer. Psychoanal. Assn.*, 46:365–388.

Stein, R. (1990), A new look at the theory of Melanie Klein. *Int. J. Psychoanal.,* 71 :499–511.

——— (1997), The shame experiences of the analyst. In: *Conversations in Self Psychology.* Progress in Self Psychology, volume 13. Ed. A. Goldberg. 13: pp. 109–123. The Analytic Press.

——— (2001, May/July), *A case study of case studies: Analysis of papers submitted to the Israel Psychoanalytic Institute for the last 20+ years.* Paper presented at the Israel Psychoanal. Soc., May, 2001, and at the 43rd IPAC, Nice, July, 2001.

——— (2003), *Continuity and freedom in analytic work.* Paper presented at the Conference for Self Psychology, Dreieich, Germany.

Stern, D. (2003), *Words and Wordlessness.* Unpublished manuscript.

Symington, N. (1983), The analyst's act of freedom as an agent of therapeutic change. *Int. Rev. Psychoanal.,* 10:283–291.

Wallerstein, R. (1990), Psychoanalysis: The common ground. *Int. J. Psychoanal.,* 71:3–20.

Winnicott, D. (1947), Hate in the countertransference. In: *Collected Papers: Through Pediatrics to Psycho-Analysis.* London: Tavistock, 1958, pp. 194–203.

Part II

New Ideas, New Voices

The seven chapters in "New Ideas, New Voices" were chosen to introduce some of the younger generation of relational writers. In line with the progressive spirit we embrace, the majority of these chapters cover the neglected topics of race, class, and politics as they come to life in the clinical situation.

Opening with Steven Botticelli's (chap. 7) thought-provoking "Return of the Repressed: Class in Psychoanalytic Process" the chapter presents class as occupying a limenal space in our awareness, that which is known and not known simultaneously. Botticelli captures the haunting quality of class and its elusiveness by replicating in the chapter the struggle to capture the manner in which class contributes to therapeutic failure. As with his previous writings (Botticelli, 2004) he forces us to confront the ways in which the political state of the world are inseparable from the relational conflicts in the consulting room.

Anne Cheng (chap. 8), like David Eng, has extended the work of Judith Butler on gender melancholia to an understanding of racial melancholia. In "Intimate Refusals: Racial Melancholia and the Politics of Objecthood" she explores the subjectivity of the melancholic object, the racial Other, whose racial identity is introjected in the form of an inarticulable loss that informs white subjectivity. Taking some of these ideas further than initially presented in her book *The Melancholy of Race* (2001), she calls for a rethinking of subjecthood as a fundamental basis of political action. Formulating an ethics of relationality rather than an ethics of intersubjectivity, Cheng courageously attempts to find a way to go beyond the subject–object construction of racialized identities.

David Eng and Shinhee Han (chap. 9), following their seminal work "A Dialogue on Racial Melancholia" (2000), take us into the domain of transnational adoption in "Desegregating Love: Transnational Adoption, Racial Reparation, and Racial Transitional Objects." They impel us to revise Freud's notions of melancholia to include the constructive holding on to lost racial objects, Klein's idea of positions as racial positions, and Winnicott's concept of transitional objects as racialized objects. Their brilliance often lies in the unorthodox interpretation and reformulation of psychoanalytic concepts. Envy is considered by them to be a creative "melancholic racial coping mechanism" that preserves the goodness of the lost Asian mother and allows for some spoiling of the goodness of the idealized whiteness of the adopted mother, a move that ushers in a reparative position for race, where both birth and adopted mothers, Asian and white, can be good and bad.

Continuing the theme of incorporating the cultural into the intrapsychic, Katie Gentile (chap. 10) ventures into the realm of eating disorders. By analyzing 18 years of diary entries of a white, upper-middle class British woman, Gentile struggles with the paradox of resistance and its underlying desire for transformation. Eating disorders are simultaneously self-destructive and an attempt to defiantly resist the social order imposed on the bodies of women. Skillfully, she holds the tension of the diametric oppositions throughout the piece. Only when shifting into a critical analysis of power to explore the many levels in which submitting and resisting co-exist can the analyst appreciate how the body/mind emerges through self-destruction.

Robert Grossmark (chap. 11) presents an innovative chapter, "From Familiar Chaos to Coherence: Unformulated Experience and Enactment in Group Psychotherapy." This is the first chapter to articulate a specifically relational approach to group psychoanalysis. As he takes us into the grips of a group enactment, he shows how the unthought and unformulated aspects of the internal world become enacted in the group, not as formed unconscious material awaiting projection onto the group but that which can only emerge and be formulated through the group experience. The analyst is, of necessity, intertwined in the enactment, looking for the snare to disentangle and using the group themselves to create meaning and shift the dynamics of the enactment.

Returning to class, Stephen Hartman (chap. 12) takes a completely different approach to that of Steven Botticelli, situating class in the body, as he explores the mutual engagement of material and psychic worlds. Titled "Class Unconscious: From Dialectical Materialism to Relational Material," Hartman depicts the unformulated experience of class in the unconscious domain. With theoretical complexity and skill he weaves Marx, Foucault, Laplanche, with Aron, Benjamin, Stein, Fonagy and Target to produce an interesting exposition of his own interpellation into the class structure and the unfolding of class in his relationship to his patients.

In closing Part II, Marsha Hewitt (chap. 13) in "Self/Object and Individual/Society: The 'Two Logics' of Psychoanalysis" explores the emancipatory potential of psychoanalysis as a political project in cultivating a democratic mind. Moving beyond psychoanalysis as individual transformation, Hewitt infuses hopefulness into the reader, emphasizing the interconnectedness of subjectivity and social practices. She proposes that relational practices that promote self-reflexivity, intersubjectivity, and mutual relatedness offer the potential for creating democratic ways of social life.

References

Botticelli, S. (2004), The politics of relational psychoanalysis. *Psychoanalytic Dialogues, 14*(5):635–651.

Cheng, A. (2001), *The Melancholy of Race: Psychoanalysis, Assimilation and Hidden Grief.* Oxford: Oxford University Press.

Eng, D., & Han, S. (2000), A dialogue on racial melancholia. *Psychoanalytic Dialogues, 10*(4):667–700.

7

Return of the Repressed:
Class in Psychoanalytic Process

Steven Botticelli, PhD

At the mention of class, all progressive heads reverently bow—yet within psychoanalysis, few can think of anything to say about it. About a dozen years ago psychoanalysis discovered gender, and since then journals and conferences have been filled with papers and presentations on the topic. More recently, analysts such as Leary (2000) and Altman (2000) have begun to consider race. Within the family of "gender, race, class, and culture" beloved of a thousand conference organizers, class decidedly has been the neglected child. I think this is no accident. To state my thesis at the outset: Where class appears in psychoanalytic process, it may mark the presence of intractable, perhaps insoluble conflict; of thwarted possibility; of failure—and this is something that we American analysts, in our boundless therapeutic optimism, have difficulty coming to terms with.

Of course, it is not true that psychoanalysis has had nothing to say about class. Freud believed that psychoanalytic treatment should be made available to the poor. His proposal led to the establishment in the 1920s of the Berlin Clinic, where, according to Peter Gay, "indigent neurotics ... were not simply turned over to candidates to be practiced on, but could count, at least part of the time, on being seen by a seasoned practitioner" (Gay, 1988, pp. 462–63). Wilhelm Reich (1934) believed that a psychoanalytically informed understanding of people's minds, especially psychosexuality, was essential in fostering the development of class consciousness among the masses so they could throw off the yoke of capitalism—though he kept this concern quite apart from his clinical interests. Decades later, in *The Age of Desire* (1981), Joel Kovel tried to theorize the relation between class and mind within the framework of traditional Marxist categories and a one-person psychology.

We might expect that the relational turn in psychoanalysis would open more space for considerations of class to enter, based on some thematic resonances. For one thing, the Marxist definition of class is inherently relational, not simply hierarchical. For Marx, class was a relationship. Eugene Debs well captured this aspect when he said "It's not just that some are rich and others are poor; it's that some are rich *because* others are poor" (1904, p. 2). Class experience bears a structural resemblance to trauma, that privileged object of relationalists' attention. In both, there is a tendency to blame the self in a situation where another individual, or forces outside one's control, have inflicted injury (cf. Sennett & Cobb's *The Hidden Injuries of Class,* 1969). Finally, there is a resonance between the relational interest in multiplicity and the idea of multiple subject positions theorized by post-Marxists Laclau and Mouffe (Dimen, personal communication, October, 2003). They believe that expanding the traditional Marxist emphasis on class position to include ethnicity, gender, and other subject positions increases the possible sites of political resistance in fighting for social change (Best & Kellner, 1991).

And indeed, to some extent, it has been the case that under the influence of relational shifts in theory, analysts have become interested in how class enters the clinical picture. Dimen (1994), for instance, considered the implications of therapists' charging for our time in the context of a case in which her patient's resentment of this fact came to play a pertinent role. Altman (1995) examined how perceptions of the class difference between himself and his patients at the clinic of a public hospital became the basis for projective and introjective processes within the dyad. With Dimen and Altman as full participants in the therapeutic interaction, we make the leap into a two-person psychoanalysis. Both authors limn a clinical process that develops out of the patient's (and analyst's) perception of "actual" class markers or the actual class difference between the patient and therapist. Yet I imagine that class also may enter clinical process in ways that do not depend on the presence of such "reality-based" elements.

Here I want to claim a much larger role for class by considering how life in class society creates structures of experience that profoundly shape us and our lived relationships. As Marx wrote decades before any psychologist had formulated a concept of internalized object relations, "the self is the ensemble of social relations" (quoted by Kovel, 1981, p. 70). Though he has often been criticized for neglecting the subjective, psychological aspect of human life, Marx here might have been suggesting that through our experience living in a class society, we develop within ourselves representations of relationships between members of different classes. As with all internalized object relations, these representations carry particular affective valences, and are reversible. The manner in which they become activated in the clinical situation, which member of the dyad takes up which representation, is not predictable in advance, and may shift from one moment to another. Perhaps the first noted appearance of internalized class relations in psychoanalysis in the sense I describe here occurs in the Dora case. Freud, receiving Dora's "fortnight's warning" of the termination of her analysis, felt he was being treated "just like a maidservant or governess" (Freud, 1905, p. 107).

We might expect that these internalized relationships would have a distinctive quality, owing to the peculiar status of class as a social category in American society. Perhaps the most salient characteristic of class is that its very existence often is denied. We are constantly bombarded with the myth that we live in a classless society. American freedom of opportunity allows anyone who works hard enough to get ahead, we are told. Certainly, there are some very rich people, and some poor people in this country, but the vast majority of us belong to a relatively content middle class. Recent statistics give the lie to this quaint notion: Since the 1970s real wages have been declining for 80% of American male workers, the total number of hours worked per household has increased greatly, and the average U.S. household is deeper in debt than ever before (Roy, 2003). Furthermore, the rate of social mobility has been falling for the last several decades, as reduced government spending on higher education and steep tuition increases at universities have limited people's opportunities for advancement (Hutton, 2003).

The mainstream media play a significant role in perpetuating misconceptions about class. For example many newspapers have a business section, but almost none have editors or reporters specifically assigned to cover labor issues, let alone a labor section. This implies that news written from the perspective of business represents the interests of all Americans, and that there are no conflicts based on competing class interests. Where class conflicts are reported, as in strikes and other labor disputes, they are often trivialized by being described as if they were individual relationships gone sour. For instance, when *The Chicago Tribune* reported on a newspaper strike in that city in 1997, its writer said little about the issues at stake but instead spoke of "the often-overlooked wounds when labor and management can't agree" and the "complexity of emotions" felt on both sides (Frank, 1997, p. 291). Such coverage misrepresents class relations as something other than the structural, irreconcilably conflictual relation that they are.

Sometimes events break through this construction and force into our awareness the fact that we live in a class society. The Enron scandal was one such example: While CEO Ken Lay and other top executives cashed in their stock in the company before it went bankrupt, regular employees lost their jobs and the bulk of their retirement savings, all of which was invested in Enron stock. This was on the front pages for all to see. Yet, most of the time awareness of class occupies a space in what sociologist Stanley Aronowitz has called our "class unconscious" (2003, p. 30). Indeed, I want to argue that it is exactly this "known but not known" quality that makes class experience especially likely to be evoked in the clinical situation. Joyce Slochower (1999) puts this idea in the now-familiar language of dissociation: "It is exactly those experiences that belong to split off self states, that remain unintegrated, that are especially likely to be reenacted within the transference-countertransference dynamic" (p. 1127).

Despite or perhaps precisely because of this unconsciousness or "split-offness," people often have powerful identifications with their class of origin. My patient Gary is such a person. Gary is a lonely, socially isolated gay man who first came to see me 6 years ago. Despite earning a professional's salary in a midlevel position at a brokerage firm, Gary, for the most part, has continued living an existence more in keeping with his working class background. In his late 40s, he lives in a rented studio apartment. Occasionally he contemplates buying an apartment or taking a European vacation. He usually becomes anxious about what his working class siblings would think about such a purchase, and proceeds to trample all over the idea.

Early in the treatment, Gary got the idea that a sexual and romantic relationship with me would be the answer to all his problems. In fact, this was the only thing he wanted from me. Somehow, he got the idea that such a relationship was not only desirable but possible. Even though on several occasions I explicitly disabused him of the notion that we could become involved in this way, he seemed to see the treatment as a kind of extended courtship that we would eventually consummate in a sexual relationship. Although his fantasies about our relationship often provided a context for us to examine his fears of closeness with another man, other avenues of exploration seemed foreclosed by his preoccupation with the question, "When are we going to do it?" The stage was set for what would come to feel like an extended conflict over the purpose of the therapy: Gary wanted a relationship with me, whereas I wanted him to be able to use his relationship with me to develop the rest of his life.

Class has felt like a shadowy presence in this treatment, most of the time looming somewhere in the background. Accordingly, in describing my work with Gary, I proceed by allusion and speculation, listening for how class is subtly threaded through the material, noting resonances of class experience where I hear them. I intend to be evocative, rather than precise.

As the therapy progressed, Gary's fantasy of our relationship came to occupy a larger role in his life, inside and outside the sessions. Often in his reveries, our budding romance began to falter on the grounds of what he perceived as our differences from one another. For instance, I have more education than he; would he be able to hold my intellectual interest? Clearly, Gary saw me as in possession of more of what sociologist Pierre Bourdieu (Bourdieu & Passeron, 1977) refers to as "cultural capital" than he, and believed that this discrepancy might present a serious obstacle to our building and maintaining a romantic relationship. Another thing that seemed clear: whenever our relationship was to take the leap into this new realm, it would be up to me to make the first move. Both inside and outside the treatment, Gary showed a strong disinclination to take any action on behalf of his stated interests, what Nina Coltart (1986) once described as a "pathological disablement of the will" (p. 197). As I once put it to him, he seemed to take a "hands-off" attitude toward his own life, experiencing it as something that was happening to him, rather than as something he might shape according to his own wishes and intentions. Although Gary had had several short-lived relationships with other men since his late teens, where I was concerned he seemed more or less content to wait. In the meantime, he kept spinning out more fantasies about us.

A notable exception to this passivity and helplessness was Gary's willingness to spend his money on consumer items, which he did freely. He would tell me about the suit he bought at Barney's, "to impress people and to hide [his] dysfunctional middle class background," the gym membership he purchased in order to appear to be "someone who is successful and can afford to do this." He frequently considered looking for an apartment to buy, but always drew back from the idea. "What if a year later it turns out that I've made a big mistake?" This fear of making a mistake seemed to contain some almost existential dread beyond anything he could put into words. As with his reluctance to take any interpersonal risks, it seemed there was something very important at stake in refusing the choices that could actually make a difference in the quality of his life and outlook on the future.

My internal response to all this had several aspects. At first blush, the emergence of Gary's eroticized transference interested and excited me, heralding his affective entry into the process of treatment and offering the promise of a lively and meaningful engagement between us. Disquiet began to build as I noticed that Gary seemed to talk about our romance as a real possibility. I wondered whether I had done something to give him this impression, perhaps by sometimes letting myself enjoy his fantasies too much. However I was not sure he literally believed this was something we could actually do, and for the moment felt disinclined to ask him to clarify. It felt as though we had entered our own version of "confusion of tongues" (Ferenczi, 1933), unsure of how to understand each other on this issue. Later on, taking a cue from a trusted supervisor, I felt encouraged to try to bracket my disquiet and to go on receiving Gary's transference in the open, playful way I had initially.

I spent a good deal of time puzzling over the possible meanings of Gary's wish. Certainly, it had a defensive aspect to it. As Steven Cooper (2003) has noted, "The eroticized transference can itself represent a defensively forged substitute for other, more realizable outside relationships" (p. 48). In addition, it seemed a counterdependent move on Gary's part: Insisting on something I could not give him prevented him from availing himself of whatever help I actually might be able to offer. In a similar sense, his demand seemed a way of maintaining distance from me, under the guise of seeking closeness. Indeed, on a few occasions when Gary believed I was signaling my intention to grant his wish to consummate our relationship, he became quite frightened. At these moments he seemed to recognize that it was not actual physical contact he wanted from me—though this realization always quickly evaporated.

Even as I struggled to understand what Gary was doing with me, I couldn't help noticing as the years went by that nothing much was changing in Gary's life outside the therapy. In fact, he was becoming more isolated and avoidant. At times he became more impatient and importunate with me about when we were going to get together—even as he continued to make it clear that it would be up to me to make the first move. The fact that this stance gave me a great deal of power over him clearly was making him increasingly angry and unhappy—and yet he remained firmly planted there. The erotic reveries that he would initiate and that I would enter with him seemed to stoke both his desire and his frustration. For Gary, I'd become Fairbairn's unsatisfying object, frustrating his need even as I continued to whet it. Let's notice that this dynamic bears a resemblance to the dynamic of consumer capitalism, which must continually stimulate desires that it keeps unfulfilled. Craving leading to consumption must be perpetually renewed, in what writer David Lenson (1995) refers to as "consumerism's metaphysics of desire" (p. 132).

According to Fairbairn (1952), "it is only the unsatisfying object that the infant seeks to coerce" (p. 111), and coercion too was becoming an aspect of my experience with Gary. Gary's demanding my love while pointing to the apparent lack of helpful influence the therapy was having on his life could at times elicit in me a feeling that I owed him something. He seemed to want to use the ineffectiveness of the therapy as the basis for a claim to some extraordinary treatment from me. I caught myself feeling that I had enlisted him in the treatment under false pretenses, that I was exploiting him, holding out the promise of a relationship I had no intention of giving him. We had entered the realm of what Ogden (1994) calls the subjugating third, in which our only choices seemed to be either submitting to or resisting the other's will and perspective.

In a widely cited 1998 article, Slavin and Kriegman offered their perspective on such intractable situations, which they frame in terms of conflicts of interest. They believe conflicts of interest arise inevitably between patient and analyst, as between any two people in relationship. They view this inevitability as a legacy of our "evolutionary, biological heritage" (p. 274), in essence as part of human nature, that "real diverging interests" (p. 263) between any two people in relationship will emerge and form the basis for actual conflicts of interest. As the open acknowledgment of such conflicts may have a disruptive effect on a relationship, Slavin and Kriegman see much of relational life as shaped by the deceptions and self-deceptions we engage in in order to manage this fact of life.

Slavin and Kriegman's ideas provide one way of considering Gary's construal of our relationship in terms of irreconcilably opposed interests. However, it is not clear why these writers naturalize this relational phenomenon as reflecting what they speculate is some "deep, natural human sensitivity to the ways in which our needs and identifications conflict with those of others" (p. 257). Bypassing history to reach for biology, they overlook the role of class society and class antagonism as the breeding ground for the seemingly unavoidable conflicts of interest they so astutely identify.

Attempting to reinscribe my interpersonal conflict with Gary within a historically specific context, we might think of Gary, in his insistence on real gratification from me, as "on strike" from the work of therapy. Meanwhile, I as his "boss" continually try to get him back to work. It certainly seemed true that, just as the working class most makes its social power most manifest when collectively withholding its labor, Gary through his refusal had found a way to maximize his psychic impact on me. Indeed, relational reconceptualizations of the concept of resistance could deepen our understanding of the phenomenon by expanding consideration of the impact that resistance has on the person of the analyst. Such consideration could build on Roy Schaefer's (1992) recasting of resistance as reflecting whatever behavior of the patient has elicited negative countertransference, by including our patients' (often unconscious) determination to have a powerful impact on us.

Slavin and Kriegman suggest that these always present, treatment-stalling conflicts of interest between analyst and patient can start to be negotiated only when analysts undertake a "struggle to reopen aspects of our own identity ... with minimal deception and self-deception, in areas that are elicited by and relate to our patient's conflicts" (Slavin & Kriegman, 1998, p. 279). When perceived by the patient, this willingness on the part of the analyst to reopen areas of difficulty within her own personality that she had provisionally settled, indicates to the patient the analyst's willingness to step away from her own preferred perspective on herself. The patient's perception of this painful effort, made on the patient's behalf, is what allows the patient to trust the analyst sufficiently to allow himself to open himself to the influence of the treatment. The patient becomes willing to undertake the often painful reworking of his own long-settled conflicts.

In fact, my work with Gary evoked just such a struggle within myself, a struggle over how deeply to enter my countertransferential identification with his childhood and early adolescent experience of being teased by other boys for perceived effeminacy. In trying to account for his current avoidance of most social situations, Gary frequently invoked his childhood harassment by other boys in his neighborhood. In one particularly painful and frequently recalled episode, Gary was taunted by a boy who mocked him, sneering that his father had told him to "stay away from that little fem." Gary found little refuge from this torment at home, where he and three sib-lings lived with an alcoholic father who alternated between sullen silence (when sober) and verbal abuse of his wife and children (when drunk), and a mother who seemed unable to offer any protection. Other boys' taunting caused him to feel a great deal of shame about himself, which blended with the shame he felt about the unkempt state of his family's home and yard. His shame moved him to efforts, so common for gay boys, to hide or shut down those parts of himself that seemed to incite other boys' scorn. In Gary's case, this included a lively, silly, playful aspect that in rare moments I had been allowed to glimpse a vestige of.

At age 48, Gary continued to live in fear of his gayness being detected and mocked. In one session, Gary worried over whether he would be perceived as gay if he were out in public with another man he was dating. He'd worked hard in his adolescence to "cover over" as much of his "queeniness" as he could, an effort he speculated had become automatic and continued to the present day. As I asked Gary the question, "What had to be covered over?," I found myself tearing up, overtaken by a wave of sadness for Gary, for my childhood self, for all gay men. Quickly noticing my misting up, Gary said he was "freaked out" by my reaction: "Steve—I thought you were the strong one!" He moved through several further reactions—thinking I was pitying him, wondering whether my tearing up was part of some manipulation on my part—before coming to the thought that maybe he and I had more in common than he had previously believed.

Prior to this session I had not allowed myself to feel this much about Gary's experiences of being teased, though we had talked about them fre-quently. Gary's feelings about the bullying, still so raw more than 30 years later, came a bit too close for my comfort to feelings I had mostly chosen to suppress about taunting I had had to endure in my adolescence. Now I found myself remembering being called "fem" when I went to school one day in sixth grade wearing a pair of bell bottoms. At that time bell bottoms had recently started to become fashionable, though apparently some of my peers had not yet realized this. Although I had a more stable situation at home than Gary, like him I had felt I had no one to turn to who could help me with the teasing and what I felt about it. I responded by withdrawing socially and emotionally shutting down. These reactions strongly shaped the person I was becoming as I entered adulthood.

In the process of writing this paper I thought of an aspect of my sixth-grade experience that cast it in a somewhat different light for me. The school district I was placed in that year brought together the kids from my middle class town with kids from a neighboring working class town. While my wearing bell bottoms got coded as effeminate, it may also have indicated that I came from a family with the money to buy such clothes. I wonder how much class resentment my taunters were expressing in their teasing me—maybe without realizing it. Perhaps, for sixth-graders just as for psychoanalysts and in fact for most people in our society, it is easier to talk about gender than class. It may be that class, in its seeming unspeakability, sometimes finds displaced expression through gender categories and hierarchies.

The therapy continued. Several months after this session, I received a message from Gary over a weekend. "Well, the cat's out of the bag—I saw you walking on the street tonight with your boyfriend. Or maybe he was your brother—he looked just like you. Anyway, it couldn't have come at a worse time—here I am alone on a Saturday night, about to stuff my face because I'm so miserable. I don't want to see you this week." When Gary came in a few weeks later, he told me how crushed he had felt seeing me in the street, thinking of me now as having a boyfriend. Compounding the injury, I had not acknowledged him. He demanded to know whom I was walking with. "Tell me more about what you felt, seeing me walking with this person, and my not acknowledging you," I encouraged him. "Forget about feelings—who was that you were with? That will settle once and for all whether we can get together." Perhaps too quickly, I explained to him, not for the first time, that regardless of whether or not I had a boyfriend, it would not be possible for us to be involved in that way. Gary sat silently for a moment. "I just can't give up the idea of our getting together," Gary said. "I'm very stubborn and I don't like change."

Gary went on to say he thought he should see another therapist, or maybe stop therapy altogether. He began to fret about the money he had already placed in a flexible spending account, earmarked to pay for therapy for the coming year. What would he do with that money now? Feeling rather hopeless at that moment about the place we had come to, I did not question or challenge him. But after I said something to him about how much feeling it must have stirred for him to see me in the street, Gary said, "I just drifted off. I was thinking I'd love to suck some cock right now—could I suck yours?" Then, a moment later, "I think what I just said about sucking your cock was a defense mechanism. I didn't like what you were saying." Surprised by his reflectiveness, I asked him what I had said that he didn't like. "That you were reminding me again that we're not getting together." That

Gary did not like to hear me say this was old news. That he was able to observe his internal reaction to my saying it, and that we could talk about this together, was a new development.

Before the session's end, Gary began to wonder what it might mean that he had never reached orgasm while thinking about me when he masturbated—something he had often mentioned, but about which he had never before seemed curious. Thinking on it now, he reflected that actually having sex with me might not feel right, considering the kind of emotional attachment we did share. We talked about whether he may have been taking his sexual feelings and wishes for me too much at face value. Here, in what might be our final session, Gary was allowing me to be his therapist.

Discussion

In making an assessment of my work with Gary, I could take some consolation in the thought that the treatment of a man as mistrustful as he would take a long time before it could be expected to have a beneficial impact on his life. One could argue that our relationship itself has been sustaining for him, providing a measure of comfort and human contact that he has not felt safe enough to allow himself with anyone else. And certainly Gary's nascent ability to observe the workings of his mind and join me in reflecting on them in our final session seemed to be a positive development. It suggested the possible opening of a space of "thirdness," a movement out of the register of power and into a space of potential mutuality. But I would like to consider that this treatment was, in an important sense, a failure. At the point at which actual therapy seemed possible, Gary went away frustrated and dissatisfied. He left treatment having gotten neither what he nor I thought he needed, even if our relationship gave him a place to locate, and rail against, all the unhappiness and thwarted possibility of his life.

On reflection, it seems that Gary used his therapy to stay the same while telling himself he wanted change. Renouncing his own agency, Gary placed all efficacy and authority in me. In his fantasy, our becoming lovers would cure his loneliness and free him from having to make a life for himself. A tacit bargain had been struck, whereby in exchange for being my patient, Gary abdicated to me all responsibility for making change in his life. In retrospect, my countertransference experience that I was exploiting him and having difficulty sustaining hope about the work might have alerted me to this sooner. That some of our patients will use their treatment with us for this purpose underscores how difficult it can be to take responsibility for change, a responsibility that always carries with it the frightening risk of failure.

In my experience, there seem to be an increasing number of patients who resemble Gary, patients who wish for magical solutions to their problems, who look to the analyst to assume responsibility for making change happen in their lives. As with Gary, this scenario (if not identified as such) easily becomes a setup for the kind of intractable impasse into which we became embroiled. I wonder whether we might think of this phenomenon as a form of learned helplessness, born perhaps of individual experiences but also out of our collective experience as people living at this particular moment in history. We live in a time when we are implicitly encouraged to let our leaders make our decisions for us, when it may feel hard for many to recall within living memory an example of a social movement that seemed to shift the course of current events. And this, at a time when social inequality is increasing, as the gap widens between rich and poor. Perhaps our diminishing sense of our capacity to influence the social decisions that affect us all is mirrored in our clinical practices, where we may encounter more patients like Gary who feel powerless to effect change in their lives and look to their therapists to rescue them, to do their work for them. (Elsewhere [Botticelli, 2004], I have argued that this loss of a sense of efficacy to impact the larger world has influenced theory development in relational psychoanalysis.)

In practicing psychoanalysis with a given patient, we cannot know in advance what we will conjure. Existing theory leads us to expect to find aspects of early relationships with caregivers—especially those which have been conflictual or traumatic, and therefore repressed or split off—in the transference-countertransference matrix. But can we imagine that repressed or split-off aspects of our collective history, as well, may come to life in our treatments? Indeed, Altman (2004) recently has suggested this very possibility, writing of how "history on the large-scale level may be reenacted on the small-scale level of the individual or the dyad" (p. 807).

Reviewing some of the salient features of Gary's treatment—his identification with his working class background; my role as a stimulating but frustrating object for him; his refusal of the work of therapy in favor of eroticizing our relationship in a fashion that turned us into adversaries as far as the purpose of the treatment was concerned—I can locate coordinates from Gary's early history of relationships. But I am also reminded of "large-scale" history—the dynamic of capitalism and the history of class struggle. Although it seems to have receded from what Zizek (1999) refers to as "the horizon of historical imagination" (p. 55), the idea that the working class would transform capitalism into a more equitable economic system—perhaps through a mass strike that generalized into a broader struggle for political power—until recently enjoyed great currency. This much-imagined historical possibility, in every instance in which an effort toward it has been made, has ultimately failed. Perhaps it is sufficient here to recall the massacre of the Communards of the Paris

Commune; the degeneration of the promise of the Russian Revolution into the nightmare of Stalinism; the cooptation of the student protests and mass strikes of the French May of 1968 into electoralism and the resurgence of Gaullism. Could it be that these failures (not of imagination but of agency, leadership, strategy) were repeated, unremembered, in my (ultimately unsuccessful) work with Gary?

The clinical implications of my speculations here are not very clear. But one might be that we could afford to have more respect for and reflectiveness about our therapeutic failures. Just as class is repressed within society, the experience of failure is repressed within psychoanalysis. Even Kohut's "optimal failure" is but a way station on the road to the repair of the patient's self. Psychoanalytic case presentations reveal a remarkable uniformity in their narrative arc: treatment impasse yields to "negotiation," the finding of a place of "thirdness," or some other resolution of one kind or another. Should we be suspicious that so many reported analyses turn out so well, when things are going so appallingly badly in the world?

If it sounds strange to hear therapeutic outcomes and the state of the world brought together as part of the same thought, I think it is because within relational psychoanalysis we currently do not have models for thinking about the linkages between our efforts to help our patients change and the need to change the world. For some suggestive efforts in this direction, we might consider Julia Kristeva's notion of "intimate revolt" (2002a), or Tony Kushner's 2004 play "Caroline, or Change," both of which show an easy fluidity in moving between the personal and the social in thinking about the need for change.

To turn my argument on its head and close with a different perspective on my work with Gary, we might ponder whether Gary's insisting on the unattainable with me reflected not just some entrenched sense of powerlessness and lack of agency but perhaps the leading edge of a utopian impulse. In his way, Gary stands with the student protesters of May, 1968, who raised the slogan, "We're realists—we want the impossible!" (quoted in Kristeva, 2002b, p. 13). Failure in one sense though it may have been, my work with Gary shows the value of psychoanalysis as a practice in which the seemingly unattainable can, importantly, be imagined, desired, and carried forward into the future.

References

Altman, N. (1995), *The Analyst in the Inner City: Race, Class, and Culture through a Psychoanalytic Lens*. Hillsdale, NJ: The Analytic Press.
——— (2000), Black and white thinking: A psychoanalyst reconsiders race. *Psychoanal. Dial.*, 10:589–606.

———— (2004), History repeats itself in transference-countertransference. *Psychoanal. Dial.,* 14:807–816.

Aronowitz, S. (2003), *How Class Works: Power and Social Movement.* New Haven, CT: Yale University Press.

Best, S., & Kellner, D. (1991), *Postmodern Theory: Critical Interrogations.* New York: Guilford.

Botticelli, S. (2004), The politics of relational psychoanalysis. *Psychoanal. Dial.,* 14:635–652.

Bourdieu, P., & Passeron, J. (1977), *Reproduction in Education, Society and Culture* (R. Nice, Trans.). Beverly Hills: Sage.

Coltart, N. (1986), "Slouching towards Bethlehem ..." or thinking the unthinkable in psychoanalysis. In: *The British School of Psychoanalysis: The Independent Tradition,* ed. G. Kohon. New Haven, CT: Yale University Press, pp. 185–209.

Cooper, S. (2003), The countertransference transformation of oedipal idealization, mourning, and erotic masochism: Commentary on paper by Jody Messler Davies. *Psychoanal. Dial.,* 13: 29–40.

Debs, E. (1904), The Socialist Party and the working class. Opening speech delivered as candidate of the Socialist Party for the President at Indianapolis, IN, September 1, 1904, E. V. Debs Internet archive, 2001.

Dimen, M. (1994), Money, love, and hate: Contradiction and paradox in psychoanalysis. *Psychoanal. Dial.,* 4:69–100.

Fairbairn, R. D. (1952), *Psychoanalytic Studies of the Personality.* London: Tavistock Publications Ltd.

Ferenzci, S. (1933), Confusion of tongues between adults and the child. In: *Final Contributions to the Problems and Methods of Psychoanalysis.* London: Karnac Books, pp. 156–167.

Frank, T. (1997), When class disappears. In: *Boob Jubilee: The Cultural Politics of the New Economy,* ed. T. Frank & T. Mulcahey. New York: Norton, pp. 289–300.

Freud, S. (1905), Fragment of an analysis of a case of hysteria. *Standard Edition,* 7:3–124. London: Hogarth Press.

Gay, P. (1988), *Freud: A Life for Our Time.* New York: Norton.

Hutton, W. (2003), The American prosperity myth. *The Nation,* Sept. 1/8, pp. 20–24.

Kovel, J. (1981), *The Age of Desire: Case Histories of a Radical Psychoanalyst.* New York: Pantheon.

Kristeva, J. (2002a), *Intimate Revolt: The Powers and Limits of Psychoanalysis.* New York: Columbia University Press.

———— (2002b), *Revolt, She Said: An Interview by Philippe Petit.* Los Angeles: Semiotext(e).

Leary, K. (2000), Racial enactments in dynamic treatment. *Psychoanal. Dial.,* 10:639–654.

Lenson, D. (1995), *On Drugs.* Minneapolis: University of Minnesota Press.

Ogden, T. (1994), *Subjects of Analysis.* Northvale, NJ: Aronson.

Reich, W. (1934), What is class consciousness? In *Sex-Pol: Essays 1929–1934,* ed. L. Baxandall. New York: Random House, pp. 275–358.

Roy, D. (2003), The myth of the classless society. *Socialist Worker,* Aug. 15, pp. 5–6.

Schafer, R. (1992), *Retelling a Life.* New York: Basic Books.

Sennett, R., & Cobb, J. (1969), *The Hidden Injuries of Class.* New York: Vintage.

Slavin, M. O., & Kriegman, D. (1998), Why the analyst needs to change: Toward a theory of conflict, negotiation, and mutual influence in the therapeutic process. *Psychoanal. Dial.,* 8:247–284.

Slochower, J. (1999), Erotic complications. *Internat. J. Psycho-Anal.,* 80:1119–1130.

Zizek, S. (1999), The spectre of ideology. In: *The Zizek Reader,* ed. E. Wright & E. Wright. Malden, MA: Blackwell.

8

Intimate Refusals:
A Politics of Objecthood*

Anne Anlin Cheng

▼ ▼ ▼ ▼ ▼

In the 1930s, social psychologists Kenneth and Mamie Clark conducted a series of experiments—the by now famous "doll tests"—designed to study how African American children perceive racial difference, if at all. In interview after interview, the majority of the African American children, including 3-year-olds, when gave the choice, found the brown dolls to be "bad" and preferred instead to play with the "good," white dolls. Several of the children went on to identify the white dolls as the ones "most like themselves." The kids not only displayed an awareness of racial difference, but also appeared to have processed the symbolic values of that difference: that white dolls connote "whiteness" and that whiteness connotes security and probity. In Kenneth Clark's words, what was most difficult for the adults to witness was in fact the depth of these children's understanding:

> We were really disturbed by our findings, and we sat on them for a number of years.... Some of these children ... were reduced to crying when presented with the dolls and asked to identify with them. They looked at me as if I were the devil for putting them in this predicament. Let me tell you, it was a traumatic experience for me as well. (Clark, cited in Kluger, 1975, p. 318)[1]

---

*This chapter is a summary and reconsideration of arguments developed in *The Melancholy of Race: Psychoanalysis, Assimilation, and Hidden Grief* (New York: Oxford University Press, 2000).

[1]Quoted by Richard Kluger, *Simple Justice: The History of* Brown v. Board of Education *and Black America's Struggle for Equality.* New York: Vintage Books, 1975, p. 318.

Clark's consternation at the moral and political implications of his findings pales in comparison with the polemics that followed this research. The notion of racial injury, its materiality and its ghostliness, will continue to the one of the most contested and vexing issues haunting American courtrooms, boardrooms, and classrooms.

As many readers have recognized, the Kenneth Clark experiment was the key but explosive evidence in the landmark case to desegregate America, *Brown v. Board of Education* (1954). Arguably the most celebrated and most vilified decision ever to come out of the Supreme Court, *Brown* and its legacy highlight our nation's continued struggle over the construction of social meaning at the conjoined site of racial injury and racial desire. And behind the struggle lies a larger question: What kind of a social claim can the psyche make at all?

The haunting specter of racial injury and its impact on both individuals and American civic life has never been exorcized even as its meaning remains contested. In the years since *Brown*, psychologists and sociologists have repeatedly staged versions of the Clark experiment, producing contradictory interpretations and ongoing debate. Ten years after *Brown*, in an ironic turn, the same experiment initially deployed by Thurgood Marshall was recruited by white segregationists to challenge the *Brown* decision.[2] To this day, legal scholars struggle to redefine the place of "psychological evidence" in court.[3] And as recently as 1999, psychologist Claude M. Steele, aware of the history behind the notion of racial damage and anxious not to repeat the damage hypothesis, nonetheless posits that material factors such as socioeconomic differences are not the primary culprits in the inferior test performances of African American college students. Steele locates the psychological impact of racism in what he calls the "stereotype threat" that can haunt African American students and hinder their academic performances.[4] It would seem that more than six decades after Dr. Clark testified that "this type of [racial] wound stays raw for a life time,"[5] the "wound" endures, not only in the individual psyche, but in the American national psyche as well.

To speak of psychological injury resulting from racial discrimination is a tricky matter, fraught with political and ethical pitfalls. On the one hand, we criticize the perspective that racism has wreaked psychical damage on racial

---

[2]*Stell v. Savannah-Chatham County Board of Education*. (1963), 220 F Supp. 677.

[3]For a summary of this ongoing debate over the uses and status of social science and psychological evidence in what is known as the Brandeis Brief, see Herbert Hovenkamp (1985), "Social science and segregation before *Brown*," *Duke Law Journal,* 85 (June–September):624–643.

[4]Claude M. Steele, "Thin Ice: 'stereotype threat and black college students, *Atlantic Monthly 284,* 2(1999 August):44–54.

[5]*Briggs v. Elliot,* 342 U.S. 350 (1952). Also quoted in Kluger, ibid., 320.

minorities for its potential to re-victimize these individuals. On the one hand, there is wide agreement that the discourse of racial damage has played a key role in promoting civil rights reform during the past half century. It seems theoretically, pragmatically, and ethically important for us today as individuals and as a nation to begin to confront the psychical imprints of racial grief in ways that recourse to neither denial nor sentimentalization.

Some initial steps toward this challenge might include: the distinction of the psychical from the essential, the expansion of the discourse of injury from the solely material to the invisible yet formative consequences of discrimination, and a rigorous examination of the *constitutive* role that authority and abjection play in subject formation for *both* subjects of power and subjects of discrimination. Today, I concentrate on the last point and sketch out ways in which psychoanalysis as a school of meditation on intersubjectivity can not only elucidate the relationship between power and identification, but also supply a crucial perspective in redefining the terms of liberal politics. Indeed, psychoanalytic insights into the intimate relationship among power, fantasy, desire, and identification can offer a vocabulary for addressing racial grief that legal and sociological discourse often eschews.

It is precisely racism's affective crisis, its insidious conflation between the lack and excess of love, that requires acknowledgment. There is, of course, the truism that some discriminated subjects have internalized dominant demands, but this in fact says very little about the mechanism of psychological subjection and ignores altogether the mechanisms of identification fundamental to subjectivity itself. Indeed, more often not, evocation of this formula signals either pious indignation or simple resignation, or worse, a moralism that suggests "bad identifications" ought to be cured by "knowing better." Yet, as too many of us are aware, knowing better has rarely ever saved anyone from their pathologies or desires. Indeed, one of the most powerful legacies of psychoanalysis for modern societies must surely be its critique of utilitarianism: the wisdom that human beings do not always act in accordance with their own supposed best interests. Even more pertinently, psychoanalysis insists on the possibility that intrasubjectivity exists as a form of intersubjectivity and that intersubjectivity often speaks in the voice of intrasubjectivity: a mutually reinforcing system. And it is here that psychoanalysis can offer the most compelling intervention into discussions of minority subjectivity and the phenomenon of "internalization." For even as we recognize how deeply uncomfortable it is to talk about the ways the racialized minority is as bound to racial melancholia as the dominant subject, we must also see how urgent it is that we start to look at the historical, cultural, and cross racial consequences of racial wounding and to situate these effects as crucial, formative elements of individual, national, and cultural identities. Only then can we begin to go on to analyze how racialized people as complex psychical beings deal with the objecthood thrust on them, which to a great extent informs how they negotiate sociality and nationality. Within the reductive notion of "internalization" lies a world of complex negotiations that is as much about surviving as embodying grief.

In 1917, Freud wrote his essay "Mourning and Melancholia," which proposes two different kinds of grief.[6] According to Freud, "mourning" is a healthy response to loss; it is finite in character and accepts substitution (that is, the lost object can be relinquished and eventually replaced). Mourning is healthy because, Freud tells us, "we rest assured that after a lapse of time, it will be overcome" (p. 280). "Melancholia," on the other hand, is pathological; it is interminable in nature and refuses substitution (that is, the melancholic cannot "get over" loss.) The melancholic is, one might say, psychically stuck.

Moreover, "loss" exists as a very curious condition in melancholia. In order not to have to recognize loss, the melancholic introjects and takes in the lost object, creating at once a crypt and an identification within. Freud goes as far as to call this process a form of psychical cannibalism. If the story ends here, this might make melancholia a pretty effective, if selfish, way of dealing with loss. But of course the "swallowing" does not, cannot, go down easily. By taking in the object, the melancholic has taken in also all the ambivalent feelings he/she has for that object: no longer just love or longing but also profound resentment. Although the source of the resentment is the object, if we were to follow the logic of the consumption, that the thing-within is now the ego, then we would also have to see that the plaint can no longer properly belong to either subject or object since the two are now intrinsically (con)fused. In a sense, the melancholic is not melancholic because he or she has lost something per se but because he or she has introjected that which he or she at once denigrates, longs for, and is constituted by.

I am interested in what Freudian melancholia (both its articulation and aporia) can contribute to our understanding of the process by which the introjection of an other constitutes self-identity. For one of the most provocative aspects of Freudian melancholia must surely be what it says about the intimate connections among loss, its compensation, and subjectivity itself. What kind of subject lives with—maybe even *through*—loss?

Let us begin by reexamining the condition of pathology to which melancholia has been assigned, for one of the most curious things about this essay comes from Freud own penchant for the pathological. This is not

---

[6]Sigmund Freud (1917), "Mourning and Melancholia," *Standard Edition,* 14:239–260 (London: Hogarth Press, 1955).

just another example of Freud proclivity for the "abnormal"; instead, something crucial happens to the status of the pathological in this essay about melancholia that will prove to be the key to much of Freud thinking about identification and ego formation. Specifically, what starts out in the melancholic paper as a diagnosis of a pathological form of grief slowly turns into a potential description of subjectivity itself. Not only does mourning and melancholia start to resemble one another within the essay as many of Freud binary terms tend to do *and* not only does Freud himself later in life admits this binary opposition to be false, but in fact the mechanisms of melancholia as developed by Freud in this essay start to look uncannily like the very mechanisms of identification itself. That is, the apparently abnormal way of digesting loss in the condition of melancholia turns out to occupy an inversely primary role in psychical formation. Indeed, Freud tells us that melancholia affords us the rare chance of viewing "the constitution of the human ego" (Freud, 1917, p. 247). It is as if melancholia serves as something of a latchkey in the unveiling of the ego. Freud writes,

> An object-choice, an attachment of the libido to a particular person, had at one time existed; then, owing to a real slight or disappointment coming from this loved person, the object-relationship was shattered. The result was not the normal one of a withdrawal of the libido from this object and a displacement of it on to a new one, but something different.... [T]he free libido ... was withdrawn into the ego ... to establish an *identification* of the ego with the abandoned object. *Thus the shadow of the object fell upon the ego....* (Freud, 1917, pp. 248–250; emphasis added)

In this account, the ego comes into being as a psychical object, as a perceptual object, only *after the "shadow of the object" has fallen on it*. As Judith Butler and others have pointed out, this melancholic eating of the lost object may say something about not only the peculiar condition of melancholia but also the very constitution of the human ego.[7] By taking in the other-made-ghostly—through the profits of impoverishment—the melancholic subject fortifies him or herself and grows rich. Melancholia thus designates not just *a* but potentially *the* mode of ego formation. This also suggests that the history of the ego is the history of its losses, just as the history of identification is the history of ghosts. (This, by the way, is one reason why I called psychoanalysis a theory not of intra- but of intersubjectivity, a perspective that highlights subjectivity itself as already a political ground.)

---

[7] Judith Butler, *The Psychic Life of Power: Theories in Subjection* (Palo Alto, CA: Stanford University Press, 1997); Elin Diamond, "The Violence of 'We': Politicizing Identification." In: *Critical Theory and Performance*, ed. Janelle G. Reinelt and Joseph R. Roach (Ann Arbor: University of Michigan Press, 1992); Diana Fuss, *Identification Papers* (New York: Routledge, 1995).

What Freud does not explicitly address but what must be a consequence of this psychical drama is the continuous *work* required to sustain this elaborate structure of loss-but-not-loss: that is, the multiple layers of refusal and exclusion that the melancholic must exercise in order to keep up this system. The melancholic must first deny loss as loss in order to sustain the fiction of possession. The melancholic would then have to make sure that the "object" never returns, for such a return would surely jeopardize the cannibalistic project that, one might note, is a form of possession more intimate than any material relationship could produce. Thus although it may seem reasonable to imagine that the griever may wish for the return of the loved one, once this digestive process has occurred, the ego may in fact not want or cannot afford such homecoming. As Thomas Mann once observed:

> The calling back of the dead, or the desirability of calling them back, was a ticklish matter after all. At bottom, and boldly confessed, the desire does not exist; it is a *misapprehension* precisely as impossible as the thing itself, as we should soon see if nature once let it happen. What we call mourning for our dead is perhaps not so much grief at not being able to call them back as it is grief at not being able to want to do so. (1969, p. 596)

Read against Freud thesis, Mann account of grief dilemma really elucidates a melancholic ambivalence toward the object. In short, at the juncture of having to legislate loss, *loss* turns into *active exclusion* in the melancholic landscape.

In a sense, exclusion, rather than loss, is the real stake of melancholic retention. Indeed, Freud's text itself may be considered quite melancholic in *its* ruthless exclusion of the object. For the ego is not the only ghostly presence in this essay. That is, the melancholic ego is a haunted ego, at once made ghostly and embodied in its ghostliness, but the "object" is also ghostly—not only because its image has been introjected or incorporated within the melancholic psyche—but also because Freud is finally not that interested in what happens to the object or its potential for subjective conditions.[8] The melancholic ego is formed and fortified by a spectral drama, whereby the subject sustains itself through the ghostly emptiness of a lost Other.

This peculiar and uneasy dynamic of retaining a denigrated but sustaining loss that resonates acutely against the mechanisms of the racial imaginary as they have been fashioned in this country. Although psychoanalytic

---

[8]It is beyond the scope of this brief chapter, but I should note that in psychoanalytic theory, incorporation and introjection have for the most part been understood as similar processes, and here I am using the terms interchangeably. There are, however, theorists (such as Nicolas Abraham and Maria Took) who have argued for a differentiation between the terms, although I would argue that the differentiation of these terms tend to reproduce, rather than disturb, the original Freudian binarism of the normative versus the pathological.

readings of melancholia have been mostly theorized in relation to gender formation,[9] melancholia also presents a particularly apt paradigm for elucidating the activity and components of racialization. To put it bluntly, racialization in America may be said to operate through the institutional process of producing a dominant, standard, white national ideal, which is sustained by the exclusion-yet-retention of racialized others. The national topography of centrality and marginality legitimizes itself by retroactively positing the racial other as always other and lost to the heart of the nation. Legal exclusion naturalizes the more complicated "loss" of the unassimilable racial other.

Melancholia offers much more than an analogy for thinking about how racial exclusion works in American sociality. It provides a critical paradigm for understanding how American nationality narrate and legislate—both materially and as a cultural memory—the "loss" of the unassimilable racial other. Freud notion of this melancholic, uncomfortable swallowing and its implications for how loss is processed and the secured as exclusion lend provocative insights into the nature of the racial other seen as "the foreigner within" America. In a sense, the racial other is in fact quite "assimilated"

---

[9]Psychoanalytic melancholia has mostly been read in relation to gender identities in the works of Judith Butler on heterosexual melancholia in *Bodies That Matter: On the Discursive Limits of Sex* (New York; Routledge, 1993), Kara Silverman on femininity and the melancholic nature of the negative oedipal complex in *The Acoustic Mirror: The Female Voice in Psycho-Analysis and Cinema* (Bloomington: Indiana University Press, 1988), and Juliana Schiesari's *The Gendering of Melancholia: Feminism, Psychoanalysis, and the Symbolics of Loss in Renaissance Literature* (Ithaca, NY: Cornell University Press, 1992). Franz Fanion in *Black Skin, White Masks* (New York: Grove Press, 1967) is the first to gesture toward the conceptualization of race as melancholic, even though he never talks specifically about melancholia. In his discussion of "narcissism," he refers to the "black body" as "distorted, recooked, clad in mourning" (p. 112). Butler theorizes specifically about "drag" as a melancholic incorporation fantasy, whereby gender performance allegorizes a loss it cannot grieve but must act out. For Butler, homosexuality is the unreeved loss for heterosexuality, the melancholia at the heart of heterosexuality: "Heterosexual melancholia is the melancholy by which a masculine gender is formed from the refusal to grieve the masculine as a possibility of love" (p. 235). Heterosexuality is thus constantly resurrecting and burying the gay figure ... hence the guilt about homosexuality. Heterosexuality is the "lost, proper" identity that represents the melancholia of homosexuality—a loss that can only be acted out as the desire for "straightness." Silverman's chapter on "Disembodying the Female Voice" in *The Acoustic Mirror* conducts an especially close reading of Freud and points out that the Freudian definition of female-gingering is essentially melancholic: the Oedipal complex by which a "girl becomes a girl," when she is asked to repudiate and disidentify with the mother even as she suffers from continual cultural pressures to identify with the mother, creates a melancholic condition of unreeved loss and self-denial/denigration. Silverman works to revalue a sustained identification with the mother.

into—or more accurately, most uneasily digested by—American nationality. The history of American national idealism has always been caught in this melancholic bind between incorporation and rejection. If one of the ideals that sustained the American nation since its beginning has been its unique proposition that "all men are created equal," then one of America's ongoing national mortifications must be its history of acting otherwise. Although all nations have their repressed histories and traumatic atrocities, American melancholia is particularly acute because America is *founded* on the very ideals of freedom and liberty whose betrayals have been repeatedly covered over. Even as the economic, material, and philosophical advances of the nation are built on a series of legalized exclusions (of African Americans, Jewish Americans, Chinese Americans, Japanese Americans, and so on) and the labor provided by those excluded, it is also a history busily disavowing those repudiations. In his essay "The Two Declarations of American Independence," Michael Rogin suggests that this paradox erupts on the very surface of the Declaration of Independence:

> The Declaration of Independence, demanding freedom from enslavement to England for a new nation built on slavery, is the core product of that m alliance in political theory.... [The Declaration] bequeathed a Janus-faced legacy to the new nation—the logic on the one hand that the equality to which white men were naturally born could be extended to women and slaves, and the foundation on the other of white freedom on black servitude. (Post, 1999, pp. 75–76)[10]

Melancholia thus may be said to describe both an American ideological dilemma and its constitutional practices.

It is at those moments when America is most shamefaced and traumatized by its betrayal of its own democratic ideology (the genocide of Native Americans, slavery, segregation, immigration discrimination) that it most virulently—and *melancholically*—espouses human value and brotherhood. In his *Notes on the State of Virginia,* Thomas Jefferson, for example,

---

[10]Michael Rogin, "The Two Declaration of American Independence," collected in *Race and Representation: Affirmative Action,* edited by Robert Post and Michael Rogin. Berkeley: University of California Press, pp. 75–76. In an essay in the *Washington Post,* Roger Wilkins proposes that there has been a price for the Declaration's doubleness: "By the time Thomas Jefferson wrote into the Declaration of Independence the sweeping egalitarian claim that underlies our myth of classlessness, the colonies had nurtured a slave culture and the psychic distortions required to sustain it for more than a century. A decade later, the Founding Fathers wrote slavery and its attendant racism into the Constitution, thus giving our racist ideology a legal standing that our egalitarian aspirations—set forth in our non binding Declaration—did not have. Racism was thus lathered into the foundations of our nation, and nothing—not the Civil War, not Reconstruction, not the Civil Rights revolution—has been able to blast it out of our culture and our psyches." (Wilkins, Dec. 5, 1990, p. A25)

meditates on his discomfort about the apparent discrepancy between the Declaration of Independence and the colonial practice of slavery only to console himself by reassuring himself and the readers that the inhumanity of blacks exempted them from considerations such as human rights, freedom, and equality. blacks were seen as lost to moral and human concerns. Through this consolation of philosophy which exemplified his melancholic relationship to blackness Jefferson disentangles the new republic from the ideological burdens of slavery and at the same time reconciles slavery to the ideology of the new nation.[11] American values therefore tend to acquire their sharpest outline *through,* not in spite of, the nexus of investment and anxiety provoked by slavery and other institutions of discrimination. As Eric Lott and Michael Rogin have so well demonstrated in their works on blackface minstrelsy, the dominant culture's relation to the raced other displays an entangled network of repulsion and sympathy, fear and desire, repudiation and identification. It is this imbricated but denied relationship that forms the basis of white racial melancholia.

But having laid out the structure of white racial melancholia, what about the so-called racialized Other? What is the implications of this critique of white racial melancholia for the so-called minority subjects? Are they mere objects of dominant melancholia or are they also melancholic? If so, how? In short, let us ask the question that Freud does not ask: What is the subjectivity of the melancholic object?

I propose that the racial Other is not just the so-called object of white racial melancholia, but he or she is also a subject of racial melancholia, whereby his or her racial identity is imaginatively reinforced through the introjection of a lost, never-possible perfection, an inarticulable loss that comes to inform the individual's sense of his or her own subjectivity. This incorporation of and identification with a never-possible ideal, however, does not necessarily imply compliance and victimization. As we have already noted, this "consumption" is neither easy nor stable even as it is constitutive. Much more than a mere analogy for what is commonly called the "internalization" of discriminated subjects, Freudian melancholia unpacks the mechanisms of loss, management, and compensation that underwrite that condition.

---

[11]Both violent vilification and the indifference to vilification express, rather than invalidate, the melancholic dynamic. Indeed, melancholia offers a powerful critical tool precisely because it theoretically *accounts* for the guilt and the denial of guilt, the blending of shame and omnipotence in the racialist imaginary. Segregation and colonialism are internally fraught institutions not because they have eliminated the other but because they need the very thing they hate or fear. This is why trauma, so often associated with discussions of racial denigration, in focusing on a structure of crisis on the part of the victim, misses the violators' own dynamic process at stake in such denigration. Melancholia gets more potently at the notion of constitutive loss that expresses itself in both violent and muted ways, producing confirmation as well as crisis, knowledge as well as aporia.

Let me offer an example of how insights into the melancholic dynamics of American race relations can help deepen our readings of scenes of racial rejection and subjection. To do so, I want to evoke a "classic" text about the nature of racial subjection in American literary history, that is, Ralph Ellison's 1952 novel *Invisible Man*. At first glance a text that thematizes the invisibility of blackness, *Invisible Man* in close examination offers us a rather complicated and enigmatic vision of the nature of blindness and disenfranchisement. In the opening sequence to the novel, after telling us that he is invisible "because [white] people refuse to see [him]" (p. 48), the narrator relates a violent confrontation between himself and a white man:

> One night I accidentally bumped into a man ... he looked insolently out of his blue eyes and cursed me ... I yelled, "Apologize! Apologize!" But he continued to curse and struggle, and I butted him again and again until he went down heavily ... I kicked him profusely ... when it occurred to me that the man had not *seen* me, actually; that he, as far as he knew, was walking in midst of a walking nightmare ... a man almost killed by a phantom.[12]

I call this scene enigmatic because the description opens up a range of questions about the difference between perception and projection, between action and reaction. To begin with, from the narrator's perspective, we see the white man's "insolence" as anger from having to confront what he presumably did not want to see. The white man's curse, on being bumped, expresses an active wish to deny the invisible object now demanding a competing presence. According to the narrator subsequent reading, what troubles the white man is the "bumping"—that *point of contact with invisibility*—that has in fact historically ensured the white man's ability to see and to not see. In a sense, this white man both sees and does not see the black man in that alley. In describing a white store owner who had difficulties seeing a little black girl right under his nose trying to buy candy from him in *The Bluest Eye,* Toni Morrison depicts a similar moment of seeing/not-seeing. She describes the man as having been "blunted by a permanent awareness of loss" (p. 48). In this subtly turned phrase, Morrison has located the precise and peculiar nature of "loss" in white racial melancholia: teetering between the known and the unknown, the seen and the deliberately unseen, the racial other constitutes an oversight that is consciously made unconscious—naturalized over time as absence, as complementary negative space. It is precisely the slippery space between *loss* and *exclusion* that racial myopia effects. Part of the central dilemma of dominant racial melancholia—since its authority is constituted, sustained, and made productive by this system of the suspended other—is

---

[12]Ralph Ellison, *Invisible Man* (New York: Vintage, 1990), p. 5. All further citations from this text come from this edition.

that it does not really want the lost other to return (or demand its right of way).

At the same time, when we enter Ellison scene more fully, we have to ask: Is the white man the only one suffering from not-seeing in this scenario? The writing is ambiguous: Who is the invisible one? If the narrator bumps into the white man, is not the white man the one who is invisible to the black man? The narrator bumps into what *he* did not see and then accuses the other of blindness. If we do not take the narrator's account at its surface value, it is conceivable that the white man cursed the black man for his clumsiness rather than for racist reasons (that masculinist rather than racial confrontation may be at stake) and that the narrator's interpretation of "insolence" may be itself a melancholic response to the (historically) incendiary sign of "blue eyes" and his own self-denigration and wounded pride. That invisibility is rarely a one-way street is one of racial melancholia most insidious effects. In this confrontation, there is potential mutual invisibility and mutual projection. Indeed, the racial moment is born out of this dynamic locking of the two men in mutual antagonism. In a response that is both macho and hysterical, the narrator demonstrates that he is trapped, not by having been seen as invisible *but by suspecting himself to be so. This* is racial melancholia for the raced subject: the internalization and anticipation of rejection—*and* the installation of a scripted context of perception. Within this script, the invisible man's racial radar must be seen as *simultaneously* perspicacious and paranoid. The invisible man is both a melancholic object and a melancholic subject, both the one excluded and the one performing the exclusion, the one lost and the one losing.

Thus if the white man in Ellison's "Prologue" represents, so to speak, white racial melancholia, then the invisible man dramatizes the other face of racial melancholia. In an intense response at once macho and hysterical, Ellison narrator reveals that he is trapped not only by having been seen as invisible but also by *suspecting himself to be so.* His perception is subject to a script that he is unable—and indeed cannot afford—to ignore. To overlook the racist potential in the scene is to be blind to history, but to assume that potential is to be enslaved by that history. If the white man is caught in a melancholic bind of denying that which fortifies his authority and integrity, then the black man is caught in a *double* melancholic bind: he is *both* a melancholic object and a melancholic subject, the one lost and the one losing, the one excluded and the one performing the exclusion. This internalization of the dominant ideal and its accompanying denigration dramatize racial melancholia for the raced subject: the taking in of a rejecting other, creating a negative self-perception that one must continually negotiate in some form or the other, whether it is to be complied with or resisted. Only in the light of this double melancholia can we understand the narrator racial radar as at once paranoid *and* perspicacious. The invisible man is caught by the web of history, a history at once past and still unfolding. And history itself must be understood as not just material but also psychical reality.

What makes this reading of Ellison writing uncomfortable for many is the fear that it takes away from the impact of white racism in the scene. I would argue instead that it is only in seeing the psychical as well as the historic stakes in the scene that we can truly begin to grasp the expansive and profound effects of racism. Furthermore, what I am calling the invisible man's double melancholia alerts us to, not the impingement of sociality into psychology, but the interdependence of the two, suggesting that we must develop more nuanced vocabulary for thinking about the power and effects of discrimination than one of pious disapproval. By essentially critiquing the ideal of uncompromising individualism so often evoked as the solution to discrimination, our insight into the imbricated, melancholic dynamics of both racist and racial (in the affirmative sense) identification should motivate us to redirect or reframe how we think about political agency.

Instead of debating the politics of identity, we ought to examine the material and psychical conditions under which an identity can take place. In short, the political ground is not identity, but *identification*. As "the psychological process whereby the subject assimilates an aspect, property, or attributes of the other and is transformed, wholly or partially, after the model the other provides" (Laplanche & Pontalis, 1973 p. 205).[13] identification provides the cornerstone on which subjectivity is made possible. It is the underlying process that enables an individual creation of and faith in his or her "identity." As the mechanism that subtends the possibility and the limit of any given identity and as the subjective corollary—indeed, the *vehicle*—for interpersonal negotiation, identification is pivotal to discussions of racial identity and dynamics, because it refers to the elaborate, mediating process that relates self to other, subject to object, inside to outside. *This* site, above all others, must b the place from which we begin to imagine an ethical relationship to the other.

The most intriguing and vexing aspect of identification, as suggested by Freud's work on the complex nature of melancholia, lies in the very confusion between subject and object that occurs in its processes. Contrary to being politically disabling, this confusion signals the importance of exploring identification as a potential site for reimagining an ethics of intersubjective relations. It holds the key to understanding the inherent imbrication between sociality and psychology, an imbrication that identity is designed to disguise. Because "identity" carries the burdens of so much recognizable

[13]Jean Laplanche and J.-B. Pontalis, *The Language of Psychoanalysis* (D. Nicholson Smith, Trans.; New York: Norton, 1973).

social and institutional work, it often ends up acting as something of a red herring preventing us from performing the equally important task of unraveling the deeper identificatory operations—and seductions—producing those identities in the first place. Rather than thinking about what identity can or cannot do, what if we were to ask questions along a different line: How does understanding the potentially intimate relationship between subjecthood and objecthood translate into insights about racial discrimination and denigration?

This problem of mediating the meanings of objecthood or objectness haunts the history of psychoanalysis itself, where the relationship between subjecthood and objecthood has always been ambivalent—ironic because psychoanalysis continues to provide one of the most sustained bodies of work that meditates precisely on this supposed difference. Part of the difficulties of "politicizing" psychoanalytic thinking can, in fact, be traced to the ambiguous status of the so-called "object," especially when that object refers to a person. When analysts such as Freud, Winnecott, or Klein refer to an object, they are more often than not referring to a structural position occupied (be it by persons, ideas, or matter) in psychical pattern of desires (that is, the object of a drive or affection). As I already noted, Freud himself is notoriously disinterested in the "realness" or the potential subjectivity of the object.[14] To be a psychoanalytic object is, by definition, to have already relinquished certain subjective properties and to have been entered into the subjective, fantasmatic landscape of another imaginary. Part of the task of bringing psychoanalysis into conversation with sociopolitical history lies in expanding and nuancing the very notion of the object. It is my proposition that the facile elision between the material and ghostly status of "being an object" calls most urgently for the rethinking of the notion of agency as a fundamental basis for political action.

Much of the philosophical formulations of the notion of political agency rely on subject-based thinking, for obviously good reasons. That is, given the objectification of certain groups of persons, the counteroffer of subjecthood surely appears as a good antidote. I am thinking of Jessica Benjamin's clinical notion of intersubjectivity, which attempts to replace the subject–object relation with a subject–subject relation as an ethical paradigm for patient-analyst dynamics; Drucilla Cornell's reworking of "mimesis" as a nonviolent ethical relation to the other; and Kaja Silverman's vision of "heteropathic identification."[15] All these meditations recourse with sincerity to some notion of will or intention—or, at least, some privileged position in which one can determine one action in relations to another. The ethical

---

[14] In Freud mapping of the "lost object" in melancholia is a peculiarly murderous one, in which the supposedly long-for return of the lost object would in fact seriously jeopardize the *jouissance* of melancholia, hence sabotaging the ego-constituting mechanism that *is* melancholia.

position in the face of a history of objectification thus coincides with the injunction to recognize the other as "like subject," to borrow Benjamin words. In a sense, we can describe the ethical calls being called for by the writers just mentioned as demanding the duty to purify one desires. There is, of course, much to be gained by this search for this proper, self-corrective subject. And perhaps in everyday life the most we can hope for is the ability to discipline ourselves in light of our desires. Yet one of the insights offered to us through understanding the melancholic constitution of the racial subject precisely reminds us that such a self-corrective position may not be possible. How do we confer "subjecthood" on a subject whose subjectivity has already been seriously compromised, especially if the conferral of recognition paradoxically *rests on* that subject status as injury itself? (This is one of the fundamental paradoxes of the liberal "recovery" of "minority" subjects: more often than not, the rescue merely renames the injury.)

Understanding the melancholic imbrication in the heart of racial identification presses us to ask: What happens in contexts where such a privileged position of choice is not possible? How do we conceive of choice and ethical action in a crisis of consent? More significantly, these moments of crisis may not be as exceptional to our everyday living as we would like to imagine. It is precisely at the moments of most quotidian and most jeopardized individuality (when we discover that our subjective mastery is indebted to the imperial and compulsive taken in of the Other) that we discern most urgently the need for and the difficulties of formulating an ethics of intersubjectivity. The politics of vision and of agency clearly calls for terms beyond "subject" versus "object."

I suggest that psychoanalysis is most politically cogent when it gestures toward that third term beyond subject and object. That is, it is precisely psychoanalysis critique, rather than consolidation, of subjecthood that I think renders psychoanalysis a most compelling *political* discourse.[16] Given the compromised precondition behind subjective certitude, the answer is obviously not to claim access to either full subjective agency or complete subjective relinquishment, but to acknowledge that human relations are structured along that difference. We might conceive of ethics, not as solving, but as pro-

---

[15]Jessica Benjamin, *Like Subjects, Love Objects: Essays on Recognition and Sexual Difference* (New Haven, CT: Yale University Press, 1995); Drucilla Cornell, *Beyond Accommodation: Ethical Feminism, Deconstruction, and the Law* (New York: Routledge, 1991); Kaja Silverman, *The Threshold of the Visible World* (New York: Routledge, 1996.)

[16]It is beyond the scope of this chapter, but the work of Jacques Lacan, I would suggest, offers a powerful springboard from which to develop the notion of an ethics that is *not* subject-based. His work on the Gaze, for instance, unravels our illusions of subjective mastery even as it re-asserts the importance of understanding that subjective *failure* as precisely the very foundation for ethical and political action. See my essay "Passing, Natural Selection, and Love Failure: Ethics of Survival from Chang-rae Lee to Jacques Lacan," *American Literary History,* Fall, 2005, (17:3), 553–574.

ceeding from the basis of this subjective dilemma. In short, melancholic complicity encapsulates the ethical dimension in the realm of desire.

To me, this misrecognized, traumatic, and imbricated encounter with the Other lies at the heart of the political. The realization of one radical susceptibility to the Other that is lived as a division/alienation within the Self must be the very foundation on which to rebuild an ethics of relationality. As Copjec (1994) elegantly puts it: "It is always and only this division of the subject that psychoanalysis insist on, not only because of the attempt to establish an ethics on the basis of its disavowal is a mistake but, more importantly, because it is unethical" (p. 98).[17] And it is precisely the collusion between "lack" as the precondition for subjectivity and "loss" as material condition of racial abjection that requires acknowledgment. There is no political "remedy" for this complicity between psychical and material impoverishment. There is only the ethical injunction to acknowledge this imbricated relationship.

Is there a way to fundamentally and radically reimagine agency freed from an attachment to subjecthood? Can we perhaps imagine freedom *through* objectness? I suggest that the answer is—must be—yes, given that objectness is the historic precondition for the "minority" subject. But this answer also means that we would have to reimagine altogether the meaning of self-making, as well as altering a host of explicit and implicit terms about race relations in the socio-historical realm: compensation and loss, love and hate, mastery and subjection. If we were to acknowledge the racialized subject as truly a subject, then we must also be willing to acknowledge those inevitable moments when sovereign subjectivity fails. What remains to be thought through is the possibility that the answer to the political dilemma of identification may not rest in trying to wrestle out a space of distance between self and other, subject and object, but to go instead for the opposite, to undertake the difficult task of *immersion*. If we were to be courageous or patient enough to relinquish the need to rectify, moralize, or idealize a subject–object relation and seriously entertain the implications of separating ethics from its rootedness in the notion of ideal individualism, then I think we will be able to reimagine political freedom in such a way as to still accommodate political conditions—to be able to imagine a future that is not merely, as Toni Morrison once wrote about liberal progress, "adjustment without improvement."

The shadow of the object fell upon the ego. What are truly insidious and difficult to address about systematic discrimination and denigration are the ways in which they *mime* psychical modes of identification. This *is* the precondition of subjectivity and hence the precondition for ethical and political

---

[17]Joan Copjec, *Read My Desire: Lacan Against the Historicist* (Cambridge, MA: The MIT Press, 1994), p. 98.

considerations. The only ethical relationship we can imagine in relation to another must account for rather than deny our melancholic intimacy to that other. In short, the crisis of love must be the condition for an ethics of love.

References

Benjamin, J. (1995), *Like Subjects, Love Objects: Essays on Recognition and Sexual Difference*. New Haven, CT: Yale University Press.
Briggs v. Elliot. (1952). 342 U.S. 350.
Brown v. Board of Education, 347 U.S. 484 (1954).
Butler, J. (1993), *Bodies That Matter: On the Discursive Limits of Sex.* New York: Routledge.
Cheng, A. A. (2005), Passing, natural selection, and love failure: Ethics of survival from Chang-rae Lee to Jacques Lacan. *American Literary History,* 17:3, 553–574.
Copjec, J. (1994), *Read My Desire: Lacan Against the Historicist.* Cambridge, MA: The MIT Press.
Cornell, D. (1991), *Beyond Accommodation: Ethical Feminism, Deconstruction, and the Law.* New York: Routledge, 1991.
Diamond, E. (1992), The Violence of "We": Politicizing Identification. In *Critical Theory and Performance,* ed. J. G. Reinelt & J. R. Roach. Ann Arbor: University of Michigan Press, pp. 390–398.
Ellison, R. (1990), *Invisible Man.* New York: Vintage.
Fanon, F. (1967), *Black Skin, White Masks.* New York: Grove Press.
Freud, S. (1917), Mourning and Melancholia. *Standard Edition,* 14:239–260. London: Hogarth Press.
Fuss, D. (1995), *Identification Papers.* New York: Routledge.
Hovenkamp, H. (1985), Social science and segregation before *Brown. Duke Law Journal,* 85:624–643.
Kluger, R. (1975), *Simple Justice: The History of* Brown v. Board of Education *and Black America Struggle for Equality.* New York: Vintage Books.
Laplanche, J., & J.-B. Pontalis. (1973), *The Language of Psychoanalysis* (D. Nicholson Smith, Trans.). New York: Norton.
Morrison, T. (1994), *The Bluest Eye.* New York: Plune.
Rogin, M. (1999), The Two Declaration of American Independence. In: *Race and Representation: Affirmative Action,* ed. R. Post & M. Rogin. Berkeley: University of California Press, pp. 75–76.
Schiesari, J. (1992), *The Gendering of Melancholia: Feminism, Psychoanalysis, and the Symbolics of Loss in Renaissance Literature.* Ithaca: Cornell University Press.
Silverman, K. (1988), *The Acoustic Mirror: The Female Voice in Psycho-Analysis and Cinema.* Bloomington: Indiana University Press.
——— (1996), *The Threshold of the Visible World* New York: Routledge.
Steele, C. M. (1999), Thin Ice: "Stereotype Threat" and black College Students. *Atlantic Monthly,* 284:2, 44–54.
Stell v. Savannah-Chatham County Board of Education. (1963). 220 F Supp. 677.
Wilkins, R. (December 5, 1990), "White Racism Is Still the Problem." *Washington Post,* final edition, p. A25.

9

Desegregating Love: Transnational Adoption, Racial Reparation, and Racial Transitional Objects

David L. Eng, PhD
Shinhee Han, PhD

▼ ▼ ▼ ▼ ▼

Although it may read like a single-authored essay, this article is part of an ongoing collaboration. We—a Chinese American male humanities professor and a Korean American female psychotherapist—discussed and wrote this case presentation and critical commentary together. Investigating how a more speculative humanities-based approach to psychoanalysis might enhance and supplement its clinical applications, and vice-versa, is crucial. In the context of race and racial difference, which continue to remain undertheorized across various disciplinary deployments of psychoanalysis, such a critical venture is all the more urgent.

Transnational adoption involves the intersection of two very powerful origin myths—the return to mother and to motherland. In this case history of a Korean transnational adoptee, Mina, problems relating to Asian immigration, assimilation, and racialization are absolutely central to the patient's psychic predicaments. First-generation Asian immigrant parents and their second-generation American-born children typically negotiate problems of immigration, assimilation, and racialization as intergenerational and *intersubjective* conflicts. However, the transnational adoptee often struggles with these issues in social and psychic isolation. In Mina's case, she mourns the loss of her birth mother and motherland—a repressed past prior to her "official" arrival and history in the United States—as a profoundly unconscious and *intrasubjective* affair.

Moreover, we witness in Mina the ways these significant losses trigger a series of primitive psychical responses such that we are forced to rethink Melanie Klein's (1935) theories of infancy—of good and bad objects, as well as good and bad mothers—in terms of good and bad *racialized* objects, as well as good and bad *racialized* mothers. Mina's case history demands, that is, a consideration of racial difference as constitutive of, rather than peripheral to, Klein's fundamental notions of splitting and idealization, depression and guilt, and reinstatement and reparation. In short, we come to recognize that Klein's developmental positions are also *racialized* positions. For Mina, the reparative position ultimately entails the *racial* reparation of the lost and devalued Korean birth mother.

Finally, we focus on the ways Mina's case history draws attention to the materiality of the psychotherapist as a raced subject. In particular, we consider how the transference-countertransference dynamic between the transnational adoptee patient and her Korean American therapist is framed not only by the "public" fact of their shared racial difference but also by the "public" nature of Han's pregnancy during the course of the patient's treatment. We examine how Han's pregnancy constitutes her, to reformulate D. W. Winnicott (1951), as a "racial transitional object" for Mina. In the process, we reconsider Winnicott's theories about "object usage" in relation to Mina's "use" of the therapist to transition into a reparative position for race—one that allows her to resignify her vexed identifications with not only a disparaged Koreanness but also an idealized whiteness. Ultimately, psychic health for the transnational adoptee involves creating space in her psyche for two "good-enough" mothers—the Korean birthmother and the white adoptive mother.

Case Presentation

Mina is a 23-year-old transnational adoptee from Korea. She is a dancer in a renowned New York City ballet company. One of Mina's mentors referred her to me (Han) as she was beginning her first year with the ensemble. (After a couple of white therapists, Mina was specifically seeking a Korean therapist.) Mina carries herself with the natural grace of a ballerina. During our consultations, however, she often sat at the edge of her seat. She is a smart and articulate, though rigid, young woman who sought psychotherapy to understand better the problems in her romantic relationships as well as the "whole adoption thing." She believes that the two are somehow connected.

In her presentation, Mina recounted that, since age 13, she had had a series of white boyfriends. Every relationship was marked by some degree of abuse, mostly verbal. Furthermore, though she boasts of her "sexual power" over men, Mina believes that she was often coerced into sexual relationships with her partners much sooner than she desired. At the start of her sessions with me, she was not in a relationship because she felt that she needed to "figure out" herself first. Mina had a theory that her birth mother had been a college student when she found herself in a precarious and perhaps abusive relationship with a boyfriend. This boyfriend subsequently abandoned her mother when she became pregnant with Mina. Mina spoke angrily about her previous boyfriends and recounted her fantasies concerning the circumstances by which her birth mother had become pregnant. At the same time, Mina blamed herself for consistently choosing "bad boyfriends." Collectively, these failed relationships have had a negative impact on Mina's self-regard. Despite her formidable artistic talents, she suffers from low self-esteem while often displaying excessive intolerance of others.

During our initial consultation, Mina asked how much I knew about Korean transnational adoption as well as "what kind of Korean" I was. She immediately wanted to figure out my attitudes toward adoptees: she wondered if I was adopted, a recent immigrant, born in the United States, from an affluent background. She believes that the overwhelming majority of Koreans in Korea as well as in the U.S. are prejudiced against Korean adoptees. She stated that she does not like Koreans at all. In particular, the Korean nationals with whom she attended dance school "made her sick" with their "Gucci, Louis Vuitton, and Chanel accessories," as well as with their "garish" and "ugly" makeup. She felt especially disconnected from them because they spoke only Korean to one another. "They are in America," she remarked. "Why don't they speak English?" Finally, she accused them of behaving disingenuously. "These girls all have white boyfriends. And they sleep around all the time," she stated. "But they act virginal around other people, as though no one can tell how slutty they really are."

Before I could respond to Mina's statements, she told me that she thought I was a Korean American, but not the type she described. (I am, in fact, a "1.5 generation" Korean immigrant, having moved to the U.S. when I was 13.) I took this as a warning not to carry my Gucci purse to work. At the same time that I wondered if I were going to be a "good-enough" Korean for Mina, I also realized that in all likelihood she did not consider herself a "good-enough" Korean for me. I decided to share with Mina my prior experience with Korean transnational adoption, in particular, my specialty as a postadoption social worker assisting both transnational adoptees and their parents. Skeptically, she replied, "Good." Because of her angry, aggressive, and defensive attitude, I felt unsure whether our relationship would continue beyond our initial consultation. "She's a tough one," I concluded. I thought to myself that I should be careful, or she would group me with those Koreans she hates, or even worse, create a new negative category of Korean just for me.

A white couple from Philadelphia adopted Mina when she was 11 months old. She has a younger brother, also adopted from Korea, who is now a first-year student in a small liberal arts college in the Northeast. Mina describes her brother as an "easy-going kid" who does not seem to have many issues concerning his adoption or Koreanness. She is not very close to him. Mina's mother is a free-lance journalist who often writes for travel magazines. Though her mother was once a full-time reporter, she quit her office job in order to raise Mina and her brother at home. Mina describes her relationship with her mother as very close. They talk on the phone at least once or twice a day. She discloses "everything" to her mother, including her boyfriend problems as well as adoption issues. While Mina feels that her mother offers solid advice, she also worries that her mother "knows too much" and is biased about these topics. Mina looks and sounds confident when she says that her mother would do "anything and everything" she wants her to do. Mina's father is a professor of applied mathematics. She describes him as somewhat distant and "clueless" about her life. However, both are actively involved in Mina's flourishing dance career and often travel from out of town to attend her performances.

Mina reported that her adoption file contained very little information. She was found in a tattered basket at the doorstep of a church in Inchon City, near Seoul, in South Korea. The minister and his wife took Mina to a local police station. From there she was taken to an orphanage. One week after Mina was found, a young woman visited the church to inquire about the infant left at the doorstep. Mina wonders if this woman was her birth mother. She hypothesized that her birth mother was perhaps not a college student, after all, but a "poor whore" who lived in a nearby city. And she stated angrily, "Why didn't the bitch leave just a little more information about me? Like, my name and her name! Did she even think to give me a name?" Mina stated that she has two questions for her birth mother if and when she finds her: "What's my name?" and "Why did you give me up?" After these answers are furnished, she claims she wants nothing further to do with her birth mother or with Korea. Mina's anger toward her Korean birth mother is notable. Unlike other transnational adoptees I have previously treated, youths as well as adults who often created idealized pictures of their lost birth mothers, Mina's negative attitude toward hers is remarkably raw and unrelenting.

During the years at her dance academy, Mina's engagement with her adoption issues was often displaced by school demands. She was the only one of her classmates chosen to join her ballet company upon graduation. Mina was surprised by this achievement. Her teachers had been telling her that, while her technique was superb, she needed to work more on her emotional expression. Shortly after joining the ballet company in the fall, she began treatment with me. Four months later, Mina started seeing a young choreographer, Henry, who was already in another relationship. It started off as a friendship, which quickly evolved into a romantic relationship. This relationship spun Mina's emotions wildly. Her volatile moods were largely contingent on Henry's continued but failed promises to break up with his girlfriend.

As their tumultuous affair progressed, a noticeable pattern emerged. Mina became increasingly dependent on Henry. She organized her daily schedule around his while also taking care of Henry's laundry and cleaning his apartment. Gradually Mina grew exhausted and resentful, though she could not bring herself to end the affair. She wondered if her birth mother had found herself in similar circumstances, resulting in her pregnancy with Mina. A couple of months later, Henry abruptly ended the relationship by announcing that he had decided to become engaged to his girlfriend.

At the time Henry broke up with Mina, I was four months pregnant. As I was in my second trimester, my pregnancy had become noticeable to a few patients. I wondered if Mina had noticed my physical change. I was due to give birth at the end of summer, around the time that Mina was scheduled to return from her summer tour. However, before she departed, I decided to discuss my pregnancy with Mina. When I told her, Mina's reaction was very controlled and polite. And when I asked Mina directly how she felt about my pregnancy, she answered, "Oh, it's fine. You having a baby has nothing to do with my adoption. You're a professional. You'll come back to the office and we will work together as usual."

Despite her initial nonchalance, as my belly swelled, Mina often asked how I was feeling, how much weight I had gained, and whether my pregnancy had been planned. "I know nothing about you," she said. "But I know that you are well educated and independent. So, I don't know if you're having this baby alone, with a man, or even a woman." On further exploration of her fantasies about me, Mina added, "I think you're married and this is a planned pregnancy. You wouldn't be so stupid and just get knocked up." It seemed important to Mina that my baby have two parents who would love and care for him and, most important, keep him.

As her summer tour approached, Mina wanted to know if we could schedule phone sessions while she was away—"just in case." I reassured her that I would be available until I gave birth. At the moment, I wanted to explore with Mina any possible feelings of abandonment, of unacknowledged feelings of envy toward my unborn child. I feared that my pregnancy might raise doubts about our relationship as well as her not feeling "special enough." But as much as I attempted to raise these topics, Mina showed little interest in discussing them. She left for her summer tour soon after these conversations.

During Mina's tour, we more or less kept to our weekly sessions over the telephone, until a couple weeks before I gave birth. After giving birth, I took maternity leave and was not in contact with Mina for two months. After resuming our sessions in late fall, Mina immediately asked if my baby was a boy or a girl and offered warm congratulations. She then delved into her big news: she had just attended an adoption camp. Following the dance tour, Mina had decided to volunteer as a camp counselor for adopted children from Korea as well as China. There, for the first time, she spent an extended period with other Korean adoptee volunteers who had either found their birth mothers (and families) or were contemplating such a search. She experienced an inexplicable drive to absorb their stories, and she began to reconsider her own search for her birth mother. Mina's shift in attitude made me wonder how much of her recent actions were connected to my pregnancy and motherhood.

That fall, Mina joined a Korean adoptee support group as well as a mentoring group for young adopted Chinese girls in New York City. While she expressed envy toward the social and cultural support that these white parents collectively provided to their Chinese daughters, her feelings toward her adoptee support group were quite negative. She described them as a "bunch of screwed-up Korean adoptees who are obsessed with their adoptions." She fears that there is something deeply wrong with her because, like these "screwed-up" peers, she too was adopted.

Indeed, throughout her treatment, Mina expressed blatant prejudices against most minorities—African Americans, Latinos, Jews, Asian Americans, as well as gays and lesbians. For instance, she characterized African Americans as "those lazy blacks who are all in gangs and only know how to steal and kill." She described Latinos as the "dumbest racial group" and Jews as "those who sniff money all day." As for Asian Americans, she embraced the (ostensibly positive) model minority stereotype. She observed, "At least Asian Americans are academically successful and work hard and don't bother anyone." Finally, gays and lesbians were "abnormal" and "flamboyant" people obsessed with sexual display.

It was extremely difficult for me to endure Mina's tirades and rants against these various groups. Mina's prejudices waxed and waned over the course of treatment, and I continued to hold her anger without any direct verbal confrontation, though I grew increasingly concerned about the ways my negative countertransferences might affect her. As I learned more about Mina, however, I began to understand that her bigotry was deeply connected to the fear of being seen by others, and of accepting herself, as a minority. Mina's emphasis from the very beginning of our work together had been, "I'm an American! I have an Asian face but I'm white! My parents are white, and I grew up in a white suburb, and I feel most comfortable around white people." However, under this tough and brittle surface, Mina felt extremely vulnerable and conflicted about her own racial identity, as evidenced not only by her aversion to Koreans in general but also by her vexed identifications with her new friends as "a bunch of screwed-up Korean adoptees." Hence, as I began to feel more empathetic and protective toward Mina, I made a conscious effort to police my disapproval as it arose.

During that fall, Mina spent more and more time with her new Korean adoptee friends. She reported that most of their conversations revolved around what they all called "the search" (for their birth mothers) and the ways in which "the search" often provoked intense rivalry and envy around the amounts and quality of information discovered. For the first time, I began to notice Mina's deep struggle with the idea of beginning her own actual search for her birth mother, one motivated in part by competitiveness with, as well as by a desire to belong to, this group. It became increasingly clear that Mina was starting to come to terms with the great psychological difficulties associated with initiating the search process.

During this period, Mina also volunteered to be a spokesperson at a local adoption agency. There she meets with potential parents to talk about the "do's and don't's" of transnational adoption. Mina tells these potential parents to "embrace the culture and language of their children as their own." In our sessions, she began to express new feelings toward her adoptive parents: "I'm so angry at them for not exposing me to Korean things. I told my mom maybe I'm screwed up because I didn't have anything Korean when I was growing up. I asked her why she didn't do this, and she just says she doesn't know why. It didn't occur to her. How can she say that?"

It seems that Mina's deidealizing of her adoptive mother stems from a feeling that she had intentionally kept Mina away from all things Korean, including her birth mother. In fact, as Mina has become more involved in these various adoption activities, it has become increasingly noticeable to me that she has been regressing and is in greater conflict with her adoptive mother. Nonetheless, Mina calls her every morning and evening to complain about being lonely and unhappy. She blames her mother for her agitated state of mind. But, at the same time, she feels more dependent on her. As a result, her mother has made extra visits to New York.

A year and a half into our sessions, Mina's desire to take action on "the search" congealed. She decided to go to Korea for a big adoption conference during the upcoming summer, and she planned to stay afterward to search for her birth mother. Again, Mina expressed her frustration and anger about having such limited information about her adoption. She also had a long list of anxieties and complaints: "How long will it take? Where will I stay—in Seoul or Inchon City? How will I get around when my Korean is barely good enough for ordering food in restaurants? I'll be so lonely. I don't really know anyone there and I don't want to see anyone from the dance school. Who will really help me? How will I know if someone is really genuine or just wants to take advantage of rich Americans?" I replied, "It sounds as if you'd feel more secure if I went there to search with you." She smiled and quietly acknowledged, "I guess so." When I asked her how she felt that I could not go with her, she immediately responded, "Oh no! I wasn't asking or thinking that you could go with me. Besides, you have a baby to take care of."

Trying to refocus our discussion on the issue of her birth mother, I suggested that, if we followed Mina's fantasies about her, she might currently be around my age. Mina looked at me with great surprise and said, "Wow, that could be true. I just never thought of it that way." My comment seemed to introduce to Mina the idea that her birth mother is a real, living person rather than a fantasy. Mina added, "I just always imagined her as a twenty-something-year-old girl like me ... but I guess she isn't anymore." On further exploration, Mina admitted, "I want her to be married but with no kids. I don't want any siblings, not even half-siblings. I don't want to be the one she didn't keep." Mina hoped that her birth mother was okay, "living a normal life, but not too happy." Despite her curiosity about her birth mother's current circumstances, Mina continued to feel angry that her mother had not tried to search for her. And she envied those adoptees whose birth mothers had sought them out first. She feared that she had been erased from her birth mother's memory the moment after she was dropped off at the church doorsteps.

In the following session, Mina introduced yet another fantasy: her stuffed animals. Mina has been collecting ducks since she was a toddler. Mina takes one female duck, Suzette, with her wherever she goes. Indeed, Suzette has now traveled around the world with Mina on tour (lucky duck). When Mina was nine, Suzette got "married" to Tommy and gave birth to three baby ducklings. However, Suzette did not like her babies because all they did was whine and cry, demanding attention. Suzette pecked and hurt them, and finally she abandoned them. As a consequence, Tommy was left to take care of these "ugly ducklings" along with another duck, Jane. Mina describes Jane as a sort of nanny. It was only recently that Tommy, Jane, and the ducklings have been reunited with Suzette, joining her in Mina's New York apartment. Still, Mina asserts, Suzette "hates" these babies.

Mina told me that she also "hates babies" because they are such helpless creatures. When I suggested that perhaps she feels that her helplessness as an infant contributed to her birth mother's abandoning her, Mina expressed great shock. After some silence, she asked, "How could I not have thought of this possibility? I have been blaming myself all this time without realizing it. My mother gave me up because I couldn't do anything. I didn't have any skills." Mina understands that this is the reason why she has become so independent—strong willed and intent on taking care of herself and no one else, not even a husband if she later marries.

I asked Mina what kind of "skills" she could have possibly possessed as an infant. She replied matter of factly, "I should have known how to feed myself and how not to rely on my mother. Be toilet trained, so she didn't have to change my dirty diapers." She speculated that perhaps she cried too much, and, as a result, her birth mother had to give her up. After this revelation, Suzette stopped abusing her ducklings. Instead, she "bathed and cleaned them up."

Currently, our primary focus is on Mina's preparations for "the search." Mina plans to put advertisements this coming summer in Korean newspapers. In addition, she has brought in her adoption file to share with me, to look for "possible clues." As Mina mentioned earlier, there is little information in the file that we could use to make her advertisement distinct. Finally, Mina has decided to participate in a Korean television program that reunites lost relatives. She repeatedly states, "I'm all for results. That's all I care about, and I don't care what I have to do to find her." In this regard, Mina requested that I call and talk with the church couple who discovered her. She has also asked her adoptive mother to go with her to Korea to help with her search. Mina is determined to find her birth mother and to demand answers about their brief life together. She has become increasingly agitated about her abandonment. And she wants answers.

Commentary

Transnational Adoption

Is the transnational adoptee an immigrant? Is she Korean? Is she Korean American? Are her adoptive parents, in turn, immigrants, Korean, or Korean American?

Mina's case history provides some provocative and vexing answers to these questions. Mina does not consciously see herself as an immigrant, as a Korean, or as a Korean American. She insists that, like her adoptive parents, she is an "American." Although she has an "Asian face" she nevertheless feels "white." "My parents are white, and I grew up in a white suburb, and I feel most comfortable around white people," Mina reasons. Indeed, she despises Koreans as a categorical whole—the "ugly," "garish," and "slutty" Korean nationals at her dance school who speak only Korean to one another, as well as Korean and Korean Americans who are "prejudiced against Korean adoptees."

We know that such extreme feelings of hate and disavowal often represent for the patient unconscious and ambivalent identifications with the ex-
coriated object. In this regard, Mina's struggles with the "whole adoption
thing" raise a number of issues concerning immigration, assimilation, and
racialization that are entirely consistent with the psychological problems of
many Asian immigrants and their second-generation children. Not unlike
Mina, these second-generation Asian Americans often exhibit ambivalent or
conflicted relationships to race and racialization—for example, identifying
with a dominant white mainstream while disidentifying with their immigrant parents as "raced" others.

Departing from these observations, how might we bring some psychic
specificity to Mina's case history and to the phenomenon of transnational
adoption in particular? Elsewhere, we have elaborated the concept of "racial melancholia," which we consider here in the context of transnational
adoption (see Eng and Han, 2000; Eng, 2003). Briefly, as Freud's (1917)
privileged theory of unresolved grief, melancholia presents a compelling
framework to analyze the sustained losses attendant to processes of immigration, assimilation, and racialization for Asian immigrants and their second-generation children. In "Mourning and Melancholia" (1917), Freud
tells us that mourning comes to a definitive conclusion with libido withdrawn from the lost object, place, or ideal to be invested elsewhere. In
contrast, melancholia is temporally extended into an indefinite future; it
is a mourning without end. Interminable grief is the result of the melancholic's inability to resolve the various psychic conflicts that the loss of the
loved object effects, and the inability to direct psychic investment into
new objects.

Here it is important to remember that experiences of immigration are
based on structures of mourning and melancholia. When one leaves one's
motherland, either voluntarily or involuntarily, one must grieve a host of
losses both abstract and concrete. These can include family and language,
homeland and property, customs and cultures, status and community—the
list goes on. Moreover, to the extent that Asian immigrants and Asian Americans are never fully assimilable to normative regimes of whiteness and remain socially consigned to perpetual foreigner status (like Mina, they may
"feel" white but not "look" white), they must work through a host of losses
and encumbered investments that may not be fully resolvable.

From this perspective, though Freud initially formulates melancholia as a
pathological psychic condition, we describe racial melancholia as a depath-
ologized "structure of feeling" (Williams, 1977), one exemplifying the everyday psychic lives and struggles of Asian Americans. In short, if
experiences of immigration, assimilation, and racialization in the U.S. are
fundamentally circumscribed by the relinquishing of lost but unspeakable
Asian ideals as well as foreclosed investments in whiteness, then we must

not slot racial melancholia under the sign of pathology, permanence, or damage. Instead, it must be considered a normative psychic state involving everyday conflicts and negotiations between mourning *and* melancholia, rather than, in Freud's estimation, mourning *or* melancholia.

How does Mina mourn the loss of Korea? Her Korean birth mother? How does she negotiate her vexed identifications with both Koreanness and whiteness in her adoptive country? Mina mourns and negotiates them in social and psychic isolation.

In Asian American cultural politics, the numerous political, economic, and social conflicts arising from the difficulties of immigration, assimilation, and racialization processes are often configured as *intergenerational* and *intersubjective* struggles. These conflicts, that is, are usually interpreted in terms of master narratives of intergenerational *cultural* struggle between immigrant parents and their American-born children, between the Asian-born first generation and the U.S.-born second generation. Reducing such conflicts, including those resulting from institutionalized racism and systemic exploitation, to intergenerational cultural struggles threatens to displace them into the privatized space of the family as personal issues and problems. In the process, such displacements often serve to deny what are necessarily public issues and problems by absolving the state or community from political response, economic redress, and social responsibility (see Lowe, 1996).

While we flag this palpable danger, what we must emphasize in Mina's case history is the suspension of this intergenerational and intersubjective process, the loss of the communal nature of racial melancholia. To the extent that Mina's parents do not recognize her as either an immigrant or a Korean/Korean American ("I'm so angry at them for not exposing me to Korean things. I told my mom maybe I'm screwed up because I didn't have anything Korean when I was growing up."), and to the extent that Mina herself does not affectively *feel* herself to be an immigrant or a Korean/Korean American, the numerous losses relating to her birth, birth mother, abandonment, adoption, and immigration remain unaffirmed and unacknowledged by her own family or self. All the more, they remain unaffirmed in the face of the "public" nature of her adoption. That is, unlike the biological Asian immigrant family, which is seen (if not always felt) as an integrated racial unit, the transnational adoptee disrupts the aesthetic continuity of the white nuclear family. She cannot pass, and her presence draws attention not only to her racial difference but also to the fact of her adoption (see Anagnost, 2000).

Mina mourns these significant losses in solitude. She negotiates them not intersubjectively but, rather, *intrasubjectively* and, equally important, *unconsciously.* Furthermore, to the extent that adoptive white parents in general recognize their transnational adoptee as immigrants or racialized subjects (Mina envies the Chinese adoptees whose white parents provide social and cultural support for their young daughters), but do not consider themselves immigrants or racialized subjects, in turn, we witness an affective cleaving of tremendous significance within the privatized space of the family. In other words, while transnational adoptees identify with their parents' whiteness, their parents do not necessarily identify with their adoptees' Asianness. Such a failure of recognition threatens to redouble racial melancholia's effects, severing the adoptee from the intimacy of the family unit, emotionally segregating her, and obliging her to negotiate her significant losses in isolation and silence (see Borshay-Liem, 2000).

As Freud reminds us in "Mourning and Melancholia" (1917), melancholia is one of the most difficult psychic conditions to treat, as it is largely an unconscious process. "[O]ne feels justified in maintaining the belief that a loss of the kind occurred," Freud observes, "but one cannot see clearly what it is that has been lost, and it is all the more reasonable to suppose that the patient cannot consciously perceive what he has lost either. This, indeed, might be the case even if the patient is aware of the loss which has given rise to his melancholia, but only in the sense that he knows *whom* he has lost but not *what* he has lost in him" (p. 245, Freud's emphasis). Mina knows that she has lost her Korean birth mother, but she does not know what she has lost in her. And through the unspecified and thus ungrievable nature of this loss, we come to witness in Mina the psychic forfeiture of the embodied humanity of this lost maternal figure. Hence, in attempting to outline some crucial psychic issues attendant to the practice of transnational adoption, we might consider how, in its particular configuration for the transnational adoptee, racial melancholia can manifest itself in particularly severe and unconscious psychic forms.

Here let us emphasize that Mina's adoptive white mother is, in fact, a warm and caring person. She is an extraordinarily empathetic, conscientious, and responsive woman. Mina not only discloses "everything" to her adoptive mother, but she also feels that her mother would do "anything and everything" for her. Indeed, as Mina's treatment has evolved over time, and as Mina has come into greater conflict with whiteness and her adoptive mother, Mina's mother has been able to hold effectively her daughter's rage. She does not retaliate against Mina's frequent and angry attacks but, in fact, provides increased emotional support to her by making herself available for extra phone calls as well as by making numerous visits to New York City. She has also agreed to go with Mina to Korea to search for her birth mother.

The adoptive mother's "failures," if they can be labeled as such, are less individual than social. That is, what Mina's case history underscores is the necessity of analyzing her psychic struggles not only in the context of her particular individual family dynamics but also in relation to larger social issues concerning immigration, assimilation, and racialization as they affect the developmental trajectories of the transnational adoptee and configure her mourning as an isolated psychic enterprise.

Racial Reparation

What we so strikingly witness in Mina's case history is that the "return" to origins—the return to mother and to motherland—that invariably marks the psychic development of the transnational adoptee occurs through the very dissociation of mother from motherland through primitive mechanisms of splitting and idealization. This process might be productively analyzed in relation to Melanie Klein's notions of infant development. We might say that, in mourning her unacknowledged losses, Mina deploys a psychic strategy of gender and racial segregation such that she *idealizes* the *white* adoptive mother while simultaneously *deidealizing* the *Korean* birth mother. Hence, the "reparative position" that Klein associates with an infant's reinstatement of the mother as a loved object—as whole, separate, and good—is, in Mina's case, unquestionably a *racialized* position.

Mina's case history insists that we consider Klein's concepts of good and bad objects as theories about good and bad *racialized* objects, her concepts of the depressive and reparative positions as theories about *racial* reparation. Indeed, Mina's case history more broadly demands the consideration of how racial difference is figured and narrated within primal fantasies of infant development, fantasies that are too often analyzed and recounted solely in terms of gender and gendered development. Mina's "whole adoption thing" implicates a terrain of infant development—a primal territory of splitting and idealization, depression and guilt, reinstatement and reparation—that haunts her into adulthood. It casts a long and profound psychic shadow over all her relations with others, romantic and otherwise, and it overdetermines her racial antipathies and prejudices.

From a slightly different angle, we might say that Mina's case history insists on a rethinking of Klein's concept of good and bad mothers through a more refined theory of good and bad *racialized* mothers. Psychic health, therefore, would entail a reparative position for race that accounts for the psychic possibility of two good *racialized* mothers—not the white *or* Korean mother but the white *and* Korean mother. Mina's continual negotiation between these two maternal figures, similar to our notions of mourning *and* melancholia as an everyday struggle for Asian Americans, constitutes one psychic locus of the racial melancholia with which the transnational adoptee struggles.

In "A Contribution to the Psychogenesis of Manic-Depressive States" (1935), Klein describes the ways a patient deploys psychic mechanisms of splitting and idealization so as to preserve a "beautiful picture" of the mother in the face of a "real object" felt to be wholly inadequate. Klein writes:

> In some patients who had turned away from their mother in dislike or hate, or used other mechanisms to get away from her, I have found that there existed in their minds nevertheless a beautiful picture of the mother, but one which was felt to be a *picture* of her only, not her real self. The real object was felt to be unattractive—really an injured, incurable and therefore dreaded person. The beautiful picture had been dissociated from the real object but had never been given up, and played a great part in the specific ways of their sublimations. (1935, p. 125)

The Korean birth mother, the "bitch" and "poor whore," who abandoned Mina on a church doorstep without proper explanation or name comes to assume the status of this unattractive creature, this "real object." She becomes "an injured, incurable, and therefore dreaded person." Such dread opens upon the affective terrain of hate and envy. It poisons Mina's relationship to Koreanness and accounts for her radical devaluation of all things associated with her "motherland"—from her "slutty" Korean classmates at dance school to Korean/Korean Americans who are all "prejudiced against Korean adoptees," and from the other "screwed-up" Korean adoptees Mina encounters at adoption camp and in her local support group to the Koreans in Korea who will take advantage of "rich Americans" as they initiate "the search" for their birth mothers. This dread not only threatens her therapeutic relationship to the Korean American therapist—whom, from their very first session, Mina puts on warning not to be like these disparaged others—but also shapes her bigotry toward numerous other racialized and minority groups.

If, as Klein insists, "the beautiful picture [of the birth mother] had been dissociated from the real object but had never been given up, and played a great part in the specific ways of their [the patients's] sublimations," then we come to witness in Mina's case history the particular *racial* forms and defenses that these sublimations assume: Mina's excessive idealization of whiteness and of the white adoptive mother, a figure of plenitude who would do "anything and everything" for her, coupled with her excessive devaluation of the Korean birth mother and racial otherness as a categorical whole. In short, Mina displaces the "beautiful picture" of the Korean birth mother wholly into an idealized whiteness, an idealized white mother who possesses all the qualities—education, privilege, independence—the birth mother decisively lacks.

The extreme nature of Mina's idealizations and deidealizations suggests how racial difference can function phantasmatically in primitive processes of splitting, projection, and introjection around the maternal figure. In addition, it indicates how, for Mina, good and bad objects become racially segregated into white and Korean and how this splitting forecloses the possibility that good and bad can simultaneously pertain to both racialized maternal figures at once. Only by coming to such an affective position, only by renegotiating a "beautiful picture" in relation to Koreanness, can Mina begin the work of racial reparation.

Mina is prepared to undertake this task. For, in all her various tirades against Korea, the Korean birth mother, and Koreanness, we can nevertheless detect a "beautiful picture," albeit deeply repressed and unconscious, of the lost birth mother and motherland not fully circumscribed by whiteness. For instance, by describing the Korean birth mother as a "poor whore," Mina belies a level of ambivalence that opens upon the psychic terrain of not just hate but love. (Importantly, Freud [1917] tells us, ambivalence not only is *the* psychic mark of melancholia but also holds unique ethical possibilities.) Through this turn of phrase, Mina not only condemns the "whore" who abandoned her but also displays a degree of sympathetic identification with this devalued figure—the double meaning of "*poor* whore" assuming an economic as well as an emotional inflection in relation to the birth mother's imagined plight.

Indeed, throughout the course of her treatment as well as in her many regressions into racial antipathy, Mina has displayed a remarkable psychic fidelity to the Korean birth mother. Mina's repeated failures with abusive and unavailable boyfriends; the imagined duplicities of her Korean classmates; her bonds with the mother duck, Suzette, who "pecked," "hurt," and finally "abandoned" her ugly ducklings; and the deep-seated fear that she ultimately instigated her own abandonment because of her lack of "skills" all underscore the ambivalent identifications that Mina preserves in relation to the lost Korean birth mother as both "bad object" and "good object."

Klein reminds us that extreme feelings of persecution and hate do not necessarily foreclose the possibility of love; indeed, they are its preconditions. Mina's racial tirades could simultaneously indicate a type of psychic desperation, a defense against a feeling of imminent loss, the loss of the good object and of goodness itself. In this respect, Mina's racial persecution anxieties are psychically complex insofar as they indicate an attempt to preserve not only the ego but also the "good internalized objects with whom the ego is identified as a whole" (1935, p. 124). Her excessive idealizations of whiteness can, at the same, denote that persecution is "the main driving force" (1956, p. 217). Klein observes, "infants whose capacity for love is strong have less need for idealization than those in whom destructive impulses and persecutory anxiety are paramount" (1956, p. 217).

In short, Mina's extreme affective polarities—her excessive idealization of whiteness and her excessive hatred of Koreanness—might, in fact, belie a great psychic effort on her part to preserve unconsciously the "goodness" of the lost Korean birthmother, a figure whose existence is felt to be in crisis, if not entirely irrecoverable under the idealized palimpsest of the good white mother. Klein observes, "The stronger the anxiety is of losing the loved objects, the more the ego strives to save them, and the harder the task of restoration becomes the stricter will grow the demands which are associated with the super-ego" (1935, p. 123). Mina's case history thus raises the possibility of an ethical death drive at the heart of Klein's theories of infant development, one preserving a space of "goodness" for the Korean birth mother and mapping the psychic parameters under which we might begin to theorize a reparative position for race.

In our prior work on racial melancholia, we suggest that the melancholic's absolute refusal to relinquish the lost other—to forfeit alterity—at any costs delineates one psychic process of an ethical death drive in which the loved but lost racial object is so overwhelmingly important to the ego that it is willing to preserve it even at the cost of its own psychic health (see Eng and Han, 2000). In other words, racial melancholia indicates one way that lost and socially disparaged racial others live on unconsciously in the psychic realm.

From this perspective, the racial melancholia configuring the psychic limits of Mina's paranoid-schizoid position might be said to demand a more politicized understanding of Kleinian processes of (racial) idealization and splitting. Ultimately, it might be said to underwrite a type of ethical fidelity to the Korean birth mother. Such an ethical hold on the part of the melancholic ego becomes the precondition for racial survival, a psychic strategy for living and for living on. In the transferential aspects of melancholic identifications, Freud writes, "is the expression of there being something in common which may signify love" (1917, p. 250). The redistribution of this love across a field of foreclosed, repressed, and unconscious objects—the desegregation of this love such that Mina can apportion to the devalued Korean birth mother some of the affect she reserves for the idealized white mother—constitutes one social and psychic project for racial reparation.

Klein is even more emphatic about this paradoxical connection between hate and love, of profound psychic violence, melancholy, and the death drive as the constitutive basis for (racial) reparation. She speculates:

> But, while in committing suicide the ego intends to murder its bad objects, in my view at the same time it also always aims at saving its loved objects, internal or external. To put it shortly: in some cases the phantasies underlying suicide aim at preserving the internalized good objects and that part of the ego which is identified with good objects, and also at destroying the other part of the ego which is identified with the bad objects and the id. Thus the ego is enabled to become united with its loved objects." (1935, p. 131)

According to Klein, successful psychic negotiation by patients who exhibit extreme anxieties of persecution or excessive mechanisms of idealization requires that they revise their relation to "their parents—whether they be dead or alive—and to rehabilitate them to some extent even if they have grounds for actual grievances" (1940, p. 173). Patients who fail in the work of mourning have been "unable in early childhood to establish their internal 'good' objects and to feel secure in their inner world. They have never really overcome the infantile depressive position" (1940, p. 173). Perhaps the most crucial element in Mina's slow psychic evolution—her gradual move toward a reparative position for Koreanness and the Korean birth mother—is the transferential relationship that she builds with the Korean American psychotherapist. Han is a figure Mina has specifically sought out for treatment and one she ultimately constitutes as a *racial* transitional object.

Racial Transitional Objects

D. W. Winnicott's theory of transitional objects proves especially useful in considering Mina's transference. In "Transitional Objects and Transitional Phenomenon" (1951), Winnicott outlines his concept of the "transitional object," that "first possession" of the infant (the thumb, the doll, the tattered blanket) serving to open up a "transitional space," an "intermediate area between the subjective and that which is objectively perceived" (1951, p. 3). Winnicott writes: "It is not the object, of course, that is transitional. The object represents the infant's transition from a state of being merged with the mother to a state of being in relation to the mother as something outside and separate" (1951, p. 15). The transitional object is neither strictly internal nor strictly external. "It is never under magical control like the internal object, nor is it outside control as the real mother is" (1951, p. 10).

On the whole, transitional phenomena "give room [to the infant] for the process of becoming able to accept difference and similarity," and thus they become the "root of symbolism in time" (1951, p. 6). Transitional phenomena negotiate the invariable frustrations of the infant as it comes to terms with its compromised autonomy in a world of others it cannot fully control. By providing a psychic third space between inner and outer worlds, transitional phenomena permit the subject to negotiate what are hitherto felt to be mutually exclusive options: inside-outside, subjectivity-objectivity, unity-separation. Indeed, we might say that transitional phenomena allow the infant the means to negotiate not only Freud's pleasure and reality principles, as well as Freud's later life and death drives, but also what Klein describes as primitive positions of love and hate that must eventually be resolved by the integration of the mother as a whole, separate, and good object. The transitional object, as Adam Phillips points out, "is always a combination, but one that provides by virtue of being more than the sum of its parts, a new, third alternative" (1988, p. 114). This transitional third space is not a space of obstacle but one of psychic possibility.

Significantly, the fate of the transitional object is gradual decathexis. "In the course of years," Winnicott writes, "it becomes not so much forgotten as relegated to limbo …. It is not forgotten and it is not mourned. It loses meaning, and this is because the transitional phenomena have become diffused, have become spread out over the whole intermediate territory between 'inner psychic reality' and the 'external world as perceived by two persons in common,' that is to say, over the whole cultural field" (1951, p. 5). For Winnicott, the domains of play, artistic creativity, religious feeling, and dreaming become those privileged zones of transitional space wherein the recurring burdens of reality are negotiated throughout a person's adult life. The task of reality-acceptance, as Winnicott underscores, is "never completed.… [No] human being is free from the strain of relating inner and outer reality, and that relief from this strain is provided by an intermediate area of experience not challenged (arts, religion, etc.). This intermediate area is in direct continuity with the play area of the small child who is 'lost' in play" (1951, p. 13).

Importantly, Winnicott observes, in patients who were not started off well enough by their mothers, the fundamental task of the psychotherapy is to open up this transitional space for creative play. "Psychotherapy takes place in the overlap of two areas of playing," Winnicott insists, "that of the patient and that of the therapist. Psychotherapy has to do with two people playing together. The corollary of this is that where playing is not possible then the work done by the therapist is directed toward bringing the patient from a state of not being able to play into a state of being able to play" (1968, p. 38).

While it is clear that Mina draws great sustenance from practicing her art—dancing—it is also evident that such a privileged realm of artistic creativity does not fully allow her the successful negotiation of her "inner psychic reality" and the "external world." Her dance teachers repeatedly tell Mina that, although her technique is "superb," her "emotional expression" remains blocked. Moreover, Mina's enactment of her adoption and abandonment fantasies through the parable of her ducks, constituted by the patient as literal transitional objects that remain to be decathected, underscores the extent to which her capacity "to play" with her racial predicaments, her ability to negotiate productively her inner and outer realities, is circumscribed. Under such conditions, the role of the therapist is to bring her patient into a state of being able to play such that racial difference can be reinstated and repaired and ultimately spread out over the whole cultural field.

Winnicott's (1969) distinction between "object relating" and "object use" between the patient and therapist in the clinical setting further illuminates Mina's situation. Whereas Winnicott associates "object relating" with orthodox Freudian notions of transference—the analyst as blank screen on whom figures from the past (mother, father, siblings) are projected—"object use" not only takes into account the question, "Who am I representing?" but also raises the important question, "What am I being used to do?" In other words, it is not enough to say that the analyst stands in for the mother, unless we specify what particular aspects of the mother are being revived and worked through and for what purposes.

For Mina, issues of object relating and object use come together in crucial ways that are intensified by the Korean American psychotherapist's pregnancy. The visibility of the analyst's pregnancy (like her race), as the literature on this topic broadly indicates, makes the pregnancy "public property" between analyst and patient while intensifying the transference and countertransferences between them. Often, pregnancies can also lead to resistance and reaction formations that place inordinate strain on the therapeutic relationship (see Friedman, 1993). It is clear that Mina cannot "use" the lost Korean birth mother in any productive manner to negotiate her racial antipathies. However, the return of this figure in the transferential guise of the pregnant Korean American therapist/mother provokes a particular psychic reaction that allows Han to become for Mina what we would describe as a "racial transitional object," one spilling over from the psychic territory of "object relating" into "object use."

What is the therapist being "used" to do? She is being used by Mina as a transitional object allowing her to resignify her vexed racial identifications with the lost Korean birth mother, not as a bundle of hated projections, but as a whole person, a "thing in itself." From this perspective, Mina might also be seen as "using" the young Chinese transnational adoptees that she mentors as "racial transitional objects," too. Through them, she negotiates her more complicated identifications with her Korean transnational adoptee peers—a kind of psychic coalitional identity politics.

By disclosing her pregnancy to her patient, the Korean American therapist becomes the "good-enough" Korean mother, to borrow another concept from Winnicott. Han not only keeps her child but also, and most importantly, does not abandon her patient in the process. In this regard, Han is both a good-enough mother and a good-enough analyst. She is an educated, privileged, and independent Korean woman (with qualities similar to Mina's idealized adoptive white mother) who, in Mina's estimation, planned her pregnancy and "wouldn't be so stupid and just get knocked up." As a racial transitional object, Han introduces into Mina's psyche the notion of similarity *and* difference in regard to the figure of the deidealized Korean birthmother. Moreover, Han allows Mina a way to reintegrate the hated qualities of the bad (Korean) mother and the good qualities of the loved (white) mother into one figure. "You're a professional," Mina avers to the Korean American therapist. "You'll come back to the office, and we will work together then."

By providing a space for Mina to explore any potential feelings of abandonment and jealousy ("Oh, I wasn't asking or even thinking that you could go with me [to Korea]. Besides you have a baby to take care of"), and by suggesting that Mina's Korean birth mother might "currently be around my [Han's] age," the therapist becomes a screen on which the birth mother can take shape as a real, concretized living person rather than a set of fragmented illusions, hated projections, or merged fantasies. She becomes, in short, a person with a separate reality. In "using" the therapist in this manner, Mina is finally able to resignify both her affective stance and attitude toward the Korean birth mother. "I just always imagined her [my birth mother] as a twenty-something-year-old girl like me," Mina admits. "But I guess she isn't anymore."

Mina "uses" the Korean American therapist as a racial transitional object that allows her to renegotiate her attitudes toward the Korean birth mother, Koreanness, and racial difference. A significant psychic shift occurs in regard to her transitional objects, her ducks: Suzette ceases to abuse her ugly ducklings and has instead "bathed and cleaned them up." Exhibiting such care toward her abandoned ducklings represents for Mina an altered identification with a lost Korean birth mother of significantly different affective capacities. Moreover, Mina opens the book of her past. She decides to share with the therapist her adoption file and thus her "unofficial" history prior to her "official" arrival and history in the U.S. At the same time, Mina decides to begin a search for the lost Korean birth mother, a search that she does not initiate in social or psychic isolation but with the support of others, including her adoptive white mother. Thus Mina arrives at a psychic position in which her racial melancholia might be "repaired" and the lost Korean birth mother reinstated and reintegrated into a world of loved objects. Mina sets the psychic stage for her to emerge as a good-enough mother.

Conclusion: Whiteness and Envy

The capacity to "use" the analyst, as Winnicott points out, "cannot be said to be inborn." It is the task of the therapist to abet the transformation from object relating to object use, to "be concerned with the development and establishment of the capacity to use objects, and to recognize a patient's inability to use objects, where this is a fact" (1969, p. 87). Analysts, like mothers, Winnicott observes, "can be good or not good enough" (1969, p. 89).

Han's transformation into a "good-enough" mother/analyst allows Mina to constitute her disparaged Korean birth mother and, in turn, her idealized white adoptive mother as "good-enough" mothers, too. How does this happen? Mina's transition hinges on several factors regarding the recognition of race and the analysis of racial difference in the clinical setting, as well as the importance of the therapist's material, raced body in the course of treatment. Arguably one of the most undertheorized aspects of psychoanalytic theory, race cannot be seen as merely additive or symptomatic of more primary psychic conditions. Mina's case history insists on an understanding of race (not just gender) as constitutive of the earliest forms of object relations and subjective development. Her story underscores the ways in which transnational adoption as a contemporary social phenomenon opens onto a psychic terrain of intense splitting and idealization—primitive psychic processes that are apprehended by Mina only through sustained critical attention to race and racial difference. This racial re-turn must become a central concern for psychoanalytic theory and practice.

Mina's case history forces us to revise in fundamental ways Freud's notions of melancholia as an everyday structure of feeling, Klein's idea of the paranoid, depressive, and reparative position as racial positions, and Winnicott's concept of transitional objects and the good-enough as negotiating the pain of racial history and reality. For Winnicott the cultural and creative domain is the privileged dominion of transitional space. But we learn from Mina's case history that culture and cultural difference may also be the source of racial upheaval and unrest, not just the panacea for, but also the poison of, reality. Mina's case history also suggests that we must consider how hate and envy, Klein's most toxic of psychic positions unfolding upon the terrain of the death drive, may, in fact, represent to minority patients a form of mental gymnastics to which they must subject themselves in order to preserve and to protect their socially-disparaged loved objects, objects felt to be lost or under imminent social erasure.

Mina's intense aversion toward the Korean nationals at her dance academy—unconsciously in her mind, young Korean women who are cherished rather than abandoned by their affluent families—might be analyzed in this light for, as Klein reminds us, "a very deep and sharp divide between loved and hated objects indicates that destructive impulses, envy and persecutory anxiety are very strong and serve as a defense against these emotions" (1956, p. 217). In "A Study of Envy and Gratitude" (1956), Klein defines envy as "the angry feeling that another person possesses and enjoys something desirable—the envious impulse to take it away or to spoil it" (p. 213). For Klein, envy is the most poisonous of psychic states; it is pure psychic destruction. Unlike jealousy, in which the subject feels deprived by somebody else of an object he or she loves, envy focuses aggression not on rivals but on the object itself. Envy entails not only the desire to possess this loved object but also the desire to "spoil" the goodness of the object with "bad parts" of the self. In an infant, envy simultaneously involves robbing the good breast of its positive qualities while "putting badness, primarily bad excrements and bad parts of the self, into the mother … in order to spoil and destroy her" (1956, p. 213). For Klein, envy thwarts all attempts at reparation and creativity. Representing senseless aggression, envy threatens mental development itself for it impairs the infant's ability to build up the good object and, instead, opens onto the psychic terrain of antisocial and antilife tendencies.

For Mina, however, envy does not assume such negative capacities. Proving instead to be resourceful if not indeed creative, it might be considered a kind of melancholic racial coping mechanism that *preserves* the goodness of the lost (Korean) object insofar as it does not hamper but abets Mina's entry into a reparative position for race. To the extent that Mina's primitive psychic processes of splitting and idealization segregate "good" (white) and "bad" (Korean) along a strictly racialized divide, her case history allows us one way of perceiving how envy might not be entirely psychically destructive or socially debilitating. That is, her hate and envy might be said to encompass an ethical death drive, one that facilitates a psychic strategy by which she can spoil just a little the "goodness" of whiteness and the white adoptive mother she idealizes. Through this spoiling of whiteness, Mina can create some room in her psyche to begin to repair the "badness" of Koreanness and the Korean birth mother. In other words, through envy's spoilage, Mina can begin both to undo and to redress the psychic displacements that configure whiteness as a kind of racial palimpsest masking the lost and deeply unconscious goodness of the Korean birth mother.

Mina begins to address and to repair her racial melancholia by returning to the light of consciousness the lost goodness that had been encrypted in this dreaded maternal figure. In short, she begins to come to terms with not only the lost Korean birth mother but also the goodness that she has lost in her. Thus, Mina unfolds in her psyche the lost Korean birth mother as a different type of historical subject, one who can come to occupy the place of the "good enough." In the process, Mina simultaneously creates psychic room for the idealized white adoptive mother to emerge as "good enough," too. She creates a reparative mechanism through which "good" and "bad" can exist and move across racial divides.

Admittedly, such an interpretation of Kleinian envy is unorthodox. However, the racial exigencies of Mina's case history demand such creative infidelity, such a melancholic bridge between envy and an ethical death drive that preserves a space of "goodness" for the lost Korean birth mother. Ultimately, as Mina comes to discover a reparative position for race that is productive rather than debilitating, psychoanalysis as a clinical process and a theoretical enterprise also begins to address in more programmatic ways the profound and difficult legacies of racial pain.

Acknowledgments

We would like to thank Muriel Dimen, Carrie Hyde, Teemu Ruskola, Kaja Silverman, Melanie Suchet, Leti Volpp, Serena Volpp, and Hiro Yoshikawa for their helpful feedback and suggestions. We had the opportunity of presenting earlier versions of this essay at Institute for Contemporary Psychotherapy and Psychoanalysis in Washington, DC, University of Washington at Seattle, Wellesley College, and Emory University. We would like to thank Janice Gump, Ann Anagnost, Gillian Harkins, Jodi Melamed, Ta Trang, Alys Weinbaum, Geeta Patel, Martha Fineman, Elissa Marder, José Quiroga, Rick Rambuss, Ralph Roughton, and Deborah Elise White for their hospitality and engagement.

References

Anagnost, A. (2000), Scenes of Misrecognition: Maternal Citizenship in the Age of Transnational Adoption. *Positions,* 8(2):389–421.

Borshay-Liem, D., Dir. (2000), *First Person Plural.* San Francisco: National Asian American Telecommunications Association.

Eng, D. L. (2003), Transnational Adoption and Queer Diasporas. *Social Text 76,* 21(3):1–37.

Eng, D. L. and Han, S. (2000), A Dialogue on Racial Melancholia. *Psychoanalytic Dialogues,* 10(4).667–700.

Freud, S. (1917), Mourning and Melancholia. In: *The Standard Edition of the Complete Psychological Works of Sigmund Freud, Volume XIV.* London: The Hogarth Press, pp. 243–258.

Friedman, M.E. (1993), When the Analyst Becomes Pregnant Twice. *Psychoanal. Inq.,* 13:226–239.

Klein, M. (1935), A Contribution to the Psychogenesis of Manic-Depressive States. In: *The Selected Melanie Klein,* ed. Juliet Mitchell. New York: Free Press, pp. 116–145.

———— (1940), Mourning and its Relation to Manic-Depressive States. In: *The Selected Melanie Klein,* ed. Juliet Mitchell. New York: Free Press, pp. 146–174.

———— (1956), A Study of Envy and Gratitude. In: *The Selected Melanie Klein,* ed. Juliet Mitchell. New York: Free Press, pp. 211–229.

Lowe, L. (1996), *Immigrant Acts: On Asian American Cultural Politics.* Durham: Duke University Press.

Phillips, A (1988), *Winnicott.* Cambridge, MA: Harvard University Press.

Williams, R. (1977), *Marxism and Literature.* New York: Oxford University Press.

Winnicott, D. W. (1951), Transitional Objects and Transitional Phenomena. In: *Playing and Reality.* New York: Routledge, 1989, pp. 1–25.

———— (1968), Playing: A Theoretical Statement. In: *Playing and Reality.* New York: Routledge, 1989, pp. 38–52.

———— (1969), The Use of an Object and Relating Through Identifications. In: *Playing and Reality.* New York: Routledge, 1989, pp. 86–94.

10

Resisting to Survive or Self-Destructing to Resist? The Ongoing Paradox of Transformation

Katie Gentile

Resistance is complicated. In psychoanalysis, it is usually pejorative, as "the name given to motivational forces operating against growth or change" (Ghent, 1990, p. 110). In feminist theory, it involves liberation. Resistance is bound by context to the psychological and social structures that are being resisted (Hoy, 2004), and not all forms of resistance are readily identified as such.

Eating disorders are a perfect example of the paradox of resistance. Viewed clinically, they are self-destructive and often resistant to treatment. At the same time, eating disorders are a defiant thorn in the cultural body's side. Through them, women resist traditional female gender roles. Women become too thin to reproduce, too fat to fit into the feminine ideal of beauty, too controlling and distant to fully penetrate. If the social order relies on the capacity to split off disavowed experiences and contain them within identified female bodies, then when women take any kind of control over their bodies (eating with one's hunger, sleeping when one is tired, deciding when, if, where and with whom one will have sex, or binging and purging, starving and cutting oneself) it is defiant resistance. This control not only functions to resist external pressures, it creates an experience of a skinned body with a coherent temporality, which can help counter the impact of trauma. Binging and purging or waging a "hunger strike" (Orbach, 1986) can bring feelings of control in relation to overwhelming memories and experiences.

But by locating the struggle in the body, women with eating disorders enact the cultural mandate to sacrifice the (female) body for the safety of the (male) psyche, reinscribing the dynamics of trauma. They deny their own sense of, and entitlement to, their embodied appetites and subjectivity, instead, using the female body as currency as clearly and destructively as does the culture.

Resistance functions simultaneously as both traumatic and subversive repetition; which version appears central depends on our focus. Thus, resistance can be conscious and unconscious, self-destructive and growth-promoting. Most importantly, it may only be through an act of resistance that we are able to know what it is we need to resist. Indeed, even when it appears to be complicity, resistance can open new possibilities for being (Hoy, 2004).

This chapter is an excerpt of a larger project exploring time, space and resistance in one woman's diaries (Gentile, 2007). Hannah, a white, upper middle class British woman, wrote 16 diaries in 18 years. These diaries can be split into three books written in her adolescence (from 14–17 years of age), and 13 as an adult (from 30–33 years of age). These diaries describe her emotionally and sexually invasive parents, her relationships with abusive men including her husband, her development of bulimia, and the radical transformation of her healing. Here I am focusing only on her emerging forms of resistance represented in the first five adult diaries.[1]

When these diaries begin, both of her parents have died of cancer and as an only child, Hannah is left with no close relatives outside of her marriage. She has been married to Eric for 9 years. He is emotionally and sexually abusive and controlling. She binges and purges regularly, shoplifts, and compulsively masturbates. She is unable to do daily tasks such as remembering her way home in the car. She is entirely dependent on Eric in order to move within the world. Even within her diaries, stories about her marriage dominate the narrative. Their relationship creates the skin within which she lives, and without it, she ceases to exist. But an in-depth analysis of her entries highlights some cracks where Hannah's intentionality and resistance peeks out from underneath this smothering relationship.

There are also no boundaries of time in these diaries. All her previous abusive relationships are current and ongoing within her present relationships, so that just reading her narrative, it is unclear which events are past or present.

Time and space are the foundation for development (see Gentile, 2007, 2000). Time imbues space with meaning, and space enables time to be experienced. Time is not narrativizing or ordering experience (Butler, 1993;

---

[1]Hannah was never my patient. I analyzed her diaries only. For more information, please see Gentile (2007).

Reis, 1995; van der Kolk, 1995), but creating the capacity for experience to emerge. Hopkins (1997) describes capacity as roominess, to have "room for," a simultaneous taking in and creation of. Thus, capacity is not just an internal space or interiority, it is a functioning potential space where self, other, and culture simultaneously come into being. It is inner and outer. This roominess emerges with the creation of embodied temporal linking. This linking literally makes meaning, creating experience, self-regulation, symbolization and secondary process, and the capacity for differentiation.

In this chapter, we follow a Hannah who does not have this capacity. There is no embodied temporal linking, no differentiation, no self-regulation and no meaning making of experience. Events are thrown up onto the page with no reflection. I focus on the main body of the story—the relationship between Hannah and Eric—and how it appears to function at this point in her diaries. I outline the ways in which Eric seems to contain, control and dictate Hannah by "keeping" her desires, her image, and her affective experiences. But as the chapter unfolds, it becomes quite murky as to who is dictating this "keeping."

Eric as the Keeper of Hannah's Desire

- *On the road again from 1.30 to 4.30 and then a quick tea stop. Had a cup of tea and again E. said "I think you should have something to eat" had a slice of hazelnut cake. I know he means well, but I can't always bring myself to take a piece initially.*
- *I had salad as second [course]. Shared with E. and his choice. I really wanted pasta. Didn't eat much salad; said too cold for it. Couldn't eat all meal. E. ate small and I couldn't eat any more than him.*
- *Out for dinner after tears of talking. E. and I both chose chicken salad; I ate half. Felt trapped and tearful—wanted to run out as full and knew had to eat desert and cheese. As tearful E. said could have drink and no food. Still sad. On way home wanted to vomit, felt sick and wanted to feel happy feeling after sickness. E. wanted me to eat tea and choc biscuits. [I] Said he'd said I didn't have to eat. He said [that] was only in restaurant. Felt trapped again.*
- *Towards end of meal E. said "I didn't have to eat all" so I left rest. Just what my Dad said. Towards end had enough savory was interested in a dessert and E. said "are you sure. I'm very full. You're not on a binge are you?'" [E's comment] meant I couldn't eat.*
- *When I'd gone to the restaurant. I chose asparagus salad, boiled chicken; beans; peas; ratatouille. He said "gosh you've got a lot on*

*your plate—don't eat it all if you can't" He refused a bread roll so
hard for me to eat.*

In these entries Eric clearly acts as the keeper of Hannah's desires. He
tells her what and how much to eat. He chooses food at restaurants, usually
making them share entrees. When she eats more than he thinks she should,
he asks "Are you sure? You're not on a binge are you?" which stops Hannah
in her tracks. When she does not eat as much as he thinks she should, he
forces her to eat. When they are at a restaurant Hannah ends up in tears because Eric will not let her leave until she has finished her desert. And when
they return to their hotel room he changes the rules and forces her to eat
more. Eric dictates her hunger in confusing and unpredictable ways. He
makes her eat one night, stops her from eating the next, then accuses her of
binging when a hint of her own desire creeps out. She feels trapped, and, indeed, like a caged animal, she is unable to control not only her eating, but
even her access to food.

Hannah can never eat more than Eric, even if he is not hungry and she is.
Her body ceases to exist and they live only through his, enveloped by one
controlling, tightly wrapped, "limiting membrane" (Winnicott, 1971). In
this body she does not have to hold or even experience desires around
food, her hunger, or satiation, as he does it for her. There is no space between, no need for the capacity for temporal linking. Like a conjoined twin,
Eric's body processes and creates all experiences. This is not an entirely bad
deal. Eric can grant Hannah permission to eat. When they stop for tea, she is
not able to ask for a piece of cake until Eric says she should eat one. She says
"I know he means well, but I can't always bring myself to take a piece initially." There is relief in not having to make the decisions that come with the
creation of experience.

Having been raised by two parents who made no room (literal space) for
the development of her own recognition of (let alone regulation of), her appetites, she needs Eric's "capacity for." He minds her temporal linking for
her. He creates her experience. Consequently, she never learns to differentiate her appetites and she does not have to take responsibility for eating.
This process of externalizing her appetites perfectly supports her bulimic
endeavor, as she continues to dissociate her experiences of her appetites
and her body, allowing Eric to dictate and control them. The only rule is that
they exist as one body.

Erasing Hannah's Desires for Sex

- *Had sex and can accept and don't need to come.*
- *Had sex by sucking E. and then settled to go to sleep.*

- *Feel sick again today. Had sex last night and didn't really enjoy.*
- *Worried about the sex. The thing is I find it hard to say no. Ironically the first thing I did last night was give him sex—yet I don't want, enjoy, or like myself for it. Today feel depressed and ate cake and vomited. A pattern?*

Given Eric's role of keeping Hannah's appetite for food, it is no surprise that he also keeps her appetite for sex. The entries above typify how Hannah describes sex in her diaries. Brief snippets such as these are plopped at the end of an entry, unlinked and disconnected from the rest of the content. Not surprisingly given this dissociated presentation, there is also no written subject of the action. Unlike with eating, where it appears clear that Eric is in the lead, with sex, it is unclear who is initiating what activity or what exactly is happening. Does she want to have sex? Does Eric want to have sex? What is sex? Is it oral sex? Intercourse? Is there a difference? Who decides what kind of sex to have? Is she being forced, coerced? Is it like with food and she needs him to give her permission? Among all these questions, I have only one certainty: She does not write of enjoyment or pleasure. In fact, the only time she writes a subject of the action is when she uses the pronoun "I" as she is describing not wanting to have sex, not being able to say "no," not enjoying it. So given this observation, Hannah does have desire in the diaries, only it is not wanting to have sex.

As the diaries progress, Hannah's desire appears less in the negative as she writes:

- *Had sex but I didn't have an orgasm. Need more time for me and sad it's not made all the time.*

Here it becomes apparent that, as with food, sex involves only one body and one orgasm—Eric's. But although Hannah's appetites for food are inextricable from Eric, it appears that with sex, Hannah is able to create some separation. She knows she needs more time. Indeed, she seems to have a notion that she, too, should have an orgasm. So perhaps her desires for sex are not so much in the negative, that she does not want to have sex. She does not want to have what constitutes sex in their relationship, that is, an activity that results in Eric's orgasm only.

- *Worried about sex and affection. Will tell E. at a nonsensitive time about fears of being rejected if initiate sex. Also will say am going to discuss sex topic in FT (family therapy which is couples therapy) on Monday so he is warned.*

When Hannah considers discussing sex with Eric, she plans to do it during one of their family therapy sessions. This discussion requires preparation, which involves "warning" Eric ahead of time. But this warning must be done at a "nonsensitive" time. She must mold her fears, desires, and needs around his moods and sensitivities. It is fatiguing just reading how much controlled, careful planning is required for Hannah to relationally position herself in order to discuss sex "properly." All this work and she does not even get to have an orgasm.

- *Got to talking about sex I said I have no feelings of desire but ok when started. He said I should do it for him. I asked how often he'd like sex and he said 5 times a week. I feel that's ~~excessive~~ unreasonable when I'd choose nil. We agreed to start with 3 times a week—maybe 1x intercourse, 2x oral sex and start with. I put in cap when I want. If either of us definitely don't want sex we should say when we get into bed so other knows and we can go straight to sleep.*

When they do finally discuss sex, it is a business negotiation where Hannah is working hard to hold her ground. They plan not only the amount, but the type of sex they will have. She will give him oral sex twice a week and then have intercourse once a week. The deal is set and neither partner was distracted by desire during the negotiation. But there is still no orgasm for Hannah.

At this point in the analysis of Hannah's diaries, I find it is impossible not to feel a parallel process of frustration, control, invasion, and desire. Reading entry after entry with Hannah not wanting sex, robotically having it anyways, saying it is ok, then saying it is not, not wanting to eat, eating anyways, feeling fat, feeling relieved Eric made her eat, I get frustrated. What does she want? I wonder where she is, what is her passion? Oddly, as much as I hate Eric's control and sadism, I find myself identifying with him, wondering what it is like to live with Hannah. Is his sadistic control released due to frustration or an inability to please Hannah? Or does he not even notice? What a powerful relational position it is to live with no desires, no way to be pleased.

This is invisible but potent resistance. It is profoundly disruptive to the system (e.g. Eric's invasions of her body), and although it is not so effective at lessening Eric's control over her, it does seem to shift her relationship to his control. So, as these diaries proceed, Eric's hold on Hannah's desire appears to crack further, when she details what is clearly her own sexual desire.

- *I feel abused by so many men that even with E. I sometimes feel guilty. Maybe when in my fantasies it is either forced or not me i.e.*

another role or times gone by. Maybe only then can I accept myself in
sex [She fantasizes about being forced to have sex and/or she dissoci-
ates and imagines someone else is having sex].
Find I need fantasies to enjoy sex.
sexuality w/E—can cuddle/kiss
—not interest in sex
abuse issues—sexual turn on
—still sexual interest
—satisfy myself

We see her struggling here, not necessarily to identify her desires, but to
allow herself to hold them. As she writes, "maybe" her fantasies involve
forced sex, "maybe" she needs fantasies to accept her desire. This tentative
voice gets solid when she shifts to a list. The importance of lists is discussed
elsewhere (see Gentile, 2006a, 2006b), but suffice to say the structure of
lists provides a tighter limiting membrane than mere prose. Here she
clearly states three different times that her sexual desire is linked to her fantasies, not to Eric, and that these fantasies are often re-creations of past
abuse. These re-creations indicate that time and space are abundant here,
as Hannah is experiencing sex in multiple times and places at once. She may
be having sex with Eric in the present, but she is also fantasizing about being
overpowered by someone, re-creating various situations of her past abuse,
or she imagines she is watching someone else having sex.

Although she may feel she deserves an orgasm, Hannah cannot allow
herself to hold her sexual desire. Fantasies about being overpowered allow
Hannah to enjoy sex by placing her guilt or disturbing feelings about sex in
the fantasized situation and not in her physical response. This way, it is not
her body that is betraying her with its desire, but the other person. This
other person exists only in fantasy, thus, he or she is under her control this
time. These different fantasies also allow Hannah to split her emerging sexual desire into different scripts, times, and places, ensuring that one does
not overpower her. She can buffer one desire with another, a made-up fantasy with reality, enabling Hannah to act out different roles.

Davies and Frawley (1992, 1994) have written about these various configurations of relational desire, allowing a survivor to play the abuser, victim, or rescuer in an attempt at integration. Similarly, Freud (1919)
described the masochist being beaten simultaneously identifying with and
fantasizing that she is the sadist doing the beating. Meanwhile, the sadist is
fantasizing that he is the masochist being beaten.

In her fantasies, Hannah can play the roles of masochist/victim, sa-
dist/abuser, rescuer and witness. She can enjoy sex in one, be disturbed by it
and create a different dyad having sex in another, she can absent her body

altogether and just watch the action, or she can struggle to integrate the past in a re-creation. Through all these fantasies, she avoids having sex with Eric in the moment. She can keep herself from being temporally pinned down by being in a number of different times simultaneously. The problem is that wherever she is in the fantasy, she is still allowing herself to physically have sex with Eric when she does not want to. She is still being pinned down in space, even as she is escaping in time.

This analysis demonstrates the fact that just creating an embodied experience is probably traumatic for Hannah, for it necessarily entails connecting with her experiences of abuse. Her fantasies are potentially re-traumatizing based on their violent content, but they may create a space for her to claim some desire. So she does have desire, and in some ways she clearly knows her desire, but she does not speak it or place it within a relational space. It is projected onto Eric one moment, contained in lists the next, spoken in the negative when she desires not to have sex with Eric, then it is seen peeking out from behind a memory of abuse that she describes as being sexually exciting. Desire is a hot potato that must be thrown into another. In doing so, Hannah, in relation to Eric, retains the power of having no desire. She does not need another body for an orgasm. She can evacuate all of her desires and watch them work on Eric, how they make him want to control her. She can emerge the victor in this sexual negotiation, while remaining his captive in their marriage.

Hannah has learned how to refract her desires, getting around the cultural dictates abnegating female desire, so her subjectivity is quite slippery. She is there and not there simultaneously. Because she must constantly project her desires onto others, her only form of temporal linking casts these desires as emanating not from within, but as an invasion from the outside. Consequently, her projected desires and Eric's desires are probably indistinguishable, leaving her feeling as a powerless object to his whims.

Eric as the Keeper of Hannah's Image and Experience

- *Went to bed and he saw my nails—hand and toes—I'd cut them very low in anger one evening. I said it's 'cos I don't like myself and don't care about my appearance. He was quite angry and said if not for me I should make an effort for him.*
- *E's view was I need to pull myself together—eat normally, put on makeup daily and especially when I get home, [wear] sexy clothes and no knickers sometimes to feel sexy not worry if I get fatter—just do it for his sake if not mine and maybe I'll enjoy it. Also grow my*

nails and take time for myself. He suggested writing a list of positive action points carrying round with me pinning on fridge etc. and agreeing to do. I'm not sure if this is me—feels like what I'm being told to do. I suppose I can give it a try. Trouble is it's back to acting and not sorting out underlying problems.

Yet another struggle for control of Hannah's body revolves around her appearance and image. In the example above, Eric sees that Hannah has cut her nails off and is scratching her legs and making marks on them. Eric buckles down and jumps further into her to control every crevice of her experience. He details the image he wants her to project, if only for him. This is literally an image, it is not about Hannah finding or creating her self, or even deciding what image she wants to convey.

It is Eric's desire that she come home from work and stay dressed up all evening, keep her hair down, her makeup and jewelry on, with perfectly painted nails. But he moves beyond the image by stating that she should also be in a good mood in the evenings for him. He tells her how many times per week he wants to have sex and he insists that they construct a list of ways she should keep up her appearance. And if penetrating her body and mind here is not enough, he suggests that they write this list within her diaries, and then post it on the refrigerator so that they can both be reminded of her goals.

Here Eric tells Hannah to put her body, literally and symbolically, on display for him. He wants her to be an object without any desire (she should just have sex for him), or needs of her own (she should keep herself attractive to and for him). But he is also penetrating her symbolic body—her use of lists within her diaries. He becomes a focus of one of her lists and she will have to rip it out of her diary, her only safe and private space, to hang it up. He will jump inside her private space, create a foreign body, make her rip is out of herself, and then place it on public display. As I have described elsewhere (see Gentile, 2006a), Hannah's diaries create a "third" in their relationship, providing a relational buffer for Hannah. These diaries also serve a therapeutic function for Hannah. Therefore, penetrating her use of them is yet another violent act of domination.

Ironically, by creating the Hannah he expects, as opposed to the Hannah that exists, Eric is not getting closer to Hannah. Instead, he creates another third in their relationship. Placing this idealized body on the refrigerator creates space between the real Hannah and himself As described of repetitions, Eric's action creates both further trauma and the potential for subversion.

First, Eric's action is an additional, insidious invasion of Hannah that succeeds in further splitting her psyche and soma. When a caretaker is not attuned to the infant, development proceeds only by splitting the psyche and soma, with the psyche dominating the desires of the soma (Winnicott, 1958, 1970).

Here Eric is taking advantage of this split that was created by years of abuse. He enters and travels freely within this space, further splitting them apart by creating an objectified, idealized version of Hannah. His role as the one who knows how often to have sex, how much to eat, what she should look like, solidifies his position within this triangle, fueling her already potent distrust of her body, and enhancing her dependence on him as the expert psyche. As such, Eric provides the space, quite literally, for Hannah to remain bulimic. He stands in the way of her recovery, not only with his openly sadistic control of her appetites and appearance, but because their relationship is based upon a triangulated way of relating that necessitates a huge split between Hannah's mind and her body. She cannot trust her body and remain with Eric because he cannot tolerate her having her own sense of her body and her own relationship with her body. He has to remain a translator intercepting and distorting communications. Thus, she must remain sick in order to remain married to Eric.

By fueling her distrust of her body, Eric sides with the abusive parent persona (Davies & Frawley, 1992, 1994) that Hannah has internalized. By supporting her identification with the aggressor (her parent), he reinforces that she deserved to be abused, so, her body—the container of her memories of trauma and abuse—must be innately bad. Thus, she cannot possibly rely on it for any form of knowing and she must continue to dissociate it and its contents. By supporting the strength of her internalized abusive parent, Eric reinforces that she cannot trust her memories or her body. There is no possibility for Hannah to integrate her psyche and soma or for her to develop the capacity to experience herself as being real. And living in and of the world as a dissociated being means that she has no internal compass, no sense of who she is, what she wants. It requires that she continue to look to Eric to tell her all about herself, thereby solidifying the circle of her abuse.

But creating the ideal Hannah also functions to help Hannah. As Davies and Frawley (1992, 1994) contend, healing from trauma requires that the adult persona acknowledge both the dissociated embodied memories of the abused child and the part of herself that allied with the abusive parent to blame herself for the abuse. With Eric standing as the gatekeeper between her body and her mind, she does not have to tackle this frightening and potentially fragmenting rapprochement. She is not threatened with integration. The importance of this function cannot be overemphasized.

Existing without agency (the capacity for temporal linking), is like walking through a world of chaos with no sense of where to begin, the direction to take, what is up, down, or sideways. Self-destructive violence can stand in to link internal intentional states with external events (Fonagy & Target,

1998). This violence can create the skin, the limiting membrane, differentiating inner–outer, self–other, enabling the emergence of spatial orientation. Cutting, binging and purging, and other forms of self-destruction also become a concretized, physical representation of cause and effect, time. But because this time and space, temporal linking, operates literally on the skin, or in the food taken in and expelled, it does not require the creation of an internal space, a capacity for.[2]

Given this, it is not surprising that each time Hannah is suddenly faced with integration, she reinscribes self-destructive violence as temporal linking. Here, as Eric becomes aware of her growing attempts at self-mutilation (which are occurring as she is beginning to speak about sex in family therapy), he reinserts himself as the keeper of her desires. Although this reinsertion does keep her from creating her own links, it also saves her from further self-destructive violence. He is saving her from having to experience her self prematurely, without having developed her own capacity for temporal linking.

Second, by creating an ideal Hannah, Eric has inadvertently created a larger space for Hannah's resistance. With each decree he hands down, Hannah creates a secret space (Khan, 1993) within which to encapsulate her self in hiding. Through her secrets, she creates a space to begin to hold herself. So when he tells her to stop writing in her diary she hides it and writes in the middle of the night while locked in the bathroom. When he tells her to keep up her appearance for him, she undermines this control by noting that he is asking her to act, not to "sort things out" more deeply. She uses Eric's order to differentiate between "manufacturing the feelings of being a genuine person" (Guntrip, 1971, p. 149), and working toward being able to be one. With each attempt at control, Eric seems to create the space for Hannah's differentiation.

Eric as the Keeper of Affective Experience
or Hannah Using Eric as a Container?

I have alluded to the possibility that as controlling as Eric is, Hannah may participate in this control by using Eric to contain her experiences. This complex process requires a more in-depth look, which is provided by focus-

---

[2]Fonagy and Target (1998) seem to assume the presence of internal intentions, which implies the existence of an internal space. For Hannah, I wonder if she has had the opportunity to create such an internal space. Even when such a space does exist, the use of self-destructive violence indicates that this space has been dissociated and is unavailable to access for the creation of temporal linking. The process then is transferred to the skin or into other physically self-destructive behaviors, where linking becomes concrete and visible.

ing on one of the rare family therapy sessions when Hannah gets angry. As she writes:

- *E. was asked his greatest fear. Was that if he was critical, I would leave him. That he is being tested—if he doesn't agree to address problem areas (e.g. anger, and sex) I will leave him. I replied they are problems and part of why I'm in therapy. He was very literal—"you came into therapy due to your mum not our marriage." Explained slowly—in. mental shorthand and less literal then E. [I] Said I did come in and addressed childhood/eating issues but feel there is dysfunction in sex life and anger and I cope through inappropriate images [fantasies] and food. Want to give up old ways and have healthy new ones. E. was very scared of my response even though I'd heard his fear before.*

  Lili explained he had choices too. I wasn't one with all power—he could say what he wanted too. Then L. asked what I feared, round anger—E.'s at me; my hurt of him as "child"; my "failure" of him as a mother and repeat of his mother leaving him after he had trusted her. As he pushed a little about anger. I was tearful and my mind became chaotic—I couldn't think logically anymore—just cried. E. said [I] couldn't say anything yet as I'm too vulnerable—clearly I am and L. talking very slowly. E. also explained we don't get angry—I've taught him to speak to "personnel" speak and we both intellectualize issues. Don't ever express true anger—indirect; patterns around each other; snap at each other etc.

In this entry, Hannah gets angry at Eric for saying he thinks if "he doesn't agree to address problem areas" she will "leave him." She describes having to use "mental shorthand" in order for Eric to understand her thoughts. Eric becomes "scared." Lili, the family therapist, then asks Hannah what she fears around anger and Hannah responds that she fears hurting Eric. Eric "pushed" her about her anger and she literally, immediately decompensates within the entry. "I was tearful and my mind became chaotic—I couldn't think logically anymore." And as she is decompensating, Eric steps in to protect her from Lili, saying she is "too vulnerable" to continue, and explains that as a couple, "we don't get angry."

This interaction seems to demonstrate the dynamic of Hannah taking the role of the sick child as if to make herself impotent in relation to Eric's power. But by doing this, she does not have to experience her anger, indeed, she is not allowed to experience her anger. Instead, she decompensates and he takes care of her by ending the inquiry. Eric gains control through Hannah losing her voice and becoming mentally chaotic. And in her chaos, Eric emerges as the rational logical one who knows about their interaction patterns. He can be the one to tell Lili how things are in their marriage, because Hannah is too sick to continue, even though only two lines before, Hannah was the one using "mental shorthand" trying to explain something he was unable to understand.

This is only one example of many where Hannah seems to defer power to Eric by becoming a sick, helpless, vulnerable child to his omnipotent parent. As she hints within the family therapy session, her anger is so powerful she can hurt Eric. Indeed, turned inward, it causes her to decompensate. Harris (1997) contends that more than anything, women fear hurting others with their anger, and they often do not have the opportunities to develop the capacities to create temporal links to help self-regulate and symbolically express their anger. In which case, Hannah's anger might be so powerful that she is too frightened to hold onto it even within the family therapy environment. It is easier to be a sick child in relation to a powerful parent than to be an angry woman in relation to a weak man.

Hannah is not only decompensating under the weight of her anger, she is desperately attempting to cover Eric's sudden vulnerability, apparent when Hannah must use "mental shorthand" with him. Here the restrictions on gender limit Hannah to either/or experiencing. Either she is strong and he is weak, or she is weak and he is strong. There is no way to share power or to empower one another. It is a dog-eat-dog relationship and she knows to let him emerge as the strong man and he knows how to help her emerge as the weak woman. This line-by-line analysis indicates that the dynamic of power in their relationship is not so clear cut.

Who Leads in this Sado-Masochistic Dance?

In order to explore who is leading in their sadistic-masochistic dance, Hannah's masochism, submission, and attempts at surrender (Ghent, 1990) must take center stage.

Novick and Novick (1987) describe masochism "as an *adaptation* to a disturbed environment" and "a *defense* against aggression" (p. 354; emphasis in original). So in the face of a controlling and invasive mother (the father's participation is left untheorized), the child uses her self, becoming the container for the mother's aggression. Using her own body to gratify the mother's needs maintains the mother as the idealized object. The "omnipotent aggression" (p. 367), experienced as such by the child who cannot yet symbolize and regulate it, must be turned against the self and not toward the mother. This turning against the self may take the form of beating fantasies, or I would add, relating to others who will literally or symbolically do the beating for you.

Certainly, Hannah grew up in a disturbed household where her mother's terrifying nightmares and "unpredictable moods" scared her and threatened to push her father out of the house. As she writes, "I had never felt secure at home because mum was so unpredictable." So Hannah grew up with a model of anger not only being bad, but literally being "omnipotently" destructive, with the power to annihilate relationships. Additionally, she emerged in relation to a mother and father who were invasive and controlling, both using her body to gratify their needs.

Ghent (1990) claims that some instances of masochism involve a "passionate longing to surrender" (p. 115). Ideally, surrender recalls Loewald's (1980) notion of eternity, where one "plunges into no-differentiation," (Milner as quoted in Ghent, 1990, p. 113), emerging more whole, more linked, more plumped up with meaning, and more vital. But submission and masochism can masquerade as surrender. Unlike the creativity of surrender, submission typically operates in the service of maintaining the status quo, reinforcing traumatic repetitions. Instead of the blissful, vitalizing unity of surrender, submission requires being a puppet to another.

When an individual is emerging within an environment of extreme impingements, she "develops as an extension of the shell rather than of the core, ... [she] then *exists by not being found*" (Winnicott, 1950–1955, as quoted in Ghent, 1990, p. 117). These impingements become the sole organizing pattern around which she is able to relate to herself and others. This pattern creates a model of self-regulating by externally using the other as if he or she is a self-state. This complex maneuvering illustrates that masochism is not traumatic repetition in the service of mastering the original experience, but a desperate bid to integrate it (Ghent, 1990), to create meaningful temporal links, to resist the pattern of trauma. As Ghent notes, "the intensity of the masochism is a living testimonial of the urgency with which some buried part of the personality is screaming to be exhumed" (p. 116), penetrated and recognized. Unfortunately, this desperation in the absence of faith in temporal linking results in submission.

Given the "disturbed" environment of aggression and impinging control within which Hannah was raised, she may feel she needs to be in a relationship with a man who can physically and symbolically hold and contain her omnipotent, unorganized, unsymbolized anger, and not let it annihilate him as the idealized, merged-with Other. This is submission in her quest to surrender. Indeed, when she is listing what qualities she wants in a man, she notes that he must be tall and bigger so she can "respect" him. She cannot feel safe enough to surrender unless her male partner is large enough to pin her down and save herself from her own aggression. This is a classic case of Ghent's submission. Hannah's seemingly masochistic participation in a sadistic relationship may be in part an attempt at keeping her aggression from annihilating others and herself, as well as being the only relational way she can feel recognized (Benjamin, 1995).

But any discussion of masochism, submission, or surrender is incomplete without addressing the cultural inability to symbolize female anger and aggression. Harris (1997) notes that girls fear their anger and aggression because they are not taught how to express and experience them. Thus, we have a transgenerational cycle of being gendered by having indigestible omnipotent aggression passed from mother to daughter (Harris, 2005). This cycle can only be broken in relation to a nonsadistic parent who can contain and not retaliate, in the face of the child's unsymbolized aggression (Harris, 1997). Certainly both male and female children benefit from this nonsadistic parent, but for girls, this parent is key. The culture creates many different avenues for male aggression to be digested, temporally linked or acted out. The fields of competition and aggression are greatly limited for girls, and they generally take the form of self-destruction. Thus, experiencing and expressing aggression not only destroys relationships, it threatens ones identity as a female in our culture. This cultural deficit, in addition to her family history, leaves Hannah with no space within which to hold or conceptualize her aggression.

So, as an adult, the dynamics of Hannah's marriage work to turn all of her anger into an enactment of being the sick child. When she is angry she vomits, attempts to overdose, or gets upset and tearful. Eric, then, becomes the omnipotent parent who helps to maintain Hannah's location as the sick child, reinforcing her inability to speak her anger. She can remain the infirm, helpless woman in relation to her powerful husband. So the masochistic dynamics of her marriage help her regulate her affect while they function to reinscribe her gender.

Given all that is hanging on Eric and Hannah's relational dance, it is no surprise that there is a high price to pay for disrupting their perfect rhythm. As Hannah writes of her marriage,

- *If our relationship does not survive, I can't live without him so I must die. Truly believe now if family therapy does not work I am not worthy of living.*

There is a great deal of potential power being enacted by the masochist, Hannah, in order to keep sadist, Eric, on a pedestal. She is willing to die to maintain his status as the omnipotent parent. Having said this, I am stuck in a dangerous feminist dilemma. If I acknowledge her power and control, I am saying she is asking for it. If I disavow her power and control, I leave her as a helpless victim. Even couching these statements within her history and bringing in a cultural analysis of female aggression, still leaves me treading dangerous misogynist waters, where the onus of change rests on Hannah learning to symbolize her aggression "properly," as if that would end Eric's abusive behavior.

Masochism, sadism, submission and control all boil down to power, another term that is gendered male (Harris, 1997). To be powerful as a woman is to abnegate gender. Within a patriarchal culture, women are literally named as the property of men, both as daughters and wives. When Hannah married Eric she said she knew she had to take his name and "obey" him. Indeed, it was probably in the vows they took. In other words, Hannah's sadomasochistic relationships with men are not only the result of her familial disturbances, her desires to submit in an attempt to surrender, or her inability to culturally symbolize female anger. These relationships are supported by a culture that considers women the property of men, where movies, books, and advertisements sexualize and romanticize women's suffering, martyrdom, and masochism. This makes surrender a very tricky concept. After all, power and aggression can only emerge gendered male in relation to victimization which is gendered female. One can surrender in the moment with a partner, but if that partner has more power within the culture (based on identified gender, race, class, sexual orientation, etc.), then one is also necessarily submitting to them.

Within this cultural set-up, surrender is also always submission for women. Culturally based power creates the space between, that is, the relationship, thus, it, too, must be a subject of (psycho)analysis.

So Hannah can lose herself within Eric who will jump inside her to save her from her own experiences. Hannah submits to Eric's needs for dominance as Eric submits to Hannah's needs to be penetrated and controlled. As Hannah is being penetrated, symbolically and physically by Eric, in the moment of penetration, it is Hannah who suddenly may hold the power, while Eric, in the act of penetrating, is left momentarily vulnerable. He needs Hannah to penetrate.

However, given this last addition to the analysis, we can see that their versions of submission are not equitable. Eric emerges as a male dominating a female in a patriarchal world, while Hannah emerges as a female submitting to a male in the same patriarchal world.[3] Hannah's submissive role will always rely on dissociating her capacities, while Eric's will always rely on dissociating his vulnerabilities. And although neither is particularly healthy, by

---

[3] I am creating a false sense of simplicity by focusing on gender to the exclusion of race, class, and ethnicity. One can see just how complicated power as race, ethnicity, class, and gender operates relationally, and how imperative it is to create the means to explore it. In this chapter, I have focused on gender, with the implicit, albeit often unwritten, understanding that Hannah is walking through what appears to be a white, upper-middle class British world, relationally constructed by a white, middle class woman from the United States.

playing the game, Eric gains status and power whereas Hannah must cautiously constrain hers and project it onto Eric. Eric's strength depends on Hannah's weakness, and he is willing to tie her up, hit her, colonize her body, to maintain this arrangement. And he can do this, without police intervention or criminal charges of battery. She is his property. This trade-off works so well because it follows the traditional cultural narrative of heterosexual relationships that temporally link vulnerable women with strong heroic men and strong women with castrated men, his behavior (the effect) as her responsibility (the cause).

Thus, the symbols through which women and men come into being as temporally linking people, are those that teach women early to hide their strength and power in order to maintain their bonds with others, especially with men. This means that the position from which Hannah makes such choices about her behaviors is not at the same level of privilege and freedom as that from which Eric chooses his behaviors. It may take two to tango, and her behavior necessarily impacts and influences his, but relational equality is distorted.

Although freedom of choice is a myth for both of them because their responses are generated from gendered, raced, classed, pallets of potential relational interactions, he has the privilege of much wider freedom of movement both within their relationship and in the outside cultural world. Within her relational world, Hannah may have a great deal of power, but her freedom of choice in terms of expressing, experiencing and relationally enacting this power is severely constrained so that, like her resistance, it most often takes the form of self-destruction, traumatic repetition, submission and the creation of secrets.

As this analysis demonstrates, submission, masochism, and sadism not only masquerade as surrender, they co-exist. One is always submitting or surrendering in relation to not only individual bodies but also the cultural bodies that provide meaning for experience. Thus, a critical analysis of power is imperative in order to explore the many different levels of submitting/surrendering. Resistance, goes hand in hand with power, often functioning to make it more visible (Hoy, 2004).

In these five diaries, Hannah was submerged within Eric's will and body. His appetites were her appetites. Only when I shifted focus to explore the hints of her resistance, did her body/mind begin to appear. This body/mind emerged through self-destruction. In doing so, she struggles to resist not only Eric, but also cultural bodies that recognize and identify "female" primarily through submission (the forms submission takes may vary according to race, class, ethnicity, and religion). Sussing out some of the many different layers and manifestations of power, control, submission, resistance, and surrender in relation to individual and cultural bodies, then, was key to recognizing Hannah's potential capacities for transformation and healing.

References

Benjamin, J. (1995), *Like Subjects, Love Objects*. New Haven, CT: Yale University Press.

Bulter, J. (1993), *Bodies That Matter: On the Discursive Limits of "Sex."* New York: Routledge.

Davies, J. M., & Frawley, M. G. (1992), Dissociative processes and transference counter-transference paradigms in the psychoanalytically oriented treatment of adult survivors of childhood sexual abuse. *Psychoanal. Dial.,* 2:5–36.

——— (1994), *Treating the adult survivor of childhood sexual abuse: A psychoanalytic perspective*. New York: Basic Books.

Fonagy, P., & Target, M. (1998), Mentalization and the changing aims of child psychoanalysis. *Psychoanal. Dial.,* 8:87–114.

Freud, S. (1919/1958), "A Child is Being Beaten": A contribution to the study of the origin of sexual perversions. *Standard Edition,* XVII:175–204. Collected papers, Vol. II Chap. XVII.

Gentile, K. (2007), *Creating Bodies: Eating Disorders as Self-Destructive Survival*. Hillsdale, NJ: The Analytic Press.

——— (2006), Timing development from cleavage to differentiation. *Contemporary Psychoanalysis*, 42(2).

Ghent, E. (1990), Masochism, submission, surrender. *Contemp. Psychoanal.,* 26:169–211.

Guntrip, H. (1971), *Psychoanalytic Theory, Therapy and the Self*. New York: Basic Books.

Harris, A. (1997), Aggression, envy, and ambition: Circulating tensions in women's psychic life. *Gender and Psychoanalysis,* 2:291–326.

——— (2005), *Gender as soft assembly*. Hillsdale, NJ: The Analytic Press.

Hopkins, B. H. (1997), Winnicott and the capacity to believe. *Internat. J. Psycho-Anal.,* 78:485–497.

Hoy, D. C. (2004), *Critical Resistance: From Poststructuralism to Post-Critique*. Cambridge, MA: MIT Press.

Khan, M. M. (1993), Secret as potential space. In: *Between Reality and Fantasy: Winnicott's Concepts of Transitional Objects and Phenomena,* eds. S. A. Grolnick & L. Barkin. Northvale, NJ: Aronson, pp. 259–270.

Loewald, H. W. (1980), *Papers on Psychoanalysis*. New Haven, CT: Yale University Press.

Novick, K. K., & Novick, J. (1987), The essence of masochism. *Psychoanalytic Study of the Child,* 42:353–284.

Orbach, S. (1986), *Hunger Strike: The Anorexic's Struggle as a Metaphor for Our Age*. New York: W.W. Norton.

Reis, B. E. (1995), Time as the missing dimension in traumatic memory and dissociative subjectivity. In: *Sexual Abuse Recalled,* ed. J. Alpert. Northvale, NJ: Aronson, pp. 215–234.

van der Kolk, B. (1995), The body, memory, and the psychobiology of trauma. In: *Sexual Abuse Recalled,* ed. J. Alpert. Northvale, NJ: Aronson, pp. 29–60.

Winnicott, D. W. (1958), *Through Paediatrics to Psycho-Analysis*. New York: Basic Books.

——— (1950–1955). Aggression in relation to emotional development. In: *Through Paediatrics to Psycho-Analysis*. New York: Basic Books.

——— (1970), On the basis for self in body. *International Journal of Child Psychotherapy,* 1:7–16.

——— (1971), *Playing and Reality*. London: Tavistock/Routledge.

11

From Familiar Chaos to Coherence: Unformulated Experience and Enactment in Group Psychotherapy

Robert Grossmark, PhD

▼　▼　▼　▼　▼

Many relational psychoanalysts conduct group psychotherapy and group psychoanalysis, but few have applied evolving relational thinking to the theory and practice of group psychotherapy. There has yet to be such an attempt in the contemporary psychoanalytic literature. Within the group therapy field there is a gradual recognition of relational ideas such as therapist openness and authenticity (Wright, 2004), and intersubjectivity (Cohen, 2000). However, a broader consideration of the potential integration of the postmodern and hermeneutic emphases of contemporary psychoanalytic theory into the group therapy field is still lacking. This chapter is an attempt to build this integration and to illustrate how group therapy can be informed and transformed by relational psychoanalytic theory.

I believe that the following relational ideas add a new dimension to the understanding and practice of group psychotherapy: the focus on the interpersonalization and enactment of the patient's internal object world within the group matrix; the conceptualization of the unconscious as unformulated experience (Stern, 1997); the emphasis on multiple self states (Bromberg, 1998), and the dissociation and enactment of those states (Bromberg, 1998; Davies, 1996; Stern, 1997). These ideas offer an exciting addition to and rethinking of the major approaches in the group psychotherapy that influence my work. Foulkes (1948) developed the Group Analytic tradition that is founded on the idea of the social and communal nature of the individual. The group is viewed as a communicational network and all patterns of interaction within the group are seen as manifestations of unconscious communication. The shared work of understanding the group together creates a dynamic group matrix within which psychological healing can take place (Pines, 1983). Bion (1961) pioneered the theory of the group-as-a-whole, wherein the group is seen as an entity in its own right that is greater than the sum of its parts, with its own mental states (basic assumptions). The task of the group is to become a "work group" oriented to its goal rather than to be lost in the unconsciously driven basic assumption life where the primitive needs of pairing, fight–flight and dependency predominate. Agazarian (1992) applied general systems theory to the theory of the group-as-a-whole and outlined the developmental processes of the group, emphasizing the importance of subgrouping. The group therapist treats the group itself and may talk directly to the group-as-a-whole, rather than individuals within the group. Object relations approaches have conceptualized the group as the container into which the internal objects of the patients are projected, and have highlighted the crucial role of projective identification in all group interactions (Alonso & Rutan, 1984; Ashbach & Schermer, 1987). Self-psychological approaches (Harwood & Pines, 1988) address the repetitive and pathological ways in which group members strive to meet their self-object needs within the group situation and work to help patients develop more mature and stable means of sustaining themselves within the group. The evocation of the experience of shame in the group is given particular attention (Morrison, 1990). The Modern Group Analytic approach developed from the work of Hyman Spotnitz with very disturbed patients (Spotnitz, 1969) and addresses resistances to emotional communication, intimacy, and change in the group (Cohen, 2001; Ormont, 2001). Group members are asked to communicate their emotional responses to each other in the here and now. Failures or difficulties in doing so are regarded as resistances that are addressed in the moment, with particular attention given to resistances to the expression of aggression.

The Work of Group Therapy

Patients come to group therapy and engage in being themselves within the context of the group in such a way that both reveals and obscures who they are, and both opens and closes the path toward the emergence of new, growth-enhancing and potentially surprising experiences of themselves and others. The group members engage together in their well-worn pathways of being, of knowing and of not knowing, while simultaneously hoping for and searching for a new way to be.

As the group therapist, my task is primarily to create and maintain the safe, productive, and transformational space within which the group can do its work. I set the boundaries of the group in terms of attendance, confidentiality and acceptable behavior within the group. I tell the group members that their task is to talk to each other about themselves, their worlds, and each other. In particular, I try to promote honest and direct feedback about their feelings *toward each other* and toward me. That is, I ask group members to articulate as best as they can, the effects that they are having on each other and that the whole group experience is eliciting in them. The aim is to foster a living and breathing environment within which the members can experience themselves and others in both old and new ways. I emphasize to group members that this is an experience that asks a lot of them and I work hard to support them individually and collectively in the group. By working together the group members become part of a dynamic group that is itself the agent of change. Rather than therapy *in* the group I am working toward a situation where there is therapy *by* the group.

It is not uncommon for the group to engage in what feels like chaotic, painful, or numbing interactions with each other and with me. Invariably these interactions are variations on the very damaging, deadening, and mystifying dynamics of the group members' lives and minds. When these internalized modes of experiencing themselves and others unfold, it is often as familiar, repetitive patterns in relationships that are experienced as unthought "things that happen." They leave the individuals with a dead and helpless feeling about themselves and the sense that this is "the way things just are." My work is to help the group find what is meaningful and coherent in these chaotic interactions and to allow the emergence of what has until now been unformulated and stuck in the realm of what cannot be thought and felt. Let me give an example from a recent group session that illustrates the emergence of meaning and relatedness from a repetitive, deadening and unthought state.

Kevin has been talking in the group with an intense rigidity that the group is familiar with, about how it is impossible for him to not see the world as full of the certainty of failure and retribution. He has such overwhelming anxiety in every area of his life that he cannot think of it being any other way. The group seems impatient; they have heard this from Kevin many times. There have been comments that Kevin is getting on "one of his rants." The group has made many attempts to find a way to communicate with Kevin in these moments but often becomes deadened and incapacitated by the intensity and rigidity of these "rants." He will not let anyone in. He and the group are enacting the very dynamic that is being described. The group have called it "getting trapped in a Kevin-hole." I feel anxiety that we will be trapped again. This feeling mounts quickly within me to a kind of panic, and I begin to hate every moment that he is talking. Such reactions tell me that I am containing something painful and unbearable for Kevin and the group, but I too am locked into the group dynamic in that moment and cannot yet find a good way to release us. Hannah, a relatively new member stands up for Kevin and says, leaning in towards him, with much emotion that she feels strongly for Kevin's struggle with anxiety. She herself has intense struggles to overcome anxiety just to function from one day to the next. Kevin's face is fixed and he responds by talking even more compulsively about the overwhelming nature of his anxiety. It appears to me that he has used Hannah's comments to amplify his ideas and his hopelessness. He has found an injection of mirroring for his solipsistic and stuck struggle and has deepened his isolated hole. He has been unable to feel the humanity of Hannah's reaching out to him, and the pain in her words. I interrupt him and ask him how he feels toward Hannah herself at this moment, not about her words but about her attempt to reach him. He stops, looks at Hannah and tears well up in his eyes. He is lost for words and cries for a while. He tells the group that he has no words to express the loneliness that he feels. The group is completely with him in this moment. For Kevin, these moments capture the emergence of a new experience that had been locked away by the terrified, rigid nonthought of his psychic orientation in the world. The group itself was freed from the "Kevin-hole" wherein Kevin was experienced as dead and unreachable and the group became hopeless, repetitive, and inert. Having seen the pain that Kevin was capable of feeling, group members were able to work in a different key with him, asking more questions and anticipating more feelingful interactions with him. The subsequent group interactions were infused with a vitality and aliveness.

In this example, we see the power of focusing the group on the emotional communication in the moment. My intervention highlighted the affective interpersonal aspect of Kevin's state. Kevin had been locked into a fixed and rigid view of himself and his object world. He could only receive Hannah's empathy as purely a mirroring of his repetitive dead state. His body, meanwhile, and in particular his eyes, had other ideas, and yearned for an emotional connection: a noncritical and nonanxiety-producing connection. This was not something, I believe, that was known to him, nor thought and then repressed. Rather, it was yet to take shape for him. It was unformulated. Like Emmanuel Ghent's patient who was not aware that she was cold until he offered her a blanket (Ghent, 1995), Kevin did not "know" that he was lonely and crying out for someone to be empathic to, and containing of his pain. Furthermore it was only in experiencing it with others, rather than the talking or thinking about it, that this revelation could come to be. One cannot know a new object relationship until one has it, and in these kinds of moments we can see how the group experience can foster the regeneration of a new object world.

The work of finding meaning rather than deadness is itself a reparative and restorative endeavor. The group can be a space and an object in and of itself that contains the qualities of mirroring, relatedness, and reparation.

Group members respond to and internalize these qualities over time. My hope is that they not only have an encounter with situations that promote the making of meaning out of their repetitive and empty experience but also that they will internalize and develop the reflective function and the ability to mentalize that emerge in the group, and that are initially embodied in my being and presence. These will be the building blocks in the restoration of themselves as empathic and intersubjective agents in their own lives. The group becomes a place where meaning and coherence emerge from what has been chaotic, dead, and meaningless, where the processes of thinking, relating, and mentalizing can grow. Group members begin to find experiences of agency and vitality where before they had non-experience and dead nonthought. The meaning of the group interactions is not regarded as fully formed unconscious material awaiting interpretation by the therapist in the group. Rather, the meaning is regarded as unformulated (Stern, 1997) and must be allowed to emerge in the work of the group. The emphasis is on helping the group to work to make that meaning with and for itself.

The thing that is inescapable in group therapy is the engagement with others and with the context of group. Group members are not solely working on their own issues and focusing on themselves. They are asked to contribute. Specifically, they are asked to have and express their feelings about what other members are talking about, their experience of the other members in the moment, and of the group as a whole. In this way they enter an intersubjective matrix wherein they can develop the capacity to experience other members and themselves as subjects in their own right. For instance, in the example just cited, Kevin initially responded to Hannah with no connection to her as a subject herself, but rather as a mere mirror for his repetitive and isolating state of grievance. Only when he was urged to respond to her, as a subject, with her own intense anxieties and her own need to connect to him as a subject himself, could he find a more intersubjective realm of interaction with her and the group. Simultaneously, she found an experience of having a meaningful impact on Kevin, the group, and me, and effectively began to introduce her subjectivity to the group.

In session, group members wait for their turn to speak, and work at finding the right moment and way to bring themselves into the process. They "give to" the group as well as "receive from" the group. My sense is that this not only evokes their family dynamics and the roles they have become locked into, but also mirrors the now-me–now-you turn-taking rhythm and emotional interpenetration of early mother–child interaction (Leal, 1983; Pines, 1998). In this way, the group is implicitly a context with the potential for the making of coherent meaning and psychological growth.

Enactment, Dissociation and Multiplicity
in the Group Situation

My approach differs from other approaches to group therapy that empha-size the centrality of both individual and group resistances and their analy-sis in the group. Ormont (2001) and others in the Modern Group Analytic tradition have most clearly placed resistance analysis at the center of their approach. Other classics of the group therapy canon, such as Yalom (1975) and Rutan and Stone (2001) integrate resistance analysis into a larger theo-retical frame. Overall, there has been a general acceptance in the group therapy field of the drive and defense model that underlies the focus on re-sistance analysis. In contrast, from an object relations approach, the group's behavior is regarded as the enactment of the inner world of the pa-tients in the group setting. Internal objects are projected onto other mem-bers, the leader and onto the group as a whole, in a constant kaleidoscope of mutual projective identification. Group behavior is not regarded as resis-tant, but as the externalized enactment of internal object relations or as the enactment of the actual object relationships of the patients' world.

In addition to thinking about the enactment of object relations in the group, I try to build on a hermeneutic and constructivist approach to psy-choanalysis that does not regard the unconscious as a storehouse of com-plete and inert memories, objects, and experiences waiting to be unearthed and brought to consciousness. The goal is to facilitate the creation of the meaning embedded in group behavior and, in so doing, the group makes new and transformative experiences. Individual and group behavior is not regarded as resistant and therefore a block to the true material that would become manifest once the block is removed. Rather, I assume that all the behavior of and within the group is some kind of communication of both the inner worlds of the members, and their unformulated experience, and can only be accessed by allowing the full enactment of these dynamics with-in the group setting.

Furthermore, I focus on the role of the enactment of dissociated self-states (Bromberg, 1998) in the group. These may be dissociated self-states of the individuals themselves or of the group as a whole. I try to help the group to find and then symbolize the self-states that are being enacted and to enable the group to "stand in the spaces" (Bromberg, 1998) within and between the different self-states that emerge in this process and therefore to help the group create a new, coherent, and meaningful experience. In the example just discussed, Kevin was mired in a dead self-state that had no access to a more alive self-state of pain and yearning. Hannah was able to detach from the group's hopeless and defeated self-state and find her empathic, energized self-state, also fused with real longing for connec-tion. These moments when there are sudden and visceral shifts in the state of the group, point to the presence of dissociated experience in the group and in this example, with Hannah's inspiration the group and the other members are finding ways to stand in the spaces between previously dissociated states.

When patients enter a group they experience something utterly new and unlike anything in their lives, yet also completely familiar and known. Stern (1997) borrows the phrase "familiar chaos" from Paul Valery. He describes a "state of mind cultivated and perpetuated in the service of the conservative intention to observe, think, and feel only in the well worn channels—in the service, actually of the wish not to think" (p. 51). Such a state of mind feels familiar and therefore a comfort, and yet is chaotic in that experience and thoughts are yet to be developed or formulated. The as-yet-unformulated experience is not accessed through interpretation, because there is nothing there yet to interpret. It becomes known as it is enacted in the group setting through the interactions between members or between members and the leader, or through group-as-a-whole phenomena that involve the whole group entering a state of mind—similar to Bion's (1961) ideas of Basic Assumptions in group life—often dedicated to not thinking or feeling and foreclosing the emergence of new thoughts. The leader is often involved unconsciously in the enactment along with the other group members, either in a dyadic manner or in terms of a group-as-a-whole enactment. The task of the leader and the group is to try to notice when these enactments are occurring—in everyday speech, "to figure out what's going on"—to describe the experience and then to try to make sense of it. In the above example, I think that Kevin, the group and myself were all caught in a version of Kevin's "familiar chaos." There was no thinking occurring, just the repetitive non-experience of his pain and the group's and my frustration and helplessness. I do not believe that interpretation of this process could have accomplished much beyond injuring Kevin further and perhaps the group members as well. It was Hannah who made the first new and fresh approach and enabled myself, and then Kevin to find some new experience. What emerged is the unspeakable and unformulated pain and longing that have been disintegrated in Kevin's rigid and aggressive stance in the world.

So how does the group therapist know when he or she is caught in an enactment? Stern (2004) has described the work of the individual analyst who tries to formulate his or her own experience when unconsciously engaged in an enactment. This asks much of the analyst. How can we see ourselves in a conscious way when we are unconsciously engaged in something? Stern suggests that one becomes aware of a "snag" in one's experience, like getting your sweater caught on a branch while walking in the woods. Careful attention to that kind of experience enables one to recognize that one is involved in an enactment. Once known, one tries to make sense of and extricate oneself and the patient. In order to extricate him or herself from the self-state that is engaged in the enactment, unable to think and vulnerable to the press of the patient's need to replay this particular object relationship, the analyst has to struggle to find the self-state that allows for perception, thought, and formulation. That is, the analyst has to be able to be in both self-states at once, to be lost in the patient's world and to be able to occupy one's role as analyst, simultaneously.

In the individual situation the multiplicity that both analyst and patient bring to the task is the key and the pathway to the resolution of enactments. In the group situation, we have not only the therapist and patient and the potential for multiple self-states that they bring, but there are actually many multiple selves in the room, if you will. In the example just cited, Hannah's self-state that strives to relate and make contact was available to her when the group and I were stuck in the self-state generated by Kevin's world. Often when the group-as-a-whole is engaged in a blind and total way, the group analyst is unable to maintain his or her analyzing function and stay in the self-state that will offer insight or at least some connection to the task of the group, to try to understand their experience. Unlike other approaches to group-as-a-whole phenomena (Agazarian, 1992; Bion, 1961), and unlike other approaches to group therapy, a relational approach does not assume that the group analyst can stay outside of the enactment with the clarity that enables accurate and meaningful interpretations of the group process. Indeed the idea that the group therapist is immune to group-as-a-whole processes and can maintain clarity of consciousness while the group members are swept away in the unconscious group process is seen from a relational perspective as both undesirable and actually impossible. Mitchell (1993, 1997) has persuasively reconsidered the analyst's authority and knowledge as entirely mediated by the analyst's own experience and subjectivity. It is only by becoming lost in the total experience of the group, or as Stern (1989) puts it, the "grip of the field" (p. 15) even if that involves a temporary destruction of thought processes (Gordon, 1994; Hinshelwood, 1994), that one can find and create meaning in the enactment. In situations such as this, the analyst has to work hard to help the group stay in touch with the task and to try to find one or some parts of some of the members who can begin the process of mentalizing and reflective function that will guide the group out of their temporary darkness. Experiences such as these are drenched in pain and struggle for the group members and the group analyst, but are the *sine qua non* of a group therapy experience that will be real and vital and will actually bring about change.

An Enactment in the Group

The example that follows illustrates how I integrate the concepts of enactment, dissociation and multiplicity into my approach to running a group.

Since Maggie had begun group, she was on the verge of leaving. She came to the group having graduated from the Day Program she had attended since discharge from the psychiatric hospital where she had been admitted after a descent into overwhelming suicidal despair and a complete inability to control or regulate her emotions and her state. She had recovered sufficiently to return to finish the last semester at Law School and subsequently found employment and has advanced at a reputable firm. She has tremendous academic and intellectual abilities that can temporarily offset her deep emotional vulnerabilities when she is in the work environment. In her personal life, she has little except her family to be involved with. Since her first session in the group she has often announced with little warning, often breaking into ongoing dialogue, that she is going to leave the group. The group at first was flustered and upset by these outbursts, typically giving her all of the attention for the rest of the session. She would talk of feeling unsafe in the group, of feeling that it is just not the place for her, that her work makes too many demands on her, and that the group just cannot understand her. She would often interrupt dialogue in the group, and say that she has something terribly important going on, and would then shift into mumbles and silence, saying "I can't; I can't," leaving the group in a state of desperation. On one occasion she got out of her seat to leave and once actually left the group in a rage only to return the next week and blithely apologize by saying that she knew what had happened and was now over it, offering no other substance. On another occasion she became so agitated she could only calm herself with medication right then and there, making quite a show of searching for and then gobbling the medication. At other times, she was a wonderful contributor to the group. She had insightful, kind and meaningful input to give to other members and often seemed to keep in mind details about other members that was greatly surprising to them. The group expressed their appreciation for her and their utter distress and helplessness when she would return to the intolerable state.

My feeling was that this was an enactment of emotional and physical abuse. My experience was of a physical body-blow when she would do these things, and certainly she succeeded in inducing profound distress, fragmentation and torture in the group. It seemed as if the group was the container within which the various roles of abuser–torturer, abused–tortured comforter–protector and so on were being played out in a dissociated manner as described by Davies and Frawley (1994). I decided to hold and contain these experiences and not to interpret this to the group. I believed that to interpret would have injured Maggie and the group by having their experience interpreted and known about before they themselves had come to their own understanding. An interpretation would have precipitously shifted the experience to the mental realm of knowledge that is *given*, rather than what can *emerge* in experience. I therefore understood that only by allowing these enactments to be fully realized and "lived out" (Joseph, 1989) could they become formulated and the dissociated self-states be integrated.

In the meantime, I feared for and tried to protect the group members from these capricious and hostile attacks on the group and on the minds and souls of the group members. I encouraged the group members to speak directly to Maggie and tried to do so myself, not flinching from calling her behavior "destructive" and "hostile" I was also mindful to be supportive and protective of her and her other self-states, always inviting whatever reparative gestures she might make, however weak, and suggesting to her and the group that I felt that she was terribly scared of getting too close to the group. Eventually after one particularly vicious attack, meted out in her typical dissociated manner the group, began to engage with her on a different level. Jane had talked tearfully for the first time, after some years in the group, about her gradual discovery of her father's infidelities when she was a child and how she had had to hide them from her mother, and was torn apart. She wept and the group members were uniformly touched and empathic, except for Maggie who sat silently seemingly uninvolved.

With about 10 minutes of the group remaining, I was concerned what effect this story of betrayal and fragmentation was having on Maggie and I asked her what was going on. She responded with a coldness that was quite viscerally shocking "Oh; quite honestly, I don't give a shit. I mean I don't want to offend anyone but I don't give a shit. I've got some really important things on my mind. None of you would understand. This is going to be my last group." She snarled and grimaced. Jane broke down, wailing, "How can you do such a thing. That's so, so cruel." Maggie was unfazed: "We're here to say what we're feeling, right, so I'm just saying what's on my mind!" I could feel violence inside me. Not intellectually, but coursing through me. I was paralyzed momentarily by the intensity of this violent feeling. I felt she was doing violence to the group, to group members for whom I have deep affection and admiration after much work and struggle. Michael took up the struggle in the group. He addressed Maggie: "Look; you're obviously doing something which is really screwed up and we are all here to take a look at ourselves and to try to learn something, so can we talk about what it is you're doing." Maggie said that no one in the group could possibly help her and that she was going to leave. Michael said with a deeply wounded and angry voice "You don't have any idea how much you hurt people, how much you are hurting us. So leave! If you can't handle it we should just be left to get on with things here." Maggie looked down an imperious nose at Michael and scoffed. Michael protested that he was just trying to help. I was distraught. I was glad that Michael was at least trying to make some connection here. I was still struggling to get over the body-blow feeling of violence: no doubt an enactment of the abusive violence that impacts the body and attacks mental processes, that Maggie must have suffered. I was, however able to find the self-state that enabled me to stay with the task of the group and to remain in touch with a sense that Maggie was in excruciating psychic pain. I was absolutely determined to try to not allow Maggie to simply leave the group, and certainly not like this, with no chance for reparation. I spoke to her and the group saying that this was a difficult passage, but that I was sure it would be useful for everyone to hang in and to keep trying to communicate with each other. I addressed her directly, with firmness and kindness saying that I understood that she was compelled to leave and that she was struggling with something unbearable, but I emphasized that I had the conviction that she would gain real benefit from staying the course, however difficult. I tried to give her a sense that I understood that she was in terrible pain and terrified.

Driving home, I reflected on these events and though still filled with a sense of disruption and disturbance, I felt that by finding my own self-state and voice that could reach out empathically to Maggie and the group I had begun to find my way into a space that was both in and between the pain and torture of this group moment, and my own ability to be self-reflective and mindful. I did not know whether she would return but I felt that she would. I trusted her other more related and less damaged self-states. The next week continued in a similar vein. My feeling was that Maggie's warring internal object world was now becoming interpersonalized and enacted in the group and that this was the only way that she could communicate her story and her world. For the next few sessions, she and Michael were at each other. Any time one would speak the other would roll their eyes, disagree and attack the other. They—and we—were in the grip of a vile and assaultive enactment. Michael was consumed with Maggie's attack on the group and her constant threats to leave. He felt utterly bound to her and completely tortured by her. She was enraged with him; she felt he willfully misunderstood her and was trying to twist her words and her intentions. The vociferousness of their conflict was disturbing to the group, but was absolutely gripping. During these weeks everyone attended and arrived early, without fail. For Jane, issues of guilt came up. She, in her own familiar chaos, felt guilty. Somehow this ugly state of affairs was her doing, even though rationally, she could say that that did not make sense. Harry was overcome with fear, of his own violence and of the "family" breaking apart as his had done when he was a teenager. At one point in despair, during a very heated exchange between Michael and Maggie, he began to beat his own head with his fist. I quickly jumped in: "Stop! This is painful but you don't have to damage yourself! I know if you can stop and think, you can try to put into words what's going on for you rather than hurt yourself!" Harry stopped hitting himself and wept, shaking with fear. He said that he was terrified; that conflict in his family was always so scary and was never anything but painful. This was a turning point, because both Michael and Maggie seized the task together of helping Harry through this storm. Both implored him to understand that however intense this seemed, it was healthy; no one was going to actually get hurt, and in fact their conflict was a way to work something out. It was the first sign of a thaw in the ice between Michael and Maggie, the first sign that both had some empathic awareness of the other and that each was beginning to be able to, at least momentarily, bridge from the dissociated torture/tortured self-state to a more reflective, reparative and comforting state: to find the space between and within these dissociated self states and to occupy it. I added to their impassioned attempts to reach and help Harry. I told him that I understood that from his past experience he assumed that it was inconceivable that talking and expressing emotion could be productive or anything but destructive, and that people who express anger at each other are unable to have any other thoughts. I urged him to try to digest what Maggie and Michael were telling him and try to consider that even though they were locked in this angry conflict they also had spaces in their mind to know that this would be productive and most importantly, to be caring and thoughtful about him. I was addressing Harry and also talking to Maggie, Michael and the whole group. Anger does not have to obliterate other experience.

During this period in the group, I found that I needed all my energy to simply hold the group. My priorities had shifted. All my energies were involved with ensuring the actual and emotional survival of the group; I had no mental energy available for anything more such as linking comments that might have clarified the enactment. Here again, we see the beauty of the group situation. I could not come up with the intervention that would free the group from this impasse—and by the fourth week it sure felt like an impasse—but other group members could. When once again Michael and Maggie locked horns and angered each other, Jane interjected. Managing to free herself from the guilt that paralyzed her mind in the group and in her life, she was able to find the clearing in her mind that allowed her to *reflect about* the situation while still being in it. She said "Don't you see; both of you are just locked in your old family dynamic here!"

The group stopped in its tracks. Both Michael and Maggie took up this idea as if it were the first time anyone had ever said anything in the group about behavior relating to their family dynamic. Michael related this to his mother. He talked about how this felt just like how he is locked into his damaged and needy, yet abusive and self-involved mother. He keeps returning to spend time with the family and it's always the same. It is confusing to the point that he doesn't know if he starts the abusive cycle provocatively, or if he's responding to it. All he knows is that he's exhausted and has to find a way to change. Maggie spoke similarly about the cycles of abuse and neglect in her family between her and her parents and between the siblings. More significantly, some weeks later she spoke for the first time in her life about memories she has had for years and never shared with anyone, of being sexually abused as a child by a distant relative in the presence of her mother. This is work that she has now begun and continues in her individual treatment as well as the group. She still periodically feels the impulse to leave the group but is more able to find the space between that self-state with its blind impulse and her reflective and related self. The enactment of the abusive relationship, and the ability of the group to experience it, not intellectually, but by *living* it with her, has allowed her to experience it in the present and begin to apply her mind to understanding it. When Maggie and Michael found the bridge together to the space between the tortured dissociated selves and the comforting reflective selves in their response to Harry's terror, they forged a new area of experience together with the group. This allowed them a space into which to receive Jane's comment about the replay of their family dynamic. Prior to this, neither they nor the group had access to such a space and hence any words could only be heard as assault and domination, rather than as helpful communication. Since then, Maggie and Michael became a kind of unit in the group. As if their relationship had been forged in fire, they have been supportive and extremely understanding of each other. These events are often called up in the group as an important and productive time for the group.

There is much that can be said about the example just discussed. It serves to illustrate the value of facilitating the emergence and unfolding of an enactment within the group itself. I believe it would have foreclosed the experience if I had conceptualized Maggie's constant leave-taking of the group as resistance, or interpreted it prematurely as the projection of violence and abuse into the group. It was vital for her to feel contained by me and by the group so that she could continue to enact the torture that she had suffered in her past, and lives with in her internal world. The torture dynamic was not repressed, but existed in her in an unintegrated dissociated space that could only be accessed and made available for mentalization and understanding via *the living of it in a safe and containing space*. The same can be said of Michael who previously could describe quite well the craziness of his family, but who had never come close to letting himself feel and experience the degree of damage and torture that is embedded in him and his family. I believe that a crucial part of the creation of the space within which such a powerful enactment can be realized has to do with my containing the unformulated parts of the experience and allowing them to disturb a part of my mind. This is the only way to "know" that one is engaged in an enactment. I knew something was brewing within Maggie, but did not know what it was. I knew there was a "snag" that kept pulling at me in a disturbing and unsettling way from the first time that she spoke of needing to leave the group. I knew that whatever it was, it would unfold in due course, if I could just hold the frame. To have placed myself outside the group and interpreted from such a "perch" (Modell, 1991) would, I believe have abandoned the group to the terror that was about to unfold. That would have foreclosed the emergence of these dynamics for Maggie, Michael, Harry, Jane, and the rest of the group. They were not yet ready to contain the level of cruelty and terror that was about to emerge. It needed to be contained within my self as well as the group. We shared the burden. To interpret or explain would have actually been a sign of my fear that I could not stand the pain of what I was containing and wished to evacuate this pain in the form of therapeutic knowledge or "material" to be understood, as described by Betty Joseph (1989). Further, as suggested by Reis (2006), an interpretation would have compounded the group's dissociation from the pain that we were all struggling to countenance. In other words, to interpret the dynamic would, I believe have been an attempt on my part to dissociate and to evacuate the violence and disturbance from my being, back into the group (Joseph, 1989), before it took the clear shape and meaning that emerged in the group. I would not have lived through it *with* them and would have deprived them of the experience. In a prescient observation, Foulkes and Anthony (1965) noted: "There are times when the therapist must sit on his wisdom, must tolerate defective knowledge and wait for the group to arrive at solutions" (p. 153).

Often the phrases "holding" and "containment" are used to suggest something quiet and perhaps even passive. As these examples illustrate, there are times when "holding" is very much a "doing." I responded to Maggie's threats to leave and Harry's attack on himself with very active and impassioned interventions. During enactments such as these I am very aware that I am *doing* therapy, and *doing,* I believe is an essential part of engagement in an enactment. To allow group members to engage in self or group-destructive behaviors such as threatening to leave or hitting oneself is to neglect the group and re-traumatize them. Mentalization does not grow out of neglect, but out of containment, holding, and safety. If I may conflate Winnicott and Heidegger: to go on being is to go on doing.

This vignette also illustrates the power of helpful insight and meaning that comes from another group member rather from the therapist. Michael and Maggie found an experience of knowing themselves in a deeper way, through being known by another, Jane, and subsequently the rest of the group. Locked in their tortured embrace they could not access the other or themselves as subjects. Everyone becomes objectified in the perverse relationship of torture. They were first able to see Harry's own subjectivity when they joined to help him in his terrorized moment, and were subsequently able to be available when Jane addressed them as subjects themselves. One can only develop one's own subjectivity when related to as a subject by another (Benjamin, 1988). Together with the internalization of my role and my capacity for reflective function, the group members were able to find each other's subjectivity. In this way the intersubjective matrix of the group was restored, and the un-thought familiar chaos was transformed into intersubjective meaning.

From Familiar Chaos to Coherence

Each of the group members in the examples just cited created their own familiar chaos in the group. They enacted in unthought and unformulated ways their internal worlds and the well-worn channels of their repetitive need to not think. I have illustrated how, when appropriately contained and held, these enactments can become intensified, experienced and then thought about. The familiar chaos becomes seen for what it is, and new experiences emerge in the group interaction. One of the compelling aspects of enactments in group therapy such as that involving Maggie and Michael is the profound effect they have on the group dynamic. I mentioned that the relationship between Michael and Maggie became strengthened, but so too did the relationship of the whole group to itself, following these events. The group members were much closer to each other having lived through and attempted to understand such a potentially traumatic experience. In his classic text, Yalom (1975) highlights "group cohesion" as one of the crucial "curative factors" in group therapy. He describes how over time and by virtue of shared experience a natural group cohesion or "warm group feeling" prevails. This seems to me to be only a part of the complexity of what happens when a group becomes integrated as a unit. In an interesting and illuminating commentary on Yalom, Pines (1998) notes that cohesion implies a "sticky" unity, such as cement or mortar and does not describe a principle of dynamic organization. It implies inertia and nonthought, much as I would describe "familiar chaos." Pines prefers the term "coherence" because it highlights "the unity of parts brought together in harmony with one another" (Pines, 1998, p. 61). It stresses the process of formation of meaning as in the coherence that is found in the disparate details of a picture or the parts of a story. The emphasis here is on the formation of meaning, the hermeneutic process, and on the recognition of multiplicity. I believe that this describes quite well the way group therapy progresses in my work. In these examples, we can see the shift from the "cohesion," inertia and familiar chaos of each member, to the ability of the members and the group as a whole to find a flexible and multiple coherence in the group experience. Coherence and meaning were found in the unthought chaos of these familiar enactments and along with this came greater relatedness and genuine intimacy in the group—a surprising and new experience for all of us!

References

Agazarian, Y. M. (1992), A systems approach to the group-as-a-whole. *Internat. J. Group Psychother.*, 42(2):177–205.

Alonso, A., & Rutan, J. S. (1984), The impact of object relations theory on psychodynamic group therapy. *Amer. J. Psychiat.*, 141:11, 1376–1380.

Ashbach, C., & Schermer, V. L. (1987), *Object Relations, The Self and the Group*. New York, NY: Routledge.

Benjamin, J. (1988), *The Bonds of Love: Psychoanalysis, Feminism and the Problem of Domination*. New York, NY: Pantheon Books.

Bion, W. R. (1961), *Experiences in Groups and Other Papers*. NY: Basic Books.

Bromberg, P. M. (1998), *Standing in the Spaces: Essays on Clinical Process, Trauma and Dissociation*. Hillsdale, NJ: The Analytic Press.

Cohen, B. D. (2000), Intersubjectivity and narcissism in group psychotherapy: how feedback works. *Internat. J. Group Psychother.*, 50:2, 163–179.

Cohen, P. F. (2001), The practice of modern group psychotherapy: working with past trauma in the present. *Internat. J. Group Psychother.*, 51:4, 489 503.

Davies, J. M. (1996), Dissociation, repression, and reality testing in the transference: The controversy over memory and false memory in the psychoanalytic treatment of adult survivors of childhood sexual abuse. *Psychoanal. Dial.*, 6:189–218.

Davies, J. M. & Frawley, M. G. (1994), *Treating the Adult Survivor of Childhood Sexual Abuse*. NY: Basic Books.

Foulkes, S. H. (1948), *Introduction to Group Analytic Psychotherapy*. London: Heinemann.

Foulkes, S. H., & Anthony, E. J. (1965), *Group Psychotherapy: The Psychoanalytic Approach* (2nd. ed.). Baltimore: Penguin Books.

Ghent, E. (1995), Interaction in the psychoanalytic situation, *Psychoanal. Dial.*, 5:479–491.

Gordon, J. (1994), Bion's post-"Experience in Groups" thinking on groups: A clinical example of – K. In: *Ring of Fire: Primitive Affects and Object Relations in Group Psychotherapy*, ed. V. L. Schermer & M. Pines. London, Routledge, pp. 107–127.

Harwood, I., & Pines, M. (Eds.). (1998), *Self Experiences in Group: Intersubjective and Self Psychological Pathways to Human Understanding*. London: Jessica Kingsley Publishers.

Hinshelwood, R. D. (1994), Attacks on reflective space: containing primitive emotional states. In: *Ring of Fire: Primitive Affects and Object Relations in Group Psychotherapy*, eds. V. L. Schermer & M. Pines. London: Routledge, pp. 86–106.

Joseph, B. (1989), Transference: The total situation. In: *Psychic Equilibrium and Psychic Change: Selected Papers of Betty Joseph*, eds. M. Feldman & E. B. Spillius. London: Routledge, 1989, pp. 156–167.

Leal, M. R. M. (1983), Why group analysis works. In: *The Evolution of Group Analysis*, ed. M. Pines. London: Jessica Kingsley Publishers, pp. 183–196.

Mitchell, S. (1993), *Hope and Dread in Psychoanalysis*. New York: Basic Books.

Mitchell, S. (1997), *Influence and Autonomy in Psychoanalysis*. Hillsdale, NJ: The Analytic Press.

Modell, A. (1991), The therapeutic relationship as a paradoxical experience. *Psychoanal. Dial.*, 1:13–28.

Morrison, A. P. (1990), Secrets: A self-psychological view of shame in group therapy. In: *The Difficult Patient in Group: Group Psychotherapy with Borderline and Narcissistic Disorders*, eds. B. E. Roth, W. N. Stone, & H. D. Kibel. Madison, CT: International Universities Press, pp.175–190.

Ormont, L. R. (2001), *The Technique of Group Treatment: The Collected Papers of Louis R. Ormont*. Madison CT: Psychosocial Press.

Pines, M. (Ed.). (1983), *The Evolution of Group Analysis*. London: Jessica Kingsley Publishers.

———— (1998), Psychic development and the group analytic situation. In: *Circular Reflections: Selected Papers on Group Analysis and Psychoanalysis*, ed. M. Pines. London: Jessica Kingsley Publishers, pp. 59–76.

Reis, B. (2006), Even better than the real thing. *Contemp. Psychoan.*, 42, 2.

Rutan, J. S. & Stone, W. N. (2001), *Psychodynamic Group Psychotherapy*. New York, NY: The Guilford Press.

Spotnitz, H. (1969), Resistance phenomena in group psychotherapy (overview). In: *Group Psychotherapy Today*, ed. H. M. Ruitenberg. New York, NY: Atherton Press, pp. 203–217.

Stern, D. B. (1989), The analyst's unformulated experience of the patient. *Contemp. Psychoanal.*, 25:1–33.

———— (1997), *Unformulated Experience: From Dissociation to Imagination in Psychoanalysis*. Hillsdale, NJ: The Analytic Press.

———— (2004), The eye sees itself: dissociation, enactment and the achievement of conflict. *Contemp. Psychoanal.*, 40(2):197–237.

Wright, F. (2004), Being seen, moved, disrupted and reconfigured: Group leadership from a relational perspective. *Internat. J. Group Psychoth.*, 54:2, 235–250.

Yalom, I. D.(1975), *The Theory and Practice of Group Psychotherapy*. New York, NY: Basic Books.

12

Class Unconscious: From Dialectical Materialism to Relational Material

Stephen Hartman

▼ ▼ ▼ ▼ ▼

My father and I are estranged. I first presented this chapter on his 70th birthday.[1] I wrote it as part of an ongoing project to describe how the political world enters psychic life and, also, to work on our relationship. Ours is a struggle that bears the strains and injuries of class. There were moments between us when the father–son compact upended, moments when who provides and who depends blurred. This confusion was only articulated through our approach to my father's work. Work, between unemployed father and analyst-to-be son, was where the material world of dependence and obligation could be felt deep inside each of us and between us. When I reflect on our troubles, I can think of two patients with whom I have what one might call an eroticized transference that is wholly mediated by work. In psychoanalysis, we are quick to attend to the sexual body—not so the working body. But more of this in time.

Layton (2002) offers a relational view of the unconscious. She writes that an analyst greets her patients with a history—not just a personal or family history, but a history of conflictual class, race and gender relations that are inextricable from the position that she inhabits and the practices in which she engages. We generally take this "objective" history into account, but we tend to treat it as secondary to "subjective" emotional and "intersubjective" biographical life. Our way of working, face to face or analyst to analysand,

---

[1] A shorter version of this chapter was presented at the Spring, 2004, meeting of Division 39, American Psychological Association, March 19, 2004. A slightly different version was published in *Psychoanalysis, Culture & Society* 2005, 10:121–137.

leads us to privilege direct contact among thinking people. We listen for our patients to evoke a history that took shape in the way that we now work: person to person, mind to mind, perhaps asymmetrical but nonetheless empathic (Aron, 1996).

In this chapter, I suggest that we consider working like a person who labors in a context determined not by minds but by bodies: in a context where class, race, and gender relations lend what seems like objective structure to subjective life. I want to give the early history of material relations a place of primacy in the unconscious and in the development of our sense of self and other. I don't intend to suggest that the material world structures the psychic world but, rather, to explore how it engages it. At the same time, I want to avoid reiterating mind-society, base-superstructure dualisms or determinism by emphasizing a third place where material and psychic life interact. I will call this the *class unconscious*. I consider the material world to influence all manner of embodied and verbal experience. In psyche and in soma, in speech and in affect, in language and in culture, we are always articulating aspects of material experience. The material world may not govern the flow of consciousness, but it certainly permeates it as bodies and minds meet through the medium of work. As we move from preverbal to verbal experience and from pre-oedipal to oedipal and post-oedipal relations, we encode implicit then explicit knowledge of bodily material life. Insofar as that knowledge is accented by class experience, we enter the political world.

As this chapter unfolds, I describe how material relations color "mother"–infant and "father"–infant interactions.[2] Mystified by the objective demands of work, these intersubjective relations are carried in our bodies but rarely formulated in thought. I use the term *class unconscious* to describe the unformulated experience of class in unconscious territory (Stern, 2003a). I argue that class functions as a kind of "thirdness" that is surprisingly neglected in the psychoanalytic literature.[3] With notable exceptions, (Altman, 1995; Cushman, 1995), *thirdness* is reserved to describe cognitive phenomena or the cognitive component of social interaction. Material reality is not factored into the dialogue between intrapsychic and interpersonal experience that opens intersubjective space. Although thinking and language certainly give us the ability to reflect on experience, I believe that important parts of material experience are negotiated in bodily form. The class third would be a material Other: not a father who observes and

---

[2]*Mother* meaning the primary and *father* meaning the secondary providing parent. I want to attenuate these gendered terms while drawing attention to the undertheorized role of the paternal body in pre-oedipal development.

[3]For reviews of this literature from the perspectives of diverse psychoanalytic writers, see the special issue of *The Psychoanalytic Quarterly* (2004, Vol. LXXIII no. 1) devoted to "The Third in Psychoanalysis."

thinks about the mother–child dyad (Fonagy & Target, 1995), not an intersubjective dialectic generated by the distinct subjectivities of analyst and analysand within the space of treatment (Ogden, 1994; also Aron & Benjamin, 1999), and not a set of cultural performances (drag for example) that disturb assumptions that we knowingly or unwittingly share (Butler, 1991). This third is not a zone of thought, but a set of bodily, material practices that are only known to us (to the extent that they can be known by us) through work. I argue that our ability to develop subjectivity and engage others intersubjectively is in no small part framed by our engagement in the seemingly objective world of work and class.

It may come as a surprise that Karl Marx never defined "class" even though his materialist dialectic hinged on the unfolding of class conflict (Lukacs, 1971). Marx used the term conceptually, that is, to theorize about material and social relations, rather than descriptively, to classify or codify them. Contemporary usage of the term *class* in psychoanalysis is rather vague and tends to be descriptive for lack of theoretical development. While our understanding of the "unconscious" has shifted from a descriptive structure that regulates drives to a relational matrix of internal and real world experiences, our understanding of class has not been similarly revised. Ghent (1992, 2002) warned that we misuse the term *relational* when we summon it to describe interpersonal relations rather than to conceptualize them; *class* remains a descriptive term. In much recent relational writing, class (when cited) is seen to be descriptive of—but not inherent in— intrapsychic and interpersonal experience.[4] As a referent, class is mentioned to identify an individual's background but it is rarely considered to be a site where the material outside and the psychic inside meet. Class is left out of the dialogue among internal personifications and representations that we call the unconscious.

To begin to conceptualize class from a psychoanalytic perspective, we would need to consider how class, like gender, race and other "objective" components of social relations are absorbed into the psyche. I define "class" as a signifier of a person's ongoing experience of social relations and of their history with regard to work. I propose that a child receives early knowledge about class through an unconscious communication from his parents about work.[5] I argue that parents communicate "enigmatic messages" (borrowing the phrase used by Stein, 1998) about class to their children in the form of spoken or unspoken attitudes about work that the child discovers in his parents' bodies, affects, and thoughts. These unconscious messages are usually undecipherable because they are received as facts of

---

[4]This literature is reviewed in Botticelli (2004a).

[5]Although *work* and *class* are not isomorphic terms, I sometimes use them interchangeably so as to lend the term *class* enough ambiguity to capture its unconscious quality.

life that need not be contested. Work (for alienated laborers and for those for whom work equals career) stands outside conscious reflection. It is typically disassociated from material and social reality so that its profits can be enjoyed. But, in its dissociated, reified state, work cannot be mentalized. Even though parents work for their children's welfare, the work may or may not communicate to the child the parents' care. Here the vicissitudes of class relations are as important as the vicissitudes of personality. Early in the development of identity, then, class is a dissonant (if not repressed) element (Botticelli, 2004b). Even though class imbues our attitudes toward work and regulates much of our interpersonal commerce, it is hard to reckon with class because class experience remains so doggedly unconscious.

I use the term *class* in the manner of Lukacs (1971) to posit a dialectical relationship between material reality and consciousness. Unlike Lukacs, I do not assume that class relations have an objective history. Rather, I want to consider the intersubjective communication of class experience between parents and children and among adults through work as manifest between psychoanalyst and patient. I argue that some of the communication we cite in the "intersubjective" field is ambiguously objectifying because it contains the stain of material relations, but I do not take those relations to be objective in and of themselves. I propose we think of class as a sometimes reified, sometimes generative expression of material experience rather than as an objective drive with a logic of its own. My explanation of class communication is "materialist" by comparison to most current intersubjective theory (see Beebe, Knoblauch, Rustin, & Sorter, 2003a) insofar as I situate intersubjective communication within a broader discourse of material and social relations that are written on the body and in the psyche through work. To this end, I consider the child's interaction with both the maternal and paternal body.

I discovered the power of my class unconscious by accident. Jim is my first patient of the day, a banker who pays full freight. He is a very congenial, thoughtful man—the type of patient who makes going to work on dark mornings tolerable. Jim often works well into the night and then is late to therapy. Because he travels for work at a moment's notice, he often misses sessions. In order to have more frequent sessions, I agreed to meet him an hour earlier than my usual first appointment. Jim is always polite about calling to apologize for no-shows, though often days later after I have agonized over his disappearance, and he always pays promptly while expressing sincere regret at missing the sessions.

I am a night person. You name it, I'd rather do it after midnight, off the clock. I get grumpy, pacing my office in the early morning light, wondering whether Jim will eventually show up. I wish I were back home in bed. I contemplate napping before my next patient though I guess that napping will make me even sleepier. I saw a full day of patients yesterday and then accompanied my boyfriend to a business dinner. His wealthy clients are almost as demanding as my most difficult patients. Another night with too many cocktails and not enough sleep. If Jim shows up, I will be happy to get my workday started. I'll feel like I have my life back, like I am able to think. If he doesn't, I will hover in limbo worrying about my practice and imagining that when I go to my analyst later in the morning, I will tumble asleep on her couch.

So we make a deal. If Jim is running late or at the airport, he will call me on my cell phone before I leave for the office. It works. At first, my mornings are less bleary-eyed. Not only does Jim call when he will be absent but, soon, calling organizes him to get to my office on time more regularly. However, on my end, the new arrangement quickly becomes irksome. Instead of pacing my office, I pace the kitchen. If Jim calls to cancel, I drift into hazy half-sleep for an hour. If not, I will rush to beat him to my door. How long to wait before deciding to go to work? Taxi or subway? I feel mostly dread until I get to the office and settle in. I remark that it is extraordinary how my attitude to work changes once an analytic hour has begun. I feel grateful for my patients and for a job that allows me to get to know people intimately. Work awakens me but, until then, I feel the deadening punch of the time clock.

Only months later, on a morning when I was particularly sleepy during my own analysis, did I remember this scene from my childhood. I grew up in Ohio. My father was an industrial roofer. Beginning soon after my birth, he had a series of industrial accidents, falls and burns that left scars on his aching body and that left me in fear of the ambiguous space between accident and suicide. In the winter, we regularly had upwards of 10 feet of snow piled alongside our driveway. Snowfall meant icy roofs and months of unemployment for my father, who rued the winter, hated his job, and resented having to work to support a family. In the dark mornings, my father would pace the family room waiting for the phone to ring. The union dispatcher would call to say where my father should report to work, weather permitting, when it permitted. On a lucky day, my father would have to scramble off to a job. I had missed the school bus, because I sat patiently by the phone lending silent support to my father as he worried. My father would have to drop me—at school and from his guilty thoughts. We drove to school preparing to slog through a long pleasureless day of labor. I would be relieved to be at school, though worried that my father might slip on ice or into depression. It was worse if the phone didn't ring. And, most days, it didn't. While other kids built snow forts and made snow angels while waiting for the bus, I remember mostly waiting for the phone and the feeling of sinking into piled-up snow forever.

To understand how I made this arrangement with Jim, I needed to understand how I made this arrangement with my father, which brings me back to the subject of class unconscious. We are accustomed to thinking about how anxious mothers communicate affectively with their children, but we rarely think of them communicating their experience of work. A father comes home from the factory; he's angry and has little to say to his child. What does the child learn about labor? This raises an additional question: Does parents' affect teach children about class, or does class structure perpetuate itself through parents' affect? We might think of a person who feels weak and who attaches himself to stronger characters as having dependency needs. But might dependency needs reflect class experience reproducing itself in primary attachments? Do we not discover the hidden injuries of class in our parents' bodies just as we do other traumas? (Caruth, 1995; Harris, 2004; Laub & Auherhahn, 1993).

How, then, do we know our class? Or does our class know us? How did we learn that our parents' economic class somehow belonged to us? Presented us with a narrative of social status, an economic regimen with bodily and mental consequences and a set of attendant affects? As I said earlier, I propose that parents communicate enigmatic messages about class to their children in the form of attitudes toward work. Sometimes these attitudes are spoken; more often, they are embodied. Let's not forget that parenting is an occupation that preoccupies not only mothers and fathers but also doctors, nurses, nannies, teachers: A wide swath of society works with children. Parents who work out of the home bring their day jobs home with them. Children are exposed to work from the moment their mothers begin labor. Implicit awareness of class and race accrues when Jim's mother places her overstimulated, crying baby in the black nanny's hands. Explicit class awareness that will become awareness of class conflict begins to gel when the anxious father, in this case mine, reaches to answer the union dispatcher's call. Patterns of affect regulation are manifest in pre-verbal and "verbalizable" moments of parental work. Each can be observed occurring simultaneously in the "intersubjective field" between Jim and me.

Jim grew up in an environment where titles are used to create space among intimates of different class standing. Work is something men (who don't have to work) do to get away from their stay-at-home wives. Work clarifies the separateness of interdependents and diminishes any anxiety prompted by fantasies of co-mingling bodies. When coworkers respect the boundaries of employment, the dependency of subordinate on boss trumps any desire that circulates between them. In the interests of a safe workplace, the class hierarchy (and the primacy of the family) is sustained when any erotic possibility between employer and employed is renounced. Neither dependent nor superior can slip out of defined roles. Lust as they might, they need not worry that the status quo will collapse. The same is true of an erotic transference when sex is limited to talk in the interest of the patient and the work. Jim always addresses me as "Doctor Hartman" even though we are the same age and travel in overlapping social circles. Our sessions can become uncomfortably familiar and erotically charged when some turn in the conversation draws attention to our bodies. Our use of my job-specific title steadies affects that rock off-kilter in some space between sexual possibility and mutual dependence.

Jim rues the fact that his sexual partners always want intimacy to be coupled with emotional dependence; he expresses contempt/(envy) for his parents who are prone to declare "I will always need you" somewhat falsely. Jim argues that dependence extinguishes desire and justifies relationships of convenience with similar insincerity. By calling me "doctor," Jim can flirt with me and safely imagine that I do/don't need him. "Doctor" signifies worker, which signifies dependent for Jim. By being the doctor, I am someone who helps Jim regulate the panicky affects that sexual (read dependent) strivings stir. Jim can depend on and believe my feelings for him are expressed directly or withheld for good reason. This is work, not sex. (Doctor Hartman is not in bed waiting for me; he is waiting by the phone—like his dad—which makes Doctor Hartman aware of just how dependent we each are). Work keeps our bodies apart enough to be thinking together. Just as Jim and I learned explicitly how work correlates with dependence and class position from our fathers, we likely learned much earlier to establish emotional regulation in implicit interaction with our mothers. When Jim calls me "Doctor," that is, "worker," to defuse an erotic spark, I think of Beebe and her colleagues' (2003b) work on infant–mother matching during moments of overarousal. But I'm not sure who is holding Jim: his mother or his nanny. The message is surely love. But is it also work?

The parent's body is a site of work.[6] Here I want to build on an argument made by Stein in her writing, *The Enigmatic Dimension of Sexual Experience* (1998). Stein elaborates an idea originally raised by Laplanche (1999) who noted that "sexuality, which was at first entirely grounded in the nutritive function, undergoes a movement that enables it to dissociate from the vital function and to constitute itself" (p. 597). Stein describes the enigmatic signifier as a place of surplus knowledge. The mother cares for her child with her whole body and personality, including her unconscious. This obscures the fact that "the sexual object is not identical with the object of the function, but is displaced in relation to it" (p. 597). The functional object has an enigmatic aspect that is contained within the sexual body. As the mother cares for the child, "the process of the infant's appetite being satisfied arouses love in the baby, and desire is the experience of the gap that stretches between love and need satisfaction" (p. 599).

---

[6]That the primary caretaker and primary breadwinner roles are gendered by cultural practice is evidence of the unconscious reproduction of what Bourdieu (1991) calls "symbolic power."

Now, let's suppose that the mother holds her baby with more than her sexual body, but also her body at work. My friend Chitra had trouble producing milk in the initial weeks of breast-feeding. After being counseled this way and that by advocates for and against formula feeding, she worried that she was not quite "up to the job" of feeding her baby. She had to work at it to the point of exhaustion. Watching her play with David is a joy, but watching her feed him feels like inspection time on an assembly line. Soon, as her husband Roland points out, they will have to find a nanny so Chitra can return to work at her office. Roland concedes, as I've heard many parents do, that parenting is "mind-numbing" work, and he is eager for Chitra to have intellectual stimulation again. For now, Chitra balances working at home with David's feeding schedule. Might we say that her desire to feed David and the pleasure she derives from it (as well as the frustration) is not only part of her sexual body, but, also, a material marker of maternal work? This work is a labor of love but also a site of ambivalence: Our culture alternatively idealizes and devalues it like all feminine functions. When Chitra feels pressed to work beyond her ability to feed David, her love for David is bound up with the regulatory discourse of sexuality (Foucault, 1980a, 1980b) that is voiced by the nurses who are employed to coach her to keep working.

Stein (1998) writes that, "after being awakened in the child by the mother, the aspects of sexuality that have not been understood or assimilated become repressed and add to the feeling of strangeness and mystery we have about sexuality" (p. 601). But might not this enigmatic message also relate to that which we do not understand about David's implicit understanding of work? Indeed, might the implicit knowledge David will soon assimilate in all areas of intersubjective commerce be in part structured by his mother's body at work? Were David born in India, where helpers of all kinds would have been enlisted to assist in mothering, his mother would have had a different job than she has here as a mother/web designer. Her enigmatic message to David contains unconscious messages about race and gender as well as class and caste. Her body tells him what is possible and what is not as she works to feed him. The enigmatic signifier is carried in her material body at work. Yes, as Stein says, moments of ineffable mutual recognition have an erotic power that enhances the pleasure of intimacy. Yes, some patients who are especially sensitive to the analyst's personality and idiom "may be particularly sensitive to any kind of excess that is similar to what the sexual part of the mother may have toward her child" (p. 618). But precocious patients may also be sensitive to the parts of analyst and mother that work to care for the child. Is that labor given freely or coerced? Is it a joy and privilege or/and a career? Is a mother's sexuality even separable from her work at mothering?

We must wonder, to go a step further, whether the gap between love and need satisfaction belongs to the individual whose body contains it. Is not this gap the space of sexuality that Foucault (1980a, 1980b) described—that part of sexuality that belongs to a host of practices that regulate the interchange of body functions in the service of certain disciplinary regimens? The enigmatic signifier may well carry what Foucault called "the dark shimmer of sex" (1980a, p. 157), that part of desire which cannot be separated from the interests of technologies: of doctoring, mothering, psychoanalyzing, pornographizing, militarizing, laboring. We might say that the enigmatic message could be written as an equation: Sexuality equals desire minus the interventions of work and other cultural practices on the body. Laplanche (1999) implied this when he alluded to that part of surplus desire in the transference that is the site of "cultural interpellation" (p. 233).

If psychoanalysis lacks a theory of how class works on the body, on the psyche and between psyches, we might add that psychoanalysis lacks a theory of how the State penetrates the psyche. This is particularly surprising when we consider that contemporary theories of intersubjectivity owe so much to writers such as Habermas (1968) and Taylor (1989), whose theories of the relational subject evolved in an effort to describe the political subject. A traditional Marxist would spare no ink involving the State and its ideology in the regulatory practices of childrearing (Althusser, 1994). Lacanian psychoanalysis has weighed in on this point by naming moments that loosen the hinge between Self and Other "a unit of work." Here is where the Father enters the scene as the surrogate for that part of experience which seems objective yet always has, quoting Zizek (1994), "a leftover, a stain of traumatic irrationality and senselessness sticking to it" (p. 43). This is the space between the subjectivity of the worker and the disassociated objectivity of work. My dread of waiting for Jim's call places me in a familiar, disquieting position. I am identified with my father, trying to prop him up, and willing to submit to the tyranny of the phone on his behalf, perhaps to rescue him in my imagination as a father who is happy to provide for his family, though I know otherwise. He is beaten down and, in these moments, I only exist for him as a material dependent—for he is unable to be both father and worker. I am interpellated by the scars on my father's arms: A burned worker's son who will ultimately fail his father. My father can't accept that I think for a living when he tunes out to survive. I become a campus radical and then a lefty academic, always with a sense that my work won't quite support my lifestyle. I need Jim's money, I imagine, more than I can afford the liberty to define my mornings.

Psychoanalysis imagines a very cognitive father. A clear example of this can be found in the work of Fonagy and Target (1995) on the use of the body and the role of the father. Fonagy and Target locate the development of the psychological self in the mother's capacity "to demonstrate to the child that she thinks of him as an intentional being whose behavior is driven by thoughts, feelings, beliefs, and desires" (p. 54). When the mother is able to "mentalize" her child, she grants the child interiority. The child understands his body as the container of his mental state. The father observes the child in relation to others, and places the child's experience in a broader context of subjects. Hence, "the child needs to experience the father as somebody looking at his relationship with the mother, and at his attempt to find a viable image of himself in her mind" (p. 65). The father, functioning as a third in the field of mentalization, "provides an external perspective on the child's primary object relationship" (p. 66). His ability to hold this relationship in mind spatializes different subjects in different bodies. The father is not oedipal rival so much as an external witness.

This is the father who observes and thinks. His body is a 3-D container of beta function. But what of the father whose ability to view another subject is limited by the way work has taken over his body and structured his ability to think? This is the father who comes home angry from the factory and kicks the dog. He loves (works, provides) / hates (into the dog), drinks, and then seems to become himself again. A familiar analytic stance would cite a split between two positions toward self and other objects that he holds within: one malignant, one generative (Bollas, 1987). But, if we know one thing from Marx, it is that the idea may not belong to the person thinking it. An affect may not belong to the individual feeling or acting on it. Thoughts and feelings may be structured intrapsychically by material experience. If the "intrapsychic," as Ghent (2002) explained, is in fact "a dynamic structuralization of the interpersonal," here, the "interpersonal," that is, relations codified by labor, are obscure. Fonagy and Target, like Aron and Benjamin (1999), Benjamin (2004), and others, assume that the third is an independent, autonomous agent—or agentic stance—that has ideas and fantasies that belong to it. Perhaps the father's ideas don't always belong to him. Perhaps there are times when the father's ideas are not markers of his observing stance but emblems of reified social relations. In the manner of "false consciousness," might it be possible that psychoanalysis embraces the "father as witness" because it allows a fantasy of external agency to thrive in a context of objectifying work? Before and beyond an oedipal father of intentionality, we need to engage an embodied parent whose will is empowered or disempowered by work. And we must ask, is the father's witness, then, thirdness or ideology?[7] This is the double bind inherent in the parent's command to the child to "mind your own business" as if "business" belongs to the mind.

The same might be said of the Basic Rule. Is the command to say whatever comes to mind a means to cleanse object-relations of material ones?

---

[7]Perhaps this enigma gives "trade" its erotic thrill. It is too easy to assume that trade fantasies are only about power and domination (Bollas, 1992) or paternal identifications (Isay, 1989) and not about the ambiguity of the paternal body as a site of both sexual and material labors that are partly owned and partly reified.

Do analysts invest subjective verbal communication with dialogic function because this enables them to do their work? Does their way of working, then, prevail over parts of the patient's utterance that they fail to engage dialogically or theorize critically? Aron and Benjamin (1999) emphasize the capacity in development for the child to hold two thoughts in mind at once and in relationship to each other. Self-reflexivity, they write, "refers to the ability to grasp two sides of a dialogue or maintain an internal dialogue among multiple aspects of self or multiple self-states" (p. 4). In the meeting of minds, a child comes to the "third point" of "taking the self as object without losing one's own perspective as a separate subject" (p. 6). They conclude that, "it is precisely this opportunity for adopting a multiplicity of positions in relation to the other that signifies a transformation in mental structure" (p. 7). Benjamin in her way (with attention to recognition) and Aron in his (by focusing on mutuality) describe the psychic mechanisms at play in the development of intersubjectivity.

Aron and Benjamin err by assuming that mental structure develops unimpeded by social structure. Though they mean to describe dialogic relations, they allow "no play of the context framing it" (Bakhtin, 1981, p. 346). The perspectives on experience that they consider to be in dialectical relationship belong to thinking people. Aron and Benjamin privilege "identification" and "recognition" in the cognitive domain of subjectivity, free of its more opaque reflection in material relations. This leads them to overestimate the degree of autonomy working subjects (including analysts) can imagine themselves to occupy in self and other's minds.

For Aron and Benjamin, thirdness breaks down in enactment to a state of "complementarity" when interactions are governed by a projective stance. This occurs when a person engages with others as if experience is "done to me." They write: "relational options are narrowed and interpersonal roles are rigidified" (p. 10). This is true, but it is not the same thing as having to wrangle internally with residua of social relations that are "done to me." There are likely self-states that appear to mark "regression" to schizoid object relating, states that may indeed present an opening to political consciousness even while they enact self–other roles that seem foreclosed. The problem is not that rigid thinking sets in; it is that work interpellates the worker according to its own logic. A relational theory of the subject must include a political analysis of that subject's relative autonomy within economic structures and discursive frames. Aron and Benjamin located reified states in the character of the rigid person, when, in fact, it may emerge from the role within material relations that the person occupies. Not all of the perspectives a subject can identify with in the object are "subjective." So although I second Aron and Benjamin's position that "we can virtually define the quality of relationships by what kind of thinking we can do in them" (p. 12), I want to emphasize that sources of thinking often emanate from identifications clad in material relations that resist recognition. It is possible to identify with a subject who is, at least in the material part of his or her experience, an object. "Thirdness" can be established when we take a perspective on our interaction that is part yours, part mine and part something "done to me"—or by me—as a matter of material necessity.

The tragedy of the class unconscious is that, in its reified state, it cannot be mentalized as a third point of view in the space where we carve out self. Otherwise, we would be mindful of work and its inextricable history (Layton, 2002). Having renounced conflict models of the mind, perhaps we ought to pin our hopes on class conflict! To take Stern (2003a, 2004) in a political direction, the knowledge of class we discover in our parents' working bodies seems to be "done to me" because in its unformulated state, it resists articulation. We are at a standstill that "is not necessarily maintained by a rigidly enacted conflict between conscious and unconscious aims, but by the *absence* of the conflict we need to be able to experience if we are to sense the availability of choice" (2004, p. 229). Maybe our unconscious resists reification in just this way: we yearn to wrangle with the enigmatic signifier—to transform an object of work into a subject of desire.

George and I share this yearning to address the father whose love was compromised by his duty to provide. This is played out in the transference as George seeks to work with me in a way that engages needs that were dissociated between him and his father. We have an erotically charged rapport that comes into focus when we use explicit sexual metaphor to describe affect states. We use these moments to recognize how intensely desire and dependency are intertwined. I will conclude by describing a recent turn in our work that led us to understand how embodied these needs are and how resistant to formulation between working father and desiring son. Now articulated in words, George and I share a wish to love the father whom we, each in our own way, mourn.

George is a 60-year-old African American furniture designer. His work is considered first-rate: he is widely published, often invited to present his work at conferences, and his loyal clients, many of whom have become friends, are among the wealthiest benefactors of art and design in New York City. Few people know that George lives close to the brink of financial collapse. His resources are entirely consumed by his firm that, though successful, has never been profitable. Behind George's intense professional bearing is the determination to always make payroll. Even George does not recognize the father in his inscrutable composure.

George is a ruggedly sexy man who moves decisively with a confident stride. He can appear brash and intentionally intimidating. When we first spoke to arrange a consult 4 years ago, he told me he sought a therapist who could make him work. His intense manner had the effect of making me wonder if I could work hard enough for him. Over the years, I have come to love George and he me. We have moved beyond bravado. George sheds tears while describing his love of fragile materials. We have had stalemates when sex comes up that were broken with tears as we each dealt with the limits of our arrangement. George can see that I love my work, that I take it seriously as he does his work. We have shared our experience in families where work signaled something more like death.

George's father was a foreman at a factory in Atlanta. He was an angry, rather silent man who is best remembered by the command "know your place." George was a sensitive boy who brought home paintings from school and, at age 5, already declared himself an artist. "Who do you think you are!" was his mother's reply as she went back to work in the kitchen. In his teens, George was a precocious, sometimes flamboyant young gay man who nevertheless was fiercely loyal to his parents. He was strikingly aware of their anxiety and fragility and he was unwilling to rock the boat. On the occasion of his high school graduation, George's father shaved his son's arty hairdo in an angry scene. "Know your place" was what he had to say. George still considers himself an artist in that he works with his hands. One of the reasons his business loses money is that he bills design tasks and manual labor at the same rate. Were he to bill appropriately for his time, he imagines, his client/friends would remind him to know his place.

Four years into our relationship, George developed prostate cancer. His surgery was scheduled for the first day of my vacation. George arrives at the first session after his surgery sullen and defeated. Though the surgery was successful, George is terribly shaken. I had left him a message wishing him a speedy recovery, but he did not receive the message for a week (it went into his alternate voice mail and he forgot to check it). All week, George felt terribly betrayed by me. Did I only have the stomach for his pain if I was at work, he wondered. Perhaps, outside of my office, I can't tolerate his pain. It's not that I was on vacation that kept me from thinking about him, he told himself, it's that I wasn't at work. Perhaps I am not the ideal father who is enlivened by work after all. Am I any more dependable than the father who was exhausted by work? He challenges me in our first session after the break:

> G: If I fall apart and become a puddle of shit, you won't be able to pull me back together.

I ask how that is? George replies first by shifting the topic. He tells me how concerned he is that he can't work a full day yet. He reminds me that he is afraid that his cum is forever changed, devoid of semen, thin and insubstantial. He can think of nothing else. He has been "fucked over" by cancer. I express my sadness and encourage him to be patient in recovery before suggesting that he is worried that I stop being substantial when I am not at work: maybe I can't handle thinking about impotency? Maybe I don't get how dependent on me he feels? Maybe I can't imagine his not being able to cum?

> G: It feels like being forced into submission! (he scoffs, but there is a glint of desire in his plaintiff tone that suggests he might like to turn his weakened body over to me).
> S: Like being fucked over when you want to get fucked (I say—we have our lingo).
> G: I just feel so goddamn weak but I have to be strong in everyone's eyes.

George goes on to list all the people who are being supportive, very "chin up," and he is pissed off. He repeats my observation: "I want to be fucked not told how lucky I am! I'm sick of hearing it. I just want to give in to this goddamn thing and no one will let me. They tell me how well I'm doing and all I can think about is not being able to cum."

> S: You want to feel weak. And I was not at work. So, I guess I couldn't take you being weak either.
> G: No, and I can't know that you can take it unless you are.

I am struck that the erotic language we use conveys George's embodied desire for me to recognize the inevitability of weakness. Being able to "take it" implies being poised in body and mind to accept surrender (Ghent, 1990) to human frailty. I remind George that for each of us, work is a haven, a place where we are able to think and to feel—unlike our fathers in whose bodies work was a cancer. I suggest that he is worried that when I'm not in my work mode, I can't or won't take it. He can't take it unless I could be the father that he wished for: one enlivened by work. George reminds me that, as a child, no frailty was tolerated. His parents showed love by providing food and shelter, but they just couldn't give affection with their bodies. George tried to figure out how they could be so loving yet aversive to affection and he guessed that work took the love out of them. I remind George that workers aren't allowed to express frailty. Even if they could, it would be to surrender and that, I say, is unthinkable. George's fight against weakness is at odds with his desire to be recognized as weak.

> G: If only I could have not been so fucking sensitive! I should have stood up for myself and been more demanding.
> S: You? Or your dad?
> G: And my mother! She was so angry and anxious. She'd be hovering over the stove creating meals out of nothing, trying to hold

the family together. (We revisit the scene of him feeling needy, wanting recognition, getting reprimands).

S: I'm sure she wanted to hold you together but she was overwhelmed by her work.

G: (after a pause) You held me together. (The flirtatious tone is gone; he is looking over my shoulder as if someone else is in the room and it sounds like an effort after repair).

S: But when I couldn't, I was a father thing, a work thing, not him either.

G: Yes.

S: (after a pause) George, what would your father say if you told him how frail you feel after the operation?

G: As I feared then or as I know now?

S: Both.

G: I feared he would say "get out of my sight," but he said "come here baby. It's okay to be afraid."

George had always feared that should he express need, he would invite contempt for being weak. His parents, hard at work, expressed the love they were able to offer, but George had wanted something more: a sign that they understood his fragility and cherished his sensitivity. He looked to his parents for affirmation of the pleasure he took in the world around him but, in their working bodies, he found only reserve and regret. This legacy of class in unspoken territory made it difficult for him to offer love—or seek recognition—in ways unrelated to work. Once cancer left him no choice but to experience ambivalence in his own body, he turned to me for a show of strength. But given the inevitable limits of analytic work, he found dependency instead and with it, paradoxically, his parents' love.

Acknowledgments

I wish to thank Steve Botticelli, Ken Corbett, Jody Davies, Muriel Dimen, Adrienne Harris, Lynne Layton, Melanie Suchet and Henry Urbach whose strong voices guided my work on this chapter.

References

Althusser, L. (1994), Ideology and ideological state apparatuses (notes towards an investigation). In: *Mapping Ideology,* ed. S. Zizek. New York: Verso, pp. 100–140.

Altman, N. (1995), *The Analyst in the Inner City: Race, Class, and Culture through a Psycho-analytic Lens*. Hillsdale, NJ: The Analytic Press.

Aron, L. (1996), *A Meeting of Minds*. Hillsdale NJ: The Analytic Press.

Aron, L., & Benjamin, J. (1999), *The development of intersubjectivity and the struggle to think*. Paper presented on a panel entitled "Changing Your Mind: Relational Perspectives on Thinking" at the Spring Meeting, Division (39) of Psychoanalysis, American Psychological Association, April 17, 1999, New York City.

Bakhtin, M. (1981), *The Dialogic Imagination*. Minneapolis: University of Minnesota Press.

Beebe, B., Knoblauch, S., Rustin, J., & Sorter, D. (2003a), Introduction: A systems view. *Psychoanal. Dial.*, 13:743–776.

———— (2003b), An expanded view of intersubjectivity in infancy. *Psychoanal. Dial.*, 13:805–842.

Benjamin, J. (2004), Beyond doer and done to: An intersubjective view of thirdness. *Psychoanal. Quart.*, 73:5–46.

Bollas, C. (1987), *The Shadow of the Object: Psychoanalysis of the Unthought Known*. New York: Columbia University Press.

———— (1992), *Being a Character: Psychoanalysis and Self Experience*. New York: Hill and Wang.

Botticelli, S. (2004a), The politics of relational psychoanalysis. *Psychoanal. Dial.*, 14:635–651.

———— (2004b), *Return of the repressed: Class in psychoanalytic process*. Paper presented on a panel entitled Class Unconscious at the Spring Meeting, Division (39) of Psychoanalysis, American Psychological Association, March 19, 2004, Miami, Florida.

Bourdieu, P. (1991), *Language and Symbolic Power*. Cambridge, MA: Harvard University Press.

Butler, J. (1991), Imitation and gender insubordination. In: *Inside/Out,* ed. D. Fuss. New York: Routledge, pp. 13–31.

Caruth, C. (1995), *Trauma: Explorations in Memory*. Baltimore, MD: Johns Hopkins University Press.

Cushman, P. (1995), *Constructing the Self, Constructing America: A Cultural History of Psychotherapy*. Reading, MA: Addison-Wesley.

Fonagy, P., & Target, M. (1995), Understanding the violent patient: The use of the body and the role of the father. *International Journal of Psycho-Analysis, 76*:487–502.

Foucault, M. (1980a), *The History of Sexuality*. New York: Vintage.

———— (1980b), *Power/Knowledge*. New York: Pantheon.

Ghent, E. (1990), Masochism, submission, surrender. *Contemp. Psychoanal.*, 26:169–211.

Ghent, E. (1992), Forward. In: *Relational Perspectives in Psychoanalysis,* eds. N. Skolnick & S. Warshaw. Hillsdale, NJ: The Analytic Press, pp. xiii–xxii.

———— (2002), *Relations: Introduction to the First IARPP conference*. Paper presented at the IARPP Conference, January 18, 2002, New York.

Habermas, J. (1968), *Knowledge and Human Interests*. Boston: Beacon Press.

Harris, A. (2004), *Gender as Soft Assembly*. Hillsdale, NJ: The Analytic Press.

Isay, R. (1989), *Being Homosexual*. New York: Avalon.

Laplanche, J. (1999). *Essays on Otherness*. New York: Routledge.

Laub, D., & Auerhahn, N. (1993), Knowing and not knowing massive psychic trauma: Forms of traumatic memory. *Internat. J. Psycho-Anal.*, 74:287–302.

Layton, L. (2002), Cultural hierarchies, splitting, and the heterosexist unconscious. In: *Bringing the Plague: Toward a Postmodern Psychoanalysis,* eds. S. Fairfield, L. Layton, & C. Stack. New York: Other Press, pp. 195–223.

Lukacs, G. (1971), *History and Class Consciousness.* Cambridge, MA: MIT Press.

Ogden, T. (1994), *Subjects of Analysis.* Northvale, NJ: Aronson.

Stein, R. (1998), The Enigmatic dimension of sexual experience: The "otherness" of sexuality and primal seduction. *Psychoanal. Quart.,* 67:594–625.

Stern, D. (2003a), *Unformulated Experience: From Dissociation to Imagination in Psychoanalysis.* Hillsdale NJ: The Analytic Press.

——— (2003b), The fusion of horizons: Dissociation, enactment, and understanding. *Psychoanal. Dial.,* 13:843–873.

——— (2004), The eye sees itself: Dissociation, enactment and the achievement of conflict. *Contemp. Psychoanal.,* 40:197–239.

Taylor, C. (1989), *Sources of the Self.* Cambridge, MA: Harvard University Press.

Zizek, S. (1994), The spectre of ideology. In: *Mapping Ideology,* ed. S. Zizek. New York: Verso, pp. 1–33.

13

Self/Object and Individual/Society: The 'Two Logics' of Psychoanalysis

Marsha Aileen Hewitt

[A] psychoanalysis that does not accommodate the social arguably makes, thereby, a statement of indifference to social issues or of collusion with the established order.
Neil Altman (1995)

But the human essence is no abstraction inherent in each single individual. In its reality it is the ensemble of the social relations.
—Karl Marx (1845)

As a theory of the individual psyche and its development, organization, and pathologies, psychoanalysis is at the same time a theory of society, because individuals are mediated by the social/cultural contexts into which they are born. "[T]here is no such thing as a human nature independent of culture," writes anthropologist Clifford Geertz (1973, p. 49). Psychoanalysis is both a clinical treatment for the disturbed individual as well as a theory of society, its institutions, and social relations, whether analysts themselves are conscious of this fact or are in disagreement with it. Psychoanalyst Robert L. Pyles's (2003) critique of managed health care is relevant to this issue when he challenges all analysts to engage in social and political activity for the benefit of their patients and profession: "I see each member in each of our societies and institutes becoming a vigorous voice for social and political change and for bringing psychoanalytic ideas into the community. We must become, not quite citizen-soldiers, but analytic scholar-activists" (p. 34). He also wondered why most psychoanalysts have "taken flight from the kind of social activism, community involvement, and political activity that flow naturally from the basic premise of psychoanalysis–individual freedom?" (p. 24).

Although the minority, there are a number of psychoanalysts who would agree with Pyles and are clearly troubled by the indifference toward, and lack of interest in, social and political issues on the part of most analysts (Altman, 1995; Castoriadis, 1997; Dimen, 1994; Roudinescu, 2001). Yet, even a brief consideration of the history of psychoanalysis shows that this was not always the case; social theory and political activism have been a part of psychoanalysis since its beginnings. Otto Fenichel, Wilhelm and Annie Reich, Edith Jacobson, and Erich Fromm, to name a few, were all interested in a social psychoanalysis and were themselves associated with socialist movements in Europe prior to the Second World War (Jacoby, 1983). These analysts and others, including Freud, understood that psychoanalysis was not limited to clinical treatment, but could also be an emancipatory force for social transformation. A reforming and social impulse runs throughout even much of Freud's writing, especially concerning themes of human sexuality and social-sexual mores. Freud advocated that psychoanalysis could liberate humankind from its debilitating enslavement to religious ideas and beliefs that undermine the capacity for a mature and independent life by keeping people in a state of infantile emotional stagnation (1927; 1933). Freud also supported free psychoanalytic treatment for the poor (1918) along with the training of lay analysts. He was interested in the contributions that psychoanalysis could make to transformations of culture and liberation from socially restrictive *Weltanschauungen,* such as religion, that undermine maturity and independence of thought (1930; 1927; 1913). Freud did not wish to limit analysis to therapy alone (Jacoby, 1983; Marcuse, 1962).

Otto Fenichel articulated the implications of psychoanalysis for social change more directly and, although adhering to the classical concepts of Freudian drive theory such as the unconscious, transference, resistance and repression, he was also interested in the relationship between social institutions and individual neuroses. At the end of *The Psychoanalytic Theory of Neuroses,* Fenichel states that neuroses are "social diseases" and are "derivative of social conditions and institutions" (1945, pp. 586, 584). He goes on to write that, "Neuroses are the outcome of unfavourable and socially determined educational measures, corresponding to a given and historically developed social milieu and necessary in this milieu. *They cannot be changed without corresponding change in the milieu"* (p. 586; emphasis added). Along with Freud, Fenichel (1985, p. 587) understood the task of psychoanalysis as cultivating freedom and independence of thought; he further recognized that these values were central to a democratic society. However, a democratic society requires democratic minds, which is where psychoanalytic theory and practice become politically and socially relevant in ways that reach far beyond the consulting room.

Although not many of the analysts associated with Fenichel and interested in socialist ideas developed a psychoanalytic social theory (with the exception of figures such as Erich Fromm and Wilhelm Reich), their contemporaries in the philosophical area of critical theory associated with the Frankfurt School[1] had been interested in Freud's theories since the 1920s. Psychoanalysis was of great interest to the critical theorists, in part because of its theory of the instincts, resistance, and repression, which they found useful in their analysis of the dynamics of domination and submission in the individual and society. Theodor W. Adorno, a central member of the Frankfurt School collaborated on a study of "the authoritarian personality" that sought to answer questions about what inclines people toward prejudice, fascism, and murderous hatred of different others, and what internal psychological forces render them responsive to totalitarian dictators (1982). Psychoanalysis, along with philosophy and sociology, provided a useful resource for the exploration of the contradictions of enlightenment, where technological advances are accompanied by increasing forms of barbarism (Horkheimer & Adorno, 2002). Max Horkheimer, another leading figure in critical theory, was in a short analysis with Karl Landauer, a student of Freud (Jay, 1973, p. 87). Landauer founded the Frankfurt Psychoanalytic Institute, whose members included Fromm and Frieda Fromm-Reichmann. Fromm, influenced by the thought of Marx, used psychoanalytic concepts as mediating ideas in his effort to understand the relationship between individual identity formation and society. Fromm's humanistic psychoanalysis emphasized the importance of culture and history on individual psychic development (Mitchell, 1997, p. 63). His statement that, "Every neurosis represents a moral problem" (cited in Jay, 1973, p. 100) anticipates Loewald's idea that in the therapeutic process, the analysand learns to take responsibility for his unconscious desires and conflicts. Fromm remained inspired by the commitment to social justice and peace articulated by the Hebrew prophets, which was perhaps one of the elements, along with the influence of Ferenczi and Groddeck, in his advocacy of more egalitarian analyst–analysand relationships. He did not support a therapy whose goal was adjustment to the "moral inhumanities of contemporary society" (Jay, 1973, p. 98). For Fromm, "destructiveness is the outcome of unlived life" (cited in Jay, 1973, p. 112).

---

[1]For an intellectual history of the Frankfurt School and its representatives, see Martin Jay (1973), *The Dialectical Imagination: A History of the Frankfurt School and the Institute for Social Research, 1923–1950*, Boston: Little, Brown and Company and Rolf Wiggershaus (1994), *The Frankfurt School: Its History, Theories, and Political Significance* (Michael Robertson, Trans.). Cambridge, MA: The MIT Press.

Critical theory and psychoanalysis, particularly in its contemporary, relational form, share an understanding of the mutual constitutiveness of subjectivity and objectivity, such that psychoanalysis, in its exploration of the internal world of an individual, reaches society. "It is here," writes Russell Jacoby, "where subjectivity devolves into objectivity: Subjectivity is pursued till it issues into the social and historical events that preformed and deformed the subject" (Jacoby, 1975, p. 79). This understanding of the relationship between the individual and society does not rest on a simple correspondence theory of the individual and society identity formation; the underlying premise of such an approach would inevitably lead to a clinical practice oriented to adaptation of the individual to prevailing moral norms and political, social structures that negate the possibility of psychoanalysis as an emancipatory theory and praxis. The important issue here is not so much clinical practice and technique as it is a question of how psychoanalysis theorizes its own emancipatory potential that has implications for psychoanalytic practice. What form of psychoanalytic theory and practice contributes most to the cultivation of a democratic mind, and should psychoanalysis be intentionally committed to this political project? Some analytic writers argue that psychoanalysis must help in struggles against all forms of discrimination, especially given its own history of being discriminated against (Roudinescu, 2001, p. 121). Psychoanalysis must reclaim its original "subversive force" (p. 14) by contributing to new forms of freedom as it helps individuals make meaning out of their life histories and experiences. Although psychoanalysis is culturally constructed, given its development within specific historical and social contexts (p. 123), its nature is to foster and sustain a questioning, critical self-reflective attitude, which means that psychoanalysis is also discordant with the societies in which it develops.

The work of the French analyst and social theorist Cornelius Castoriadis (1997) provides an important resource for theorizing the relationship between the individual and society; for him, the psychoanalytic task of "gaining knowledge of the Unconscious and transforming the human subject" is entirely related both to questions of "freedom" and "philosophy" (p. 125). Like Hans Loewald (2000), Castoriadis, too, insists on the more accurate translation of Freud's famous dictum, "Where id was, there ego shall *become*" (p. 127), which emphasizes that therapeutic change is a process of becoming, such that subjectivity emerges into being and is not a fixed entity waiting to be unearthed; nor does it move toward a completed, finished state of being. The "I" becomes a "self-reflective subjectivity, capable of deliberation and will," not a "socially adapted machine" (p. 128). The capacity for self-reflection that posits the self as a "nonobjective object" (p. 158) requires the development of autonomy that paradoxically does not yet exist in the individual, nor in the society (p. 131).

In psychoanalysis, the human being is posited as its own subject, as a "participant in the constitution of its own experiences" (Abramson, 1984, p. 115). The analytic couple work cooperatively together to create an autonomy within the context of a heteronomous society, where people struggle to become autonomous while paradoxically absorbing and internalizing existing institutions and social arrangements. Viewed in this way, analysis must negotiate treacherous emotional territory so that the patient is not repathologized or retraumatized in an unconscious enactment of submission to the analyst's agenda. Stephen Mitchell (1997) recognizes this perilous contradiction that exists within the analytic relationship as well, pointing out that, although this contradiction is implicit in the analytic relationship, it must always be resisted through probing reflection by both parties. Identifications with the analyst as an internal object can enslave the patient in a nexus of "unconscious loyalties" that produce newer, perhaps more subtle forms of submission for the patient rather than transformation (p. 26). Both Castoriadis and Mitchell, as well as Loewald (2000) are committed to a psychoanalytic process that fosters and nourishes creativity and personal freedom. The only way for internalizations of domination and submission to be overcome is through the intersubjective experience in the analytic relationship. For Castoriadis (1952), psychoanalysis moves against the grain of prevailing social forces since this process takes place in a society whose purpose is to mold a compliant ego that preserves, maintains, and reproduces the very social institutions that created it (p. 131). In this respect the interests of psychoanalysis and society are at odds given that the main purpose of social institutions is the production of the "conformable individual" (p. 132) who lives according to what the American psychoanalyst Robert Lindner called that "vicious and fatal idea: the notion that the optimal way of life is the way of adjustment" (p. 297).

Miss G.

Miss G.'s relations with her family and co-workers were organized primarily around her feelings of guilt and, at times, betrayal whenever she sensed a conflict between her own desires and the expectations of others. "It's not that anyone dictates to me, or directly tells me what to do," she said. "It's just that I know they expect certain things of me and I feel really bad, really guilty, if I can't or don't do what they want. I can't remember feeling any different." Miss G.'s mother was depressed and dissatisfied for most of her life; her dependency on Miss G. increased when she and her husband divorced. Although Miss G. longs for a life of her own, she feels a powerful "obligation" to help her mother, to listen to her endless complaints and to comfort her even when Miss G. can hardly bear to listen to her. Miss G. does not understand why she feels so compelled to parent her mother, but is aware of feeling if she doesn't, her mother will suffer more. She cannot help but abdicate fulfilling her own needs for those not just of her mother, but of most people in her life. All of Miss G.'s major life decisions have been made in compliance with the demands of others: her choice of university, her choice of career, the long, arduous hours she puts in at her work, even when she is sick. Her workday typically starts at 7 a.m. Only recently has she felt emotionally strong enough to leave work "early"—6 p.m.—to make her analytic appointments, although she still has feelings of guilt that she is doing something "wrong." She imagines her co-workers are disdainful of her lack of "commitment" to work, or that they think she is "not very good" at her job if she puts in anything less than a 12-hour day. The effect of this is to make her an even more obliging, compliant employee. For a long time, Miss G. could not state directly her own wishes and desires in our sessions; she could only express them in an arduous detour through multiple layers of apologetic explanations and rationalizations that clouded the realization not only that she wanted things that were at odds with the expectations of others, but that their demands were at times unreasonable. She remains frightened of what other people think of her because as she put it, "my identity has always been defined by other people." A large part of the therapeutic work with this patient focuses not only on helping her reflect on *what* she thinks and wants, but on the *thinking process itself* because many of her desires are largely unformulated. As they become formulated, powerful feelings of guilt become inevitably aroused.

One of the difficulties in working with people who are emotionally organized in this way is to provide a sense of safety for the patient so that the analyst is not experienced as humiliating or judging her. At the same time, the analyst must accept that she will inevitably do this at times despite her best therapeutic intentions. Miss G. feels deeply ashamed when she "buckles" under the pressure of another's demands, thinking she has disappointed me, and she becomes anxious. The countertransference here can become quite complicated because the analyst realizes she is one more person the patient has to please. When this happens, it is important that the analyst explore with the patient how she has humiliated the patient, which involves the analyst acknowledging that she has hurt the patient. As the patient experiences the analyst as humiliating and hurtful, it is necessary that the analyst realize that she has indeed inflicted the injury despite her conscious intentions. In this way, the analyst comes to understand what it is like for the patient and can share the patient's experience; in other words, the analyst comes to see their relationship from the patient's point of view as well as her own, not merely cognitively, but affectively as well. The analyst must carefully negotiate her way between the Scylla of humiliation and the Charybdis of domination of the patient while helping the patient connect with her own needs. We must recall Mitchell's caution that analysts must attend to the ways in which we participate in pushing the patient further into deeper webs of submission for our own agendas for therapeutic change. The analyst works to foster a democratic relationship wherein the patient begins to experience democracy internally and interpersonally. Psychoanalysis facilitates the development of the democratically constituted individual.

Social Theory and Psychoanalysis

For Castoriadis (1997), democracy is only possible in an autonomous society which is "a self-instituting and self-governing collectivity that *presupposes the development of the capacity of all its members to participate in its reflective and deliberative activities*" (p. 132; emphasis added). If democracy means "collective reflectiveness," and if there is no democracy without the democratically constituted individual (p. 133), then the question is, how does such an individual come into being, especially within the conditions of heteronomy? It is the task of psychoanalysis to help individuals find in themselves the emotional capacity for "reflective and deliberative activities." However, psychoanalytic theory does not address itself seriously enough to this issue because it tends to be more focused on itself as the object of its own interest. Although psychoanalysis requires a social theory, it is also true that social and democratic theories require a strong psychoanalytic component as well.

As psychoanalysis has detached from its early interest in applying its own insights to social transformation, so too has contemporary critical theory distanced itself from its earlier commitment to psychoanalysis as a key element in social analysis. Unfortunately, some leading democratic theorists, such as Juergen Habermas either have a very rudimentary concept of psychoanalysis or demonstrate little interest in it as a central element in democratic theory and practice. This is especially ironic given that one of the key assumptions of Habermas's theory of deliberative democracy (1998) assumes without psychoanalytic elaboration that human beings cognitively possess the capacity to hold a plurality of perspectives in the process of communicative action, where members of a community engage in open, critical discourses that require each member to adopt the role or point of view of others. In assuming that all human beings involved in discourse are able to decentre sufficiently from their own subjectivity and interests so that genuine communicative action can take place, Habermas is able to propose the possibility of an intersubjective public space whereby everyone who will be affected by the decisions of the communication community has the chance to fully participate in the decision making process (Habermas,

1984, 1987). In the discursive process of the justification of truth claims and the adjudication of contested norms, the emphasis is on mutual understanding rather than consensus. The participants agree that "all affected can freely accept the consequences and the side effects that the *general* observance of a controversial norm" may have and that "only those norms can claim to be valid that meet (or could meet) with the approval of all affected in their capacity as participants in a practical discourse" (1990, p. 93).

This entire communicative process requires that all parties conduct themselves in a respectful manner that is cooperatively and peacefully directed toward the search for truth relevant to their community. Moreover, key to this process is the ability of each of the participants in communicative action to see the situation that affects them all from the point of view of each other. What Habermas's carefully elaborated theory of communicative action and deliberative democracy tends also to neglect, however, is the affective and emotional realities of the interlocutors in the communication community, that whole dimension of the nonrational unconscious within human beings that is inevitably mobilized in the communicative process as in every other form of relating. Desire, aggression, hatred, prejudice, sexuality, envy, fear, and rage will inevitably arise to one degree or another in the communicative effort to resolve contested norms, yet he never takes these emotional realities seriously into account. Not to mention the fact that not everyone in a communication community necessarily enjoys full mental health. "Habermasian man," writes Agnes Heller (1985), "has ... no body, no feelings; the 'structure of personality' is identified with cognition, language and interaction" (p. 22).

Not only Habermas, but many theorists interested in promoting more democratic ways of living together presume an already existing democratic mind that is oriented toward intersubjective relatedness that somehow becomes mobilized through reason and linguistic capacity alone. Being able to see the world from the perspective of another, especially an "alien" other, is a hard-won achievement that, for many people, requires psychoanalytic treatment. Living peacefully together in complex, pluralistic, and diverse societies requires the ability, let alone the desire, to understand how and why people think and believe the things they do. This cannot be taken for granted. Yet consider the following passage from Hannah Arendt (1993), which captures the spirit of Habermas's idea:

> The power of judgement rests on a potential agreement with others, and the thinking process which is active in judging something is not, like the thought process of pure reasoning, a dialogue between me and myself, but finds itself always and primarily, even if I am quite alone in making up my mind, in an anticipated communication with others with whom I know I must finally come to some agreement.... And this enlarged way of thinking, which as judgment

knows how to transcend its individual limitations, cannot function in strict isolation or solitude; it needs the presence of others "in whose place" it must think, whose perspective it must take into consideration, and without whom it never has the opportunity to operate at all. (pp. 220–221)

How, we must ask, does an "enlarged way of thinking" "know how to transcend its individual limitations?" Like Habermas, Arendt also, and rightly so, thinks of democratic relationships as intersubjective, in that reasoned thinking cannot operate in isolation from encountering other minds. However, where does this capacity for an "enlarged way of thinking" where the participants are engaged in a sustained, self-reflexive communicative process come from? How is it generated and cultivated, or is it more basically an inherent "genetic" given? Without a psychoanalytic theory, the kind of individuals that democratic theory by necessity presupposes must remain abstract entities that float above history and society.

Psychoanalysis, with its focus on the concrete human being in his or her context of psychosocial/sexual development reveals that the kind of individuals necessary for the creation and maintenance of democratic societies must have a sufficiently developed ability for "mentalization" (Fonagy & Target, 2003, pp. 270–282). Mentalization is a developmental achievement where the growing child learns to differentiate self and other, internal and external worlds, and to regulate affectivity. Most important, it underlies the capacity for self-reflection, for "putting oneself into question" as Castoriadis would say. Without the capacity for mentalization, there is no chance that one can adopt another's perspective or understand how he feels and why he may feel a certain way, whether we like it or not. The capacity for mentalization develops within specific historical, social, and familial contexts that provide—or negate—the conditions of its very possibility. Democratic societies, with their value commitments to tolerance, support for diversity, traditions of civil liberties, religious freedoms, constitutional protections, and other similar norms are best suited to promoting and fostering "mentalization" processes in individuals. In healthy emotional development, this capacity for mentalization or self-reflection helps the "socially embedded self" maintain a "critical perspective on its own embeddedness" (Altman, 1995, p. 41). It also involves the ability to imagine what another person might be feeling, how the world might look from another's perspective that is different from one's own without having to annihilate or control it. Being able to tolerate different perspectives, and even clash with them in ways that lead to deeper forms of mutual understanding rather than destructive action, often means having to hold feelings of dread, anxiety, confusion, and uncertainty as we confront and meet each other in our difference and otherness. If such feelings can be sustained without lapsing into a struggle for control or mastery of self and other, then the space between them can be negotiated toward mutual understanding and reciprocal recognition that is at the heart of a democratic sensibility that promotes values and life forms organized around intersubjective relationships.

Mr C.

By the time I saw Mr C., he had already made a number of suicide attempts that were the result, he said, of a life of depression, at times unbearably severe. Some time into our work together, I began to see that underlying Mr. C.'s depression was a narcissistic rage that, among other things, could not tolerate different points of view from his. He lived an isolated life, in large part because of this intolerance; he often took extreme offense where none may have been intended and he absolutely refused to consider that another person's behavior might not necessarily be an attack on or rejection of him. He would write scathing, humiliating e-mails to people he actually liked if he felt in any way hurt by them. I was the recipient of several such messages. Mr. C. was a well-educated though unpublished novelist with a background in literature and the arts, and he would often refer to novels to illustrate his point. Early on in the analysis, I ventured an interpretation of a scene in a novel that differed from his, and he categorically insisted I was wrong. Dialogue was not possible. I neither pushed my own view nor did I acquiesce in accepting his, rather being content to let the disagreement be because at the time, I did not realize just how important it was to him. Mr C. returned to our discussion of the novel repeatedly in subsequent sessions, sometimes months later, finding more ways to "prove" he was right and I was wrong. In each instance, he became progressively contemptuous and dismissive of my interpretation of the novel even though I did not attempt to justify my ideas further.

As the analysis progressed, Mr. C. became increasingly intolerant of anything I had to say and then of my saying anything at all. His intolerance was rooted in an unbearable anxiety that was aroused when I made interventions. When I tried to speak, he would roll his eyes or look impatiently at his watch or out the window. I said less and less during our sessions until I said nothing at all. Only then did he seem to relax. Slowly I began to realize that not only my expression of an alternative perspective, but any expression of my professional subjectivity at all, was intolerable to him. Eventually, I understood that underneath all that contempt and arrogance that often left me feeling humiliated and helpless was a terror that he would be overwhelmed or possibly destroyed by having to face and consider the mind of another since he barely had a mind of his own. Throughout his life his caregivers had forced him to accommodate not only to their values and their vision of how he should live, but to their version of reality. They told him his father went away on a trip when in fact he was dead, a mystification that went on for two years during his childhood. He wanted to be a writer, they wanted him to be a lawyer. For a time during young adulthood, Mr. C. accommodated his family in his education and career choices, and that is when his hospitalizations for depression and suicide attempts began. In telling me about his family's refusal to take seriously his ambition to become a writer, he would mimic his grandmother's facial expression, which I recognized as the same look of contempt he had shown me many times. Incapable of recognizing another, Mr C. could sustain no close relationships and lived in rigid isolation, needing to control everything and everyone around him.

A deliberative democratic society fosters intersubjectivity, participation, and mutual relatedness, which is grounded in mutual recognition between self and other. Psychoanalysis, especially in its contemporary relational form, offers a potential resource for creating democratic ways of life because of its emphasis on therapeutic action as facilitating "a collaborative inquiry into the nature of the analytic interaction … (developing) awareness of the patient's active role in creating interpersonal patterns, without denying the analysts's contribution … (fostering) flexibility where there was rigidity" (Altman, 1995, p. 56). From a relational perspective, psychoanalysis is participatory and cooperative, a performative enactment of a democratic principle that encourages reciprocity, recognition, and respect, and where the patient's desires are acknowledged as worthy of understanding and being heard. So many patients come to us who have never had the experience of being asked what they want or think about things. Many of our patients have learned early in life that the price of connection with others is to abdicate their own desire before it has had a chance to become known to themselves. Some patients, when asked what they want often report feeling anxious and uncertain at the very question; one patient reported "going blank." She would momentarily dissociate, and ask me to repeat the question. Some years later, this patient, a highly successful professional, no longer dissociated but reported powerful feelings of fear when she tried to imagine herself taking her own decisions in opposition to the wishes of the father she felt compelled to please. Especially when accommodation to the demands of others has been wrought in conditions of psychic trauma in early life, the emerging experience of desire and a fledgling sense of agency can arouse a terror of inexpressible isolation and even physical annihilation. Another patient told me that when she thinks of living her own life in ways that would please herself (and thereby displease her mother) she immediately becomes deeply frightened: "It feels like death, like falling into a black hole. I am dying." Such patients often demand that the analyst tell them what to do or give them "the answers," and become distressed and frustrated if the analyst tries to refocus their entreaties in terms of what *they* want.

238 Marsha Aileen Hewitt

The experience of being dominated and controlled has its comforting as well as its painful side—not because the patient likes to be hurt, but because she needs to be loved, and being loved means being acceptable to the other by conforming to the other's demands. It is a question of survival. Attachments organized around domination and submission to the expectations and needs of others establishes a way of being in the world that structures not only most relationships, but moral values, beliefs, and worldviews. The individual's capacity for resistance and critical thought are seriously impaired when one cannot experience oneself as an agent whose desires originate within oneself.

Relational psychoanalysis can provide our patients with an experience of democratic relationships that, over time, may become internalized, thus replacing rigidly organized emotional structures with more flexible, relaxed ones, where the patient acquires a stronger sense of his own agency and desire while being less threatened by others. With their emphasis on therapeutic action taking place within the analytic relationship that involves two people engaged in a process (Mitchell, 1997, p. 193) oriented to more critically self-aware and authentic meaning-making that puts the individual patient's needs ahead of the primacy of theory, relational psychoanalysis has much to contribute to the promotion of democratic minds. From this perspective, the enlarged mentality required for democratic social practices appropriate to complex, diverse modern societies cannot exist in the absence of human beings who have a strong sense of personal agency and the imaginative capacity to see the world from the perspective of the foreign other. As the individual gains the experience of becoming "increasingly self-authorized" in psychoanalysis, she becomes increasingly capable of expanding her desire for an enriched personal life that includes the creation of those social conditions without which a non-alienated, more satisfying life is not possible. Psychoanalysis is inspired by the hope that personal transformation is possible in the direction of an individual becoming the most she can become (Freud, 1917, p. 435). But hope in individual transformation is not enough. Analysts must resist the tendency widely present in psychoanalysis to "insulate subjectivity from social practices and discourses" (Abel, cited in Altman, 1995, p. 74). As Jessica Benjamin (1988) writes, "the personal and social are interconnected, and to understand that if we suffocate our personal longings for recognition, we will suffocate our hope for social transformation as well" (1988, p. 224).

Psychoanalysis and the Hope of the Individual

Joel Whitebook's (1985) observation that today, psychoanalysts are treating a "new patient," holds increasingly true. He writes, "As the self has failed to adequately coalesce, it cannot be taken for granted in psychoanalytic treatment. Rather, the consolidation of the self itself becomes a primary goal of that treatment.... The old metapsychology has simply proven inadequate—theoretically and clinically—for dealing with these new phenomena" (p. 150). The "consolidation of the self" cannot occur when the child has learned that submission to others is the price of survival before he or she has had a chance to develop emotionally. Certain fragments of self-development may occur—Miss G. is an extremely successful woman professionally—while other parts of the self remain in a more primitive, infantile state. Such people cannot develop a sense of themselves as independent individuals who establish a comfortable measure of control over their affective states because they remain largely unintegrated, unconsolidated, shifting parts of a self. This is the psychic effect of emotional enslavement to the demands of others, and the prospect of disentangling and separating oneself from internalized oppressors may be too frightful to bear. Like Winston in George Orwell's dystopian novel *Nineteen Eighty-Four,* human beings raised in environments of domination and submission, both familial and social, are "squeezed empty" in order to be filled with alien forces before they have a chance to develop any sense of autonomy, distinctness, or individuality. Only individuals who experience themselves as such are capable of resistance and protest, both on their own behalf and that of others.

Politically, fear and destruction constitute the emotional sources of fascism, whereas eros belongs to democracy (Jay, 1973, p. 86). Fear may be soothed by external forces of rigidity and control, even though it produces emotional deadness in human beings. Fear cannot tolerate diversity or welcome otherness, nor can it negotiate difference. It cannot be and let be, but must control and dominate everything around it, bringing the world to submission in its insatiable urge to destroy ambiguity and the unknown. If psychoanalysis is about any one thing, it is about freedom, freedom for human beings not only to love and to work but to become while feeling reasonably comfortable with the becoming of others. Psychoanalysis is a call to morality, responsibility, and autonomy-in-relationship that are crucial to becoming truly human beings who are open to themselves and to others in all their complexity and diversity. In this respect, psychoanalysis is thoroughly modern as it challenges humanity to critical self-reflection without which tolerance, cooperation, and peaceful living together are impossible. This challenge cannot be limited to the consulting room; it is a political project as well as a project committed to healing mental illness. At its heart, psychoanalysis is *both* a social theory of democracy as well as a clinical treatment oriented to individual change whose goal is inevitably the cultivation of a democratic mind.

References

Abramson, J. B. (1984), *Liberation and its Limits: The Moral and Political Thought of Freud*. New York: The Free Press.

Adorno, T. W., Frenkel-Brunswik, E., Levinson, D. J., & Sanford, R. N. (1982), *The Authoritarian Personality* (Abridged Edition). New York: W.W. Norton & Company.

Altman, N. (1995), *The Analyst in the Inner City: Race, Class, and Culture Through a Psychoanalytic Lens*. Hillsdale, NJ: The Analytic Press.

Arendt, H. (1993), *Between Past and Future: Eight Exercises in Political Thought*. Harmondsworth: Penguin Books.

Benjamin, J. (1988), *The Bonds of Love: Psychoanalysis, Feminism, and the Problem of Domination*. New York: Pantheon Books.

Castoriadis, C. (1997), *World in Fragments: Writings on Politics, Society, Psychoanalysis, and the Imagination*. Stanford, CA: Stanford University Press.

Dimen, M. (1994), Money, Love, and Hate: Contradiction and Paradox in Psychoanalysis. *Psychoanal. Dial.*, 4:69–100.

Fenichel, O. (1945), *The Psychoanalytic Theory of Neurosis*. New York: W.W. Norton & Company.

Fonagy, P., & Target, M. (2003), *Psychoanalytic Theories: Perspectives from Developmental Psychopathology*. New York: Brunner-Routledge.

Freud, S. (1913), Totem and Taboo. *Standard Edition,* 13:1–161. London: Vintage, The Hogarth Press.

Freud, S. (1917), Transference. Introductory Lectures on Psychoanalysis. *Standard Edition,* 16:431–447. London: Vintage, The Hogarth Press.

Freud, S. (1918), Lines of Advance in Psycho-analytic Therapy. *Standard Edition,* 17:159–168. London: Vintage, The Hogarth Press.

Freud, S. (1927), The Future of an Illusion. *Standard Edition,* 21:5–56. London: Vintage, The Hogarth Press.

Freud, S. (1930), Civilization and its Discontents. *Standard Edition,* 21:64–145. London: Vintage, The Hogarth Press.

Freud, S. (1933), New Introductory Lectures on Psychoanalysis. The Question of a Weltanschauung. *Standard Edition,* 22:158–182. London: Vintage, The Hogarth Press.

Geertz, C. (1973), *The Interpretation of Cultures: Selected Essays*. New York: Basic Books.

Habermas, J. (1984, 1987), *The Theory of Communicative Action* (Vols. 1 & 2; T. McCarthy, Trans.). Boston: Beacon Press.

Habermas, J. (1990), *Moral Consciousness and Communicative Action* (C. Lenhardt & S. Weber Nicholsen, Trans.). Cambridge, MA: The MIT Press.

Habermas, J. (1998), *Between Facts and Norms: Contributions to a Discourse Theory of Law and Democracy* (W. Rehg, Trans.). Cambridge, MA: The MIT Press.

Heller, A. (1985), Habermas and Marxism. In: *Habermas: Critical Debates,* eds. J. B. Thompson & D. Held. Cambridge, MA: The MIT Press.

Horkheimer, M., & Adorno, T. W. (2002), *Dialectic of Enlightenment: Philosophical Fragments,* ed. G. S. Noerr (E. Jephcott, trans.). Stanford, CA: Stanford University Press.

Jacoby, R. (1975), *Social Amnesia: A Critique of Contemporary Psychology from Adler to Laing*. Boston: Beacon Press.

Jacoby, R. (1983), *The Repression of Psychoanalysis: Otto Fenichel and the Political Freudians*. Chicago: University of Chicago Press.

Jay, M. (1973), *The Dialectical Imagination: A History of the Frankfurt School and the Institute of Social Research 1923–1950*. Boston: Little, Brown and Company.

Lindner, R. (1952), *Prescription for Rebellion*. New York: Rinehart.

Loewald, H. W. (2000), *The Essential Loewald: Collected Papers and Monographs*. Hagerstown: University Publishing Group.

Marcuse, H. (1962), *Eros and Civilization: A Philosophical Inquiry into Freud*. New York: Vintage Books.

Marx, K., & Engels, F. (1976), Theses on Feuerbach in *Collected Works* Vol. 5, 1845–1847. New York: International Publishers, pp. 3–5.

Mitchell, S. A. (1997), *Influence and Autonomy in Psychoanalysis*. Hillsdale, NJ: The Analytic Press.

Pyles, R. L. (2003), The Good Fight: Psychoanalysis in the Age of Managed Care. *J. Amer. Psychoanal. Assn.*, 51/Supplement: 23–41.

Roudinesco, E. (2001), *Why Psychoanalysis?* (R. Bowlby, Trans.). New York: Columbia University Press.

Whitebook, J. (1985), Reason and Happiness: Some Psychoanalytic Themes in Critical Theory. In: *Habermas and Modernity,* ed. R. J. Bernstein. Cambridge, MA: The MIT Press, pp. 140–160.

Part III

Experiments in a New Key

"Experiments in a New Key" opens up the domain of experimental writing. By playing with voice, creation of a narrator, language and writing styles, we hope to give a sense of what possibilities psychoanalytic writing holds, which remain, as yet, unexplored.

Jeffre Phillip Cheuvront (chap. 14) opens this part of the volume with a bold stroke in "Eternal Return: Development, Repetition, and Time." In the beginning of the chapter, we read: "He dreams that the world is a world where all things emotionally felt will be repeated; a world of eternal recurrence." Cheuvront, in an evocative, mysterious fictional piece, inspired by clinical material, explores the themes of repetition and development and their relationship to time. The chapter is a major departure from traditional psychoanalytic writing, and yet the psychoanalyst is never far from the page in how the story unfolds and the depth of understanding lent to the characters. It leaves us unsettled, curious, longing for more.

In a very personal and moving paper, Gilbert Cole (chap. 15) takes us into the dreadful space of "The HIV-Positive Analyst: Identifying the Other." Adapted from his book *Infecting the Treatment* (2002), Cole explores, with remarkable openness, the implications of being known as seropositive by his patients and the analytic community. Marked for death, forced into the category of the Other, Cole captures the shame and disgust projected onto the contagious and despised in a homophobic culture. In an admirable weaving of theory, clinical material, and personal narrative, Cole highlights his relational sensibilities and the many constructive uses of the self, in the room and on the page.

"Never Mind the Equipment: A Brief and Somewhat Eccentric Interrogation of the Homo in Sexuality" (chap. 16), as the title suggests, is a playful, yet serious exploration of the way sameness is constructed solely on genitally based conceptions. Elaine Freedgood and Debra Roth, using humor, irony, and personal narrative, expose the societal preoccupation with placing the genitals in the foreground as a signifier of difference. In a subtle and masterful way, they integrate their own observations as a couple with their different theoretical backgrounds in cultural theory and psychoanalytic texts. They conclude that conventional categorization occludes other possibilities of erotic engagements less based on bodily topography. Furthermore, in an attempt to disrupt the conventional psychocultural process they argue that there is a cultural eradication of the multiple yearnings for sameness in sexual desire.

A moving and courageous piece by Sandra Silverman (chap. 17) follows. In "Where We Have Both Lived," Silverman explores the impact of having lived psychically in the same fragile and wounded place of trauma as her patient: Both have two older siblings with severe mental illness. Weaving her own childhood history with current narratives, Silverman draws the reader into her emotional space. We feel the shame, the loss, and the tragic helplessness of the situation. As the treatment unfolds Silverman explores moving out of a dissociated position and into a space where her yearnings for recognition and deep connection can be expressed.

Gillian Straker invites us to enter the experience of perversion with her as she explores a fictional text. If perversion is, of necessity, relational, then in "Enter the Perverse: Unpacking the Co-construction of Perverse Entanglements" (chap. 18) Straker brilliantly and subtly implicates us, the reader, in the perverse scenario in a similar way to how she finds herself unwittingly seduced into a visceral involvement with the text. In a creative blend of evocative emotions and incisive theoretical inquiry, Straker takes us with her on a journey through anxiety, disgust, and denigration as she exposes the mechanisms of her entanglement.

Finally, Melanie Suchet (chap. 19) closes with our second fictional piece, "Transitions." Based on clinical issues generated in her work with transgendered patients, Suchet explores the transformative journey of the analyst, how it parallels that of her patient in his quest to transition. The use of fiction allows for a deeper exploration of the analyst's psyche, her own losses and longings, the ways in which patient and analyst resonate, touch and profoundly move each other. The piece is engaging, provocative, and disturbing, evoking and creating a transitional mood that leaves the reader unsettled yet enticed, replicating that of the analytic space.

In Part III, we see relational analysts exhibiting creative and flexible uses of the self to gain deeper insights into the rich inner and intersubjective experiences of their analysands. There is no neutral, objective stance, not for the analyst, nor the reader as they are both inevitably drawn into the visceral, affective drama of psychoanalysis.

Reference

Cole, G. (2002), *Infecting the Treatment: Being an HIV-Positive Analyst.* Hillsdale, NJ: The Analytic Press.

14

Eternal Return: Development, Repetition and Time

Jeffre Phillip Cheuvront, Jr., PsyD

▼ ▼ ▼ ▼ ▼

An essential point of the clinical theory, then, is that sensual pleasure is not an autonomous experience sought after simply for its own sake. Sensual mobilization is an organismic event whose motivational importance arises from the requirements of a developing self that seeks always to perpetuate and preserve its unity, integrity, and coherence. Encounters and relationships that have linked sensual activity to self-conception and self-esteem are retained as part of the cognitive record of sensual pleasure and are thereafter very much part of the stimulation of sexual activity. (Klein, 1976, pp. 38–39)

Foreword

A difficulty with words, particularly when written, is that their precision can obscure precisely what is struggling to be communicated. This is common, too, in psychoanalytic treatment and an important point of concern for inter-subjectivity theorists (e.g., Orange, Atwood, & Stolorow, 1997; Stolorow, Brandchaft, & Atwood, 1987). The story that follows is a small attempt to stretch beyond dialectical thinking and to capture some themes regarding development and repetition—self-psychology's two dimensions of transference (Kohut, 1977)—and their peculiar relationship to time. The story, although inspired by clinical material, is fabricated. In the service of setting a tone for the story I evoke Nietzsche (e.g., 2000) and George Klein. Apologies for doing justice to neither.

I.

He dreams that the world is a world where all things emotionally felt will be repeated; a world of eternal recurrence. In this world, the swelling of the heart from the most tender kiss placed on the forehead by a beloved may sit side-by-side the abject terror and deepest despair of the most lonesome moment. Sentiments, sufferance—once experienced—are bound, expected, to return. Forever.

In this world, the man once hurt despairs, for he knows this despair will be felt again. He spends his days, his energy, watching, waiting. He asks: When will these feelings return? Will it be today? Tomorrow? The man once blessed rejoices, perhaps this bliss will surround his life, suspended, like time in a photograph. He too has reason for concern. He wonders: *When will the joy end?* And then, after it has passed: *When will the joy return?*

In a world of eternal recurrence, a man, once abandoned, finds solace in martyrdom and for life is bound, eternally, to act the sacrificial sufferer. An addict, many years a user, has long forgotten what brought him to drug use, but continues to use as each occurrence imparts the tender familiarity of unfulfilled hopes of prior highs. An old woman is warmed by a flirtatious gesture she gives a young maitre d' as she leaves a restaurant, the same warmth that she has felt since first enacting these movements as a girl. And so on. Bound, eternal, repetition.

And yet: Right now, on a park bench on a warm autumn day a young woman notices the aroma of dry fallen leaves. She tips her head back, eyes closed, and feels the sun warm her face. For this moment she is transported to another time. She remembers an Indian summer day from her time at school. On this day she lies next to a young man who is to be her first adult love. They become lost in conversation. They clutch hands. They miss literature class. Later, in his studio, he gently undresses her. It is now nighttime, cooled air passes through an open window and tickles their bare skin. For a moment she feels cold, reluctant. But the warmth of the young man's lips soothe her chill, quiet her unease. Pressed against him she feels safely cocooned. A happiness, previously only imagined, is present. And in the protective shelter of the young man she allows herself to be absorbed in contentment, lost in delight, wishing time would stop.

Of course time does not stop, and the woman finds herself, throughout the better part of 20 years, thinking of this moment, hoping to recapture this safe feeling. And so when she is with men she is often met with disappointment. She craves duplication of this previous excitement, the return of the young man's touch. And this feeling, so easily remembered, imagined, proves so easily elusive in her present, lived life. And when she is alone the memory keeps her company, quieting her loneliness, assuaging concerns about her desirability, providing a mooring for her identity.

But today, as it happens, her mind does not rest on this moment. She begins to think about her neighbor's 19-year-old son whom she has watched grow and is now in his second year at college. He is handsome and earnest, and awkward and self-conscious, and reminds her of the young man from her past. She thinks of her father, now dead for some 4 years, and remembers feeling duplicitous as she laid cocooned with the young man. And then, as if rotating the lens of a camera, the memory, so often remembered and replayed, comes a little more into focus, and she sees the young man—a boy, really—pale, awkward, nervous. She sees two adolescents stumbling through the yet-learned rhythms of seduction, sexual desire, and consignation. And with this new recollection she tips her head a little further back, feels the sun's warmth, smiles, and begins to quietly laugh.

At the same time in Nucla, Colorado, a 53-year-old woman tends the Montrose County Mining Museum. She straightens literature printed on colored sheets of paper. On summer days two or three groups may visit the two-room exhibit, but by early September, visitors are less frequent. Now a man has entered and, in his arms, an infant. The man and woman exchange greetings. The woman can see that the baby, no more than 6 or 7 months old, is asleep.

The man studies the antique maps. He moves to the display case containing locally mined rocks and gems. As he moves he gently, and without thought, places his free hand on the infant's head, caressing, supporting, and protecting the child from disturbance. The woman is drawn to the grace of this small gesture. She is reminded of her son, now away for 16 months. His father, she remembers, had held him with the same confidence, the same smooth elegance. Where she had felt clumsy, he moved with her son as if the motions were practiced, choreographed. Even now, with her son, his father displays an open, natural manner that she cannot. And although her love for her son feels absolute, she cannot escape the feeling that, where this communication is effortless for the boy's father, for her expression of this sentiment feels arduous, clumsy, blocked; almost as if she were struggling to speak with someone only partly familiar with her language.

The man with the infant turns to inspect a large antique glass jar with an aluminum screw-top lid. Inside the jar is a chunk of rock containing uranium ore mined long ago. The woman tells the man that she and others have been trying to unscrew the lid and remove the rock for years. Many visitors, she tells him, many strong men have tried to dislodge the lid, but the jar remains sealed. Here, with the same grace, the man shifts to raise his face from the jar to meet the woman's face. For a moment the woman is concerned he might ask her to hold the child while he tries the jar, but quickly the concern fades. She finds herself, bolstered by the man's relaxed, graceful nature, hoping she might hold the peaceful child. Instead he asks the woman what keeps her from simply breaking the jar to remove the rock. What would be the point, replies the woman, it is the container I value.

The man and infant leave. The woman returns to arranging her colored papers but finds herself distracted. Her hands, she notices, are dry, almost cracked, and the discolorations that had previously been almost invisible seem a shade darker. She inspects them and remembers the hands of her grandfather. She moves towards the back office where she stores her hand cream, but instead reaches for the telephone and dials a number she knows by memory, but is seldom used. *Perhaps,* she thinks, *my son is home*.

II.

Just outside Iowa City, autumn emerges like cluster-fires. The summered greens (owing to a particularly moist season) of the grasses, trees, crops fade to harvest browns on their way to winter grays. But the trees, scattered like islands in a sea of autumn wheat, cannot bring themselves to rest. Or so this is how Taylor sees it. They mount one last gesture, pulling themselves, at least momentarily, away from the inevitable sleep of winter, and here is where they explode: brilliant crimsons and oranges aflame, like bonfires on a beach at dusk.

Taylor sees this from the porch of the house he is living in. It is an old house as houses go on the Plains. It was built in 1905 by an idyllic, hard-working, and hopeful young farmer who imagined a large home that he and his wife could fill with children, warmth, and fond memories. And so, in addition to its grand size, he constructed a porch covering two sides of the house that, in its enormity, connected the house to the land and, in this manner, the house extended invitingly outward such that the boundary between structure and terrain blurred. Home, land, work, shelter, and family were as one, and here the farmer and his family lived (even after the sale of the land for development as part of the expanding Iowa City) until his death the previous year.

These qualities (idealism, softened boundaries, family) immediately appealed to Taylor's mother who could not be dissuaded from its purchase even with a tight financial situation and an abundance of personal difficulties plaguing her husband and family. They appealed, despite her husband's modest protests, because she is a woman for whom inner experiences, personal suffering, and financial restrictions are unimportant; Success lies in appearance, and so it is the façade—the appearance of family, achievement, wealth—to which she is most dedicated. And so the house, having previously been inhabited by the successful farmer and his family, and carrying (the way objects sometimes can when long possessed by spirited people) the character of the prior owners becomes the medium through which success is established, *must* be established, for Taylor's mother.

But it is not quite right to say that "she is a woman for whom inner experiences, personal suffering, and financial restrictions are unimportant." In fact, it is more accurate to notice that each of these qualities are of the utmost importance. It is true that her marriage to Taylor's father was in no small way an attempt to satisfy both her inner emptiness and feelings of vulnerability. As a younger man, her husband was full of promise—academically heralded, mentored by the most well-known people in his field, impassioned about his work—she was immediately struck by his suitability. He was not so much like the house (infused with importance, meaning) as he was like the house's builder (idyllic, hopeful) and this inspired her own regard; She imagined herself bathed in the light of her husband's success, seizing her part as the celebrated intellectual's hostess wife. Yes, she would capture the esteem and envy of the other university women: Comparing their husbands' work (her husband had already won as a student two coveted prizes!), attending cocktail parties and receptions, and perhaps (and this was the deepest secret) attaining some approval from her own mother. And here, in these thoughts, she felt the burden of her hopelessness and quiet suffering lift, lighten.

So I think we must admit that it is not disregard or shallowness with which Taylor's mother so doggedly desired this house: Husband, son (Taylor, not her eldest), and house are like food providing nourishment, medicine to her hurt and vulnerability. In this manner, her inner world is both central and sheltered from herself and the outside world.

Here is where the house holds such potential: It is reliable. How could she have imagined that her husband's precocious brilliance would become such self-destructive obstinacy? The ordeal at the California university had left her drained. Months of enduring pointed questions and tides of gossip had made simply leaving her house a chore. Oh the duration! It was more than once she had thought how simple it would be to swallow the bottle of pills. When the administration abandoned their dismissal proceedings and her husband had been allowed back into the classroom, she felt no relief. It was only after he had found the Iowa position (Iowa, imagine!) and submitted his resignation that she felt some relief and began again to script a hoped-for life with new, imagined people in new, imagined surrounds. Yes, this is the trouble with people: They cannot be relied on and so often usher in disappointment.

Let me say that which is plain: Taylor's mother's attention to her inner concerns requires indifference to precisely these experiences in others. She cannot consider her husband's feelings of financial vulnerability, nor the emotional turmoil that has possessed him since his resignation without threatening her own emotional balance. Similarly, she cannot entertain Taylor's malaise as anything other than the inevitable struggle a (gifted!) 10-year-old feels when moving to another school. No. To see, to focus on, to empathize with the inner concerns of family member's lives would be to loosen a perfectly good knot better left tied. And worse, it may hint to herself (and then, to others) that her vision of herself as the mother of such an extraordinary son and wife of such a celebrated and successful intellectual omits complexities that she finds painful, overwhelming, and shameful.

But let me return to Taylor, who we left in the autumn afternoon of 1965 on the porch of his house. The house is uncomfortable. The porch is uncomfortable. The land is uncomfortable. They are too big, sprawling, unboundaried. In California everything was close: Bedrooms were set next to each other, the garage was attached to the house, neighbors' windows were no further than the width of a driveway away. Even the drive to the supermarket took a few short minutes. On his bicycle, Taylor could pass literally hundreds of houses and encounter other kids without leaving his neighborhood. But here (and he is certain on this point owing to the house's vantage point) there are no other houses, much less children, for miles.

California was not without its own problems. Over the years his father had become increasingly remote and in his absence, his mother's bid for full possession seemed all but complete. He had always been aware of an unwritten treaty between his parents in which Taylor's brother belonged to his father and Taylor was in the domain of his mother. Here Taylor felt conflicted. As a young boy, he spent hours solicitous of his father, patiently watching him write and anticipating the moment when he would take a break and take notice of him. But as early as he could remember he had always cherished, craved the feeling of specialness lavished on him by his mother. Early on, this took the form of elaborate praise and doting for even his smallest achievements, and Taylor would flush with discomfort. But as he grew older he became accustomed to (and even to rely on) this praise, such that he himself often tried to elicit such attention. These attempts were met as often with disappointment as with success which (any undergraduate psychology student can tell you) ushered in persistent unease. And it is here that we can see how hoped-for attention from his mother did not differ particularly from his father. Valued, prized attention was available only inconsistently, which leads me to imagine that which must have felt most consistent to Taylor was the tension between patient (hopeless) waiting and desperate (anxious) solicitation.

This had been most evident during the last year in California. Where previously Taylor's father's withdrawal had been mediated by his mother's increased activity, this year had been different. His father had become a ghost, passing through their home with the scarcest influence. And his mother, too, seemed to fade. Gone was her usual (incessant) chattiness, her perfectly applied make-up, her hours and hours of daytime phone calls. And then gone was her ability to leave the house and, on certain days, her bedroom. And, most centrally, gone was Taylor's capacity to capture her attention, lift her spirits, evoke her pride. It is difficult to know how a 9-year-old might understand or explain such parental collapse. What is known is that faced with this emotional solitude, Taylor developed a solution that was as imaginative as it was resourceful: He adopted a new family.

The Kennedy family lived directly behind Taylor's house. Alone, this would not be sufficient to bring a couple in their mid-40s together with a 9-year-old boy. But the Kennedys had just sent their youngest son off to college, and their home (devoid of boys for the first time in more than 20 years) seemed disturbingly quiet. And so it came that, after school, Taylor would pass by the Kennedys where he would accompany Mrs. Kennedy on her late-day activities. They would cook, clean, play cards, run short errands, garden. But (and this is most central) mostly they would chat: Mrs. Kennedy seemed truly interested in the boy's school day and his unending curiosity. And the precocity of his manners! She had never met such a well-behaved boy. Some days Mr. Kennedy would arrive home early and join them, often clutching comic books or pastries he had purchased for Taylor.

For Taylor's part, the generosity and availability of Mr. and Mrs. Kennedy was precious, but not without discomfort: As adults, we know that there is no understanding of possession without an understanding of loss. And here is where Taylor (unlike other children who have never needed to think of parenting in this manner) gained much of what Mrs. Kennedy perceived as his well-mannered precocity: Taylor's visits were always performances. They were performances (and I use the word "performance" in the most colloquial way, to mean an act, a recital, a show) because they were crafted with the central intent of maximizing his intimacy with the Kennedys while not bringing attention to the desperateness of his circumstances. The boy who visited with Mrs. Kennedy was not so much the delightful, well-behaved neighborhood youngster she imagined, but a very troubled little boy who was forever (even during beloved activities!) assessing his impact and dreading the time when her availability would come to an end.

Let me be more accurate: Taylor could lose himself in these moments and, indeed, there were many moments with the Kennedys in which his troubles dissolved, if only for that instant. An example: A game of cards with Mrs. Kennedy on a rainy afternoon in which she declared Taylor would not leave the house and Mr. Kennedy would wait for his dinner until she had won at least one round. In these moments, the performance was effortless and, in fact, felt unlike a performance at all. The fantasied familial relationship with the Kennedys was unequivocally the real relationship: The Kennedys were his family fully for those moments and his usual disbelief and ruminative attendance to the quality of the unfolding relationship were stilled. And, I venture to say, within these moments Taylor felt happy, lifted, lightened.

Taylor felt two ways when his mother moved out of the bedroom she and his father shared and began sleeping in his bed. First, he felt excited: Her attentiveness, long absent, had returned! And indeed each evening he could look forward to his mother's recitation on how special Taylor was to her, how, were it not for him, she would have no joy in life, and how disappointed she felt towards Taylor's father and brother. But he also felt reluctant: His mother's presence did not always imply her attention. And in this respect his mother felt demanding, intrusive. And there was this other feeling, more difficult to pinpoint, perhaps owing to its complexity. It was a feeling evoked when his sleeping mother's foot or arm would make contact with him. Or when he would allow himself to reflect on the peculiarity of his mother sleeping with him rather than his father. It was a feeling that no matter how many times he tried to articulate it he felt a shortage of words, and slightly surprised, even embarrassed, at the word which seemed to best fit. To use his word, Taylor felt *creepy*.

Do not be so quick to presume this notion is so easily understood: The temptation, in our unease, to connect the feelings of creepiness with Taylor' feelings of intrusion and our own concerns about the blurred familial boundaries, is understandable. No, to capture Taylor's meaning of creepy we must look further. True, as Taylor's mother's leg presses against her son's he feels intrusion, even trapped, constricted between the edge of the bed and his mother. And he feels guilt: It has not escaped his attention that most children sleep separate from his parents. But it is the nature of the present that the reality of it can never be assessed: The present can only be viewed as an abstraction, as a condensation in memory (just try and recall a conversation you had earlier today if you need convincing). And it is here, in this condensation, that the intrusive feelings mix with his greater milieu: The wish to feel the special alliance with his mother, to obtain her praises, to lift her spirit (enlivening her and, thus, himself) simply by meeting her expectations. So we can see that the creepy feeling expresses more than discomfort (for there is no discomfort!). Creepy, in the form of the intrusive, perhaps even the forbidden, only enhances and highlights the specialness of his mother's nighttime attention. Creepy represents the bond between the special and the forbidden.

The Iowa house is everything his mother promised and everything he has dreaded. True, his mother's spirit seems to have repossessed her body after the move. Even his father seems to have come back to life. But everything about the place feels empty. And on this autumn afternoon with no one around this feeling is amplified. His father is keeping the long hours of a new faculty member. His mother has been called to a meeting at his brother's school where (already) he has been disrupting and falling behind the other kids. And so Taylor is left to sit on the stairs to the porch of the too-large, empty house and fret. He thinks of the Kennedys and the precariousness of foraged relationships in general. He thinks of his mother, the excitement of her attention and the unpredictability of her availability. He thinks of his father, how he had seen him crying at his office desk in their California home and how invisible he can be. He thinks of his brother, how his mother's contempt for her older son fuels her pride for the younger, and how this has always prevented him from risking closeness with him. He thinks of the old home, his old friends, his old school. And then he thinks of the new house, new school, and the new kids he has met and becomes filled with dread and anxiety. All of these possess his thoughts, swirl in his head, mixing, folding onto each other until the thoughts themselves have thickened and all that is left is a feeling best (and simply) described as fear. He reaches for the gasoline can on his left and places it between his legs. The lid of the metal container sticks part way so he has to use a rag to get a sufficient grip. And then Taylor does what he has been doing since arriving in Iowa whenever he feels this despair: He bends over the uncapped tin and inhales. He inhales deeply, and the sweet smell of gasoline rushes in. At first he feels dizzy and considers pulling his head away. But then the vapors do their trick: They melt away his isolation, melt away his ruminative thoughts, melt away his feelings of hopelessness, fear, dread. And then (and, I suspect, most importantly) melt away his feelings of hopefulness, melt away his feelings of want, melt away his feelings of desire. Mind stilled, Taylor lifts his head, notes the Iowa autumn fires, and slumps unconscious.

III.

She dreams the grasses are tall and summered, the sky clear, the landscape sprawling. They are, in her mind, the tall grasses found on the plains of Colorado, her childhood home. A dirt road, she dreams, parts the grass field and gently rises to top a small hill where she has parked her truck, and from where she stands in the field she can see the truck, the truck up top. She, in the field, and the truck on the hill, she dreams, a hill maybe in the Colorado foothills but no specific location, no real place, it is a dream place, a new familiar place. She spots her small dog in the window of the truck. He has stood up on his hind legs and placed his front paws on the glass, the window is cracked open, his nose seeks outside air. Now, she dreams, the truck on the hill begins to move, to slowly roll, then gains momentum together with an inside feeling, a real feeling inside her, the blossoming of this awareness: That she did not set the parking brake. And as the truck careens downward with her little dog she is consumed by feelings of guilt over her carelessness and inattention. And this is when, horrified, she wakes.

IV.

Everywhere cotton dust has settled; a tang of burnt sulfur hangs in the air. It is quiet. The discharge of the shotgun had destroyed the mattress and box spring, splintered the bed frame, and torn part way into the wooden floor. It had, Taylor thinks, blown a hole right through it. An hour earlier the house was ablaze: frenzied phone calls from his mother to father, his brother barricaded in the bathroom, more phone calls to his brother's doctor. Taylor's mother busied herself with concerns about disposal and replacement of the bed, repair of the floor, and the application of her makeup. Taylor had watched this seated on the stairway. His father had arrived, fetched his mother and brother (he had easily coaxed him out of the bathroom) and they departed. Did they say anything on their way out? Taylor cannot remember. Standing in the doorway Taylor inspects what remains of his parents' bed. Blew a hole right through it, he thinks. Blew a hole right through it.

His mother's phone call to the doctor had been magnificent: Her explanation of how Taylor's brother had been cleaning and accidentally discharged the shotgun betrayed none of the frenetic ambiance pervasive in the house. She succeeded (and this was her brilliance) in communicating the imperativeness of the situation, of soliciting sympathy and concern from others, without betraying the particulars of the experience. And in this process (of discarding details, softening felt emotion) something remarkable happens: The actuality, authenticity of the experience is changed.

Let me be more explicit. When Taylor's mother lifts the receiver of the phone to call the doctor she does so, in part, out of (understandable) concern for her son and protection of her family. But as she locates the phone number, as she dials the phone, as she waits for an answer, she becomes aware of her central concern: Her son, who has become more and more withdrawn as he has drifted through his teen years, has fired a gun into her bed; not into his bed or Taylor's bed or even through a wall or window or (God forbid!) himself, but into her bed. And concurrent with this thought a wave of self-reproach washes over her. What sort of mother has this sort of son, she wonders. The wonder is short-lived as feelings of shame and self-pity flood her awareness. But just as she is reaching the height of her self-despair, there is an answer on the line and her attention is drawn to the demands of the conversation. My son, she tells the psychiatrist, has scared himself something horrible, a gun he was cleaning was accidentally discharged, it has upset him terribly. With this, she makes arrangements for bringing Taylor's brother for examination. And as she says goodbye, as she places the telephone receiver back into the cradle, she feels uplifted, self-assured, for her prior concerns have disappeared. With this disappearance, anxiety fades, and she is satisfied that the events of the morning unfolded precisely in the manner she has described to the doctor.

Blew a hole right through it: Taylor's approach is not entirely different than his mother's. He has a wish, a need to transform the unease that has been launched by his brother's lunacy. But where Taylor's mother seeks to assuage anxiety evoked by ideas discrepant with needed ways of seeing herself, Taylor's fears and anxiety are roused by feelings of loss. For Taylor, this is not a simple loss: His brother's action symbolically and decidedly mark the end of a relationship that has not only sustained him since the move to Iowa, but has served as the justification for his existence.

It is hard to say who initiated the sexual games between Taylor and his brother. But it is not difficult to say when. The move to Iowa had consumed his mother in a manner unpredictable to Taylor. True, the move had revitalized her, but the vitality seemed directed outward, away from Taylor. No longer did he sense the importance of his specialness to her, her need to see herself through Taylor's achievements. Instead she focused on crafting the (cursed!) house and attending women's meetings in town. For a time inhaling gasoline had provided some relief to his despair. But his inclination for this had been tempered by a scare he had given himself one afternoon in which he awoke in a field miles from home, unaware of having made the trek. And so sometime around age 12 or 13, as the first physical changes of adolescence appeared, Taylor and his brother found an interest and reason for each other that had previously eluded them: They began engaging in sexual activities. And like with his mother, whom Taylor clung to in order to provide meaning to his life (in the monitoring and anticipation of her availability, in the solicitation of the favor of her attention), Taylor became possessed by a similar attachment to his brother. And in finding this replacement, this new target of desire, Taylor was steadied, bolstered, returned to the familiar.

But today, this had come to an end. The significance of the gunshot into his parents' bed was not lost on Taylor. Where their early experiences had occurred in the shared bathroom, their more recent encounters had taken place here, in their parents' room. Taylor had sensed his brother's decreased availability, waning interest, even agitation in their meetings. No, it was more than this: Taylor's brother had been retreating from his family for some time. Most of his parents' interactions with his brother revolved around keeping him in school and stormy fights in the aftermath of his poor shoplifting skills. His brother seemed to be either detached and vacant or out of control and violent, and this introduced a sense of precariousness. And although this withdrawal and instability had concerned Taylor, it had also increased Taylor's preoccupation and the intensity of their sexual experiences. By becoming less available and more dangerous,

Taylor's brother had become more precious. And as with all things precious, possession (even for a short period) is exhilarating.

Blew a hole right through it: For Taylor it is a declaration of the end of their sexual life. And as the tingling feeling evoked by this loss spread through his body and passed into his limbs, as (by way of compensation) the pleasure of his brother's penis in his mouth enters his mind, as the intensity and power of holding his attention through pleasing him is remembered, and as he returns his attention to the notion that his brother will never again be available in this way, he has a memory. It is a memory that instills hopefulness. It is a memory that soothes, assuages the feelings of loss:

He is in the big shopping mall on the other side of town. He has left his mother to her errands and has wandered into a record store. A man, maybe 18 or 20 years old, has been meeting his gaze as he has moved about the store. As he passes by, the man asks Taylor if he would like to go to the restroom. Taylor follows him, trailing by 10 yards. In the restroom the man disappears into the far stall. Taylor approaches the open stall. Looking in, he sees the man is gesturing for him to join him. Taylor, excited and fearful that his mother will notice his absence, turns and leaves.

V.

Sometimes, where there seems to be nothing, there are dreams. The plane is high above the land. Looking down the land forms rolling patches, verdant swatches are water veined. It is a small, private plane and she and her dog are passengers. The pilot, she notices, has old-fashioned military flying gear, the sort she imagines were worn by some radio character she loved as a child. Below, the patched landscape gives way to an idyllic town with a white steeple church, a town square gazebo, and a brightly lit movie theater marquis. The pilot turns, as if to tell her about this town, and she now sees that the pilot is her father. The noise of the plane engines drown out her father's voice and although she struggles to sit forward so that she might hear, the motion of the plane, the restraint of her seatbelt, and now her dog barking all conspire to keep the words just out of reach. On the ground she wanders through the town. Shiny 1950s cars glide silently through the streets, people smile as they pass, her little dog shuffles at her side. A barber waves at them from the barbershop. As they move closer, she sees that the barber's face is that of a man she has recently met. It is a man who she has infused with hope, who seems strong and protective. And in the dream this man, now a barber, smiles at her and waves happily as she passes. She is heartened, and feels this warmth when she wakes.

References

Klein, G. S. (1976), Freud's two theories of sexuality. In: *Psychological Issues Volume 9*, eds. M. Gill & P. Holzman. New York: International Universities Press, Inc., pp. 38–39.

Kohut, H. (1979), *The Restoration of the Self*. Madison: International Universities Press, Inc.

Nietzsche, F. (2000), *Basic Writings of Nietzsche*. New York: Modern Library.

Orange, D. M., Atwood, G. E. & Stolorow, R. D. (1997), *Working Intersubjectively: Contextualism in Psychoanalytic Practice*. Hillsdale, NJ: The Analytic Press.

Stolorow, R. D., Brandchaft, B., & Atwood, G. E. (1987), *Psychoanalytic Treatment: An Intersubjective Approach*. Hillsdale, NJ: The Analytic Press

15

The HIV-Positive Analyst:
Identifying the Other

Gilbert W. Cole, PhD

▼   ▼   ▼   ▼   ▼

It has just happened again. Earlier this week, I had blood drawn for a T-cell test, in order to decide whether there ought to be any changes made in my medication regime. In the 20 years that I have had quarterly blood tests the same sequence of psychic events occurs. I begin by asserting once again how ridiculous it is to allow numbers that measure a component of my blood to determine how I experience myself. Then the familiar fantasy that suddenly this dreadful, two decade-long mistake will be over begins. In my fantasy, I telephone the doctor's office for the result of the blood test and an alarmed and excited nurse tells me that the reading is well within the normal range and that in fact there has been a terrible mistake: I am not HIV positive at all. Then comes the bargaining period, in which I attempt to end my reliance on this kind of denial by assessing the "realistic" aspects of the situation. I take into consideration all the clinical facts of my physical state, as well as the (by now) significant progress in treating the virus. And then, after firmly telling myself to calm down, I call the doctor's office and receive the news.

I tested positive for HIV before I began my psychoanalytic training, but after beginning my analysis, and after deciding to become an analyst. The possibility of testing positive did not seem unrealistic even as I was deciding to become an analyst, and so a cognitive dissonance emerged that had to be negotiated: Did it make sense to begin a protracted training period in order to engage in a protracted, intimate process with other people while I harbored a potentially devastating virus in my body? The intimation that such a negotiation was necessary can be regarded a prescient sign of the potential constructions of myself that seemed latent along with the effects of the virus. Perhaps it is an indication of the wish to dissociate any of these multiple and new constructions that have been inevitable that I considered only for a moment what it would be like to tell anyone I may be involved with professionally about my serostatus. I believed I could keep that more or less a secret, in my work as an analyst. That was long enough ago that the prognosis for anyone who had tested positive for HIV was at best 10 to 12 years of life. I exercised a crucial and healthy denial in order to complete my training. Then denial stopped being crucial and healthy.

In March of 1996, the William Allanson White Institute presented the first analytic conference devoted to HIV and AIDS. "HIV and Psychoanalysis" was, to my knowledge, the first organized, explicit response to HIV from the psychoanalytic community, and it occurred 11 years after the virus was isolated. Although I felt that this conference was long overdue, I was enthusiastic about attending. The individuals who had organized the event were dedicated pioneers in the analytic field. But as I read the program of conference events, I was struck by the fact that nowhere was there a hint of the existence of the HIV-positive analyst. It was as if such a creature does not exist. Yet there I sat, my presence marking this absence of reference. I felt very alone in an auditorium full of colleagues. Was this a moment when I should "out" myself, if for no other reason than to work against a dreadful feeling of invisibility?

As I prepared to raise my question, I experienced a nauseating wave of anxiety. To point out the absence of the HIV-positive analyst felt tantamount to identifying myself as one of the absented group. Although everyone, when pressed, would admit that HIV-positive analysts must exist, I believe a creeping notion, rooted in the ideal of the analyst's neutrality, has taken over the analytic landscape like kudzu, leafing out into a fantasy of the analyst's naiveté and inviolability. As far as I knew then, few mental health professionals, and fewer analysts, had made their status a matter of record. Why was I about to actively reconstruct myself in this way? What does it mean *now*, apart from what has it meant in the past, to assert one's seropositivity? As I framed my question, I wondered what potential consequences there might be in my disclosure. I had already identified myself as a therapist who worked with people affected by HIV. At times throughout the last several years, my practice has been made up predominantly of people coping with one phase or another of the spectrum of HIV infection and AIDS. Were it to be generally known that I am HIV positive, would my referrals become limited exclusively to those who are HIV positive or living with AIDS? Would I no longer see any HIV-negative patients, heterosexual or homosexual? Would all of my referral sources dry up as people feared referring patients to an analyst who may sicken and die prematurely?

Why does an analyst reveal anything about herself or himself? Is there justification for any sort of revelation as a viable course of action? Concerns with mutuality and authenticity in the analytic situation have become prominent in contemporary literature (e.g. Aron, 1996, Renik, 1995), but authenticity is hardly predicated on revealing aspects of one's personal, let alone medical, situation. A public assertion of a status that has remained, for the most part, invisible within the analytic community is not to be equated with the establishment of an authentic presence in clinical work. But the question that is raised, concerning the articulation of identity, seems particularly pressing in the circumstances in which I have found myself.

As an HIV-positive analyst, I have found it necessary to articulate responsibilities to myself about disclosure. My concern with maintaining a stance that felt false with certain patients was the impetus for my considering the question. I had for several years practiced without informing any patient of my serostatus. Then, when my work involved predominantly HIV-positive individuals, the question of disclosure became crucial. Some patients asserted that they wished to work only with an HIV-positive therapist. Does the encounter with a potentially life-threatening illness lead necessarily to a change in the analytic stance in order to gratify such a wish? The body of theory that would assert a negative reply to this question directs our attention to the patient's psychic reality, to fantasy, wishes, conflicts, and to the transference. But is there a way to consider this question without limiting one's options to the binary of disclosure versus anonymity? Are we forced into a position that somehow pits the patient's needs against those of the analyst? I believe that the tension that emerges with the effort to include both a one-person and two-person perspective on the analytic encounter generates more possibilities, and harder decisions for the analyst. For example, maintaining relative anonymity, can we assert confidently that the patient of an ill analyst does not know that something is wrong before the analyst tells her? Perhaps the HIV-positive analyst has a responsibility to reveal this fact to all patients, in the event that one's health does begin to deteriorate?

The condition of being HIV positive is, in important ways, unlike other physical conditions that may impinge on the analytic dyad. One significant difference is the fact that the state of seropositivity is invisible. However, while the HIV-positive individual is not sick, and his physical appearance is not altered in any way, there may be a pervasive sense of one's potential destructive or dangerous power. It is as if one is transformed on a cellular level when one sero-converts. One HIV-positive patient told me that he thought of his blood as radioactive. It possessed a charge, doubling the positive trait we all share, the fact of having substantial blood in the first place. Outwardly, he was aware that he looked fine, but he could not escape the sense of the imminent danger he posed to others simply by being. In his fantasy, the threat of infection occurred not through contact with bodily fluids, but through some other, seemingly osmotic process: He was, therefore he was infectious. His doubly positive existence meant that he was always already interacting, penetrating, and infecting.

This man's fantasies are determined by his idiosyncratic organizing principles, as well as by the fantasies of contagion (that often seem to be contagious, too) that circulate through the culture in which we live. It is significant that a magazine that grew out of one sector of the HIV-positive community is called "Diseased Pariah News." Recall the extraordinary notions about AIDS when the syndrome first appeared: that it was *caused* by the introduction of semen into the rectum, by homosexual activity, that it was a plot hatched by some government agency to wipe out gay men, or African-American people. Before the virus was isolated, the disease was understood as a punishment for the transgressions of those suffering from it, marked as they were as part of a devalued and hated group. Eventually, when certain others who had AIDS could no longer be ignored, such as hemophiliacs or children of the sexual partners of IV drug users, the term "innocent victim" was coined. As Susan Sontag points out in *AIDS and Its Metaphors* (1988), the invocation of the term "innocent" simultaneously evokes its partner, "guilty." In the metaphoric construction of a disease like AIDS, there is no such thing as "innocence." In one infamous incident, children who had seroconverted as a result of transfusions were forced to move away from the town in which they'd always lived when their house was burned down. Even "innocent victims" have not been sheltered from the perception of guilt, contagion, sin, and danger. There was an instant culture of shame and disgust that formed around the illness, as it became a lightning rod for all that was split off and denied about forbidden wishes and fears.

It is notable that a nodal point in this discourse is the problem presented by the man who desires to be penetrated by another man. While recent data alerts us to the fact that oral sex presents a greater risk of transmission of HIV than previously believed, it is thought that anal intercourse is the sexual behavior that puts an individual at greatest risk for exposure to the virus. What greater flash point can there be for a heterosexist culture? The fact that the avowal of such desires, one that may be implicit in the public assertion of one's homosexuality, and almost certainly is in the gay man's admission of HIV seropositivity, marks the man making these statements as guilty of transgressing the salient boundaries of our culture's construction of masculinity. In a book by conservative Boston talk show host David Brudnoy (1997), who has publicly disclosed his HIV positivity and homosexuality, his assertion that he had never engaged in anal sex was emphasized. This highlights the charged ambivalence that surrounds the notion of a man's desire to be penetrated. One need only point to the demands that HIV-positive people be quarantined, despite the relative difficulty in transmitting the virus (unlike TB, for example), for corroboration. It is not difficult to hear the echoes of my patient's private, unreasonable fears of his infectious potential in the world outside. The fantasy of a fundamental, frightening transformation is held and expressed by both the individual and by the social surround. We note too how the discourse quickly devolves into the stark and simpler world of paired opposites: positive–negative, normal– perverse, silence–disclosure, and healthy–diseased.

And so, the question: Why name myself in this way when I could easily remain invisible? Shame, fear, and the seductive power of fantasy all argue for silence. Indeed, one of my recurring fantasies has always been that my health would stay stable long enough to benefit from medical progress in treating HIV, that I could remain unmarked and nameless long enough so that the problem of naming myself would go away. In a sense, I relied on reversing the coming-out process. Tantalizing me, some researchers and doctors have for the first time begun talking about curing or maintaining HIV infection like a chronic disease, part of my fantasy may become operable. It may be that I do not progress to AIDS. But the problem of naming myself does not simply go away. Because the HIV-positive individual usually bears no outward sign of difference, he lives in the space between the conditions of sick and well. The experience of existence in this space requires a negotiation of a new narrative of self. But the stress of existing within this space between poles is difficult to withstand. There is tremendous pressure forcing the HIV-positive person into the category of Other. One of the remarks my doctor made to me at the time of my positive HIV test was that I was "joining a very large club." He reminded me that in New York, there are more HIV-positive people than live in some small cities. This is just one example of the manner in which the patient is named and set apart as Other without his volition. What felt more accurate was that I was *assigned* to a new social group. Whether that group ought to be called a "club," and whether and how a person "joins" it were questions that remained for me to explore.

In the first decade of life with AIDS, it was noted that HIV indeed constituted a category and so a means to dispose of despised groups. As Foucault (1973) has argued, one function of medical pathology has been the construction of illness as a means of social control. He showed us the manner in which the medical gaze constructs the clinical object in order to separate it from the rest of society. There was a time in the history of medicine when the ill were treated in the home and the community. Progress in medical knowledge and expertise led to the creation of the hospital, serving multiple functions. Not only was infection contained, but the fearful sight of the ill and insane was removed from daily life. When what is feared becomes stigmatized, this process demonstrates how culture requires reviled groups in order to recognize itself. If not HIV, then another marker for the Other that bears what cannot be tolerated or named, but without which we are not complete, would be constituted by and for the gaze of the defining subject. The endless and impossible struggle to obliterate what cannot be tolerated signifies our terrible struggle to recognize what we dread but cannot escape desiring.

So what would it mean to embrace this designation of Other? To name oneself as part of what is dreaded, disowned and yet impossible to live without is both a social and a private act that is inherently revolutionary. Each of us who claims the difference that is represented by our seropositivity volunteers our bodies as a site for the recognition of the Other, an act that can be rendered more potent if it is possible to straddle the categories of Self and Other. And here we note a repeated reworking of the ambivalence of the first object relationship. Lacan has argued that Desire is the desire of the Other, and that Other is the self that we struggle to recognize and not to recognize. This constructed image of ourselves occurs at what Lacan termed "the mirror stage" (Lacan, 1977). Here is the moment when the infant recognizes that the image in the mirror is he; that he is in the mirror. This is a triumph for the infant. "The mirror image is a minimal paraphrase of the nascent ego" (Bowie, 1991). But this image is a derisory illusion: a fantasy that there is an objective, substantial entity we can point to as a "self." Captivated by the spatial relationship between the reflected image and the real body, the infant is indeed captured by this decoy of a "self." At this moment we are alienated from the "self in process," or a dynamic becomingness. Such becoming cannot occupy a discrete location. The spatial relationship predicated by the illusion of the self in a discrete location initiates a conception of the self as divisible and divided. When the self is recognized by this sighting "out there," an infinite regression of images, as you see when standing between two facing mirrors, instantly comes into view. Among the reflections that bounce down that infinite regress are fantasies about the Other.

At the same time that some epidemiologists suspect the AIDS virus was silently spreading itself through urban American gay society, contemporary popular culture elaborated the fantasy of the meanings of the voluntary siting of the body as battlefield for recognition. The *Alien* movies (the first was released in 1979, the sequels, *Aliens,* in 1986, and *Alien 3* in 1992) presented an eerie metaphor for an unstoppable horror that surreptitiously enters, then grows inside one's body, making a striking rhyme with the initial constructions of HIV. In each of these movies, a terrifying, virulently poisonous creature uses human beings as living incubators for her larvae. At the point of hatching, the newly maturing monsters literally rip apart their still barely living hosts to be born. The living badness that was deposited in a human body to incubate to maturity is irrevocably and utterly destructive. As the series of movie fantasies developed, in the sequels to the initial *Alien,* the theme of the ruthless mother determined to reproduce became more elaborated. The themes expressed in the films are, of course, multiply determined, and those themes of maternal ambivalence, anxiety over narcissistic impingement in response to the process of childbearing, and fears of the terrifying bad mother are not to be neglected. What is compelling in the development of these themes as the cycle of films progressed is the dawning recognition of self in the heroine and the monstrous alien. Eventually, the heroine of the series carried an alien embryo in her own uterus, and destroyed her newly delivered creature by destroying both herself and the alien she'd incubated. Recognition of the self in the Other occurs at the moment of death. (Interestingly, the fourth film in the cycle, *Alien Resurrection,* released in 1997, manifests the omnipotent syntax of the Unconscious as the central character, Ripley, is brought back after she killed herself and the alien she'd carried in her womb: There is no death in the Unconscious.)

The power of the metaphor exploited in the *Alien* films is apparent in the return of the expelled bad Other that is expressed in some gay men's constructions of their HIV infection. Shame and guilt, although never straying far from even the most celebratory days of pre-AIDS gay culture, demanded recognition as HIV infection made its hosts pregnant not only with ripening infection, but with what had been expelled. In response to the desperate need of those suffering from an unthinkable terror, an industry arose among "alternative healers" to assist in the reintegration of this disavowed badness. Louise Hay, a New Age "healer" has been widely criticized for blaming the victims to whom she sold her balm. On the cassette recordings of her soothing, meditative sermons, we were told that because gay men valued beauty too much, we were visited by a plague that left us disfigured and ugly. The way to redemption is to value our inner beauty. Her message not only established the guilt of the AIDS-affected community for their sufferings, but implied that "healing" could occur once the guilt is embraced and the former hedonism is renounced. The polarities of the split are thus realigned, but not in the interest of recognizing the self in the Other, but in the interest of casting out, once again, what cannot be tolerated. When the party ended, the celebrants became zealous penitents, and some eagerly embraced shame and guilt in an attempt to bargain away what had been psychic Otherness, and was now a physical manifestation. A marketplace soon grew in which many varieties of reintrojection and reconstruction became available.

The transgressive means of exposure to the virus, the silent, invisible ripening of the disease and the ultimate monstrous disfiguring course of the illness is a process that inherently declares the seropositive to be pregnant with the gestating Other—that is, disavowed—self, containing the shame and badness, that the seronegative yearns and dreads to recognize. What happens when this monstrous pregnancy starts to show? At such a point, what had been known all along (perhaps) by one person, is finally either revealed, or the revelation is announced by the obvious signs of physical deterioration. An identification will be made when it is articulated by the body that carries the virus.

The newly sero-converted HIV-positive individual finds himself in a new, anomalous category. Though he may feel marked for death, superficially he is unmarked, except as he may designate himself. He is free of any sensations that intimate mortality, yet is told that there is now cause for alarm, and that the fantasy of uninterrupted life must be altered. Many have written and spoken of the remarkable gift this transition has turned out to be, how such a diagnosis provided the impetus to make changes in one's life or to pursue goals with less conflict. Working through to a remarkable realignment of denial and acceptance, life is possible with a new, renegotiated balance between fantasy and dread. A healthy, crucial denial enables this process. At the same time, vital medical information, such as test results, or studies of new drugs and their efficacy, must be assimilated, unimpeded by a need not to know, enabling the seropositive individual to make important decisions. As with any loss, the loss of sero-negativity comes with a terrible, urgent reminder of how much we take for granted.

Disclosure and Contagion

When my lover died of AIDS, our families immediately took in hand all of the many things that needed to be accomplished in those first, blurred days. Among these things was the matter of his obituary. I hesitated not a moment over whether to be listed as a survivor, although I was aware that several of the people I was treating at the time were themselves HIV positive or had lost someone they loved to AIDS, and so, like many of us, ritually scanned the obituary pages each day in a counterphobic accounting of AIDS deaths. The thought occurred to me that some patient would spot the obituary, identify me as his analyst, and wonder about my serostatus. But I hesitated not a moment to begin this process of potential disclosure. My decision to disclose an important, intimate fact about my life was folded into my desire to commemorate the relationship I had with the man I had cared for through his illness, and who had died. But it is clear that the meanings of this decision are manifold.

I have been HIV positive for so long that, until the appearance of the protease inhibitors changed the lives of many who are HIV positive, for several years I was among those who annually stretched the period of time beyond the posited theory of the expectable progression to full-blown AIDS. Because I privilege the transformative potential of mutuality, my fantasied revelation included my hope for mutual growth through the recognition of the patient's contribution to an important, real relationship. But it is noteworthy that in my fantasies I had to become ill in order for the disclosure to occur. My decision to be named in my lover's obituary countered the dreadful trajectory of my fantasy. It also led to the direct confrontation with how my disclosure affected my work with patients.

Kent

Kent is a 44-year-old man whom I'd been seeing for a month before he read the obituary in which I was named as a survivor, and that my lover had died of AIDS. Kent is himself a longtime asymptomatic HIV-positive man who came to this treatment, his third, depressed over the deaths of most of his friends as well as two of his physicians, of AIDS. He was isolated, extremely passive, and presented himself as unable to do anything for himself. He was filled with shame over his perceived inadequacies. Shame permeated all his reminiscences of childhood. The salient event concerned his severely depressed father, who had a history of multiple psychiatric hospitalizations, and who had been arrested several times for soliciting sex in highway rest stop men's rooms, and, given the choice of jail or psychiatric hospitalizations, opted for the latter. Kent's parents were Southern Baptists, and homosexuality was a grievous sin to them. Shame about the father's homosexuality poisoned the lives of the entire family.

Kent had found no acceptable way to express anger other than in a passive aggressive style, which could, at times, be quite provoking. My experience of Kent was dominated by his use of me to contain rageful feelings that he could not tolerate in himself. There was also a tremendous conflict between his wishes to depend on another, and his fears of what would be repeated if he were to depend on another.

When I telephoned Kent to inform him that a death in the family had occurred and that I would not be seeing patients that week, he told me that he had read the obituary and offered his condolences, asking whether there was anything he could do for me. When I returned to work, he reiterated this offer. Kent found the role of caring for others much more congenial than asking directly for anything for himself. We learned that he felt that if he could perform some caretaking task, then the cared-for might reciprocate. All relationships entailed this sort of quid pro quo. Underlying his solicitousness was concern for my physical health. He repeatedly said that he felt that his need to talk about his own health concerns would be harmful to me, evoking the possibility of losing another person. He admitted that he fantasized that talking about his own seropositivity would make me get sick, and he couldn't stand to lose someone else. He asked me to tell him if it was all right with me for him to talk about HIV concerns, adding that he wouldn't take it personally if I told him I couldn't work with him any longer.

In the weeks that followed, Kent stated that he felt self-conscious complaining about anything, when I had just lost my lover. He struggled with the question of whether treatment could be helpful to him at all. His fears about my inability to withstand his complaints or neediness suggested to me that he had reached some conclusions as to my health based on the information he'd learned about me. I repeatedly pointed out the theme of his difficulty trusting that I'd be reliable, able to tolerate all of his feelings and needs. But I felt that there was another question that Kent was trying not to formulate—the question of my seropositivity.

On the date of the anniversary of the death of his physician, Kent reported his most recent blood work results, and added that he was concerned about my health:

> K: I—I hope I'm not out of line, but, I don't know for sure, but you look as if you've lost weight recently. Have you?
>
> G.C.: Possibly, I don't know for sure. I look different to you?
>
> K: Yes, you look. Well, drawn, tired.... Are—are you all right? Is your health.... I'm sorry....
>
> G.C.: I look as if I might be ill.
>
> K: Maybe it's just the light in here.
>
> GC: Possibly, but you are also struggling to ask me something I think has been on your mind from time to time for a while.
>
> K: Well, yes, I guess so. But I have always thought that it was really none of my business.
>
> G.C.: That what exactly was none of your business?
>
> K: Well, it's hard for me event to say it. That you might get sick with AIDS. That you are positive and not doing very well.
>
> G.C.: You've been wondering about that for a long while.
>
> K.: Well, yes, ever since reading about Mason.
>
> G.C.: Maybe I ought to have been more forthcoming then.
>
> K.: I don't think so. It's your private business. It shouldn't really affect me.
>
> G.C.: Well, knowing that you've lost so many friends, and two doctors, one a year ago today, it seems to me that it is very much your business whether someone you've asked for something from, to help you in some way, is going to get sick.
>
> K: Well, I ... yes, I do wonder about your health.
>
> G.C.: How would it be if I were HIV positive?
>
> K: Oh ... [he grows tearful] I would be very sad. I don't want anyone else to be sick. I feel like I couldn't stand it. But it wouldn't change anything about working with you as my therapist.

The moment had presented itself to me to confirm his long-standing suspicion. Though he had told me that he'd feel sad if I were HIV positive, I felt strongly that there were other unformulated feelings about my seropositivity. When Kent spoke of his worry that I'd get sick if he talked about his health, I had speculated to myself that there was a part of Kent that would be quite satisfied if I *were* HIV positive, that he felt himself to be infections, and that he needed to work very hard to keep this awful conflict from being heard, either by himself or anyone else. But it was clear to me that Kent's treatment would continue to unfold regardless of what I told him, and that the ways Kent organized our relationship would indeed be affected according to what I told him next.

Is the confirmation of my seropositivity best conceptualized as countertransference acting-out? Seen in this way, my telling him this fact could be interpreted in many ways: as a counterphobic attempt to demonstrate that no matter what, I was going to be hardy enough to tolerate his needs; in a hostile/competitive demonstration of how much better I am at managing my health than he is; as a way to undermine his idealization of me as an authority figure. Are any of these possible themes made less analyzable or potentially useful in my work with Kent following my confirmation of his suspicion?

One way of approaching this question is to consider whether it is the content of a disclosure or the process leading to and from a disclosure that inhibits or promotes analytic work. For example, a major theme in our work had been his passive–aggressive style of relating. "Passive–aggressive" was a label that Kent himself had affixed to his behavior, and he recognized it as a way to try to elicit a particular response from others, including me, without appearing to be demanding. He had described how others had identified his characteristic style of self-presentation as indicating that he was too weak to defend himself, so that he could make covert attacks without fear of retaliation. Perhaps I was responding to the pressure I felt in response to his withholding style by revealing more of myself. Or, it could be that my disclosure was a retaliation of my own, in a similarly passive–aggressive style. In either case, a different response to Kent's wondering, such as an interpretation of his wish that I be HIV positive, was forestalled.

So I told him:

> G.C.: Well, I want to let you know that I am HIV positive.
>
> K: How are you doing? Your numbers. Are you on medication? Is—is it all right to ask?
>
> G.C.: Well, what I'd like to tell you is that I've been positive since before 1982, that I'm lucky enough to not need medicine at this point, and that I've never had an opportunistic infection.... How is it for you, that I've let you know all this?

K: Thank you, for telling me. I'm glad you're doing well. I've wondered, I think I knew before now. But I didn't…. I didn't think you'd tell me.

G.C.: Why wouldn't I?

K: Because … to keep a distance.

G.C.: From you?

K: From all your patients.

G.C.: You especially?

K: I'll have to think about that.

[Material from sessions with patients is reconstructed from notes taken after the sessions were over.]

Through my confirmation I spoke directly to Kent's positioning himself toward me as a subordinate who has no "rights" in our relationship, and this opened out into an exploration of this theme. In retrospect, I believe that if I had remained opaque and chosen not to disclose my serostatus, this may have amounted to a confirmation of Kent's experience of himself as "having no rights," of barely existing as a subject in our relationship. Instead, we were able to move toward a verbal understanding of this relational pattern, rather than a reliving of it.

Kent seems unconsciously to claim responsibility for the deaths of his doctors and friends. He had told me about an upsetting feeling he had on a Fourth of July picnic on the roof of a friend's building when he had unaccountably felt the impulse to push a sick friend off the edge. It may be that knowledge of my status has permitted Kent to acknowledge sadistic and aggressive fantasies about me with less cost exacted in guilt. If something bad were to happen to me, it might not be his fault. In addition, it may be that the fantasy of his doing damage to me will become foregrounded.

At this point in our work, Kent began dreaming intensely, and brought in many dreams that he spent the bulk of our sessions describing and interpreting. He expressed a good deal of satisfaction in exploring his dream material, and I felt that it was clear that, despite his stated apprehensions about my ability to be reliable, he had begun to be able to use our relationship in a more intimate way. As Kent's involvement in his unconscious material grew, we both agreed that the use of the couch and increased frequency of sessions would be helpful. One way that I sensed Kent's growing use of me as an object was a greater capacity of my own to recognize and eventually interpret my presence in unconscious derivative material, such as his dreams, in ways that were expressive of crucial self and object representations.

Kent's first dream after he moved to the couch took place at a flea market that was in the same neighborhood as my office. He was there with a companion whom he could not identify. They went into one booth that sold various Asian food stuffs and other items. An old woman sat near a large tub, over which hung a large shark, so that the shark's head dangled behind and above the old woman's head. From time to time, the shark took bites out of her head. Among Kent's associations to this dream was the connection he made between the spatial relationship of the woman and the shark, and the way it resembled his relationship on the couch to me, seated above and behind him. This was the first time he was able to identify his fears and anger with me for "taking bites out of his head"—intruding with my endless quest to understand what he had to say to me. Perhaps this dream also expressed something of his response to my contaminated state, that I was dangerous and hostile.

I am confident at this point that my disclosure did not deter Kent from using his treatment effectively. I do believe that far more was accomplished with my disclosure than was sacrificed, but as to whether the content of the disclosure was as important as the process of disclosing, is a subtle question. Surely Kent and I seek to recognize in each other some ideas about our fears about HIV infection, and fantasies of the "living badness" we each have inside us. This content-related experience is unique to the dyad where HIV infection is disclosed.

In time, our positions with regard to hope and lived experience were tested. Kent's routine blood-work indicated a decrease in his T-cells, and an increase in the viral load as measured by the PCR test. His doctor recommended that he begin taking one of the protease inhibitors that had only recently become available. This has involved Kent's starting AZT again, a medication that he took for several years, and that left him anemic and feeling generally terrible. (Protease inhibitors are administered in conjunction with two of the reverse transcriptase inhibitors such as AZT or 3TC, in a sort of cocktail to attack the virus at two points in its life cycle.) Kent immediately began talking about the discomfort he experiences being on AZT again, and especially about the constraints that the protease inhibitor has placed on him. For this protease inhibitor to be optimally effective, a strict dosage schedule must be rigorously followed: it must be taken 1 hour before eating, and 2 hours after having eaten anything, and every 8 hours. At first glance, this may seem a not unreasonable dosage schedule to maintain. But on reconsideration, it is clear that this limits one's options to a considerable degree. If your dosage schedule is, say, 7 a.m., 3 p.m., 11 p.m., one must have finished eating lunch, every day, by 1 p.m., and have finished eating dinner by 9 p.m. We are cautioned that missing or delaying a dose risks having the level of drug in the blood dip below a certain threshold would enable the virus to become resistant to the drug, apparently permanently. Once the virus can adapt to the reduced level of drug in the blood, it can remain impervious to even higher levels of drug; further, cross-resistance to other protease inhibitors has been shown in the early studies of the drugs. All this is, understandably, anxiety-provoking. The protease inhibitors are the first major clinical breakthrough in a long time. The studies that led to their FDA approval indicated that this new class of drugs reduces viral load to below detectable levels in the study subjects, and raises T-cell levels significantly, for the duration of the studies for some subjects. This has been the most encouraging news about the treatment of HIV in the history of the epidemic. Doctors now conjecture, with more confidence than ever before, that HIV infection could become a treatable chronic condition, and that seropositive individuals may be able to enjoy a more nearly normal life span. (I must add that since the time of the sessions summarized here, protease inhibitors and other HIV/AIDS medications have been formulated so as to make them far easier to take.)

I've gone into this in such detail because I was lucky enough, at that point in time, to have waited out a considerable period during which the various protease inhibitors were tested, and more data accumulated, before needing to start this new medication regime. As long as my blood work had indicated that I was remaining stable, I could maintain the denial that has permitted me to work with so many sick people while I have been HIV positive. Around the time Kent started his protease inhibitor, I had blood work done as well, and the question as to whether I would start a different medication regime arose once again.

As I listened to Kent express, in his characteristically mild and singsong-y way, his dismay over the problems of taking his medication, I found myself becoming more and more agitated. Often I work until 9 p.m.—and eat dinner after that. I found myself trying to figure out what kind of dosage schedule would work for me, should I have to begin taking this protease inhibitor. My family lives on the West Coast. What happens when you travel across time zones? How do you travel to Europe maintaining a strict dosage schedule?

I felt myself rebelling against the roles we've co-constructed, which have been determined significantly by my disclosure of seropositivity. How I longed for a way to deny all that is happening to both of us. How I hated feeling that Kent needed me to maintain my optimistic, reasonable state of mind, confident that he would find a way to make the dosage schedule work, ready to analyze the process unfolding between us. His underlying resistance to taking these medications was contagious. No—I wanted him to shut up, because his concerns were intruding on my precariously maintained optimism about my own potentially imminent need for this medication. I realized that, despite my disclosure, Kent and I both need, from time to time, to forget that I am HIV positive.

Among the potential selves and others that Kent and I present for each other, there are two parallel tracks along which the relationship between us has unfolded. One is the extra-ordinary track of our shared knowledge and experience of each other as HIV-positive people. The other is the ordinary track of a treatment in which Kent presents himself to his analyst for help. Throughout a given session, the parallel tracks merge, and, as I described, there is an ironic switch in our roles as to who holds the hope in our relationship. Kent reports that he is responding well to his medication regime. Sometimes I find myself worrying that, when I begin, as I feel is inevitable, my medication regime, I won't do as well. These are moments in which I can identify my denial breaking down, when I no longer can rely on omnipotent fantasy to support me in our quest to outgrow omnipotent fantasy. The paradox is inescapable.

Are There any Conclusions?

The psychoanalyst is the specialist of Otherness. This is the role we assume when we take up our position opposite the patient, or behind the couch. Poised between what is embraced and ejected, the specialist in otherness occupies a curious place as we work to enable the recognition of the Other. The question of the articulation of identity for the psychoanalyst who is HIV positive is complicated because his dual status enacts the crisis that occurs when the cultivated invisibility, or opacity, of the traditionally constructed Analyst, is disrupted when his very physicality becomes a site for the struggle for the recognition of the Other.

When I mentioned to a colleague that I was writing about what it is like to be an HIV-positive analyst, and about what happened when I told patients that I was HIV positive, he replied, "Why would you tell a patient anything?" Clearly he advocates a stance in which it always clear what is whose in the analytic dialogue. When I heard this response, I recalled one patient, who had sought out a therapist who was HIV positive, and who stated that he could not work with a therapist who was not HIV positive. After acknowledging and exploring the element of extortion in his communication, I told him that I was, and we began a lengthy treatment. Eighteen months after I had disclosed my serostatus, this patient was talking about how at times he felt ashamed of being HIV positive, and stated clearly that he thought it was remarkable that he was able to tell this to someone who wasn't HIV positive. He had forgotten what had been so important before beginning treatment with me, and that I had in fact disclosed my status to him. This is an example of the power of the unconscious; when it was important for this man to feel different from me, in this particular way, he forgot that it had once been crucial that we were the same, and that I confirmed that. He constructed me as he needed me to be.

Thus "an identity" can be seen to be an empty category prior to the co-construction of relationships, and even then remains fluid according to the patient's constructions of the analyst. For this patient and this analyst, "HIV positive" functioned, at times, as an identity. In similar ways, the designation "gay man" serves a useful function, as does "psychoanalyst." What happens when a disclosure is made? An emptiness is filled, or a potential is foreclosed, but does this action deny the further elaboration of identity? The category is filled not by the HIV-positive person, not by the gay man, not by the analyst, but by the person who has heard the disclosure, by an interpreting subject. It is secondary that the subject interprets to himself the meaning of the identity that has been chosen for him. A richer mode of relating depends on living in the tension between the intrapsychic and the interpersonal, where sameness and difference can assume an infinite number of possible meanings. The meanings that some individuals make of being HIV positive might have to do with castration, with loss, with victimhood. Others have been able to create different and remarkably generative meanings for themselves. But the identity of "Other" is an inescapable shadow that is cast of HIV-positive people from the moment they are so named.

Disclosure cannot exhaust the manner in which the infinitely capacious categories of identity can be elaborated. Actively filling in aspects of one's identity as an analyst is in no way incompatible with the further project of psychoanalysis. It is an example of a subject's capacity for making meaning. One of the potential meanings has to do with the goal of confronting the otherness of oneself. In the case of the HIV-positive person, that Otherness is often constituted by various configurations of sex and death. One goal of the recognition of the Other is to acknowledge the self-as-becoming, a turning away from the reified self that caught us all in the mirror. The self-as-becoming has limits, is separate, dies. The embrace of this becoming is the privilege and the privileged value of psychoanalysis.

References

Aron, L. (1996), *A Meeting of Minds.* Hillsdale, NJ: The Analytic Press.

Bowie, M. (1991), *Lacan.* Cambridge, MA: Harvard University Press.

Brudnoy, D. (1997), *Life is Not a Rehearsal: A Memoir.* New York: Doubleday.

Foucault, M. (1973), *The Birth of the Clinic.* New York: Vintage.

Frank, K. (1997), The role of the analyst's inadvertent self-revelations. *Psychoanal. Dial.,* 7:281–314.

Lacan, J. (1977), *Ecrits.* New York: W.W. Norton.

Renik, O. (1995), The ideal of the anonymous analyst and the problem of self-disclosure. *Psychoanal. Quart.,* 64:466–495.

Sontag, S. (1988), *AIDS and its Metaphors.* New York: Farrar, Straus and Giroux.

16

Never Mind the Equipment:
A Brief and Somewhat Eccentric
Interrogation of the Homo
in Sexuality

Elaine Freedgood
Debra Roth

▼   ▼   ▼   ▼   ▼

"No one has the same genitals."

—David Fisher, Six Feet Under

The idea for this chapter derives from an informal study conducted by the authors, in their pajamas: a survey of the wedding announcement photographs published in the *New York Times* Sunday Style Section. This may appear to be, on the face of it, a rather curious weekend pastime, but defer judgment for just a moment while we provide some background. Since same-sex couples started appearing in the Sunday wedding announcements section, we began to scan that long-time arbiter of social advancement each week, the novelty of our fellow homos' recent access to those pages giving us a mild sense of social progress on lazy Sunday mornings, something akin to the sense of muted satisfaction we felt when interracial couples began making the cut some years ago.

What we both began to notice was how often, in this homo-hunting, we mistook different-sex couples for same-sex couples. Among the straight white crowd who invariably dominated those pages, couples comprised of one male and one female partner often looked remarkably alike. "Here's one," we would exclaim on citing one of the couples to whom we imagined ourselves cultural kin, only to discover on a closer inspection—one informed by the rather ambiguous and often unreliable set of gender signifiers we all count on when genitals are out of view—that the couple was, after all, comprised of a man and a woman.

Both amused by and interested in what we began to think of as a more amorphous and shifting sociocultural definition of "similitude," we began to play with the criteria we might apply in developing a more complex and variable conception of the homo in sexuality, one that might operate outside of the rigid dictates of genital classification. So, looking to broaden our inquiry beyond the rarified boundaries of the *Times,* we took our curiosity into the street.

"Look at the couple over there," one of us would whisper into the ear of the other, "a male and a female clearly, yet they look exactly alike ... matching chiseled noses, the same long blond hair, identical styles of J Crew chinos ... if that isn't homosexuality then what is?" Or, we would banter back and forth: "maybe they comprise just another example of rampant homonasality? Or, could they be suffering from one of those unfortunately severe cases of homohaberdasheralism? No, no, clearly it's just a sadly displaced attempt at homocoiffurism." These riffs, along with our own playful conviction that we are and have always been a heterosexual couple despite our roughly identical genitalia, have slowly moved us into a more serious register; one where we have begun to see the limitations imposed by our culture's constructions of sameness and difference as they define homo- and heterosexuality. As Schwartz (1995) succinctly puts it, "... we must give up the idea that our culture's preoccupation with putting the anatomy (principally the genitalia) of the object in the foreground is 'natural' or built in to 'normal' psychological functioning" (p. 123) or, we add, that genitalia are the only means through which sexual sameness can be distinguished from sexual difference.

Here are some of the problems that began to tug at us. Despite marked shifts in recent thinking on sexuality and its multiple forms, why does the designation of homo in sexuality continue to rely exclusively on genital construction? And, more consequentially, why does the assurance of genital variation continue to function as such a powerful signifier of difference? For that matter, why does the capacity to recognize difference itself remain a developmental milestone more privileged than the ability to spot the often equally subtle but culturally devalued reverberations of sameness?

What, we began to wonder, would happen if we began to expand, bend, and remap the parameters of sameness and difference that we so reflexively employ in sizing up and labeling the sexuality of the two who form a couple? Could these challenges disrupt the conventional psycho-cultural process of assigning a particular category of sexuality to a particular kind of object choice? Might we then be forced to rethink the array of linguistic prefixes (bi-, homo-, hetero-) that are so critical to fixing and holding these various forms of genital desire at the same time as they work to insure their categorical segregation? In other words, might the homo in sexuality be made more ubiquitous and less curious at the same time that it is unmoored from its isolating, debased history?

It seems to us that the focus on genital equipment as the sole determinate of the homo in sexuality occludes a consideration of the yearning for other clearly essential forms of sameness, forms which may, in fact, be more critical to and illuminating of the multiple ways people wish to fit their various body and mind parts together to achieve the act(s) we refer to, loosely, as sex. Following transsexual theory (Bornstein, 1995), seeking difference might consolidate around the desire for the tallness or age or jewelry or body hair of the other—or we could desire some exotic internal part of our partner that we sense to be especially magnetic or stimulating or fragile. We are inviting you, our reader, to consider with us the proposition that moving away from the zoom-in-between-the-legs focus of genital myopia when designating the homo and the hetero in sexuality allows us to think more richly and expansively about the destabilizing possibilities of desire in erotic engagements of all kinds, including those we have not yet imagined. As an added bonus, these ideas can be useful in moving beyond the now thoroughly worn homo–hetero dichotomy since they create the possibility of a broader repertoire of erotic entanglements for *all* the sexualities. After all, a refiguration of the homo in sexuality simultaneously reimagines heterosexuality as a more various bodily topography, encompassing many more forms of sexual practice than it is has, thus far, been thought to encompass or, certainly, to embrace.

As we continued to play with these thoughts, we next began to wonder who else was thinking them. Some electronic research on these questions revealed that we were in a kind of uncanny intellectual synch with a large group of sociologists who study the apparently uncontroversial topic of "homogamy": the tendency of human beings to pair off with human beings who are similar to themselves. In a winsomely titled study, "Education and Attractiveness in Marriage Choices," Gillian Stevens, Dawn Owens, and Eric Shaefer used newspaper wedding photographs—sound familiar?—as evidence to demonstrate that attractive people marry other people who are at about the same level of attractiveness. Stevens and her team cut wedding photographs down the middle, pasted one half of each face on a card: "Four white college students, two males and two females, then rated each bride and each groom on a scale ranging from –4 (very unattractive) to +4 (very attractive) without knowing which groom was married to which bride" (p. 65). (No explanation was offered for the racial choice or uniformity of the student judges.)

In correlating this work with our informal study of the *New York Times,* Stevens' "cutting-down-the-middle" effect is paralleled by the *Times* requirement that couples who wish to announce their nuptials make certain that in the photograph they submit, their eyebrows are, to quote the *Times* Web site, "exactly" on the same level. Quite a demand when you think about it: Does one use a carpenter's level, a compass, or will any simple straight-edge do the job? Yet, in a serendipitous convergence, we discovered that this pictorial leveling does, indeed, create a plane on which the comparison of features is easier, and allows for similarities to be more readily detected.

Now, in fairness, the study we are citing was not trying to decide if brides and grooms looked *alike,* only if they were of similar *levels* of attractiveness. So that sameness, in this research, is more abstract, and thereby more elusive, than in our "study" of the *Times.* But the fact remains that homogamy is known to sociologists as a common fact of heterosexual life: as Lisa and Christopher Jepsen (2002) put it, "people want a mate with traits similar to their own (similar age, similar education, even similar weight)" (p. 435). In fact, the Jepsens found that opposite-sex couples actually sought after *more* similarity in their partners than did same-sex couples: Once you get by the genital equipment, a desire for other, various forms of homo-ness seems to become more pronounced, as well as more permissible, among heterosexuals.

Although the sociologists stop there, we wish to continue by wondering: What about the homofacial or the homosartorial pair? What are these culturally unremarkable straight couples who so closely resemble one another expressing or addressing through their representations of bodily sameness? Perhaps they are seeking a form of erotic linkage which, however unconscious and unintentional, resembles the identifications, recollections and recognitions that we understand to constitute the homo-genital forms of sexuality. And yet, despite their similarity, they seem, somehow, to have eluded the reproof of developmental arrest.

The couple who has gender indemnifying their difference has been historically immune from the blighted significations of sameness that have been legislated—literally and figuratively—around *genital* likeness. Even more perplexing are the numerous forms of sociocultural privilege that this exemption extends to straight couples even, or perhaps especially, when the man and woman look strikingly similar and are therefore, in some obvious and concrete sense, homo.

At the same time, we must note that the social menace that springs from excessive sameness or difference is so pervasive that even the immunity from cultural derision bestowed by heterosexuality can be precarious. If you are white, middle class, and heterosexual and decide to wed an 80-year-old Asian millionaire, for example, or an 18-year-old impoverished

African American or even someone of your own "race" and class who is markedly obese, you immediately become socially suspect as you forfeit the benefits of a deeply unstable invisibility anchored amorphously in just the right amount—even a small amount—of differentiation. So, what does it mean that our culture requires so much careful calibration of relational similarity and dissimilarity?

Sociologists, in confirming heterosexual homogamy, offer a hint, however inadvertently. To us, they indirectly and unintentionally invite a reconsideration of Aristophanes' views on mating as Plato describes them in the *Symposium*. Queer theorist Leo Bersani (2000) explains Aristophanes as he is explained by Plato: We are all, of necessity, looking for some part of our selves in our mates, irrespective of what that part looks like or where it is located. Aristophanes posited an original human race in which there were three kinds of people:

> males, females, and a combination of the two. Each spherically shaped person had four arms, four legs, two faces, and two sets of sexual organs. As punishment for these powerful and ambitious humans' attempt to vanquish the gods, Zeus had the luminous idea of cutting each person in two.... The result of this is that every human being is longing for his or her lost other half. (Bersani, 2000, p. 655)

Bersani argues that Aristophanes' fable disrupts two familiar stories about love and desire: First, the story in which we necessarily desire what we lack and therefore must seek someone who is different from us, and second, the story in which love goes wrong, becomes narcissistic, and we pick someone like ourselves in an act of aggressive, regressive, other-denying appropriation.

For Bersani, the idea of the lost half dispenses with the sin of narcissism through destigmatizing the desire for sameness; here, sameness "erases the individuating boundaries within which an ego might frame and contemplate itself" (p. 656). Because, according to this schema, we are not whole to begin with, the proposition that we somehow end and the other begins in keeping with some absolute and impermeable boundary policed by difference falls apart. Bersani leads us to the counterintuitive conclusion that within certain registers of abstract, unconscious experience the dichotomy between self and other has been imagined too readily, too glibly, even too concretely.

Bersani (aided by Lacan) concludes that "all love is, in a sense, homoerotic," because, in this upended formulation, it becomes possible to distinguish between the love one feels for one's self and the love one can feel for that which is *the same* as one's self. Through disentangling the link between the *identical* and the *similar*, this formulation disturbs the axiomatic notion that love of the same is embedded in a narcissistic love of the self. Without this linguistic disruption, it becomes impossible to distinguish between primary narcissism and primary homosexuality since "love of oneself appears indistinguishable from love of the same" (Dean, 2001, p. 126). Discriminating between that which is *replicated* and those things which may be *related* also creates an implicit challenge to the mistaken, but nonetheless pervasive, notion that homosexuality is, by definition, a debased repudiation of otherness (see Dean, 2001).

Bersani broadens his reclamation of sameness by rethinking the imaginary and idealized category of difference, envisioning it as a "supplemental benefit of a universal replication and solidarity of being" (p. 656). Here the desire for difference is converted from a normalizing developmental milestone into a bonus, an extra fillip of interest in human relations that occurs as an incidental, yet happy, by-product of replicating relations. This construction invites us to locate our selves everywhere, and because of the fortuitous lack of individuation and separateness, it invites us to find difference everywhere *at the same time*. Bersani is very nearly utopian in his conclusion, or he is utopian about the conclusion he finds in the *Symposium,* which he describes as "an account of connectedness according to which relations are initiated because they are already there" (p. 656). Here Bersani builds on the possibilities raised in Foucault's later work on the idea of "friendship as a way of life" (Foucault, 1989).

If what Bersani calls the "extensability of sameness" can offer the exquisite possibility of at-homeness, particularly in this particularly uncongenial world, why is sameness in relationships, especially sexual ones, not celebrated more widely? And given that sameness is a ubiquitous feature of all kinds of sexual relationships, why does the wish for it and practice of it seem to get culturally consolidated around same-sex relationships? Perhaps it is reassuring to confine the unconscious cultural appetite for the homo in sexuality to a group where it can be demonized and disavowed, heckled and quarantined, sent up and satirized, hunted down and killed, but never extinguished. Homosexuals have been envied, chastised, outlawed, refused marriage, religious sacraments, and even psychoanalysis because of the sin of sameness. Yet, we never seem to drop out of cultural sight. We are the people who represent the tainted luxury of developmental arrest, that seductive lapse that others must sprint past, with however much regret. We maintain and keep visible a possibility, an erotic option that heterosexuals must resolve to forsake: a moment on the itinerary of sexual development that lives in literary and cultural representations of adolescent love, of romantic friendship, of schoolgirl and -boy crushes that must be forsaken, or put away as childish things (see Nunokawa, 1991).

Homosexuals do the unpleasant and often dangerous cultural work of making manifest what we are suggesting is an unremarkable and pervasive desire for the experience of "sameness in the other." Yet as the extensive documentation by sociologists and the simple evidence of our senses tells us, we are *not* the exclusive providers of this crucial sociocultural service. Heterosexuals enact this need for sameness all around us—and do so as obviously as race, social class, weight, chinos, and "levels of attractiveness" are obvious. In other words, dissimilar genital equipment allows for the unencumbered pursuit of much that is homo in sexuality.

Homogamy has not yet become a household world, despite its routine presence in American households, and we predict that it will not soon become one. It appears that the deviance that infuses the love of sameness must, for now, be displaced onto homosexuals and kept alive as crucial cultural spice: in the queer eyes that help the straight guys, in the love that in daring not to speak its name becomes infinitely provocative and suggestive, and in the marginalized forms of identity that contribute their edginess and subversion to burnishing the insipidly-hued vanilla of mainstream culture.

Nevertheless, we wonder, why the genital essentialism that fuels the demonization of sameness hasn't been given more poststructuralist scholarly attention, particularly by queer thinkers who themselves pay so dearly for it? Interestingly, it is in the work of contemporary feminist psychoanalytic theorists that the hegemony of difference receives some of its most critical treatment.

Unlike its classical sibling, postmodern feminist psychoanalysis has been tackling, however indirectly, our challenge to the privilege of difference for some time. Benjamin's notion of identificatory love (1988, 1991, 1995), for example, rebuts the lock-step identificatory processes of classical oedipal theory that insist on "all opposite-sex love as heterosexual" (Benjamin, 1991, p. 287; see also Harris, 1991). Benjamin hypothesizes that during the period of rapprochement, the girl experiences a love for her father that is closer to a homoerotic, idealized identification with him than to the heterosexual object love that eventually (and usually) comes to exist alongside of it. For the daughter, the father[1] represents the freedom to explore the outside world: the girl would prefer to be his "son" who can explore that world with him.

Through this formulation, Benjamin moves our thinking away from the absolutism of anatomical difference that enforces heterosexuality, at the same time that she constructs a homoerotic identificatory attachment between father and daughter or, more precisely, between the father and his "daughter/son" as the daughter manifests her fantasy of son-hood vis-à-vis

---

[1]As Melanie Suchet (personal communication, December 2005) observes, Benjamin has refined her argument to suggest that while "traditional gender relationships [posit] the father as the identificatory object for both girls and boys, this function can be fulfilled by either father or mother, depending on who is the primary caretaker and who is seen as the outside subject."

her father. In theorizing a continuous tension between sameness and difference, Benjamin disrupts the notion that "identity" is either uniform or static by arguing against the notion of a "singular [genital] difference" (see also Dimen, 1991) that positions the self on one side of a homogeneously sexed identifacatory divide or the other.

Harris (1991) joins with Benjamin here when she argues that the perception of an object as like or as different is a determination which cannot be based solely on genital characteristics. Instead, Harris argues that theories of sexuality that harness the genitals (as it were) as the sole criteria for categorization paradoxically keep the experience of gender outside the system of meaning since "the relation of gender to the love object can be understood only by the act of interpretation" (p. 212). In other words, for Harris, the surface significations of any given object choice are consistently trumped by their symbolic meaning. In this way, any fully psychoanalytic account of otherness must relegate genital difference to an ancillary explanatory position because of the powerful roles of fantasy and the unconscious in determining both the specific contours of difference and their symbolic representations.

Following Harris' reasoning, Dean (2001) argues that because the unconscious knows nothing of contradiction, it, by extension, can know nothing of heterosexuality. Dean contends that difference, when conceptualized in concrete genital terms, results in a construction that subverts the overarching significance of unconscious processing along with "the psychoanalytic ethic" itself.

We have been arguing that genitally based conceptions of homo and hetero prefix sexuality in ways that allow for the cultural eradication of the multiple yearnings for sameness that contour sexual desire and practice. As they are now deployed, these prefixes constrain imagination, leaving us to routinized forms of desire and identification that may make us good citizens but perhaps less than fully realized humans. In their most utopian moments, queer theory and psychoanalysis have reimagined desire as endlessly unruly. This unruliness can create new cites from which to rework the practice of naming ourselves and our various parts: particularly that "equipment" we possess that moves in erotic relation to another, equipment that is never the same but always similar, close enough, reasonably aligned, possible to adjust and retrofit for those desires we know and do not yet know but can imagine. But all this, only after the definitions, categories and other pieces of cultural scaffolding that organize and support us all too well have been suspended. At that point, we can begin to "place at the disposal of the work that we do on ourselves the greatest possible share of what is presented to us as inaccessible" (Foucault, cited in Kritzman, 1984, p. 256).

Coda: On the Vicissitudes of Difference

In Jia Zhang Ke's film *The World* (2005), set in an eponymous theme park where one "can see the world without ever leaving Beijing," a security guard shows visiting friends from a distant and impoverished village a replica of Manhattan: "The Twin Towers were bombed on September 11, 2001," he says, "but ours are still here!" It is not clear at first where to locate the greatest share of pathos: with the viewers of the film in lower Manhattan for whom the replicated towers are absurdly inadequate and grotesque, or for the intrafilmic visitors at the theme park, for whom they are, or are meant to be, more than adequate, in fact, wondrous. The amusement park is filled with replicas of the great tourist attractions of the world, copied "exactly" but inaccurately: the scale is off; the materials are all wrong; "telling" details are nowhere to be found; the hump on the weary camel in front of the great pyramid looks as if it is about to fall off.

This is the kind of replication we react against "instinctively," the kind we immediately oppose by arming ourselves reflexively with the designations of difference like novelty, originality, and authenticity. But as we pity the impoverished peasants who admire the duplicate towers, we might also wonder about our confidence in knowing otherwise, in somehow knowing better. The reassuring variety inherent in our ostensibly heterogeneous designations may actually rely on an exaggerated celebration of small differences. In this way, the theme park in Beijing may symbolize the world, our world, where we can distinguish between things not so much by their differences, but by the ways in which they remind us of what it is we think we already know.

References

Benjamin, J. (1988), *The Bonds of Love*. New York: Pantheon.
——— (1991), Father and Daughter: Identification with Difference. *Psychoanal. Dial.,*1:277–299.
——— (1995), Sameness and difference: Toward an "overinclusive" model of gender development. *Psychoanal. Inq.*, 15:125–142.
Bersani, L. (2000), Sociality and sexuality. *Critical Inquiry,* 26:4, 641–656.
Bornstein, K. (1994), *Gender Outlaw*. New York: Vintage Books.
Dean, T. (2001), Homosexualtiy and the Problem of Otherness. In: *Homosexuality and Psychoanalysis*, eds. T. Dean & C. Lane. Chicago: University of Chicago Press, pp. 120–146.
Dimen, M. (1991), Deconstructing difference: Gender, splitting, and transitional space. *Psychoanal. Dial.*, 1:335–352.
Foucault, M. (1989), *Foucault Live*. (J. Johnston, Trans.). New York: Semiotexte.

Harris, A. (1991). Gender as contradiction. *Psychoanal. Dial.,* 1:197–224.

Jepsen, L. K., & Jepsen, C A. (2002), An empirical analysis of the matching patterns of same-sex and opposite-sex couples. *Demography,* 39:3:435–453.

Ke, J. Z. (2006), *The World.* Zeitgeist Films, DVD.

Kritzman, L. D. (Ed.). (1984), *Michel Foucault: Politics, Philosophy, Culture.* New York: Routledge.

Nunokawa, J. (1991), *In memoriam* and the extinction of the homosexual. *ELH,* 58:2, 427–438.

Schwartz, D. (1995), Current psychoanalytic discourses on sexuality: Tripping over the body. In: *Disorienting Sexualities,* eds. T. Domenici & R. C. Lesser. New York: Routledge, pp. 115–128.

Stevens, G., Owens, D., Schaefer, E. C., et al. (1990), Education and attractiveness in marriage choices. *Social Psychology Quarterly,* 53:1:62–70.

17

Where We Both Have Lived

Sandra Silverman, LCSW

▼   ▼   ▼   ▼   ▼

It's 1967. I am 6 years old and Chicago has had a record-breaking blizzard. Miraculously, schools are closed. Someone has bundled me so efficiently that I can barely move before I get outside to the sky-high snow. I get myself to the deepest spot so that I am buried to my chest in snow. A number of neighborhood kids are out playing. I see my 11-year-old brother, his red hair peeking out from under his hat, and yell to him to save me. He makes his way across our front yard, yanks me out of the snow and drags me to the sidewalk where the snow is not quite as high. "That was fun," I think to myself and then turn around and go back to the same spot and yell for him to pull me out again. The next part I remember as if it were yesterday, "Oh Sandy," he groans, "not again." Loyally, he takes big lunging steps toward me, pulls me out, and drags me to the snow-covered sidewalk. In my memory, we did this over and over again all day.

It's 2002. I am in my office with a few minutes to spare before my next session. The phone rings. I contemplate letting my machine take the call but decide to answer it. The man on the other end of the line identifies himself as Officer Kent of the Chicago police department. He tells me he has my brother at the station because he was on the street looking strange and when the police approached him, he became violent. Suddenly, my limbs feel light and my anxiety skyrockets. My brother always had a fragileness to him but over the years he has slipped into an elusive and paranoid world. There are glimmers of the brother I once knew, loving, witty, and smart. But he always slips away again, to some sort of suspicious other-land. My longings to rescue him and my feelings of utter failure in doing so have, at times, taken over my own thinking.

I tell Officer Kent that my brother has never before been violent, and that unless something new is happening, violence would be completely out of character for him. I explain that he sometimes has "problems with his thinking." Officer Kent tells me, with a tone of pride, that he and his partner detected that right away, "Oh, we could see Ma'am, that there's something not right with him, some kind of mental problem." I do not find his words comforting. I offer him a piece of advice. "If you treat him aggressively he is going to feel he has to defend himself. If you treat him kindly and with respect then he will be kind to you." We speak briefly about my brother's present situation when I say to Officer Kent, "I'm a therapist and I have a patient waiting. Can I call you back in 45 minutes? And, would it be possible for me to speak to my brother at that time?" He agrees. "Please don't hurt him," I say and hang up.

I stand in the middle of my office. The phone call, like a little bomb, explodes in my mind. Too many pieces of my life, the past as well as the present, are flying all over the room. I look at the clock. I am 5 minutes late for my next session; my patient is in the waiting room and, my brother is in jail. I try to focus my thoughts on my work and then I open my office door to greet my patient.

Much has been written about the importance of the analyst's willingness to draw on her associations, memories, and affective reactions to her patients in order to deepen the analytic work. It is not unusual for analysts to have traumatic histories. It is that very history that has lead so many of us into the field. How is my history in the room with me when I am with my patients? How do I use my history to inform and expand my thinking? How often does it shut down my thinking, contributing to my own dissociated analytic state? And how does it impact my work that my history continues to unfold into the present as both my brother and my sister struggle, in different ways and to varying degrees, with psychiatric symptoms.

The patient I saw after receiving the call from the Chicago police was remarkably forgiving of my lateness. Perhaps she sensed, consciously or unconsciously, that I was not in my usual state. Much as I tried to elicit her feelings about my lateness and to remain open to any feelings she may have had about me, she went right into the material we'd been exploring recently in our work together. The apparent smoothness of our interaction could have had as much to do with her as with me and with who we are together and was perhaps made easier by the fact that our histories are quite different from one another.

But what of the patient whose history parallels our own? What happens in the moments when these parallel histories evoke aspects of our pasts that are woven with shame and loss? How is it possible for us to be present with our patients, to be both in the experience and able to reflect on it at the same time, when our pasts converge in areas of trauma and vulnerability?

How do we proceed when our patients may not consciously recognize in us but instead enact with us an aspect of their own lives, and, when we may do the same with our patients as a result of our conscious or unconscious interactions with them?

In this chapter I present clinical material describing my work with a patient whose family history and experience of loss was eerily similar to my own. I am interested in the implications for treatment when analyst and patient share a parallel history the result of which is that both have lived in psychically similar places. What does it mean for the work when we encounter in our patients a place we have known in ourselves? And, what if this place of similarity, of psychic overlap, is one that feels shameful, one that bears a social stigma, one that is often spoken of in hushed tones of shame and alienation? In our need to be the new, good object to our patients we may feel that our less-than-perfect selves, not to mention our less-than-perfect family histories and the legacy of those histories that we carry, should be kept out of the room. But that is simply not possible when we are doing the intimate work of analysis. It may be our benevolent wish to help those patients whose struggles are so similar to our own by holding on to our illusions of fully healed wounds. But the reality is that many of our wounds are never fully healed. They live inside us, although in a different way than they once did.

When an analyst becomes aware, during her work with a patient, of the fragile, wounded places within her, it may leave the analyst feeling vulnerable and ashamed. To cope with these feelings, the analyst dissociates her awareness of those shameful places. She will feel less anxious and more professional when she instead locates all of the shame in the patient (Benjamin, 2004; Bromberg,1998; Davies, 2004), intensifying what Racker (1972) has called the myth of the healthy healing the sick. Fleeing to a distant and intellectual place becomes a dissociated imperative. She will feel safe because she will use her mind to the exclusion of her emotions. It's as if the getaway car of dissociation arrives and she jumps into it with the blink of an eye.

Davies (2004) writes about working with a patient who evokes in the analyst an awareness of her own shame-riddled self-states. It is transformative for her patient when Davies speaks of her own shameful affect states and in so doing demonstrates that she can tolerate and survive that which is shameful within her. Davies suspects she is revealing little about herself that her patient did not already know as a result of their interactions. What is most meaningful for her patient is that Davies can bear these parts of her self, can give voice to them and is willing to take the risk of speaking to her patient about her own experience.

Relational theory has made it clear that our patients often know more about their analysts than their analysts are aware of having revealed (Aron,

1996; Maroda, 1999). Cooper (2000) has written about how our patients come to know and contain our limitations and areas of conflict but are rarely recognized for doing so, thus infantilizing the patient. Frequently, it is assumed that for an analyst to be more active and to inquire about the patient's experience of the analyst (Aron, 1996) is a narcissistically indulgent act that intrudes on the patient's space and freedom. In fact, I believe we often hide behind our professional role, escaping to an intellectual place, meeting our need to be safe, secure, and free of powerful emotion in the guise of meeting our patient's needs. We have too often overlooked the narcissistic and self-serving aspects of remaining quiet and "allowing the transference to unfold" when that transference may involve a patient's awareness of the analysts shame and vulnerability, as well as an awareness that these feelings are not something the analyst is willing to acknowledge. Silence is always an act of communication and may carry within it a multitude of messages including the analyst's anxiety or discomfort with what the patient is evoking in her. Remaining silent is *sometimes* a way that we meet our own needs at the cost of our patient's needs.

In my work I have had patients who, like me, have one or more siblings whose minds have faltered. When a childhood includes a sibling's descent into mental illness that history is one that bleeds into the present. It is not finite and it may never feel distant. It is a part of the daily life of adulthood. To grow up with a sibling who has become mentally ill is to live with the feeling that mental illness cannot be escaped, that it is hovering nearby, that it is waiting. These patients feel guilt on separating, or pursuing their own lives and having what will never come to their siblings. I have had many of these same feelings at times in my life, particularly during early adulthood.

Simone was, for me, one such patient. Although our backgrounds and the atmosphere of the households in which we grew up had significant differences, the current state of our families bore striking similarities. Simone, like me, was the youngest of three children and, like me, both of her older siblings struggled to function in the world, one with greater difficulty than the other. For Simone, as for me, it was the sibling with whom she had been closest and by whom she had felt most loved, who battled the most ceaseless and incapacitating symptoms.

Simone began treatment when she was 29. She had a vibrant, engaging quality that I felt from the moment I met her. Her reason for entering treatment contradicted her energetic presence, "I'm afraid of death," she said, a few minutes into her first session. She had not experienced the death of anyone close to her but when she thought of death she was flooded with fear. She wondered what made her exist and was overwhelmed with the reality that one day she would not be here. She wondered what happens after you die. She believed in an afterlife but felt doubtful that it would be anything tangible. "How could it be, that one day you could just not even feel your feet on the ground?" Death was a thought both unbearable and fascinating.

Simone described a childhood in which she felt loved and adored, yet alone. Her brother and sister were only a year apart but she was 7 and 8 years junior to them. Much as she looked up to and admired her older siblings, particularly her sister, Simone always knew they were vulnerable in a way she was not. Her sister was brittle, quick to tears and had difficulty finding comfort socially. Her brother had no interest in a social world. Where it felt too easy to reach inside her sister and rattle what semblance of peace she held, her brother was unreachable, living in a private reclusive mystery world, never having made a friend. No one in her family acknowledged its strangeness and so Simone was alone, dissociating her awareness that something was not right at home.

When Simone was 9 years old, an uncle who lived in the apartment adjacent to her and her family molested her. Initially, her memory of being molested was hazy and much of our early work was focused on these experiences. As she recalls, the abuse happened two or three times and involved her uncle exposing himself, fondling, and kissing her. Simone never told anyone about the abuse until she was an adult. In the first phase of treatment I thought of her experiences with her uncle as the central traumatic experience in her life and the primary reason for the dissociated states she often presented. Together we considered the possibility that her overwhelming fears of death and of nothingness, had grown out of her experience with her uncle, that perhaps she coped by dissociating to a state in which she "could not even feel her feet on the ground."

I felt an incredible openness in Simone. It was as if she had a powerful desire to give herself over to the treatment. She would walk in, greet me warmly, and immediately begin talking. Words seemed to just spill out of her. However, 10 to 15 minutes into the session I would realize I could not focus on what she was saying and found it impossible to reflect on the material, which was usually about her relationships and interactions with others, including her family members. I would ask her what she was feeling and she would look perplexed and say she had no idea. She was quite curious about this experience but it was a curiosity that seemed removed from her, as if she were curious about another person. These moments of dissociated affect were a central part of our early work together. I used my own feelings of haziness as an indicator of when to stop her and inquire about her feelings, attempting to bring her, and me, back into the room.

Early in treatment, Simone described her visits home as feeling cocoonlike and safe. Not a lot had changed since she left home. Her sister lived with her parents and was unable to work, having had a series of psychotic episodes. Her brother lived reclusively in his own apartment, managing to hold on to a good job, but completely unable to interact with others.

Simone had always been particularly close to her sister, looking up to and admiring her as a child. Unlike her brother and sister, Simone had an active social life and a thriving career in which she was rapidly rising to the top of her field. Although she could acknowledge, in a joking way, being the only normal one to come out of her family, talking about it seriously seemed close to impossible. Early in our work when I attempted to explore her feelings about her siblings we never got far below the surface. It was as if she skated to another topic before I knew what happened. I believe my inquiry into her relationship with her siblings quickly unleashed shameful emotions for Simone and she dissociated to get away from them.

When I look back, I realize Simone was not the only one who was contending with shameful emotions and subsequent dissociation in order to escape them. Although I was not aware of it at the time, and in fact consciously experienced myself as eager to explore her family history, I believe I avoided exploring areas of her life experience because I feared they would dredge up shameful aspects of my own. The absence of my conflict regarding how I would use myself, and my history in the work is a clear sign that I was dissociating a part of myself that would be so central to the treatment. Stern (2004), describing the dissociated states that analysts enter, writes, "when the analyst dissociates it is because she finds herself in circumstances that make her vulnerable and she can tolerate that vulnerability only by dissociating" (p. 216).

But what is dissociated does not just vanish into thin air. It is enacted. What follows is the description of an enactment, the working through of which was pivotal in moving the treatment forward.

It was the 3rd year of treatment. I felt that our work was progressing rather smoothly. Simone had become curious about the hazy, dissociated affect she often experienced in session. She frequently brought in dreams, many of which were about carrying shopping bags or luggage filled with things that we came to think of as parts of herself that she kept out of her awareness. She also had many dreams about houses—houses that were burning or decaying or dangerous in some way. We had understood these dreams as reflective of her experiences in her family and of the struggles she was having in her relationship with Nick, a man she'd been dating since just prior to starting treatment. Nick was hard-edged, passionate, quick-witted, and inevitably disappointing. Although he expressed deep love for Simone, he never seemed to be available in a consistent and reliable way.

Simone was an agreeable and motivated patient, who related to me in a positive, often idealizing manner, which is why the session that I am about to describe represented a critical turning point in our work. Simone walked into my office carrying a magazine she had found in the waiting room. She sat down and held up the magazine, which said "HOME" on its cover in big, bright orange letters. "Finally, you have something good in your waiting room," she declared. "And so I am just going to take it." She proceeded to stuff the magazine into her bag. I sat there, stunned. Everything felt different. It felt like someone had knocked me off balance. I had never known this part of Simone. "You are just going to take the magazine?" I asked, in a tone of disbelief. "Yes," she said. It felt like she was aggressively taking something from me. I tried to inquire about what was transpiring between us but my questions only made her defensive, "What's wrong with taking the magazine?" she asked. I sat and wondered to myself how she could possibly not find anything strange in coming into my office and announcing to me that she was taking a magazine. Why didn't she just ask me for it, I wondered, or for that matter, why didn't she just take it from the waiting room without telling me. She was clearly trying to communicate something but I had absolutely no idea what it was.

Simone and I were stuck in the complementary two-ness of an enactment, the many layers of which would become apparent only over time. I remember sitting with Simone in this moment of stalemate and despairing at the paucity of ideas I could come up with to navigate a way out of where we were now trapped. I was jarred by the foreignness of this session with Simone and reached for more familiar experiences with her. I thought of how freely she brought in her dreams. I made a suggestion to her. "What if we think about what just happened in here as a dream?" I asked. Simone looked curious. I said to her, "Suppose you dreamt that you walked into my office with the magazine and said that *finally* I had something good in my waiting room and so you were just going to take it?" She readjusted her body and settled into her chair. It was as if she was literally moving into another self-state. After a few moments she said, "I guess I don't know if I can take what happens here home with me." She looked surprised, as if she had no idea from where she had pulled this knowledge. The space in the room opened.

In retrospect I feel that Simone was reassured by my suggestion that she think about our session as a dream because my ability to come up with this idea indicated that I was capable of thinking beyond our current interaction. In other words, she could "use" me, in the Winnicottian sense of the word, without the fear of destroying my mind (Black, 2003; Winnicott, 1969). Although Winnicott's concept of object usage represents a crucial aspect of any treatment, for a patient like Simone, the fear of the analyst's inability to survive the patient's impact is profound. Simone grew up identifying with and looking up to her sister's mind, a mind that faltered and then fell away. Simone has lived with the fear that she may have, in some way, contributed to her sister's illness, a fear that she was unable to articulate until much later in treatment, and a fear that probably contributed to her attraction to Nick with his tough, hard, impenetrable exterior.

As the session unfolded and Simone continued to associate to our inter-action as if it were a dream it became evident that an internal shift was oc-curring. In Bromberg's words (1998), she was moving from a place of dissociation to a place of conflict. She was able to hold in her conscious mind her positive feelings about our work as well as her feelings of despair. "I like being here," she said, "I want to do this work with you." Then she hes-itated, looking confused for a moment. "Outside of here so much is still so hard for me. I just don't know if this is going to make a real difference in my life. I don't know if I can really use what we do here." Simone expressed fears of her future, of never being able to have a meaningful relationship, "How will I ever have a normal life when I come from such an abnormal family?"

I wondered how I had kept myself from knowing how much pain Simone was in. Had I enacted the role of her mother in not allowing myself to see how she was struggling? Had I unconsciously needed her to smoothly come through losses that were so similar to my own? One thing was clear to me- I had not allowed myself to fully recognize Simone's feelings of helplessness as she watched her family members deteriorate. If I were to feel Simone's helplessness, I would have to feel my own.

Simone needed access to my mind. She needed to feel that I could hold her emotional experience in my mind and that I could resonate with her ex-perience. But I had not wanted Simone to sense my shame about the bro-ken pieces of my family and so I *thought* about our similarities but did not allow myself to *feel* them. When Simone brought in the magazine she let us both know that we needed to allow "HOME," in every sense of the word, into our work.

It is an inevitable part of enactment that the analyst will fail her patient. According to Benjamin (2004), it's largely through the recognition of that inevitability that the analyst is, hopefully, able to take responsibility without succumbing to feelings of badness and shame. The treatment is then opened up and a "space of thirdness" (Benjamin, 2004) is created. Now, there is increased acceptance of one another and a greater possibility for what had been dissociated in both patient and analyst to become conscious and available for reflection.

I began to hear Simone differently. Her history evoked so much of my own. I allowed myself to recall moments in my past that were teetering on the edge of forgotten. The haziness that I had so often felt with her became less frequent. Our work shifted and the feelings in the room were more clearly defined. It was as if we could hold them in our hands, feel them and talk about them where before they would slip right through our fingers, al-lowing us to register only the cloudiest awareness of affects such as help-lessness, loss, and fear. Simone could now speak out loud about how torn she felt between taking care of her siblings and taking care of herself.

As our work became more focused on her siblings Simone was able to consciously recognize that they are not who they once were or who she had hoped they would be in her life. It was becoming clear that the death she'd feared when she entered treatment was the death of her sister's former self, a death Simone had witnessed without anyone to help her integrate her experience. When she was able to let herself know what she had lost she began to mourn.

Simone remembered watching her sister slip into psychosis and embedded with that memory was the part of her that felt profoundly helpless. She had wished and, at times, even believed that she could have done something, provided some sort of glue, for her sister's splintering mind. Now she began to let herself know that she could do nothing to rescue her sister from her own mind. Simone equated moving forward in her own life with leaving her siblings behind. She talked most about not wanting to move ahead without her sister because it felt so lonely without her. And, she talked about not wanting to move forward because the guilt was intolerable.

As I sat with Simone I remembered the feeling of my brother slipping away. I felt the loss of him and, I felt alone without him. But what was unbearable to me, and still is overwhelmingly difficult to hold in my mind is *his* aloneness, and my powerlessness to do anything about it.

I remember my brother as sweet and funny and generous in the many hours we spent together during my childhood. But I knew, that when he was with others, things did not go so well for him. He stuttered and as he got older other kids were rarely forgiving of that. When I was in first grade we moved to a new, more upscale neighborhood. I remember my mother picking me up after my first day of school. I sat in the front seat, a proud first-grader, as we drove to the junior high to pick up my brother after his first day. I saw him come out of the school and race to the car. The door slammed shut and he exploded into tears. His pain filled the car. It seemed like there was nothing I could do for him. I didn't have the words for it then but as I look back now I think that I was wondering how I could have had such a good day when he was suffering.

When I say to Simone, that she knows her sister is unable to function, unable to live in the world as others do; when I ask her what knowing that feels like, she floods with emotion. Her face takes the shape of despair and she says, "I cannot know that all the time. I can only know it some of the time. I just can't live with that knowledge."

When Simone is with her sister she often feels a painful and vast distance between them. Her sister feels to Simone like an alien-Other, unknowable. But there are moments Simone holds tightly, moments when there is a rich connection between she and her sister and those moments glisten like a rare gem that the two of them have unexpectedly found. The past can live in the present in moments of understanding, of shared humor, of comfort. But the truth is that those times are rarer than the rarest gem. They are like a tease in that so much that seems possible will never be granted. I know those moments too, those glistening pieces of time after which so much that felt possible, feels lost.

About 6 years into our work together, Simone had begun to express the pain of putting to rest the fantasy that she could have a healthy, functioning sibling. She was overwhelmed by the reality that she was the only one in her family who could live in the world and function normally. Toward the end of a particularly mournful session, she leaned forward and said to me, "Do you think there is anyone out there who has not one but two siblings that don't function? Do you think there is anyone else?" Everything stopped for me in that moment. Was she really asking me this question? Could she expect an answer? My whole self felt stilled. "I mean, do you think there is anyone?" she said again. I looked at her. "I'm sure there is," I said. The room was quiet. I wanted to tell her more. But she continued to talk about her aloneness without asking me anything else and a few minutes later the session ended.

When she returned for her next session the room felt awkward for the first few minutes. I asked her how she had felt after the previous session. "I think you were trying to tell me something, " she said. "Were you?" "I am unsure how much you want to know," I said, feeling I needed to be careful and wondering whether this interaction was about me or her or, hopefully, both of us. "I want to know," she said.

"My family is similar to yours, Simone. There are differences, but I too am the youngest of three and I also have two older siblings both of whom, in different ways, have had tremendous difficulty functioning in the world." We looked at each other. Her face opened into tears. She expressed gratitude and relief and said she knew there was a reason she was with me. I felt vulnerable. I had been aware of feeling a kinship with Simone but in that moment I felt my long held yearnings for the recognition we now shared awaken from their stillness. We were siblings of a sort, both having survived a similar loss of our own. We were recognizing each other in the manner about which Benjamin (1988) has written, understanding how we are the same in the moment when we also understand how we are different. No matter how similar is the aloneness we have each felt in our families we are still alone within them. And yet, this attempt at bridging that aloneness is in fact a paradox—we are less alone because of it (Benjamin, 1988; Grand, 2000).

It is difficult to find words to describe the intensity of this session. It was profoundly moving. The look on Simone's face was one of amazement and gratitude. Although I knew that our histories were similar and had thought about that similarity many times over the years we'd worked together, I had thought about it within the context of our clinical work. I had thought about it as her analyst. What I did not know until that session was how it would feel to know and be known by a person who shared a background so similar to my own. We were deeply connected in that moment and in a sense, everything changed. It was not so much the information itself that I believe was most pivotal for Simone, although that would have been extraordinarily powerful no matter how she learned of it. It was my *choice* to put it into words, to say it to her, to let her know, and hence to let her in. My willingness to speak about my family history indicated to Simone that I could bear my own shame and vulnerability. I believe this made it possible for her to begin to move past her shame and face her family background in a more direct and meaningful way. And, it made it possible for me to more fully use myself in my work with her.

It was not long after she learned of my history that Simone started to struggle in a different way than she had before with thoughts of leaving Nick. She wondered aloud whether I had ever felt guilty at the thought of moving forward with my life and leaving someone behind. She was able to connect her relationship with her sister to her difficulty feeling entitled to seek a relationship with a man who would be loving in a more consistent and reliable way than the unavailable, enigmatic Nick.

There were some points earlier in the treatment when I believe my shame at being the one to evoke Simone's pain precipitated a dissociated state in me, leaving me unable to resonate with her hopelessness (Bromberg, 1998). Some of the struggles I faced in the work with Simone were sparked by my own need to come to terms with my inability to rescue Simone from the isolation she felt within her family just as I had wished I could have rescued my brother from his pain and that I could have stepped out of my own feelings of loss and isolation. In so many ways, I use my personal self within my professional role. But until I met Simone, I had not known how uncomfortable I was to use the part of myself that has lost siblings to their own faltering minds.

Davies (2004) writes about the ways in which the analyst may extrude what is unbearable for her into the patient, finding it more comfortable to see those traits in her patient rather than in herself. We all have fractured pasts, wounds that will never fully heal and about which we feel shame. What did I extrude into Simone? Did I want the rawness, the helplessness, the longing for a more normal family, and the endless and unpredictable road of having mentally ill siblings, to be one that she was struggling with and that I had figured out? Did I extrude my own fear, shame, and overwhelmed feelings of contending with the family into which I was born so that I could be the healthy healing the sick? Then I could help her to start down the road that I so wanted to believe I had finished traveling. In reality the journey feels different but I am still on that road.

There is an aggression in separating from family members whose minds are not fully functional. It feels selfish and cruel—like abandoning someone in the cold. Perhaps that is why, for so long, I kept my safe distance from Simone's parallel past. The question of just how to hold my responsibility, my disappointment and my love for my siblings is one that I am still trying to sort out.

I think of a moment during a recent visit with my brother. It was November and the air had the kind of coldness that warns of winter's close approach. We had just left the dentist's office where, after much reticence, he had a tooth pulled because of decay. We were walking down the street when he suddenly stopped. "Sandy!" he said, with a tone of alarm. "Something is not right. I feel really strange. I've had that tooth since I was 6 years old. Part of me is gone." I looked at him. I saw the gentleness in his eyes, his freckled hand against his cheek. Quietly, I told him he'd be okay. He had lost a tooth but he was still the same person. I could see his sadness. I felt sad too. We both knew something was lost.

Simone has been able to use her knowledge of my family history to think about her self in a new light. She has wondered about the ways in which our families and our experiences within them may be both similar and different. Recently, she spoke as if she had "forgotten" what she knows about my background. When I inquired about this, she said that she still found it hard to believe that my family really was like hers because, "It couldn't be as crazy." She said she found it difficult to think about my history because then she thought of me as "a little child going through such a horrifying experience." In this moment she was able to use our reciprocal recognition of each other's sibling relationships to reflect on her own experience in a way she hadn't before—horrors and all. She remembered feeling "so small" in a home that she thought of as warm and loving but was also filled with frightening and incomprehensible events. She described the feeling of secrecy, that she "just knew" that so much of what happened in her home—her uncle's abuse of her, the unpredictable chaos that resulted from her sister's episodes—should never be spoken of. When she said she could not bear to think of my childhood as having been overwhelming in ways similar to hers she was playing with the possibility of giving up her idealized view of me and instead allowing me to be human, imperfect and knowable.

Over the years, I have learned to live with the unpredictability of my brother's mind. When I see or hear from him he may be witty, generous, and acutely perceptive or he may be distant, suspicious, and silent. I don't know where he lives and I know better than to ask. But he stays connected to me and I to him. It is the nature of that connection that has been so much for me to grapple with.

In the work of psychoanalysis, it is the nature of the connection between our patients and ourselves that is so central to what we do. Our histories live in us and they impact our work in ways we cannot always know or control (Harris, 2004). From the beginning of my work with Simone, the connection I felt to her was largely made of the similarities in our family histories. We had both watched our siblings descend into an Otherness that was beyond our control or comprehension. In a family such as Simone's to feel hope for oneself and to abandon the other can feel like a single act. Simone knows that I know that feeling. She knows that I have lived where she lives, that pieces of me still live there and perhaps always will.

I cannot rescue Simone from the reality of her family, the shape it has taken and the losses it has borne. Our work has helped her to see her family more clearly and to mourn that which she has lost. But it also may have extended an illusion that our relationship can be sibling-like in such a way that it replaces the relationship she wishes she could have had with her sister. The immense relief she has experienced as a result of knowing about the similarities in our histories has diminished Simone's shame about her past. But ultimately Simone will have to accept that no one can replace or recreate what has been lost in her relationship with her sister and, that there is an endlessness to the unpredictability of her sister's daily life. This is, perhaps, the next phase of our work.

Recently, Simone has taken steps toward leaving her relationship with Nick in the hopes of finding someone with whom she can create a more meaningful and fulfilling relationship. She has been shocked by Nick's response, his anger and the way in which he has crashed into an incapacitating depression. Her guilt in leaving him is at times intolerable for her. "How can I do this?" she wondered. "How did I not know what he was made from underneath? It's like he is an egg with a really tough shell. I cracked him and the yolk came spilling out." I ask Simone, "And what about your pain?" She responds, "I am more cooked inside." The grief and guilt that accompany her survival have made it difficult for Simone to want more for herself without feeling greedy. It is this aspect of surviving, of being more cooked inside, that is still so much a part of our work.

When my brother rescued me from the snowdrifts on that day in Chicago, it was exciting and silly and fun because I knew that no matter how deeply into the snow I went, he would be there to pull me out. He did it every time. I have to live with the truth that I cannot spare my brother from what his life has brought him. There are times when I am still overwhelmed by the sadness of this reality.

As analysts, our own histories of trauma or loss can feel profoundly shameful. But our fears of being seen as flawed or scarred or still struggling with some aspect of our lives only make us less useful to our patients. Our need to be beyond shame makes us hide from our patients. Ironically, it is in the recognition that we all have areas of shame that the shame itself diminishes. It is our responsibility as analysts to allow ourselves to be vulnerable and to risk our own shame and fragility. Not to do so is to abandon and demean our patients, to sit and look at "them" from afar rather than to join with them on a scary but ultimately hopeful journey.

References

Aron, L. (1996), *A Meeting of Minds: Mutuality in Psychoanalysis*. Hillsdale, NJ: The Analytic Press.

Benjamin, J.(1988), *The Bonds of Love: Psychoanalysis Feminism and the Problem of Domination*. New York: Pantheon.

——— (2004), Beyond doer and done-to: an intersubjective view of thirdness. *Psychoanal. Quart.,* 63:5–46.

Black, M. (2003), Enactment: Analytic musings on energy, language and personal growth. *Psychoanal. Dial.,*13:633–655.

Bromberg, P. (1998), *Standing in the Spaces: Essays on Clinical Process, Trauma, and Dissociation*. Hillsdale, NJ: The Analytic Press.

Cooper, S. (2000), Mutual Containment in the analytic situation. *Psychoanal. Dial.,* 10:169–194).

Davies, J. (2004), Whose bad objects are we anyway? Repetition and our elusive love affair with evil. *Psychoanal. Dial.,* 14:711–732.

Grand, S. (2000), *The Reproduction of Evil: A Clinical and Cultural Perspective*. Hillsdale, NJ: The Analytic Press.

Harris, A. (2004), Haunted Bodies: Commentary on Melanie Suchet's "Whose Mind Is It Anyway?" *Studies in Gender & Sexuality,* 5:288–300

Maroda, K. (1999), *Seduction, Surrender and Transformation*. Hillsdale, NJ: The Analytic Press.

Racker, H. (1972), The Meanings and Uses of Countertransference. *Psychoanal. Quart.,* 41:487–506.

Stern, D. B. (2004), The Eye Sees Itself: Dissociation, Enactment, and the Achievement of Conflict. *Contemp. Psychoanal.,* 40:197–238.

Winnicott, D. (Ed.). (1971), *Playing and Reality*. New York: Basic Books.

18

Enter the Perverse

Gillian Straker, MA, PhD

▼　▼　▼　▼　▼

The term *perversion* is highly contested (Stein, 2003). Nevertheless, it does seem to have an experiential clinical utility (Dimen, 2003), provided its co-constructed nature is kept in mind (Dimen, 2001).

This having been said, the manner in which perversion comes to be co-constructed bears exploration. Through an interrogation of the author's own experience in reading a "perverse scenario," some elements that may be implicated in the co-construction of perversity are explored.

These elements include an attempted split between cognition and affect, a refusal to engage with the subjectivity of the other as an emergent property of interchange, as well as a seduction by a particular type of language.

They further include the affect of anxiety, elicited here by a feeling that the boundary between private and public has been breached, as well as the affect of disgust, which serves a boundary keeping function. The implication of these elements in the co-construction of perversion are explored, both in regard to one specific perverse scenario as well as more generally.

Toward the end of 2003, the International Association for Relational Psychoanalytic Psychotherapy engaged in an online colloquium on perversion based on Ruth Stein's (2003) paper "Why Perversion?" Its meaning was debated in terms of cultural construction, moral signifier, disciplinary weapon, psychic structure, pathology, intersubjective state, and clinical concept (Dimen, 2003). Despite the range of meanings and a number of dissenting voices, there seemed general agreement that the term *perversion* has experiential and clinical utility (Dimen, 2003).

Harris (2003) who, along with Bass (2003), was a moderator of the colloquium, incisively abstracted three sets of "unstable dichotomies" that formed the core of the debate: authenticity, clarity, and connection versus

301

malaises, masquerade, and destruction; love/hate versus indifference; and the clinical versus social meaning of the notion "perversion." Harris (2003) concluded that, despite some dissent, there was agreement that perversion is a complex clinical phenomenon in which life and death are at stake and destructiveness is in the ascendant.

In fleshing out destructiveness, Altman (2003) stresses the deadness implicit in perversion. He speaks of a false excitement that covers over futility and substitutes for excitement that sustains aliveness. This notion links with Kahn's (1979) work on perversion, which he saw as founded on a lack of real desire, and involving fucking out of intent. Other works quoted in the colloquium and by Stein (2003) included Freud (1905, 1927), Chasseguet-Smirgel (1985), McDougall (1995), and Stoller (1976).

Chasseguet-Smirgel (1985) is perhaps best known for her focus on perversion as denial of difference between sexes and generations; Stoller (1976), for his notion of perversion as an erotic form of hatred; and Kahn (1979), for his idea that perversion is about power and repetition. However, these notions were not quoted uncritically, and very seldom was perversion presented as anything other than "perversion is us" (Dimen, 2001). The ubiquity of perversion was emphasized, as was its tendency to lend flavor, sensuality, and creative excess to sexuality. The involvement of the analyst in its co-construction was stressed.

Ogden (1997) in his paper "Perverse Subjects" has written eloquently about the analyst's implication in perversion, foreshadowing Stein's (2003) insight that perversion involves us and that we need to allow ourselves to enter the relations of "seduction, domination, psychic bribery and the guileful uses of innocence" (p. 6) that characterize perversion and to experience how a pact is created which shuts out external reality (Wolff-Bernstein, 2003). Unless we succeed in experientially doing this, we will not be able to enter the perverse and transform those elements that trouble. The question of who is troubled, I leave aside for the moment. Instead, I attempt to write of my own experience when entering what may be considered a perverse scene, albeit a fictional one. In doing so I am aware of the many critical arguments against treating fiction as case study (Bronski, 2002), notwithstanding that, in another sense, all case studies may be considered fiction (Freud, 1927). However, what follows is less an attempt to analyze fiction than an attempt to use fiction to unpack how perverse scenarios may embroil one, even when perversion is defined broadly as that which I do not like that the other does (Dimen, 2001).

Before proceeding I note the argument of Gibbs(2001) that fiction, by its nature, evokes particular responses, as it is a site of cultural ambivalence, which demands a visceral form of involvement in which we become absorbed and agree temporarily to believe what, at another level, we may know is not true. Thus this particular form of reader involvement implicates disavowal (Gibbs, 2001, quoting Barthes, 1976). However, disavowal is also the defence of choice implicated in perversion (Freud, 1927), and it is this defense that I believe is mobilized in the analyst by the analysand's recounting and/or enactment of perverse scenarios.

Furthermore, I believe this goes beyond the normal splitting involved in disavowal. Indeed, the invitation to enter the perverse implicates a specific form of splitting, over and above the splitting of knowing and believing. It seems to implicate a split between affect and cognition in an attempt at mastery of the sensate. Although reading fiction may involve the suspension of disbelief, allowing absorption in affect (Gibbs, 2001), I would posit that entering the perverse provokes almost the opposite of this. That is, it provokes an attempt to suspend affect in order to have thought. In more classical psychoanalytic parlance, it invites an attempt to keep separate the experiencing ego from the observing one, but in an unproductive manner, such that a dialogue between them is impaired and integrated cognitive-affective thought is compromised.

The notion that properly functioning thinking integrates cognition and affect is elaborated by Damasio (1994) in his book *Descartes' Error,* in which he demonstrates convincingly that emotions are not a luxury, but are crucial to rational thinking. He conceptualizes feelings as a momentary view of the body landscape, but within this he argues that the brain is the "captive audience" of our feelings. However, rather than further theoretically elaborate this issue it may be preferable to describe its operation in myself in response to a story by Jane De Lynn (1990), and I would ask you to remain open to your own responses. The task is not so much to assess the scenario in terms you may use to define or negate perversion, but rather to enter the experience this scenario may elicit.

Setting the Scene

The story entitled "Butch" comes from De Lynn's (1990) novel *Don Juan in the Village,* in which she describes a series of sexual engagements of a lesbian narrator as she searches for an ideal, which at some level she knows is not attainable (Gibbs, 2001). The narrator picks up an "ugly" woman in a bar, about whom she comments "I didn't want anybody to see me with her. When I left the bar I made her walk several feet behind me, like Chinese woman used to do" (De Lynn, 1990, p. 223). She also comments that she felt relaxed, as it was up to her less attractive partner to initiate sex. The story continues with the narrator minutely observing herself while entering into an experience in which she becomes increasingly aroused as she hands control to the other, relinquishing responsibility such that she comments in retrospect "Whatever happened, happened. I didn't choose it and it was not my fault" (De Lynn, 1990 p. 224). She says this, notwithstanding that she sets up the scenario, thus undermining the very submission she craves as she controls the enacted scenario in particular ways.

The narrator is aware of the splits within herself as she observes herself being aroused by being teased, controlled, and dominated by "this being who disgusted me" (De Lynn, 1990, p. 232). In the process she is tied up, fisted, slapped, and left aroused and excited while her partner goes to the toilet and returns, leaving a question about whether she has washed her hands. Finally, she is left tied up with a dildo up her arse as her partner exits with no promise of return.

The narrator's awareness of splits in herself are revealed via her comments, for example, "at that moment there was nothing I wouldn't have let her do (though of course there was)" (De Lynn, 1990, p. 228); "Her arm pressed down on my pubic bone and I felt that I couldn't move (though of course I could)" (De Lynn, 1990, p. 227). Through these comments she reveals her desire to be out of control, but on condition that, in reality, she is in control. The skill of her partner in arousing her resides in maintaining both the needed reality and the required fantasy. Under these conditions the narrator's body responds. However, she comments upon not being totally in control of her body's response, while acknowledging that she was not entirely given over to it either.

The narrator is also aware of a split in her partner, whom she experiences as fucking more out of intent than desire, and comments "she was much cooler than me, almost clinical as she proceeded" (De Lynn, 1990, p. 228). It is this intent that the narrator finds arousing, even though she is in the grip of disgust and begins to worry about germs, and knows that what is happening "could be dangerous" (De Lynn, 1990, p. 234).

Despite her knowledge of danger, or perhaps because of it, the story ends with her feeling sad as her partner departs. She comments "It was the same sadness that was always there and it occurred to me that I must like it. Why else did I keep going to the bars if not to find it?" (De Lynn, 1990, p. 234). Thus, she acknowledges an erotic link with sadness, just as she acknowledges an erotic link with pain and disgust. She also recognizes what might take many an analysand a lifetime to recognize, that is, that she enjoys her symptom (Zizek, 2001).

As indicated, there is some agreement among clinicians that perversion might be a useful category in which to think about certain forms of sexual enactment, and I believe this would include the fictitious one just described. The sexual scenario described by De Lynn (1990) and the manner in which the narrator engages with it, her irony and analysis notwithstanding, contains many elements alleged to be perverse. I use the word "alleged" because, although I believe there is clinical value in the term *perversion,* it is difficult to both justify its definitional elements and to determine their presence in any particular scenario.

False excitement has probably consciously been produced by everyone at some time, even although what De Lynn (1990) describes is unconscious false excitement that masks futility and is not conscious masquerade. Nevertheless, masquerade, both conscious and unconscious, is also part of perversion (Stein, 2003). Fucking by intent—who hasn't ever decided to "do it" for reasons other than lust, love, or desire? Repetition—some fantasies are worth repeating more than others.

All of this notwithstanding, I came away from reading "Butch" with a sense of unease produced mainly by the eroticization of negative affects. Perhaps this simply proves that perversion is "the sex that you like and I don't" (Dimen, 2003, p. 827). But what is it that I do not like, and why?

Setting My Own Scene

In considering my response to De Lynn (1990), the circumstance in which I first read her work is important. I first read "Butch" in response to an invitation to present a paper at a Literature and Psychoanalysis Conference in tandem with Anna Gibbs, a colleague in Media Studies. I interpreted my brief to be to approach the paper from a classical psychoanalytic perspective. Prior to this invitation I had neither heard of, nor read, the work of De Lynn (1990), and my initial encounter was not unambivalent.

One of my first experiences was to feel strangely surveiled, which created an anxiety about being exposed. I felt that what was private would become public in an unwanted manner, or that my "Freudian slip" would be showing. It was only later that it occurred to me that the blurring of public and private is frequently reported on when working with the perverse. Stein's (2003) patient sets out explicitly to blur this boundary by consorting with friends of Stein. Similarly, Ogden (1997) in his paper "Perverse Subjects," reports his anxiety that aspects of his inner world would be unwittingly revealed.

In addition to this anxiety about exposure, further responses associated with the perverse emerged. From my imagined position as classical analyst, I found it hard to immerse myself in the story. There was something about it, or myself, which made me wish to distance from it, and I found myself quite quickly entering a discourse of mastery. It was difficult not to apply theories of perversion to the characters or to understand the story as an illustration of such theories. It was easy to move into an encounter of investigating and interrogating the text, allowing the characters to occupy the position of a traditionally Freudian patient, the roots of whose transference resides within.

In this response, I showed less self-conscious observation than did De Lynn's (1990) narrator. It was soon clear to me that the reciprocal requirement within the Freudian model that I, in the position of the classical analyst, should remain equidistant from id, ego, and superego in reading this text, was a position almost impossible to sustain. The temptation to go to a superego judgment was great, given the extent of eroticization of pain, including the eroticization of activities that carried physical danger as well as the valorization of negative affects such as disgust and distaste, generated by the denigration of another. However, this temptation revealed that I had been drawn into a position of odd entanglements claimed for the perverse, and that now pertained to me in the intersubjective space.

Perverse Entanglements

In the midst of these entanglements, the attempt to apply theories of perversion to the story and the narrator led me to lose any appreciation of the carefully crafted nuanced depiction of the narrator provided by De Lynn (1990). I found myself refusing any real engagement with the narrator's subjectivity and individuality, thus mimicking the narrator, for whom the irrelevance of the individual subjectivity of the participants to the unfolding of her preferred sexual scenario, is plain. What is at stake is simply a script in search of characters, a script repetitive in its particularity. A woman uglier than herself is required, preferably one whom she might consider inferior in other ways, to whom she could surrender herself as an object of desire, albeit in the mode of affects appropriate to the "Lacanian Thing," that is, disgust, horror, intense pleasure, a move beyond the pleasure principle.

In saying this however, I found myself caught up in the odd entanglements alluded to earlier. In describing the protagonist's preferred sexual scenario did I not, in some sense, enter into the very objectification ascribed to the protagonist, an objectification of the other that is also within the structure of the perverse? In doing so, did I not, like the narrator, refuse to see the emerging properties of the being of the other, mistaking for her totality the fragment reflected in the present moment? But once again, how did I come to be in this position? How did I come to co-construct with the text/narrator an engagement of this nature?

As already indicated, the story engendered splits in me, which manifested not only between knowing and believing, but between sensate experiencing and cognition. It was as if I felt a need to suspend the evoked sensate experience of disgust and distaste in order to continue to read the narrative. Rather than being absorbed into it and willingly suspending disbelief, I felt distanced from it. Despite this, I also felt seized by affects appropriate to the "Lacanian Thing."

In this split between sensate experience and cognition, I found myself in a situation similar to that of the protagonist as she observed herself experiencing disgust and pleasure from a place outside herself, that is, a split between an observing and an experiencing ego, on a couch of a different kind.

Yet, even beyond, or perhaps through this split, the experience of the affects themselves seemed suspect. The protagonist as observer, like myself, was not really in the grip of the affects. They were experienced one removed, affected affects if you like, an indication that the protagonist's intimacy with herself was compromised in much the same way as her intimacy with her partner, and my intimacy with myself. It was a rupture in going on being, not imposed as on the Winnicottian (1965) baby, but partially, at least, willingly sought. The narrator sought it with her partner and, I agreed to experience it by continuing to read. By doing so, I obliquely became involved in a mode of experience thought to be characteristic of the perverse, namely a conscription into the constriction of affect, which mimicked the feelings of the narrator for her partner.

The narrator had predetermined the affects she wished to feel, not only by a specific choice of partner, that is, one who disgusted her, but also by a specific choice of scenario, extreme passivity. She had chosen a particular form of intimacy by design, an intimacy that confines and limits the affects to those dictated by the contract, or more accurately, to those constituted by it. In Masumi's (1995) terms, these affects would be considered the antithesis of authentic affect, which eludes one's sense of control. They are affects confined by expectation, so there need be no shocking confrontation with that which escapes and flees, and is beyond omnipotent control. This evasion of autonomous authentic affect seems to be the narrator's hidden intention. She wishes to orchestrate the affects she will experience.

If we take the end of the story seriously, accepting the narrator is thinking of her next pick-up as her partner leaves, the story is an account of a specific instance of a repetitive set, where the beginning, the middle, and the end are known *a priori,* albeit there may be some variation in the sexual arousal that arises in the enactments of the predetermined theme. Although these variations allow the narrator to experience a modicum of surprise in regard to certain elements of her own response, the scenario remains an overall staged encounter with the Thing, with abjection as its excess. Each staged encounter not only attenuates the range and intensity of affects that may be experienced, but also forecloses on learning from experience, as evidenced at the end of the story, when, despite an intellectual insight into her attachment to pain, the narrator sets out to find another version of her previous partner, a repetition thought to characterize the perverse.

Exploring the Beyond of Repetition

Being stuck myself in mimicking the narrator, the question arose concerning whether it was possible to free myself from repetition, and if so, how? This required me to reflect on the nature of my experience and to articulate this with the literature. To recap, my experience involved an anxiety about the blurring of the boundaries of public and private, an objectification of the other, a constriction of affects, and the experience of affected affects. Furthermore, these responses felt as though they were occurring in tandem with the narrator, in some kind of awful mimicry.

This mimicry seemed to be facilitated by an impulse to mastery expressed via a distancing from the material and an attempted split between sensate experience and cognition, which compromised productive and creative thought. However, what in turn underpinned this attempt at mastery?

The first factor I have already mentioned. It involved an anxiety around exposure in regard to the sexual, or more broadly, anxiety about a nonvolitional boundary crossing from private to public. This motivated an attempt to distance the subjectively experienced private self by attempting to block, the somatic registration of affect, in an illusory attempt to protect it from scrutiny.

The second issue involved the specific effect of the affect of disgust on the self. Disgust, through the particularity of its somatic registration, reflexively leads to attempts to distance from that which disgusts. In the case of my reading of De Lynn, this reflexive response was connected with the third issue, which pertained to the performative nature of particular forms of language. Such language embroils one in affect even when such affect is unpleasurable, as in disgust. Because it does so, it amplifies the need to distance even while thwarting it.

In regard to the issue of exposure and boundary crossings, the context in which I read De Lynn (1990) involved an expectation that my response to the private act of reading would be made public in the act of writing and speaking. Within this, I felt anxiety about exposure and being judged and caught out, either in bourgeois morality, or in erotic perversity.

This anxiety about being caught out is one shared by Ogden (1997) in his paper "Perverse Subjects." In this paper, he eloquently describes his anxiety about exposure and of being caught in infantile sexuality as he finds himself voyeuristically reading his patient's coat label. He describes his experience as a perverse co-construction within which his capacity to think seemed compromised. Although he does not speak specifically of the effects of performative language, he does allude to being caught in the patient's narrative.

One author who does however discuss the ability of particular forms of language to create specific effects and affects is Dianne Chisholm (1995). She does this in her article "The Cunning Lingua of Desire," the title of which I quote because it is illustrative of her argument that speech can and should escape "a deployment of discursivity as an instrument/weapon in the regime of knowledge/power" (p. 21). "The Cunning Lingua of Desire" lends itself to a freefall of libidinal associations, which one may or may not enjoy, but is hard put to escape. A signifying chain of a particular flavour has been set in motion. One is spoken through the discourse of the Other, thus revealing the Other of oneself and the performative nature of language.

When arguing for "linguistic performativity" Chisholm (1995, p. 21) places herself in a project taken up more generally by queer theory. She quotes Sedgwick (1993) who speaks of utterances that do not merely describe, but perform the actions they name and who indicates how this language can produce effects of identity, enforcement, seduction, and challenge. She examines further, how linguistic performativity operates in a work of Mary Fallon's (1995) entitled *SexTec,* and proposes that this work embodies a shifting of registers from the discursive/confessional to reverie/revelation, which she believes produces effects that are not only ironic and/or paradoic, but are erotic.

I would argue that similar effects are produced by De Lynn's (1990) writing. Its effects are ironic and erotic, but not in a straightforwardly pleasurable way, because what is at stake is an eroticization of disgust. Nevertheless, the language remains performative and embroils us, in this instance, in disgust, which, like shame, is a particular kind of affect. It is an affect which brings the body or its contents closer to the surface (Rose, 2003).

However, unlike shame, disgust and distaste determine what we bring into ourselves and what we wish to eject. We experience disgust after we have already ingested the noxious. Thus, the disgust engendered while I read De Lynn (1990) signaled that I had already taken in something I experienced as noxious, maneuvered into the position by De Lynn's linguistic performativity. It is this ingestion, which occurs before we consciously know it, that perhaps makes us feel, first, that we have co-constructed perverse entanglements, and second, leads us to defend against this by attempting to keep sensate experience and cognition separate, and that, third, promotes perverse enactments.

Once More: Perversion Is Us

Returning then to the beginning of this chapter, it certainly makes sense that "perversion is involvement" (Stein, 2003) and "perversion is us" (Dimen, 2001). If the perverse is created in the intersubjective space via linguistic performativity and the evocation of affects like disgust, how could it be otherwise? Such language invoking the affect of disgust breaks the body boundary, the border between inner and outer, public and private, before we know it. Just as we reflexively remove our body parts from a flame even before we know we are being burnt but will subsequently experience the sensation of being singed, so too, in the disgust provoked by De Lynn (1990), we are caught in tongues of fire, our own and that of the other before we know it. However, we can feel its aftermath and this perhaps is a good place to end this chapter.

Perversely, however, I feel cannot end here. Despite myself, I feel drawn to return to the attempt to keep some distance from perverse entanglements, even while acknowledging this is doomed to fail. To not keep any distance from affects like disgust, means to habituate to them and agree to ingest more of what I initially wished to eject. It means to agree to tamper with the punctuation of my system, a punctation that disgust performs. Sensate experience such as disgust marks a boundary, and thus guards against a fall into abjection. It is for this reason I do not wish to claim too much ground back from disgust before I object.

Visceral disgust can and must be retained as the boundary marker it is, if having reflected on it we are still happy that our boundary ends where it does. Furthermore I believe this is possible without immediately going to a superego judgment which closes down thought and occludes acknowledgment of our own imbrication in the perverse.

I believe therefore that the analysis of the perverse requires a safeguarding of the response of disgust while simultaneously containing and exploring it. Safeguarding reactions of disgust guards against succumbing to the dead space that perversion pushes to co-construct. However, analyzing these reactions allows us the "perverse subjects of analysis" to move from enactment to fantasy, from fact to fiction.

At this point, then, I end the chapter, acknowledging that De Lynn's (1990) story allowed me some insight into perverse entanglements, albeit only in fiction, and also to fantasize or alternatively internally fictionalize the processes involved in them, thereby coming to embody perverse entanglements myself. But now, as fiction, I lay to rest both De Lynn's (1990) story, and, in a parallel process, my own.

Acknowledgments

My thanks go to Encompass Australasia for financial and collegial support. I also wish to express thanks to Doris McIllwain for helping me to reorient my thoughts, and to Melanie Suchet, Elizabeth Wilson, Susan Best, Louise Newman, Louise Gyler and Nell Robertson for helping me to hone my

***

. Thanks too to Anna Gibbs who co-presented work on De Lynn at the Literature and Psychoanalysis Conference Sydney (2001).

References

Altman, N. (2003), *Why Perversion?* Paper for *IARPP Online Colloquium*, Series: No 3.
Barthes, R. (1976), *The Pleasure of the Text*. London: Hills Wang.
Bass, A. (2003), *Why Perversion?* Paper for *IARPP Online Colloquium*, Series: No 3.
Bronski, M. (2002), Sex, Death and the Limits of Irony. In: *Bringing the Plague: Toward Postmodern Psychoanalysis*, eds. S. Fairfield, R. Layton, & C. Stack. New York: Other Press, pp. 309–323.
Chasseguet-Smirgel, J. (1985), *Creativity and Perversion*. New York: Norton.
Chisholm, D. (1995), The cunning lingua of desire: Bodies, language, and perverse performativity. In: *Sexy Bodies*, eds. E. Grosz & E. Probyn. London: Routledge, pp. 19–41.
Damasio, A. (1994), *Descartes' Error*. New York: Avon.
De Lynn, J. (1990), *Don Juan in the Village*. New York: Painted Leaf Press.
Dimen, M. (2001), Perversion Is Us. Eight Notes. *Psychoanal. Dial.*, 11(6):825–861.
——— (2002), The disturbance of sex: A letter to Michael Bronsky. In: *Bringing the Plague: Toward Postmodern Psychoanalysis*, eds. S. Fairfield, R. Layton, & C. Stack. New York: Other Press, pp. 295–308.
——— (2003), *Why Perversion?* Paper for *IARPP Online Colloquium*, Series: No 3.
Fallon, M. (1995), Sextec. In: *Sexy Bodies*, eds. E. Grosz & E. Probyn. London: Routledge, pp. 42–85.
Freud, S. (1905), *Three Essays on Sexuality*. Standard Edition, 7. London: Hogarth Press.
——— (1927), *Fetishism*. Standard Edition, 21. London: Hogarth Press.
Gibbs, A. (2001, October), *Pleasure and Perversion in the Fiction of Jane De Lynn*. Paper presented at Literature and Psychoanalysis Conference, Sydney.
Harris, A. (2003), *Why Perversion?* Paper for *IARPP Online Colloquium*, Series: No 3.
Kahn, M. (1979), *Alienation in Perversion*. London: Hogarth Press.
Masumi, B. (1995), The Autonomy of Affect. *Cultural Critique*, 31:83–109.
McDougall, J. (1995), *The Many Faces of Eros*. London: Free Association Books.
Ogden, T. (1997), Perverse subjects. In: *Reverie and Interpretation*, ed. T. Ogden. London: Aronson, pp. 67–103.
Rose, J. (2003), *On not Being Able to Sleep*. London: Chatto & Windus.
Sedgwick, E. (1990), *Epistemology of the Closet*. Los Angeles: University of California Press.
——— (1993). *Tendencies*. Durham, NC: Duke University Press.
Stein, R. (2003), *Why Perversion?* Paper for *IARPP Online Colloquium*, Series: No 3.
Stoller, R. (1976), *Perversion: The Erotic Form of Hatred*. New York: Aronson.
Winnicott, D. W. (1965), *The Motivational Process and the Facilitating Environment*. New York: International Universities Press.
Wolff-Bernstein, J. (2003), Response to Stein, R. (2003) *Why Perversion?* Paper for *IARPP Online Colloquium*, Series: No 3.
Zizek, S. (2001), *Enjoy your Symptom: Jacques Lacan in Hollywood and Out*. London: Routledge.

19

Transitions

Melanie Suchet, PhD

▼　▼　▼　▼　▼

I.

Paul doesn't strike one, on first appearance, as a man with any remarkable features. He is built on the slighter side than average, wears his thick black-framed spectacles neatly on his face, displays no more than the expected number of earrings, and carries his 155 pound, 5′7″ frame with relative lightness. When in closer proximity, his dark brown eyes hint of a different sensibility hiding behind his unremarkability. They can engage one in a playful encounter, and then quite suddenly, shift to an icy stare. Not necessarily the dissociated stare as when one's body is vacated of occupancy, but the penetrating stare that seems to say he can see everything you hoped to hide, even from yourself. And there is, quite frequently, an air of defiance that beams towards you, which makes finding a meeting place with them slightly tricky. Do you maintain the contact to let him know you can manage the blast of emotion coming your way, or do you let go, suggesting your interest is not in a battle of wills? Needless to say, as the recipient, it leaves one feeling rather unmoored, waiting to find the right moment to hold onto.

On even closer inspection, Paul's breasts too, can be quite unnerving. He usually prefers to wear layers of clothing to mask the rounded shapes, but their prominence cannot simply be dismissed. His relationship to them has never been easy to define. And, with hindsight, I can recall glimmers of the current bitterness as present in even the earliest years of our work. It is true that they have at times, when he has beared himself to be touched, provided sensations that were pleasurable, even if only slightly

313

so, yet their presence alone, weighing heavily on him, pulling him downwards, marks him. And it is this marking which he wishes to erase. He is aware that their removal will be a loss, although it is not clear if their absence will have the presence of the phantom limb of an amputee, replete with sensations and pain. It is not clear, indeed, if the desire for their removal will suffice to eliminate any future problems, whether they be sensations or his distaste for femininity. He knows, however, that these body parts must be removed. He has imagined the surgeon, calmly raising the scalpel, slicing the skin, removing the fatty tissue, reconstructing the nipple to produce symmetrical, properly positioned male areolas on a newly flattened bed. Even the scars will become undetectable with the passage of time, leaving no evidence of the female body which happened to have been the designated driver at the time of birth. Yes, in the day and age of reconstruction, which, with a note of irony, comes alongside the academic discipline of deconstruction, we are all too familiar with Botox, tummy tucks, liposuctions, breast reductions, steroids, weight training and body re-sculpting tools of all kinds. In this era of what might be called personal transformation, it is to the anatomy we turn, in hope of finding the yearned for transcendence, a satisfaction that can be apparent to all, an experience of profundity that cannot be claimed elsewhere. It would be hard to deny that we all participate, in one form or another, in personal re-modeling. But becoming a man, when you have been born a woman, is transformation in all together a different degree.

And the breasts are the site of contestation. Why the breasts you may wonder? How do they become the primary source of dismay, disgust, perhaps even revulsion, such that it is not uncommon to hear the wish to rip them out, cut them off, tear them to pieces, and destroy the evidence of their prior existence. It is as if, to be a man, or as close to an anatomical man as is possible, the solution lies not in the genitalia, but in the excision of the visible mounds that encase the mammillary glands, those organs which move to their own rhythm with each walking stride. I, in my rather outmoded thinking, which I might add does not refer to my chronological age, although at times that too, but rather to my perception of the world, had thought that it was the penis or vagina that stood to define the border between manhood and womanhood. With Paul, I am encountering a different perspective altogether, which at times has me confused, searching through the hidden crevasses of my gray matter in the hopes of finding some familiar neurotransmitter paths that will recognize and construct logic from all this data. Is it not certainty that we all need? And was it not until fairly recently, a certainty to either be a man or a woman? That may have been so. Now I find myself more like a visitor to a playground of body parts, in which what belongs where and to whom is not a given, even if originally given, but the very essence of what is at play. There appear to be no foregone conclusions as to the sex of a person occupying a particular body. "Sex is not assigned, it is created" were the words Paul used. Paul has been very clear with me as to the regressiveness of my thought processes. "Nancy," he has said, drawing out the "Naan," slowly, with a note of exasperation, perhaps a hint of contempt, "transgendering the world is transgressive. We are subverting what it means to be a man or woman and we are using the body to make our statement. You must understand that." And I have tried to understand how his body has become the focus of disrepute. Loss and longing, his father's disappearance, his mother's clinging despair, all embedded, so insidiously, in a body that must now be erased. Sitting forward on the couch, looking intently at me, the look in this case having the air of persuasion, piercing my stodgy body armor, I am told that sex, not the copulation kind, but the male–female variety, is a construction, yes, a social construction, and it is up for grabs, open for reconstruction, reinterpretation and reconfiguration in ways that will "blow my mind."

I find my mind drifting back, some forty years; Barnard College, 1965. *The Feminine Mystique* is sprawled open across my bed. There is an air of expectation, quite tangible, as my roommates dart in and out. "Help, I need somebody, help" is blaring from the radio, perched as it is, on the windowsill, opening to the cacophony of New York City. We are the second wave, rolling in, ready to transform the "Great Society" fueled by righteousness, we are emboldened and brazen. We are Amazons, in our own right, or so we thought then, and did we not, dispensing of despair, barge through the barriers, demanding our liberation from the confines of domesticity? And, indeed, as a child, I had adventured, boy in mind, through the tropical rainforests of the Amazon. Yes, I alone, in my rudimentary canoe, marveling at the pristine, forging paths through dense overgrowth, had tackled its inaccessibility. Muscular, heroic, and fearless, I stood, poised for triumph.

I had not always wished to leave Calgary, the fortress town nestled on the edge of the Rocky Mountains, but once she had died, and left me, so to speak, the parting seemed inevitable. And here I am today, in Greenwich Village, New York City, living in the imaginary space of another, charting unknown territories, once again.

As I sit, long gray hair pulled back, on my black leather chair, one of those stress-free varieties, where of course the "stress-free" refers to the burden on one's posterior extremities and never the burden of inner components, which weigh far more heavily on the frame, I might add, Paul is excitedly telling me of a new Internet game he has discovered. Apparently it is a game whose purpose is to appear as anything but a game. It is intended as a simulation of life. It is a game without an end, without a defined goal but a social world of people and play. It is advertised as "a place where creativity runs free, a world that is yours to invent and inhabit." He is delighted. He can enter the world without his body, without the body he lives in and design the body he wishes for. He can build each part, making it up, molding it, creating the fine details, cutting here, adding there, just the right nose, the eyes evenly spaced, the mouth not too succulent and feminine, but definitely not too severe and cold, and the hair a shade of darker black, clean cut and neatly positioned on his head. And then, of course, there is the body. The height would be easy, 5'10" without a moment's hesitation, he certainly doesn't want to stand out, he is all too familiar with that, but he needs to be tall enough to be reckoned with. And the shoulders. He wants to have the shoulders of a rugby player, their broad, expansive bones framing his figure, shoulders that could butt, shoulders that could carry, shoulders that could reveal a history merely by the erosion of time on their shape. Following this would be the biceps and pecs, instantly formed, without the dull, slogging work of daily visits to the gym, but large, well defined muscles, bulging in their manhood, evident for all to see, certainly not the outlandish, rather grotesque muscles of a body builder, but the architecturally balanced structures that result from careful planning. Needless to say there would be no vagina. The penis, surprisingly, would be of the standard size and shape. He has no desire for the 9-inch varieties that are advertised with much pride on manhunt.com: perhaps, once again, it is the wish to not stand out, but it may also be, in this one small detail, the remnants of the woman within the man.

Paul could be the perfectly upholstered man. He could be the Paul of his own creation, and indeed it would not be a forgery, for who would he be but the self he is to himself? I myself see the unfolding of possibility. Imagine a place to inhabit where you construct, from the very beginning, your self in your very own eyes. Would this, could this be a home, the home he yearns for?

Wait! I catch myself. I too feel confused, sometimes, when I am submerged in his world, a virtual reality of a different sort, I lose myself, with him, in the space that sucks us up. "Nancy, relax" he has said, as his eyes dare me to engage in mischief. How he loves to cajole me into coming out of myself, into pushing the analytic envelope, ever so slightly, one small step at a time. Children, he wants us to be, playing, imagining, forgetting who we are, in a world of make-believe. And in those moments, I believe too. But did not Humpty Dumpty fall? And was it not that the pieces that had come apart could not be put together again?

I had a dream, just two nights ago, in which Paul's voice had changed. Gone was the soft, feminine timbre, replaced by a crackling rumble. It had a much deeper sound, as if emerging from a long winter hibernation, and resonated, for quite some time, throughout the dream. He appeared in the dream to be smiling, as if to say, "You see, I told you so." And on his face I could make out the faint smattering of hair, an outline of a beard, made of the soft, baby hair that has never seen the likes of a razor. In contrast, his haircut, a close cropped buzz cut, gave a sharp, severe look to his face. Moving beyond his face, I noticed that he wore a short-sleeved shirt, dark red in color, and quite surprisingly, the first four buttons were undone, exposing his bare chest. Yes, indeed, it was, in the dream, a male chest. It was flat, a pinky, fleshy color, without hair and without scarring, somewhat like the chest of a 12-year-old boy. I knew that I was preparing myself, for the post-operative, post-testosterone Paul.

I wondered how would it be to have Paul, who first entered my office as the female Paula, to be a man, not only in name, but in sight and sound? Would he be the same person in a different shape? Or would the she, in becoming a he, be someone quite other? And what would happen to the person with whom I was so familiar?

I awoke and she was gone. She was there and then she was not. I had no warning. It was an early winter morning, –10 degrees Centigrade, and the wind kept trying to barge into the house. I heard its fury gusting up, then dropping off, defeated. I lay frozen. The heat was still off. Encased in layers of blankets, duvets, covers, I remained very still. She was gone. It took a long time to register. Perhaps I am still registering.

II.

I wondered, since I am female-bodied and female identified, it may be more difficult to imagine a transition from female to male, but what if I followed the change from male to female. Quite fortunately, I had at the time just started working with a young woman, Liz, who had a particular penchant for sexual explorations. Now let me describe Liz slightly, for it will help to explain this particular situation. In appearance, Liz looks demure, much younger than her 19 years. She likes to glance at me, a sideways glance, hiding her eyes under a rather messy mop of short blond hair, she giggles uncomfortably, and reminds me of a lost fawn quivering in the slightest breeze. In describing her latest conquest, who appeared to be the most exciting partner she had yet encountered, and I was later to learn that there had been many such encounters, and having a love of language, she carefully provided detail by detail the inexplicable deliciousness of the woman's skin, the curves of her body, the touch of her breasts and the inordinate passion that had been awakened in her. After some 10 minutes of this detailed exposition, not, I might add, initiated by me, she hastened to say, rather nonchalantly, that her partner was "a woman in every sense of the word, she just had a penis." It was stated like that. I remember the words well. They struck me with their simplicity.

"She was a woman in every sense of the word, she just had a penis." Now, this announcement came without a hint of conflict, confusion, shame, sarcasm, or any other such emotion we analysts are intent on hearing. It made complete sense to her. There would be no doubt, Liz told me, that if you passed her by in the street, or even sat nearby for an entire evening at a restaurant, that she was a woman. She sounded like, acted like, looked like, and felt like a woman. The fact of owning a penis seemed irrelevant. A by-product of a previous life. An extra appendage, perhaps in the manner one treats an extra toe or finger. And moreover, it was this particular combination of anatomical components that excited Liz. To have someone whose gentle voice, soft body, smooth skin, and perky breasts come attired with the automatic rising of a functional penis, denuded of hairs I was told, was the ultimate delight. It mattered not that she, who had been a he at birth, still retained her phallic equipment. Lying on her back, this new partner would never initiate a sexual act, waiting for Liz, the demure fawn sitting on my couch, to entice the penis out from behind her legs, back to its position of stature.

If I am to be honest, and I shall try to do so, I was left a little shaken after that session. And perhaps that was partly her intent. However, there was something in what Liz had said that I could not quite dismiss. Could I rethink the composition of womanhood? Have I, embedded as I am in a patriarchal mindset, paid too much attention to the presence or absence of a penis as the arbiter of genderhood? I do fear a slippery slope into no man's land, oh dear, no woman's land, or no land at all, just quicksand. Perhaps womanhood resides in a place other than the genitals. This is not to say that the body has no meaning, it is quite evident that the body is the center of the controversy, packed as it is with residues of meaning. But it is in the translation of body to meaning that something has been lost. A literal translation may be apt for most of us, but those in the "trans world" have slipped between the lines. Their bodies do not reveal who they are.

I, too, find myself a little lost. If Paul's experience of his body transcends its physicality, one might say the psychic supersedes anatomy. Then why, in seeking a solution to this incongruity of mind and body, go back to the choice of surgical intervention, as if it is only through one's anatomy that legitimacy can be found?

For Paul it is, indeed, the body alone, which is the source of distress. A dictatorship of sorts, I have grumbled to myself, imperious and impervious, his body rules with absolute authority. He insists that it is the container and not the contained that must be altered. In contrast, I approach change as from the inside out. I had believed that by shifting the inner psychic world, the container would be experienced quite differently. And so, over the years, I tried to reveal how the psychic trauma, the losses and longings became lodged in his body, as if it were the body. Approaching from every angle, I attempted to outmaneuver the hegemony of the body. Yet, in hatred, he remains captive to its allure. Words, in all shapes and patterns; meanings, layered and complex were unveiled to reach and transform his experience of himself.

Indeed, it has been a long journey, in which we have traveled far from where we started. Nonetheless, I am succumbing, sometimes more easily than others, to an understanding that, unlike anything else, this body of his is beyond my reach.

Our last time together had started around her large kitchen table. A deep mahogany, passed down over the generations, weathered and sturdy, it held its own in a house of precious objects. I liked to run my fingers along the lines, following each one to see where it would take me.

The first time I saw her was in a classroom assigned to the study of Biology 101. She engaged us immediately holding each one of us in rapt attention. And that was, in part, due to the subject of her talk, but far more due to the person behind the subject. She carried her voice as comfortably as her body. Her compact body showed signs of the competitive athlete she had been in her 20s, in her command of it some 20 years later. And now she held court, in a performance of mastery, a performance designed as much to be admired as to impart knowledge.

I never thought that she would notice me. I, myself, don't like to be the center of someone's gaze. I prefer to watch, to be in the background. I have been told I am shy. I hide behind my long gray hair that may, indeed, have always been more of a curtain to conceal than an object of beauty to be admired. But her eyes came to rest on me. And she seemed to believe she had found something valuable, although it was not, at the time, anything I was aware of. Indeed, it was only through her attention and especially when the gaze turned to touch that something changed.

It was only a touch, but something stopped inside me. Suspended. I hung onto the moment. I had been touched. She brushed aside my hair, opened my face to her, moving her hand across my jaw, she followed the lines and the shape of me behind my covers. Her experienced hands, gentle and deft, peeled away my layers. I did not know yet what that would open up in me. I just knew that a hunger had been revealed.

My body stood up, straight and tall, its 18 years a preparation for this moment. It held itself like that, offering itself up, abandoning prior carefully constructed notions of caution. But then she was gone (an aneurysm in the night), and so, perhaps, was I.

Paul's eyes, with their piercing quality, watch me. He reads me through my body. As I turn to my body, this body I wear, I wonder how I am now reflected in this shape. I am rather large and yet oddly small, a little crumpled and though I might in height stand tall, I am a figure in decline. "You are too stiff and hunched over" he has told me, "You are hiding." My black clothes, loose and flowing, are layers of disguise, he has determined, not simply New York attire. "You do not live in your body, Nancy, you have retreated from it." I shudder a little at his insight. Am I hidden from sight as Paul has said? Have I curled myself into the cloak of my body? And what have I excised, I wonder quietly?

Taking a deep breath, I find myself at some 60 years of age, back in the comfortable office of my prior Freudian supervisor, Jeff. The office is lined with books on two sides, covering the wall from head to toe, enhancing the sense that his calm voice carries the authority of many minds who have come before him. Behind his chair is a large abstract painting with lines, curves, colors, and shapes that change in meaning each week that I appear before them, a rather imposing Rorschach canvas. I shift my focus back to his face. He has heard Liz's clinical material and her exploits. He has one eyebrow raised, ever so slightly, in a look that is not quite puzzlement, or shall I say the puzzlement does not pertain to him, rarely have I seen him in a position of bewilderment, which is why I keep returning to his air of certainty, no, he seems to be puzzling over what I might be making of this matter. Now, being both supervisor and friend, a relationship that has grown over many years, he is well aware of my proclivity towards feminist thought. He is trying to find a way to approach me. To be fair, he is curious, open-minded and has never been anything but gentle in his guidance of my work. But the silence that is growing between us, tells me he is at a loss for where to start. He is going to tell me that anatomy is destiny. How could he not? It is such a basic tenet. He must think that we relational psychoanalysts have clearly lost our footing, wandered too far from the anchor of the body. But he takes a different tack. "There is a wonderful paper by Lawrence Kubie[1] on the drive to become both sexes" he says, in a voice that does not betray his concern. I know the paper. It has a detailed analysis of Virginia Woolf's *Orlando*, and how I love Woolf, her endless sentences that pack so many sensations into a single line. The thought of a wolf in sheep's clothing comes unbeckoned, and I laugh to myself, at my own absurdity. Of course, I had not thought of Orlando, the story of a man who turns into a woman and then back and forth between the two.

I come back to the room and he is talking, slowly and carefully about the desire to be both sexes and the wish for magical bodily transformation. Ah, yes, I catch the words "futile attempts" and "irreconcilable wishes." I drift in and out. Can he really hold so many different theories, concepts, and words in mind, to be recalled, so effortlessly, at will? What does he do with irreconcilable thoughts, thoughts that clash with feelings, ideas that sound so perfect when read, but leave one untouched in the presence of human anguish

---

[1]Kubie, L. (1974). The drive to become both sexes. *Psychoanalytic Quarterly*, 43:349–426.

sitting before you? What would he do in the room? What if this woman with a penis were his patient, telling him how much better she feels with breast surgery and hormones? Would he stick to the phallic woman interpretation, the denial of difference between the sexes, or would he, too, wonder if there was something that he had been missing?

My body feels leaden as I leave his office. I notice that the rain is coming down more heavily and I cannot spot any yellow cabs through the sheets of water. Even my glasses are misting over. I start to trudge the 20 blocks back to my office, berating myself for having forgotten to listen to the weather forecast that morning. I could have been better prepared.

It is hard to see. The heat rises off the water drenching me. I maneuver the canoe with caution and dexterity. Down the smaller tributaries I duck rather suddenly as an unexpected branch looms up before me. The mist seems to be everywhere. I feel my body, poised, ready. My shirt is off, my pants are rolled up. Every muscle is on guard. I move forward, slowly, deftly, listening to the sounds, the animal warnings. They know before I do. But I keep moving, adrenalin and exhilaration blending together, cutting a path through the water.

Then the words of Jeff, alternating with the demands of the rain, intrude. I am back in my cold body, shivering as the rain penetrates my layers. Spinning in circles, the words, the fragments, repeat themselves unable to find a comfortable resting spot. *Irreconcilable drives. A magical wish to have it all.* Boy and girl. Him and I. I conjure up, in an attempt at comfort, what my relational mentors may make of all this. Would the unconscious fantasy of an idealized other through surgical transformation be viewed as resolving an inner conflict by external means and hence doomed to fail? I imagine so. The treatment, in fact, might have some similarities to interpreting the wish to erase trauma through excision of body parts. We would, of necessity, be working to give up the fantasy of transitioning through surgical reassignment. And then I wonder, are some body transformations more acceptable than others? Is it simply the notion of altering genitals that is so taboo?

A clear cut view of the world is so appealing. I seem to be stumbling about in anything but clarity. I yearn a little for the certainty of righteousness, bared and brazen marching the streets demanding justice. I now inhabit a world of mentation in an era of deconstruction, where uncertainty, fluidity and paradox dominate the landscape. And it is as if the power of words, narratives and meanings have surpassed all else. But perhaps, if a part of one is lodged in a time before words, in a space beyond words, then the body may rule over the mind. Gender, encrypted in the body, may become the material body, not as a house within which one can move freely, but as the concrete structure, fixed and immobile. And words may not be able to penetrate, they may not have transformative powers we assume so readily, even in the context of a deep and meaningful therapeutic relationship.

Reluctantly, uneasily, but nevertheless inevitably, I find myself embarking, one foot at a time, on a path I had not anticipated.

As I stand at the door, I find myself hesitating, holding onto the knob a moment too long. Paul is waiting for me on the other side. I take a deep breath, and watch as the air slips, quite effortlessly, out of my body. I begin to open the door, my sturdy, soundproof door that seals off the possibility of unwanted intrusion. Despite myself, I tremble a little. And then it is open. Yes, as I stand, poised, there is something indescribable in the air. I steady myself, preserving a demeanor of certitude. And, gathering a semblance of ease, I step out into the space between him and me, inside and outside, then and now.

Relaxed, engaged, Paul saunters in. His eyes have softened over the four years of our work together, no longer brimming with emotional intensity, waiting for any false step on my behalf to lead us into battle, or to a permanent retreat. No, they are receptive, looking to take in warmth. He tells me he has chosen the surgeon and is intent on showing me the before and after shots. Breasts of all shapes and sizes are spread out before me and then their appearance, or shall I say their disappearance, at 1-month, 6-month, and 2-year intervals are revealed. He has read hundreds of testimonials as to the satisfaction that top surgery provides. He has made up his mind. "This is a battle for my soul," he tells me:

> I know that you are uncertain, but even understanding the reasons why I feel this way about my body, and I have slowly come to agree with you on that, it does not change my need to have the surgery. You see while making sense of all that has happened in my life has helped me in every other way, it just does not change my relationship to my body. I cannot explain it to you, but I need to find a home inside myself. It will never be a perfect home, I have given up on that, but maybe I will feel, even if only a little, like I belong.

Author Index

C

Calef, V., 12, *30*
Caruth, C., 214, *224*
Castoriadis, C., 228, 230, 231, 233, *240*
Celenza, A., 35, *51*
Chasseguet-Smirgel, J., 302, *311*
Cheng, A. A., 117, *119, 150*
Chisholm, D., 309, *311*
Chodorow, N., 39, *51*
Cobb, J., 122, *133*
Cohen, B. D., 193, *207*
Cohen, P. F., 194, *207*
Cole, G., 243, *245*
Coltart, N., 125, *133*
Cooper, S. H., 106, *115,* 126, *133,* 290, *300*
Copjec, J., 149, *150*
Corbett, K., 74, *79*
Cornell, D., 148, *150*
Crastnopol, M., 39, *51*
Cushman, P., 210, *224*

D

Damasio, A., 303, *311*
Davies, J. M., 181, 184, *192,* 193, 201, *207,* 289, 297, *300*
Dean, T., 282, 284, *285*
Debs, E., *133*
De Lynn, J., 303, 304, 305, 306, 308, 309, 310, *311*
Diamond, E., 139, *150*
Dimen, M., 56, *59,* 122, *133,* 228, *240,* 284, *285,* 301, 302, 305, 309, *311*
Dor, J., 18, *30*

E

Eigen, M., 34, 38, *51,* 75, 76, 77, *79*
Ellison, R., 144, *150*
Eng, D. L., *94,* 118, *119,* 160, 166, *173*
Engels, F., 227, *241*

F

Fairbairn, W. R. D., 36, 45, *51,* 54, *59,* 126, *133*
Fallon, M., 309, *311*
Fanon, F., 84, *94,* 141, *150*
Federn, P., 78, *79*

Feldman, Y. S., 28, *30*
Fenichel, O., 228, *240*
Ferenczi, S., 125, *133*
Fishbane, M., 19, 22, *30*
Fonagy, P., 110, 112, *115,* 184, 185, *192,* 211, 217, *224,* 235, *240*
Foucault, M., 82, *94,* 216, 217, *224,* 265, *276,* 282, *285*
Foulkes, S. H., 193, 205, *208*
Frank, K., *276*
Frank, T., 123, *133*
Frawley, M. G., 181, 184, *192,* 201, *207*
Frenkel-Brunswik, E., 229, *240*
Freud, S., 55, *59, 79,* 109, *115,* 123, *133,* 138, 139, *150,* 160, 162, 165, *173,* 181, *192,* 228, 238, *240,* 302, 303, *311*
Friedman, L., 102, *115*
Friedman, M. E., 169, *173*
Fromm, E., 7, 8, 10, 11, 12, 14, 21, 22, 23, 25, 29, *30*
Fuss, D., 139, *150*

G

Gabbard, G., 35, *51*
Gartner, R., 73, *79*
Gay, P., 121, *133*
Geertz, C., 227, *240*
Gentile, K., 176, 181, 183, *192*
Ghent, E., 24, *31,* 35, *51,* 90, *94,* 175, 187, 188, *192,* 196, *208,* 211, 218, 222, *224*
Gibbs, A., 302, 303, *311*
Gillman, N., 28, *31*
Gordon, J., 200, *208*
Grand, S., 73, 74, *79,* 296, *300*
Gray, P., 107, *115*
Green, A., 56, *59,* 93, *94*
Gribinski, M., 112, *115*
Grosz, E., 18, *31*
Grotstein, J. S., *79,* 110, *115*
Gump, J., 84, 89, *94*
Guntrip, H., 185, *192*

H

Habermas, J., 217, *224,* 233, *240*
Han, S., *94,* 118, *119,* 160, 166, *173*
Harris, A., 76, 78, *79,* 82, 83, 84, 92, *94,* 187, 189, 190, *192,* 214, *224,*

Subject Index